Cover Photographs:

Top row left to right:
 Lev Esaiakovich Shestov
 Peter Yakovlevich Chaadaev
 Aleksei Stepanovich Khomyakov
 Vissarion Gregoryevich Belinski
 Aleksandr Isaiyevich Solzhenitzin
 Ignati Bryanchaninov
 Vladimir Ivanovich Dal

Second row left to right:
 Grigori Savvich Skovoroda
 Leo Nikolaevich Tolstoy
 Aleksandr Ivanovich Herzen
 Mikhail Aleksandrovich Fonvisin
 Mikhail Vasilyevich Lomonosov
 Vasili Vasilyevich Rozanov
 Nikolai Feodorovich Feodorov

Third row left to right:
 Nikolai Mikhailovich Karamzin
 Mikhail Yuryevich Lermontov
 Vladimir Feodorovich Odoyevksi
 Nikolai Ivanovich Novikov
 Feodor Nikolaevich Glinka
 Nikolai Vasilyevich Gogol
 Ivan Andreevich Krilov

Fourth row left to right:
 Vladimir Sergeevich Solovyov
 Mikhail Aleksandrovich Bakunin
 Aleksandr Sergeevich Pushkin
 Ivan Sergeevich Turgenev
 Feodor Mikhailovich Dostoyevski
 Sergei Nikolayevich Berdayev
 Boris Leonidovich Pasternak

Bottom row left to right:
 Daniel Leonidovich Andreev
 Anton Pavlovich Chekov
 Maxim Gorki
 Ilya Arnoldovich Ilf
 Evgeni Petrovich Petrov
 Aleksandr Aleksandrovich Blok
 Anna Andreevna Akhmatova
 Marina Ivanovna Tsvetaeva

RUSSIA'S WISDOM

RUSSIA'S WISDOM

Other books by Daniel H. Shubin:

A History of Russian Christianity in 4 volumes:
1. From the Earliest Years through Tsar Ivan IV
2. The Patriarchal Era through Tsar Peter the Great: 1586 to 1725
3. The Synodal Era and the Sectarians: 1725 to 1894
4. The Russian Orthodox Church: 1894 to 1990

Leo Tolstoy and the Kingdom of God within You

Skovoroda:
The World Tried to Catch Me but Could Not

Helena Roerich:
Living Ethics and the Teaching for a New Epoch

Tsars and Imposters: Russia's Time of Troubles

Monastery Prisons

Militarist Christendom and The Gospel of the Prince of Peace

Kingdoms and Covenants

Attributes of Heaven and Earth

RUSSIA'S WISDOM

A Survey and Collection of Russian Philosophic, Religious and Political Thought, Aphorisms, and Concepts, from Its Greatest Thinkers throughout Its Entire History

Selected, arranged, and translated
from the original Russian into English, by

Daniel H. Shubin

ISBN 978-0-9662757-6-6
Copyright 2014. All rights reserved.
Daniel H. Shubin

Email: peacechurch @ jps.net

11-16-2014

Table of Contents

Introduction	11
Era of Kievan Russ	
Daniel the Recluse	17
Ilarion of Kiev	21
Kirill Turovski	23
Kliment Smolyatich	25
Vladimir Monomakh	27
Yaroslav the Wise	29
Era of Muscovite Russia	
Avvakum Petrovich	33
Maksim the Greek	36
Nil Sorski	41
Sergei Radonezhski	46
Tikhon Zadonski	49
Imperial Russia – The Philosophers	
Dmitri Sergeevich Anichkov	59
Konstantine Nikolaevich Batushkov	63
Aleksandr Aleksandrovich Bestuzhev	69
Faddei Venediktovich Bulgarin	74
Gavril Romanovich Derzhavin	78
Semeon Efimovich Desnitzki	80
Nikolai Feodorovich Feodorov	83
Aleksandr Sergeevich Griboyedov	90
Nikolai Mikhailovich Karamzin	92
Vasili Osipovich Kluchevski	99
Ivan Andreevich Krilov	107
Mikhail Sergeevich Lunin	112
Nikolai Ivanovich Novikov	116
Vladimir Feodorovich Odoyevski	122

Vasili Vasilyevich ROZANOV	132
Mikhail Mikhailovich SCHERBATOV	135
Aleksandr Vasilyevich SUVOROV	139
Vasili Andreevich ZHUKOVSKI	141

IMPERIAL RUSSIA – THE POLITICAL THINKERS

Ivan Sergeevich AKSAKOV	147
Konstantine Sergeevich AKSAKOV	149
Mikhail Aleksandrovich BAKUNIN	152
Vissarion Gregoryevich BELINSKI	155
Peter Yakovlevich CHAADAEV	168
Nikolai Gavrilovich CHERNISHEVSKI	176
Nikolai Aleksandrovich DOBROLUBOV	182
Mikhail Aleksandrovich FONVIZIN	187
Feodor Nikolaevich GLINKA	194
Timofei Nikolaevich GRANOVSKI	208
Konstantine Dmitrievich KAVELIN	211
Aleksei Stepanovich KHOMYAKOV	214
Nikolai Fillipovich PAVLOV	218
Osip Ivanovich SENKOVSKI	221
Nikolai Vasilyevich SHELGUNOV	227

IMPERIAL RUSSIA · THE RELIGIOUS THINKERS

AMBROSE OPTINSKI	233
Pyotr Semeonovich AVSENEV (Archimandrite THEOFAN)	236
IGNATI Bryanchaninov	239
JOHN OF KRONSHTADT	257
Victor Dmitrievich KUDRYAVTZOV-PLATONOV	263
MACARIUS OPTINSKI	268
SERAPHIM SAROVSKI	272
Grigori Savvich SKOVORODA	276
Vladimir Sergeevich SOLOVYOV	287
THEOPHAN the Recluse	292

THE GOLDEN AGE OF RUSSIAN LITERATURE

Vladimir Ivanovich DAL	299
Feodor Mikhailovich DOSTOYEVSKI	303

Afanasi Afanasivich FET	314
Nikolai Vasilyevich GOGOL	316
Ivan Aleksandrovich GONCHAROV	329
Mikhail Yuryevich LERMONTOV	335
Mikhail Vasilyevich LOMONOSOV	338
Aleksandr Nikolaevich OSTROVSKI	342
Aleksandr Sergeevich PUSHKIN	347
Mikhail Evgrafovich SALTIKOV-SCHEDRIN	356
Vladimir Aleksandrovich SOLLOGUB	366
Leo Nikolaevich TOLSTOY	369
Aleksandr Ivanovich TURGENEV	405
Feodor Ivanovich TUTCHEV	418
Pyotr Andreevich VYAZEMSKI	422

THE SILVER AGE OF RUSSIAN LITERATURE

Leonid Nikolaevich ANDREEV	431
Arkadi Timofeevich AVERCHENKO	435
Maksim Alekseevich ANTONOVICH	438
Aleksandr Aleksandrovich BLOK	441
Valeri Yakovlevich BRUSOV	446
Anton Pavlovich CHEKOV	450
Aleksandr Stepanovich GRIN	458
Ilya Ilyich METCHNIKOFF	463
Konstantine Konstantinovich SLUCHEVSKI	465
Konstantine Sergeevich STANISLAVSKI	468
Aleksei Konstantinovich TOLSTOY	471
Evgeni Nikolayevich TRUBETZKOI	477
Constantine Dmitrievich YUSHINSKI	481

THE SOVIET ERA

Anna Andreevna AKHMATOVA	489
Daniel Leonidovich ANDREEV	491
Aleksandr Mikhailovich DOBROLUBOV	499
Pavel Aleksandrovich FLORENSKI	505
Maxim GORKI	509
Ilya Arnoldovich ILF and Evgeni Petrovich PETROV	518
Anatoli Vasilyevich LUNACHARSKI	521

Valerian Nikolaevich MURAVYOV	524
Boris Leonidovich PASTERNAK	527
Faina Georgievna RANEVSKAYA	531
Aleksandr Isaiyevich SOLZHENITZIN	535
Marina Ivanovna TSVETAEVA	539
Vikenti Vikenkyevich VERESAYEV	544
Vladimir Ivanovich VERNADSKI	547

THE EMIGRANT THINKERS

Aleksandr Valentinovich AMFITEATROV	553
Nikolai Sergeevich ARSENYEV	555
Konstantine Dmitrievich BALMONT	559
Nikolai Aleksandrovich BERDAYEV	561
Sergei Nikolayevich BULGAKOV	565
Ivan Alekseevich BUNIN	568
Aleksandr Ivanovich HERZEN	572
Ivan Aleksandrovich ILYIN	589
Nikolai Onufriyevich LOSSKI	595
Dmitri Sergeevich MEREZHKOVSKI	599
Lev Esaiakovich SHESTOV	605
Boris Petrovich VISHISLAVTZEV	608
Russian Traditional Proverbs	611
Russian Bibliography	617

INTRODUCTION

No country in the world has the depth of philosophical, religious, and political thought as does Russia, and over such a length of time – 1,000 years – from its earliest documented counsel of the Kievan Grand Princes to after the conclusion of Soviet Union. No country has as harsh an environment as does Russia, that provides contemplation with the endurance necessary to survive, and no country has had such a diversity of rulers, and many tyrannical and despotic, that has forged independent thought at the risk of the lives of its thinkers, or so many political upheavals that have provided the source for political concepts.

Over 100 of Russia's greatest thinkers are included, and almost 4,000 paragraphs of thoughts, aphorisms, maxims, axioms, prayers, petitions, confessions, have been selected. From the most serious of religious thinkers such as Nil Sorski and Sergei Radonezhski, to the extreme traditionalist and martyred Avvakum, to Tolstoy's pacifism, to Solovyov's universal unity. Likewise, anecdotes and humor from Soviet comics, such as Ilf and Petrov and Ranevskaya. Slavophiles[1] such as Belinski and Khomyakov, and westerners such as Herzen and Kavelin, and the encyclopedist Vladimir Dal and historians such as Karamzin. Many who are popular, such as Pushkin, Tolstoy and Solzhenitsin, and the not-so-popular others with equally profound conclusions or unorthodox concepts, such as Nikolai Feodorov the Moscow Socrates, or the eclectic theologian Vasili Rozanov, or the nomadic Christian humanist Grigori Skovoroda. Historians, doctors,

---

[1] A group of Russian activists who were opposed to the influence of Europe on Russian culture and wanted Russia to be more Slavic and less occidental.

military heroes, librarians, scientists, and futurists, have been selected to provide the reader with the best possible philosophic, religious and political thoughts that Russia has produced.

A collection of traditional sayings and aphorisms has also been included at the end of this volume.

Selection of Thinkers

The compiler of this volume has utilized similar volumes of quotes published in Russia for the selection of contributors, as well and many of his own, that he has concluded as valuable in his personal study of Russian history, biography and literature. A little over 100 seemed to be a large enough selection, some of them hardly contributing a couple of paragraphs, while Tolstoy and Herzen with many pages.

The Russian bibliography at the conclusion of the volume will help the reader with the sources for inclusion in this volume.

The fate of some contributors that seem to the modern reader a praiseworthy person often ended in tragedy because their concepts were suspected by the state to be formidable, such as the military hero turned philosopher Mikhail Lunin who was executed in a concentration camp beyond Lake Baikal; or the most talented and famous poet of 20th century Soviet Union, Marina Tsvetaeva, who died at her own will after the execution of her husband and exile to Siberia of her daughter, and her own repression by the Soviet state; or the mystic Nikolai Novikov, sentenced to 15 years in prison for publishing textbooks for the peasant schools.

One item that hopefully will be noticeable to the reader is that many of these contributors did not live a long life. The hardships of Russian life in general with its extreme weather conditions and environment is one reason. Another reason is the suffering of many of them in exile or concentrations camps, under police surveillance, or even their execution or suicide, as a result of their philosophies being in disaccord or threatening to either Imperial Russia or the Soviet state. Blok was 40; Gogol was 42; Muravyov was 45; Tsvetaeva was 48; Brusov was 51; Grin was 52; Florenski was 55; Herzen, Lunin and Scherbatov were 57; Dostoyevski did not reach 60, and neither did Chaadaev or Akhmatova. Chernishevski and Karamzin died at 60. The father Andreev was 48, while the son was 52. Especially the Soviet Era writers had a short lifespan. Ilf and Petrov both did not live to 40. These are just a sample, but the reader will notice more.

Dates

All the dates for the era beginning with ancient Russia and through Imperial Russia are those traditionally provided (Old Style). The compiler did not see the need to change any of the dates of the original documents to the New Style, and because most of these dates are approximations anyway, often attributed to the person long after their birth or death.

Translation

This entire volume, all of its biographies and all of the content included here, is an original translation from the contributors' Russian into English by the author. No excerpts from any other English publication of any of these contributor's writings have been used. The translator has done his best in conveying the intent of the contributor into English.

The author has also used the best spelling available for the names of the contributors, and which may vary from others.

Arrangement

The volume is first divided into the major chronological eras, while Imperial Russia is sub-divided into Philosophers, Political Thinkers and Religious Thinkers. The concluding section is the immigrant thinkers, those who fled Russia or were exiled from Russian due to their opposition to the communist ideology. Most of them continued their compositions in Europe, and some moved to the USA.

Within each section, the contributors are listed in alphabetical order.

The section for each contributor begins with a short biography. Aphorisms are listed in alphabetical order. Some of the larger passages are located first after the biography, and then the aphorisms in alphabetical order follow later.

The final section is Traditional Russian Proverbs.

The Era of Kievan Russ

RUSSIA'S WISDOM

Daniel the Recluse

12th Century

Russian Orthodox Mystic

There is no reliable data regarding dates or even the decade of the birth and death of Daniel the Recluse, except that he lived during the second half of the 12th century and into the beginning of the 13th century. He was a native of Pereaslav. His 2 extant compositions also do not provide any biographical information, except for some geographical items.

Daniel has been venerated due to his antiquity in Russian Orthodoxy and his compositions reflect the beliefs of the people of that era.

The address of Daniel the Recluse, composed personally by him for Prince Yaroslav Vladimirovich.[2] Have mercy on me, son of the great price Vladimir.

Arise, my glory. Let me disclose my enigmas in parables and I will proclaim among the people my glory. The intelligent heart is strengthened in its body through beauty and wisdom.

---

2 Prince of Novgorod, 1181-1199, most likely

A generous prince is like a river flowing without shores through thick forests. It provides water not only for people, but also for animals. While a miserly prince is like a river flowing alongside banks full of rocks. You cannot get near the river for a drink, and neither can you water horses.

A wealthy person is everywhere known and he even has friends in foreign lands, but the destitute even in his homeland walks about hated. The wealthy will speak and all are silent, but the destitute will speak, and people ignore him. Whoever wears expensive clothes is the one whose words are valued.

Do not look upon me, master, like a wolf at a lamb. But watch over me like a mother over her child.

Every person is subtle and wise over someone else's calamity, but his own he cannot decipher.

For this reason I attempted to write of the shackles of my heart and broke them with bitterness.

Geese are made capable by their feathers, while the human body is strengthened by its muscles. The oak tree is solid due to its many roots, so with our city and due to your rule. A generous prince is the father of many servants. Even some leave their mother and father to be part of your household.

Gold is purified in fire, while a person enduring misfortune acquires a mature mind.

I have been insulted by all, because I was not guarded due to fear of your threats, yet I am like a firm wall.

I saw an ugly woman with her face pasted to a mirror and smearing mascara on herself, and I said to her, "Do not look into the mirror, the more you notice how ugly you are the more that you will develop a repulsive character."

RUSSIA'S WISDOM

If your conversations become too lengthy or verbose, you will become quickly hated, just like a song bird repeating the same chirp will soon annoy its hearers.

It is better for me to bring a wild ox into my home, than to marry an unrestrainable wife. When you beat her, she goes insane, but when you are meek with her, she betrays you. She becomes arrogant if you are wealthy, but if poor all she does is discredit others.

My lord, do not deprive your lowly sage of bread and do not raise to the sky some foolish rich person.

My Lord, look not upon my outer person, but see what I am inside. Even though I am poorly clothed, my mind is dressed in majesty. I may be young, but my thinking is mature. In my meditations I fly as a eagle into the air.

My mind is like the raven at night, vigilant in the heights.

My prince, do not let your hand be miserly when you stretch it to someone destitute. You cannot scoop all the water from the ocean with a bowl, and our petitions will not deplete the treasures in your home.

So did I gather the sweetness of flowers and their nectar in many books.

To well serve your master will gain you your freedom, but serving an evil master will only force you further into slavery.

We will trumpet like gold trumpets, with all the strength of our minds, and the silver instruments will play of the pride of my wisdom.

When you send a wise man on a mission, you explain little to him. When you send a stupid person, you have to follow him all the way lest he fail.

You provide life to your people through your mercy, to the orphans and widows, those whom rulers offend.

Ilarion of Kiev

beginning of the 11th century

Russian Orthodox Prelate, Theologian

Historical and biographical information on Ilarion is meager, he died about 1055. He was Russian Orthodox Metropolitan of Kievan Russ during the era of Yaroslav the Wise.

I believe in one God glorified in Trinity: the God who is without birth, without beginning and without end; the begotten Son, who is likewise without beginning and end; the Holy Spirit who emanates from the Father and was manifested in the Son and who is likewise co-beginningless and equal to the Father and Son. I believe and confess that the Son, by the good will of the Father and permission of the Holy Spirit, descended to the earth for the salvation of the human race, but He did not abandon the heavens or the Father. He suffered for me in the flesh as a human, but in His divinity was as passionate as God. He died in order to give life to me the one who was actually dead. The holy and glorious Virgin Mary is also named the Theotokos. Honor her and in faith venerate her. Look upon her holy icon and see the Lord as a child and rejoice. Likewise look upon His holy saints.

(Another composition of Ilarion is his Address on Law and Grace, which is dedicated to the greatness of Russia and the divine selection of its rulers. In agreement with the canons of the

Byzantine fathers, Ilarion developed his views on the basis of allegorical exegesis, having as the goal the key understandings of Christian religion – law and grace, the Old and New Testaments. Contrary to the ecclesiastical scheme that viewed grace as the fulfillment of law, Ilarion considered the 2 contrary and opposite one to another: First was law, then grace; first was the shadow, then truth. He placed the Biblical slave woman Hagar and Sarah side by side. One gave birth to Ishmael first and then later the other gave birth to Isaac. The law is the slave woman Hagar, while grave is the freewoman Sarah. Between them there is no supremacy, no legacy; they are 2 completely alien and distinct belief systems. Just as Hagar the slave woman was banished with her son Ishmael, so Judaism and the law are banished. The law is alien to the concept of divine grace – freedom; the law is entirely immersed in the vanity of earthly and bodily passions. It produces no benefit or benevolence, does not cleanse, and any fruits depends on struggle, anger and transgression. The law provides little and has no knowledge of eternity. It was obvious for Ilarion that grace demolished law and brought slavery to annihilation. The Old Testament is replaced by the New; slavery is replaced by freedom.)

When the moon's light departed, when the sun began to shine, so was the relationship of the departure of the law to the appearance of grace. The cold of the night was defeated, the sun's warmth warmed the ground. And the person is no longer suppressed in the law, but he freely walks in grace. The Jews confirmed themselves in the light of the law, while Christians in their sun's grace created salvation. The Jews only established themselves in the shadow of the law, but did not acquire salvation. Christians established themselves on truth and grace, and are saved. Among the Jews is self-confidence, but among the Christians is salvation. Just as self-confidence in this world is their salvation, salvation is in the future age. The Jews were concerned about the earthly, while the Christians – about the heavenly.

Kirill Turovski

1130 – 1182

Russian Orthodox Prelate

Kirill Turovski was born about 1130 in Turov, Gomelski Province, Belarus. From what little is known, Kirill received his initial education at home, and later from Greek teachers in the region, studying science and art, and Byzantine culture, including public speaking.

At an early age he entered one of the monasteries in the Turov region, and took vows as a monk in 1161 at the Boriso-Glebski Monastery. He secluded himself soon after for reasons of contemplation and resided on top of a pillar for a while. After his religious writings were distributed, he was ordained as Bishop of Turov. In his later years, he resigned as bishop and went into seclusion to write. One of his prominent compositions are a collection of spiritual statements for every Russian Orthodox holyday. He died about 1182.

It is good, brethren, and very useful for us to understand the meaning of the Holy Scriptures. This will make the soul prudent, and direct the mind to humility, and the heart to aspire to virtue, and will make the entire person grateful. The mind will strive toward the heavens to God's testaments, and will strengthen the body to accomplish religious efforts, and develop contempt for the earthly life and wealth. This will provide you glory and cause all the mundane matters of life to depart. So I ask of you, endeavor diligently to read the holy books to be saturated with God's work, and attain the indescribable bliss of eternal life. If it is invisible, this means it is eternal and has no end; it is solid and immoveable.

Let us just not plainly talk, but recite what is written, and with discernment quote passages and strive to fulfill this with our deeds. Honeycomb is sweet and sugar is good, and each seems to be better than studying a book, but this is the treasury of eternal life. If someone should find on earth a treasure, and was to leave it all except for just one precious jewel, and that would support him without sorrow and to his death, and this is a great wealth. So is the same with the present treasure, the Holy Scriptures, and likewise the prophetic, and Psalms and Apostolic letters, and the preserved sermons of our Savior Christ. He possessed the true mind, meditating not for his personal salvation, but for many others, those that would pay attention to him.

Here applies the Gospel parable, where it says, "Every scribe who comprehends the Kingdom of Heaven is like a householder who takes from his treasury and distributes the old and the new." If this is done out of ambition, or to please the great, he will disdain the small. Or to boldly hide his master's silver, not to give it to the bankers for interest in his life, to increase his master's money – this is people's souls – the master will take back his money, because the master opposes the proud, while giving grace to the humble.

Become strong, not to have an unstable mind. Do you have a weak intellect, not able to explain necessary passages, or like a blind arrow that cannot seem to find its target, and at whom people laugh? Study the Scriptures.

KLIMENT SMOLYATICH

Died 1164

Russian Orthodox Prelate and Theologian

Kliment Smolyatich was metropolitan of Kievan Russ from 1147 to 1155. Although he was the author of many addresses and instructive circulars, only his *Letter* to Minister Foma with a supplement to a certain monk Afanasi have survived to the present.

The ideological views of Kliment are characterized in his distinction of 2 types of divine comprehension: the gracious and the influenced. The former evolves from belief and is accessible only to saints; the later provides comprehension of the divine commandments and is accessible to all those dead in sin. Recognizing the indispensability of philosophy for comprehending Sacred Scripture, Kliment referred to the ecclesiastical fathers who applied allegory and elucidation to the Lord's words. Kliment's use of philosophy pertained to his allegorical interpretation of Biblical examples. He was also consider the first native Russian Orthodox theologian.

For sins and condemnation, death is the result. For rectitude and justification, it is life.

The person who is honored of God cleanses one item using another. So we, being God's creation, act with the help of the creation that He created, then the more we subsequently meditate on God, whose mind and wisdom can hardly penetrate our mind. And not only our mind, but the mind of the holy Angels and Archangels and all the Angelic ranks. So it is proper for Him to act through His own created creatures however He wants, to steer the majestic ark of His majesty. We should not oppose His providence, but only to praise and thank it.

The richest of the rich and glorious of all glorious is the person who lives the belief in Christ and performs activities pleasing to God.

Who is merciless will likewise receive a merciless judgment.

Vladimir Monomakh

1053 – 1125

Ruler of Kievan Russia

Vladimir Vsevolodich was grandson of Yaroslav the Wise. He was called Monomakh from his mother's side of the family, her father was Byzantine Emperor Constantine Monomakh. Vladimir continued rule over Kievan Russia from his father, being prince of Smolensk from 1067, Chernigov from 1094, and Grand Prince of Kiev from 1113.

Present archives contain 3 compositions of Vladimir Monomakh: his *Instruction*, an autobiographical story, and a letter to his cousin Oleg Svatoslavich. They reflect the morality and ethic of the era of early Kievan Russ.

Depart from evil, do what is good, find peace and banish malevolence, and live for ever and ever.

Do not execute either the guilty or the innocent, and do not pass a death sentence. If a person is deserving of death, do not destroy a Christian soul.

Eat and drink without much noise; be silent in the presence of the elders; listen to the wise; be submissive to older people; have love toward the great and small; converse always without malice;

comprehend as much as possible; do not talk to foolish women; keep your eyes down but your soul high; run from vanity; do not just honor anything, but what is deserving.

Honor elders like a father; and the young like your brethren. Do not be lazy at home, but watch for all matters.

I do not need valiant men, but I want the welfare of my brethren and for my Russian land.

If you go to war, do not be lazy and do not depend on your military leader. Train yourself to be good guards and at night. Always sleep alongside other soldiers and rise early. Do not be quick to remove your weapons from you. Immediately assist a person who is injured. Distance yourself from lies and drunkenness and immorality, because this will destroy your soul as well as your body.

Lethargy seems to be mother of us all. If you have something, work harder. If you do not have something, you will never learn anyway.

Love your wives, but do not give them authority over your self.

Visit and comfort the sick; bury the dead, because we are all mortal. Do not ignore other persons, but greet them, and always have a good word to mention to them.

Yaroslav Vladimirovich the Wise

About 978 – about 1054

Ruler of Kievan Russia

Yaroslav Vladimirovich was son of the great prince Vladimir I Svatoslav. His date of birth ranges from 978 to 980. He was placed by his father as grand prince of Rostov and then he continued to expand and conquer most of what is today the western half of European Russia. By 1035 he was essentially autocrat of all Kievan Russ. Due to the effects of so much internecine strife and civil war, his attitude changed in later years and Yaroslav became an educator and promoted Christianity in Russia, including the construction of churches and monasteries.

His efforts included hiring translators to translate books from Greek into Slavic, and creating a volume of justice and legislation. Yaroslav installed the first Russian to be metropolitan of Kiev, instead of a Greek import from Constantinople.

Traditionally he died February 20, 1054.

This is not the time to think of amusements, it is time to save our fatherland.

Great benefit is acquired from studying. Sacred books instruct and teach the path of charity. Through literacy we acquire wisdom and self-control. This is like rivers filling the world; these are the sources of wisdom. With scholarship we find profound depth, and find comfort in our sorrows. They are also the bit to restrain us. Great is wisdom. If you will diligently seek wisdom in study, you will discover great benefit for your soul.

Behold, my sons, I am leaving this world. Have love among yourselves, because you are brothers from one father and one mother. And if you will live in love among yourselves, God will reside in you and will subject your enemies to you. If you will live in hate, in strife and argument, then you will perish and destroy the land of your fathers and grandfathers who earned it with their great effort. So live peacefully, brother listening to brother.

The Era of Moscovite Russia

AVVAKUM PETROVICH

1620 – 1682

Russian Orthodox Old Believer Priest and Martyr

Avvakum Petrovich played a serious and decisive role in the Russian Orthodox Church as the originator of the group to be known as Staro-Veri (Old Believers). He was born in the Nizhni-Novgorod area (today known as Gorki), in the village Grigoriev, traditionally on November 25, 1620. Avvakum at age 21 was ordained as a deacon, and then at age 23, as a priest. He was very zealous and dedicated to the original traditions and rites of Russian Orthodoxy. In 1652, Avvakum migrated to Moscow where he taught and was very influential in the original Orthodox ecclesiastical traditions, as opposed to the renovations of Patriarch Nikon. He was banished to Tobolsk in Siberia the following year for his preaching to reject the innovations and changes that were being implemented in Russian Orthodoxy. In 1663, he returned to Moscow, but was subsequently defrocked and exiled to Mezen in the far north for preaching to people to refuse any modernization of the Church, but he returned to Moscow in 1666. Again his zeal agitated the hierarchy of the Church, and Avvakum was again exiled the following year to Pustozyorsk in the far Russian north, where he was incarcerated in an underground tomb for 14 years, and released in 1681, although still confined to the monastery. Avvakum was burned for heresy at the stake with 3 other Old Believer confederates on April 14, 1682.

Pray making the cross in this manner[3] and you will never perish; but if you abandon it, your city will perish and revert to dust, and if your city perishes then this is the end of the light.

Now Sovereign bless us as we sigh unto You, as we with our tongue recite Your divine name, that is, the God who is omnipresent, close and trustworthy. These are Your essences: existence, light, truth, life, which are Your 4 qualities, and many more: master, almighty, inaccessible, inviolate, tri-radiant, tri-hypostatic, king of glory, progressive, fire, spirit, divine and many others.

As Dionysus the Areopagite spoke about You, the truth, for whoever rejects truth will face his collapse, for Your essence is truth. But a person aligned with God can never apostatize.

We speak that we have lost many adherents to the reformists, who have fallen away from the true Lord, the holy and life-providing spirit. As Dionysus spoke, Since apostatizing from truth they deny You, the existent one. No longer are You part of them, You the omnipresent. We the orthodox, uphold both names, and in the Holy Spirit, the true master and our life-giving light. We believe so and worship the Father and the Son, and for whose sake we suffer and die, dedicating our life to Him the Sovereign.

Every person who makes the sign of the cross with 3 fingers, bows first to the beast the tsar, and second to the Russian pope, fulfilling their will and not God's, and offers his soul as a sacrifice to the antichrist and the devil himself. This is a clandestine secret, the beast and false-prophet are the snake-devil. The beast is the evil tsar, while the false-prophet is the Roman pope and those who submit to his authority.

Nikon[4] is not the final antichrist, because there are many antichrists and traitors in our country. The 2 horns of the beast

---

[3] The Old Believer (Staro-Ver) 2-finger configuration of holding the hand when making the sign of the cross.

[4] Patriarch of Russia, 1652-1658.

are the 2 authorities of the patriarchate and the autocrat. One conquers and the other provides him the ability to do so. Nikon conquers and Aleksei[5] provides him the means. They work together as did Pilate and Herod who crucified Christ.

Bow to a rich person to your waste; bow to a poor person to the ground.

Deliberate on Christ's words. It is your enemies you are to love, not God's [enemies].

Do not raise yourself over another of your natural brothers and sisters, and do not insult one another, not in words or even thoughts. And the younger brother must submit to the elder, while the elder must always worry for the younger.

Do not seek rhetoric and philosophy, or eloquence, but live with a sound and healthy mind, because rhetoricians and philosophers cannot be true Christians.

Honor your brothers and sisters. Do not say anything to them vexing and crude, and do not exalted yourself in their presence. All of you are born of the same uterus and fed by the same breasts. One mother nourished all of you and the same hands carried you, and the same heart sorrowed over you identically and she loves all of you and each of you the same.

If you want to be pardoned of the Lord, be pardonable yourself. If you want to be respected, respect others. If you want to eat, feed others. If you want to take, give to another. This is equality. Once deliberating on this properly, desire for yourself the worse, and the better for your close associate. Desire for yourself less, and more to your close associate.

---

[5] Tsar Aleksei Mikhailovich

Maksim the Greek

1475 – 1556

Religious Scholar

Mikhail Trevolis become known in Russian history as Maksim the Greek. He was born 1475 of a pious Greek family. His studies occupied the years 1495-1505, and were primarily in the city Padua, Italy. Of all his teachers the Dominican abbot Girolamo Savonarola had the greatest influence on him, impressing him with a sense of piety and a high standard of morality. Mikhail was with Savonarola in Florence, and he also attended schools in Venice and Milan. From Italy Mikhail traveled to Athens, Greece, and was tonsured as a monk at Mt Athos. He entered the Annunciation Batoped Monastery, which had an immense library he utilized to continue his scholarship. For 10 years Mikhail studied and taught, and here he learned the Slavic languages. Mikhail then took the step of migrating to Moscow to translate Greek books into Russian, and was there known as Maksim the Greek.

On the philosophic plane Maksim's main interest was divine courage. He contemplated much on this virtue tying it with a person's free will, to develop it as necessary to keep all thoughts captive in silent meditation. But in order that this choice of courage does not incline in the direction of sin, the free will needs the support of divinely-provided philosophy or belief. Maksim separated belief from external knowledge or intellect. The righteous know Christ only by faith and not by artificial means such as study. At the same time Maksim did not suspend external study or secular instruction in favor of complete mystic orthodoxy. On the contrary, he summoned his readers to become wise in every intellectual pursuit and instruction in divine wisdom, using himself as an example with his own decades of personal study.

On March 4, 1518, Maksim arrived in Moscow. During this period up to 1525 Maksim wrote several dissertations against Catholicism, against any unification of Orthodoxy and Catholicism, and against astrology. His compositions also refuted the superficial piety of Russian Orthodoxy. But these compositions turned the higher episcopacy against him and Maksim was sentenced to prison. They considered him as a foreign interloper into the private religious affairs of Orthodox Russia.

In 1525, Maksim was incarcerated for the next 6 years in a prison cell at the Joseph Voloko-Lamsk Monastery. Afterwards, Maksim was confined in a prison cell at the monastery Otroch Monastery in Tver for 15 years. Then Maksim was released from confinement and allowed to become a regular monk at the monastery, and which he did for the next 5 years. In 1551, Maksim was transferred to the Troitzkoi-Sergeev Monastery where he resided as a regular monk until his death in 1556.

Of the 38 years that Maksim the Greek spent in Russia the first 7 years were as an honored scholar and translator; the next 21 years were his incarceration as a heretic; and the final 10 years were as a regular monk.

Cleanse yourselves through a sincere repentance, with warm tears, charity according to your means, and pure dedicated prayer, so that you would become worthy to enter together with the wise virgins who hold the lit lamps, and into the mental chamber of the immortal groom, who said, Come unto me all you who labor in the vanities of the mundane life and burdened with various sins, and I will provide you rest.

Born without a beginning and all-existent from the beginningless God the Father, it was by the good will of the God and by envelopment of the Holy Spirit, that the Son and God the Word be conceived in the immaculate womb of the Holiest Theotokos and

Ever-Virgin Mary, the mother of God. And he exited from her having accepted from her, her immaculate blood and holy body – a perfect human. He is also the perfect God, existing and believed as being one hypostasis in 2 substances and activities and wills, such that His deity was not lost in humanity, and humanity was not lost in deity.

By his death he displayed his humanity; in his resurrection from death he proved his divine essence.

It was his good will to suffer on the cross and be buried, attributing to himself a model and example of perfect residence to all who desire to receive future goodness. Because radiant crowns and glorious honor, they say, must be acquired by supreme effort. For a sound mind, what greater honors can be bequeathed upon a person than eternal life and God's unending Kingdom. There is no other manner to receive this, except through many accomplishments and supreme efforts.

Christ is my King, although persecuted by many, fleeing from persecution, dying, condemned, with only 12 uneducated students who know nothing else other than the vocation of fishing, he brought to the world the right belief and performing proper conduct, but not just to one nation, not 2, but to all who live everywhere in the world, wherever the lamp of this fiery-brilliant sun shines and what the oceans surround. He freed them from idolatry and every malice, not utilizing a sword or horse or shield, and not turning to some subtlety or deceit, but by means of sincere discourses and marvelous healings, addressing them in sermons regarding proper belief.

If the King of all was not especially loving toward His creation – humanity, which He created from the soil and as an intelligent entity, then he would not have created him according to His image and likeness, and when he sinned, He would not at all have spared him, but would have either destroyed him quickly, or confined him in unbreakable shackles of the torment of the netherworld. Likewise He would not have delivered a remnant of a small family in a wood ark when He cleansed the entirely world using a immeasurable amount of water that drowned the entire human race and all animals. He likewise would not have punished Egypt with death-dealing plagues and drowned Pharaoh with his entire army. In a similar manner, He would not have created an infinite number of marvelous miracles, which He openly displayed to the ancient generations. All of this as result of His concern and divine love for His creation.

That all will arise – the criminal and sinful – this is proven by many passages, especially by those that the Lord himself declared, "Those who did good will rise to the resurrection of life, while those who did bad to the resurrection of condemnation." So does this contain a contradiction? Not at all. What is made clear is that the criminal and sinful will resurrect, but not to a resurrection of life, but to a resurrection of condemnation, that is, they will resurrect not in order to inherit eternal life together with the virtuous and righteous, but in order to be judged and hear the just sentence at their trial, "Depart from me, cursed, into the eternal fire prepared for the devil and his angels." And in another passage the divine prophet declared, "Let the criminals be transformed into hell, all the nations that forget God." Based on this we learn of 2 certain supreme dogmas, in particular, that the souls of the criminal and sinful before the second arrival of the Judge are contained in hell, and that the sinful will return from there for eternal torment.

When you hear of Gehenna, do not consider it the fire of purgatory, as do the confused Latins,[6] those who follow the heresy of Origen, but realize that this fire is unquenchable, tormenting the iniquitous and unrepentant sinners for the unending ages, relative to the amount of their defilement. Because the Lord said that he has the ability to destroy both body and soul in hell, that is, endless torment in eternal death.

---

[6] The Roman Catholic Church

The present age is the time of activity, that is, the time for the display of benevolence, while the future age is the time of compensation, and not cleansing.

Like a poisonous plant when it touches any part of the body will spread and infect the entire surface, so is sin. If a person is not cautious the evil demon allows himself to approach and touch a righteous person, then difficult torments continually poison his soul, until he repents with all his soul for going astray.

Nil Sorski

1433 – 1508

Russian Orthodox Monk and Mystic

Nil Sorski was an ascetic with immense impact on Russian monasticism during the Muscovite era. He was tonsured as a monk at the Kirill Bel-Ozerski Monastery. In his zeal as a young monk he traveled to Mt. Athos where he spent time learning the practice of asceticism and especially hesychasm, silent prayer in deep meditation. He returned to Kirill Bel-Ozerski and there introduced the practice of hesychasm. Nil also taught that every monastery should be self-sufficient, and not to seek expansion and the acquisition of property, so he was labeled a *non-possessor*. The monastic prelates that accumulated property were labeled *possessors*.

About 5 miles from Kirill Monastery, Nil began his own hermitage alongside the river Sor – hence his name, Sorski. At his new monastery he would not accept any patrimony or real estate other than the grounds themselves, and the monks were to work to support themselves, in accord with his concept of being a non-possessor.

Nil Sorski died in 1508 at about the age of 75. Not wanting his body to be enshrined or divided up as relics, he bequeathed his disciples to leave his body deep in the forest after his death for it to be consumed by wild animals. His disciples did fulfill his last wishes.

Your first fortification in defeating the inner struggle, a fortification indicated in all the Scriptures, consists in not becoming timid or intimidated when we formidably battle malicious thoughts, and not become fatigued, and not to stop, and not to early terminate our further course on the path of victory. The subtlety of diabolic malice installs shame in us when we suffer some defeat from defiled thoughts, and which restrains us from gazing at God with a feeling of repentance and the need to raise our prayers to You against them. But yes, we will defeat them as a result of our daily repentance and continual prayer and we will not submit our shoulders to our enemies, that is, we will not retreat, even for one day after we receive a thousand wounds from them. We resolve to not in any manner abandon this life-provided activity even to our death. The mercy of God will visit us secretly and descend upon us after the tests and tribulations we survive.

Desire is identified as a certain inclination and a certain activity that for a long time nests in the soul, and by means of habit soon is transformed into its essence. A person arrives at this state arbitrarily and willingly, and then the thought, now established due to its frequent access and cohabitation, now warm, now nourished in the heart, now turned into a bad habit, will incessantly torment and agitate him with lust's obsessions, installed by the enemy.

This occurs when the enemy very often presents to the person some object or person that is saturated with lust, and ignites it for their attraction, and subsequently, willingly or unwillingly, a person mentally becomes enslaved to it. The reason for this occurring, as we mentioned, is due to neglect and irresponsibility, a longtime obsession by lust. The person enveloped by desire is immutably subject in all its forms to either repentance with admission of guilt, or future torment. It is worth considering repentance and prayer to be delivered from every desire.

Let this be known to all of you, that if we perform our benevolence, but do not restrain ourselves from anger, this is not pleasing to God. The holy father spoke, "If you are angered, your prayers are unacceptable to God, even if you can resurrect the dead." If such a spirit of anger languishes and torments someone, feeding the malice toward others residing in him and exciting the wrath to repay with evil and to take vengeance on the one who wronged him, then let him remember this statement of our Lord, "If you do not release your brother from his errors against you, then your heavenly Father will have your errors remain upon you." And so, every person who wants to receive forgiveness of his sins, first must from the heart forgive his brother, because only under these conditions are we allowed to ask for forgiveness from the Lord. If we do not release these errors ourselves, then it is obvious that we will not have ours released. Let us banish thoughts of anger from our heart, which is heartfelt remission of our brother.

And you, man of God, do not associate with possessors. Do not waste your time debating with them, or discrediting them, or reprimanding them, but leave this all to God. Only God is capable enough to correct them.

Do not waste time in sinful conversations; flee from watching what is inappropriate, since they arouse desires and strengthen defiling thoughts. And God will help you.

It is better to distribute funds to the needy, than to use them to decorate a church.

Just as it is impossible to live without food and drink, so it is without preservation of the mind from all that is defiling. Without observance of your heart your soul cannot attain any spiritual perfection.

Take roots of obedience, leaves of patience, flowers of purity and philanthropy. Shred them into the pot of silence, sieve them through a screen of deliberation, dump all of it into a pot of humility and fill it with water from the tears of petitioners. And when all in the pot begins to boil, add shamefulness and brotherly love, and eat it with the spoon of repentance, and your health will be restored.

The holy fathers said, "Who often devotes his thoughts to matters immoral and vile performs immorality in his heart." And if a person does not abstain from such thoughts, then the act will eventually materialize.

The world flatters us with sweet objects, but once you eat them you discover they make your stomach bitter. The good things of the world only seem good, but they are filled inside with evil. Those who sought delight in the world have lost all. Wealth, honor, glory – all passes away, all collapses, like a flower that the smoke destroys.

We are obligatory toward our close associates according to God's command: to have love and prove it in work and action.

We must protect our thinking from all that is superficial and extraneous, to make our mind smooth and malleable, our heart to be clean of all prejudice.

When I die, abandon my body in the wilderness to be eaten by beasts and birds, because it has sinned much and not worthy of a burial. I strove not to summon honor and glory during my life, and likewise after my life. I beseech you all, Pray for my soul. I ask all of you for forgiveness and forgive all. Yes, God will forgive all.

When thoughts of immorality attack us, then we must fire the fear of God within us and bring to our mind that nothing at all can be hidden from God, not even the most subtle movement of the heart, and that the Lord is judge and executor for all the wrong that we do, even the most secret and clandestine.

Who attains spiritual perfection, has not need in the singing of Psalms. All he needs is inner concentration, prayers evolving from the heart and withdrawing deep within yourself. Such are united with God, and it is not proper for them to distract their minds from Him and violate their spiritual tranquility and contemplation.

You ask how to abandon the world. Strive to accomplish this in action. This is the path to eternal life; all the saints and holy fathers, those who gained wisdom, walked this path. Whoever wants to learn to be accepted of God must depart from the world.

SERGEI RADONEZHSKI

1314/1322 –1392

Russian Orthodox Mystic and Prelate

The Russian mystic Sergei Radonezhski was born anywhere from 1314 to 1322, in the city of Radonezh about 60 miles north of Moscow,. In 1342, Sergei with his older brother departed into the forest about 10 miles from Radonezh and founded the Troitzki Monastery (the city was later Zagorsk, but today known as Sergeev Posad). Sergei became a monk that year at the age of 24, and later became abbot of his monastery.

After 2 years of living alone in his forest residence Sergei developed a reputation as an austere ascetic and began to attract disciples. Many from all over Russia requested his counsel on matters of both political as well as religious questions.

At this time Prince Dmitri Donskoi had to deal with an invasion of Moscow by the Mongol Khan Mamai. Dmitri went to Sergei for his advise, whether to attack or submit to further Mongol occupation. The mystic Sergei informed him that God would grant him victory although at a grave cost of many soldiers. The battle of Kulikova occurred September 8, 1380, where the victory was gained by Dmitri Donskoi. This prediction of Sergei increased his reputation in Russia and his favor in the royal family.

Over the succeeding years Sergei received many visions and revelations while abbot at his monastery. He died at the age of 78 on September 25, 1392.

"Father, have love toward me, tonsure me to be a monk, because I for a long while, from my youth, want this, but the will of my parents restrained me. Today, I am free from all of this. I desire tonsure. As a dear searches for a fountain of water, so does my soul thirst for the monastic and wilderness life"

We must ascend the great feat of struggle with the invisible enemy who, as a roaring lion, lurks and wants to swallow each of us.

Take charge of yourselves, brethren. First, have fear of God. Have a pure soul and body and unfeigned love. Decorate yourself with humility, preserve unity of mind with one another. There is nothing that will provide you genuine honor and glory in your life, but in place of this await the compensation from God, the heavenly and eternal goodness and consolation.

So why should my soul then be attached to this dust of the ground, for all its meditations to be of the earth and about the earth?

The Kingdom of Heaven is founded on humility and invites the humble to bequeath them eternal life.

Human life does not pass without testing and calamity, and without this there is no salvation of the soul. Tests are sent because of sins, they must be courageously and patiently endured.

Child! Do you believe that God exists? That he is judge of the righteous and sinful? The father of widows and orphans? Ready for vengeance? And that it is terrifying to fall into His hands? If so, how can you not stop plundering, causing violence, being malicious, and being harmful in darkness? Are you not satisfied with what He has given us out of His grace? We constantly want what belongs to another and test His patience. Rather do we not see that those who are unjust and malevolent in the end become destitute; their homes empty, the memory of the wealthy vanishes forever; and in the future life what awaits them is endless torment?

There is no need to worry about matters useless to you, but what is required is to depend and look upon God, who will feed and clothe us, and He worries about all of our affairs. From Him we should await all that we need, what is good and useful for our souls and bodies.

Let us pray so He will be concerned with us. Let us more be strengthened in our hope on Him, because from ancient times He fed many thousands of Israelites in the desert with manna, the hardened and unsubmissive, and not just once did He feed the many. They asked for it and quails flew into their camp. The Lord Himself from now on will be concerned over us. Or rather has His strength been exhausted, or has His concern for us, His creation, decreased? No. As in ancient times, so also today, the Lord is ready to send us food.

"God, the Father of our Lord Jesus Christ, the creator of the skies and the land and all visible and invisible, who created the human out of soil and who does not want the death of sinners, but wants to send life. We beseech you, the sinful and Your unworthy servants. Hear us at this hour and reveal your glory. As in the desert Your strong right hand performed many miracles through Moses, who brought water from the rock according to Your command, so today also reveal Your power. Provide us water at this place. Yes, let all recognize that You bend Your ears to those who fear You and who give glory to Your name, the Father and Son and Holy Spirit, now and continually and for ever and ever. Amen."

Once Metropolitan Aleksei came to Sergei with the question, "What should I do?"
    Sergei answered, "Help the land of Russia."

Tikhon Zadonski

1725 – 1783

Russian Orthodox Monk and Mystic

Tikhon Solokov of Zadonsk and Voronezh, also known as the Miracle Worker of Zadonsk, was born in 1725, the son of a poor deacon of Novgorod Province. His parents were able to send him to a seminary and then Tikhon was hired as an instructor, and where he taught for the next 5 years. Later, he became rector of the Tver Seminary, and in 1763 he became a monk and was ordained as Archbishop of Voronezh. Having been raised in poverty, Tikhon led a humble life and was especially noted for his charity.

After about 5 years as archbishop, and having considerable difficulties with raising the level of education of priests and clergy in his diocese, this being a responsibility not of his religious vocation, as well as having to deal with ecclesiastical politics, Tikhon took leave of his episcopacy and for the final 14 years of his life, he lived as a recluse. Most of this time was spent at the Zadonsk Bogo-Roditza (Theotokos) Monastery, near Voronezh. Tikhon exemplified the austere ascetic of his era: praying for hours in his cloister, reading the Bible and writings of the Holy Fathers, and writing. He produced a total of fifteen published volumes. During these years he had a constant stream of visitors, while he also participated in routine monastic chores such as chopping wood or mowing grass. He died August 13, 1783 at the age of 59.

The Holy Bible is God's word. It speaks to you, just as any person speaks to you. It is given to you so you can receive eternal salvation, so seek your salvation in God's word, the Holy Bible. Abandon curiosity, or what is occurring in this place or somewhere else. Worry about knowing what is occurring in your soul, and with the help of God's word, and what your conclusion will be at the end of your life: to perish or inherit salvation. What path are you traveling? It is the path of the saints or the path of criminals?

In order to recognize God, a revelation from above is needed. God's word preaches God, but without God it is impossible to recognize God. Our reasoning is blind and dark; it needs enlightenment from Him who brought light out of darkness. And so it is necessary to heed God's word and petition God for His enlightenment. Natural light banishes darkness. The Holy Scripture is a lamp, but only the inner and opened eye can see the light of this lamp. A blind person cannot see light; it is necessary to have opened eyes. This is the reason the prophet prayed, "Open my eyes and I will comprehend miracles from Your law." Ps 119:18.

Deceptively and maliciously the evil devil took possession of us and took us captive into his dark authority, but Christ, God's son, redeemed us from the devil's authority and adopted us, and redeemed us not with silver or gold, but by his immaculate blood.

You see the sun pleasantly shining and illuminating all under the sky and providing us with joy. Take the example of the sun and raise your mind to meditating on the eternal sun of righteousness, Christ the son of God, who faithfully enlightens his believers in a marvelous manner and will forever illuminate them and provide them joy, so they will shine like the sun in the Kingdom of their Father.

Lead your life in the following manner: Rise from sleep, thank God and pray. After you leave church services, read something from a book that is beneficial to your soul, then begin your work for the day. After you work a while, again pray. Having prayed, again read, and then again go to work. And so do alternately in everything: pray, read, work. But while you are working, in your vocation, concentrate your mind on Christ, pray to him, so he will pardon you and help you. When you acquire the routine to alternate in these areas: reading, prayer and work, you will develop motivation and zeal. Changes in your life will create motivation and increase zeal. Often remember death, the judgment of Christ, and eternity. Having these thoughts, you will banish melancholy and boredom as with a whip.

Any person, before he sins, stands between 2 contradistinctive powers – God and Satan – and he has the free volition to turn to one or the other. God summons him to goodness and rescues him from evil. Satan deceives and draws him away from goodness, inclines him to evil and sin, which is his work. And so when a person listens to God and does good, he turns his face to God. And when he listens to Satan and does bad, he turns his face to Satan, turns his back on God, and so, rejecting God, he follows after Satan.

Sacred Scripture is given to us from God for the sake of our salvation and to glorify God's name. For this reason we must read and study and heed it. But if we read and endeavor to know it just to magnify ourselves in people's presence, then it will not be of benefit to us, but actually to our detriment.

Beloved! Constantly remember, continually remember the hour of your death. This hour is terrifying not only for the sinners but also for the saints. The saints have led their entire life meditating on death. The focus of their mind and heart has been directed at the gates of eternity, at the incomprehensible expanse that just begins at these gates. They have turned toward their sinfulness, looking at it as if into a dark abyss. From a humble heart, from a painful heart, they spilled warm and incessant prayers to God for their pardon.

If you want eternal salvation to be your primary concern, then be in the midst of this world a pilgrim and visitor. Turn away from vanity and self-deception, and turn toward truth! Turn from sin and this world to God! Turn from the temporary to the eternal! Reject all empty vocations and enjoyments, and approach God's word. Cling to His life-giving word that provides salvation. It will educate you and will guide you to eternal blessing.

The most important and most necessary matter for each Christian is obtaining eternal salvation. What we need during this era of our earthly journey is clothing, food, drink, shelter, and other similar requirements. But salvation is needed more than all. It is so necessary that all that is temporal is nothing compared to it. The person who obtains salvation now possesses everything. Who does not obtain salvation, possesses nothing, although he may claim all the world is his possession.

Recognize and be convinced that luxury, parties, amusements, gambling, dissolution of life, in short, all that possesses the appellation of vanity and secular, what worries and consumes a person's entire life, all of his time, all the strength and capabilities of soul and body, is nothing else other than the deceit and entrapment of satan, contrived and constructed by him to deceive humanity. If you will not recognize this and will not be convinced of this willingly from God's word, then you will acknowledge and admit to this unwillingly at the approach of death. Whoever will not learn this will never know this. Who will strive little for something great, or not at all strive, he considers what is great to actually be of little importance, of little significance, worthless. Christians do not know Christianity as a result of not studying it: they do not read, do not ask. In general, they do not turn any attention to the redemption of humanity by the God who became human. They trample this great work of God, because they do not worry and do not think about their salvation. Disdaining God's great gifts, they entirely abandon themselves to vanity, which is deceit. And none of this has any substance. The wrath of God will burn against such Christians.

Before the flood, people ate, drank, married and were given in marriage, and all their thoughts were driven to the satisfaction of their corporeal desires. Unexpectedly the water arrived and destroyed them all. So at present do people drink, eat, travel, marry and are given in marriage, and devote themselves to every diverse dissolution, not turning any attention to the Lord's works and His judgments. And unexpectedly the archangel's trumpet will blow, "Behold, the judge comes. Arise, dead, come to judgment. This undaunted and corporeal manner of life is now concluded, because the day of the Lord is near."

Many parents, having blind love toward their children, regret having to punish them for disobedience, but after, when the children grow and find themselves at fault, they will recognize their error on their own. Other than this, children must strongly be prohibited to associate and be friends with evil people, because the malice will change their good mind, and even the parents must be cautious, so not to be a bad example and lead the children astray.

You see a ship on the sea agitating and desperate. Learn from this, that so our life in the sea of this world is desperate and agitating from the many and diverse disasters that overwhelm us like waves. By way of this you will learn to often and zealously pray and sigh to the wisest guide, Christ, so he will not allow your small ship to sink in the waves of desperation, but will keep it afloat to reach the calm and safe harbor of eternal life.

A person is blind on this own and so needs illumination; forgetful and so needs to be reminded regularly; lazy and needs encouragement; sad and melancholy and so needs comfort; inclined to fall and go astray and so need strength; inclined to doubt and so needs instruction. All of this will find its source in Sacred Scripture.

We must approach God's word with prayer, read and hear it with prayer, and begin and end its study with prayer. This is why in our ecclesiastical gathering, before beginning reading and studying God's word – the Gospels and Apostolic letters – we pray and then after we thank God for this great gift of His.

You do notice that a lender will take his debtor and torture him, put him in prison, to have him pay the debt. So does God also subject sinners to punishment for the debt of sins that are not removed due to repentance. And the person who sins the more, and adds sins to sins, the more the sinful debt increases, and he is now subject to a greater torment and judgment of God.

If the fear of temporal penalty will shake people's hearts, how much more should the fear of eternal torment shake them. Because every temporal penalty, no matter how large or long, will eventually pass. Eternity has no end, once beginning it will never end.

The narrow path is the path of humility, obedience, patience, meekness and denial of oneself, that is, your individual will. The wide path is the path of pride, disobedience, impatience and ambition. One leads to heaven, the other leads to hell. Select which path you want to take: either the narrow and lowly to heaven, or the wide and high to hell, and there is no 3rd path mentioned in the Sacred Scripture.

The kind-hearted God for the sake of His son, the Lord our Jesus Christ, who paid for all of our sinful debts with his death and blood, forgives sincerely the repentant and believer. And so they, now liberated from their debts, are liberated from the approaching penalty. This is why every person that wants to be freed from sinful debts, for which debtors will be secured in a eternal prison, must repent and run to the intercessor, the merciful Jesus Christ.

Subsequently the repentant must definitely refrain from all further sin. He must curb further sins for God to remit his previous sins. So how can a person ask for the forgiveness of debts if he does not stop increasing them and burdening himself with them? This cannot be, beloved Christians. For a repentance to be true, sinning must be stopped, otherwise a repentance is feigned and insincere.

Do you want to see a miracle every day? Then every day meditate on the incarnation and suffering of Christ.

Every gift of God will be to our detriment when we direct it toward credit of our name, and not to the credit of God.

It is embarrassing to brag of slaves, when the Lord was meek as they are.

It will be more tolerable for idol-worshipers and the Mohammedans on the day of God's judgment, than for Christians.

Love must be in the heart, and not on the tongue.

Remember, we cannot comprehend God without God, and the person who comprehends God the more is the more humble and he fears and loves Him.

The duty of rulers is to save, not to ruin.

To sin is human; but to continue in sin is diabolic.

Whoever, relying on God's mercy, does not cease sin, that person needs to fear and to sense the coming judgment of God upon him.

With what hope in mind will you pray to God, when you do not even listen to the prayers of people just like yourself?

There is nothing more damaging to a person than sin, but a person is not so inclined to anything as much as to sin. We notice 5 reasons for sin:

1. The moral decay of human nature.
2. The devil leads people to sin.
3. The deception of the world likewise leads people to sin.
4. The poor education of children leads to sin.
5. A person's bad habits strongly draw a person to sin.

All of these enemies of our salvation are bad for us. Corporeal evil with its desires and lusts rise against spirit.

IMPERIAL RUSSIA – THE PHILOSOPHERS

RUSSIA'S WISDOM

DMITRI SERGEEVICH ANICHKOV

1733 – 1788

Philosopher, Educator, Mathematician

Dmitri Sergeevich Anichkov was born at Troitzki-Sergeev Monastery in 1733. His education begin at the seminary school and in 1755 he transferred to Moscow University. He studied philosophy and mathematics and concluded studies in 1761. He continued to teach at the university and became a professor of philosophy in 1766, and he also taught Latin. He also used his talent to create textbooks in arithmetic, algebra, geometry, trigonometry as well as philosophy, and subsequently taught ethics, a topic not recognized at the time. During his tenure he wrote several books on philosophy.

From 1777, Anichkov was a member of the Masonic Lodge in Moscow. One sad event is that toward the conclusion of his life many of his manuscripts were destroyed in a fire. Anichkov died May 1, 1788, in Moscow.

A simple and uneducated people are inclined to polytheism and stagnate in it.

All that people write to ascribe perfections to God evolves from their human capacity of thinking, and as a result are not conformed to His essence and cannot be proofs of His perfection.

And this is so true, that there is nothing that cannot cause so great a harm to humanity's cognizance than an unlimited volition to fabricate something based on your own arbitrary notion, depending on solely your feelings, which are not conforming in view to the items themselves. And so not deliberating or identifying what is good and what is bad, what is useful and what is harmful, we make a conclusion solely based on our feelings, although this may impose great harm upon ourselves. And this we do not understand, that our feelings – in the manner our soul deliberates – only provide us the capability of ascertaining, just as a microscope or telescope assists the eyes.

Every truth has as its initial concept a person's knowledge of himself.

For the ignorant, every extraordinary item seems to be divine.

However there are many in Christianity who are very gentle by God's standards, who have sworn and now affirm that they in their handicaps have actually seen paradise and hell and that the former was presented to them as a most beautiful garden overfilled with joy, while the other was a terrifying kettle bubbling with some inconsumable fatty liquid and that they in the presence of all of such visions, being in body and soul in their present life, saw God whom they were not able to recognize although face to face, and the same with devils.

It is contrary to the nature of a human to believe that what is in the mind and cannot materialize in the imagination.

It is often that we who have despaired with our individual strength to defend our high opinion of ourselves then aspire to steal alien credit and honor and attribute it to ourselves and then build upon it a temple of our supremacy.

It is truly worth amazement that these very qualities by which mortal man surpasses other animals and considers himself like unto the Supreme also occasionally serve equally to his ruin as much as to the perfection of his human entity.

Our soul always has an inclination to further proceed and even as if skip from one place to another.

The antiquity of traditions much promotes the stagnation of the people in superstition.

The barbaric peoples in their knowledge of things are just a little above animals, but because of this also, they live in a natural setting and so are capable of learning much.

The ignorant and uninformed definitely are consoled by deceptions, and devising one delusion after another they increase their polytheism and their rampage against monotheism.

The ignorant nations are those who understand God in their minds as being terrifying and unapproachable.

The uneducated are amazed at things and they deify them out of amazement solely because they do not comprehend in detail the reasons why such strange activities occur in things. Among the commoners at present, the supreme drunken address that they can mumble about things incomprehensible to them does not extend any further than *God knows about this*, which they refer to what they do not comprehend.

There is noticed in every person as much inclination toward vanity, megalomania and self-interest as there is toward a lie.

We almost never deliberate about things and their essence for their sake, but for the most part at every deliberation we have our attitude directed at ourselves. But especially when we think that all our meditations and all opinions are so clear and reliable to the point that when we propose them to others and force them on others, then they agree. Those who think and deliberate otherwise we usually consider ignorant and thoughtless.

With one good quality of the soul another will follow.

With the increase of humanity's knowledge of things, humanity's knowledge of God is simultaneously increased.

Konstantine Nikolaevich Batushkov

1787 – 1855

Poet, Military Hero

Konstantine Nikolaevich Batushkov was born May 18, 1787 in the city Vologda, northern Russia, in a family with considerable wealth. He attended school in St Petersburg, and at age 16 was studying French and Russian literature, as well as Latin and the classical writers. In 1802 he went to work at the Ministry for National Education, and then in 1805 at an office of the Moscow University. His first poems appeared in print in 1805.

In 1807, Batushkov joined the military and fought in the war against Prussia, and was awarded the Order of St Anne for bravery. He was sent to Riga for recovery due to injuries. The following year he was again in active duty in the war against Sweden. After the war he was released from the military – in 1810 – and returned to his home for a short visit, and then to Moscow. For the nest several years, Batushkov circulated among different Russian literary circles and composed poetry. His health often hindered him from any further physical labor, and as much as he wanted to join the war against Napoleon in 1812, his health prevented him. However he was able to acquire a secondary position and followed the troops in 1813 to Paris. Batushkov visited England, Sweden, and Finland on his return to Russia in 1814. Now in Moscow he continued to write poetry and circulate among other writers.

In 1818, Batushkov visited Odessa to regain his health, and returned to St Petersburg, but went again to Europe: Italy and

Germany, seeking doctors to help him. But he was back in Russia in 1822. Then it was Crimea and the Caucasus for his health, and then 4 years in France. He returned to Moscow for 5 years and he decided to return home to Vologda, where he died from typhus, July 7, 1855.

A beautiful woman is always divine, especially if she is kind and smart and wants to be liked. But how is she more attractive? When holding a harp, or a book, knitting or embroidering, while praying, or dancing? None of these at all! But at the table as she is cutting a salad.

A person in the wilderness is free; a person is society is a slave. A poor person is more of a slave than a rich person.

An eloquent defender of truth (as long as truth is not contrary to his passions), a fiery deifier and priest of virtue, so often exchanges virtue and truth when discovered among the greatest of his mistakes.

Who has gone astray the most in the labyrinth of life while carrying the lamp of humanity's wisdom in his hand? Such a lamp is insufficient. One ray of belief, a weak illumination, being constant, shows us the more trusting path to the true goal than a complete radiance of the mind and imagination.

As love ages, so does respect.

An exceptional passion to some type of literature can be harmful to the successes of education.

Circumstances shape great people, and then great people shape circumstances.

Do not do anything of any sort that you would not want your enemy to know.

Great people undertake great matters, and because they are great. But stupid people do what makes them just that, idle.

Great thoughts flow out of the heart.

He was possessed by the incurable disease that only those people whom fortune early showered with gifts possesses – gluttony.

Ideas circumnavigate the world, migrate from age to age, from language to language, from element to element, from prose to prose. Finally they appear in clothes that appear nice to you, in a prosperous expression, and then they become worthy to belong to the legacy of the human race.

If you want to weigh merits and offences, then take some weight from the one side and add it to the other and then they will balance.

If your enemy is praising you, this means you have turned into a fool.

In short speak the truth as much as you can in a humorous manner, to despot and to slave, since to the former it is dangerous and to the latter it is useless.

In solitude time belongs to the sage and the sage is all to himself. In solitude, I will add, all accepts an important and triumphant appearance.

It is not by our will to have talents and often not in our will to develop what nature has gifted us, except to be honorable in our will, to be good in our will, to be condescending, magnanimous, consistent in our will.

It is possible to quarrel with women? It is possible, but you need to be bold. They have as many virtues as they do vices.

Just as the power of reproduction has its basis on warmth, so the power of civility has its basis on goodness.

Language always walks on the same level as success in weapons and national credit, with education, with the needs of society, with civil advancement and humanitarianism.

National fables always have an initial basis of truth.

No matter from what side a person looks at himself and society, he will discover that condescension must be the first virtue. Condescension in speaking, in actions, in thoughts, this provides an attraction for goodness which is considered the most admired trait in society. But condescension must also have its limit: not condoning a vice, but yet forgiving weakness. The intellect will separate vice from weakness. A person must also be condescending to himself. If you did something foolish today, do not become despondent. Now you have fallen, tomorrow you will arise. Do not wallow in mud.

Nothing gives such strength to the mind, heart, soul, than incessant integrity. Integrity is a straight line, it is closer to truth than a crooked line.

Often the best qualities of the heart are called weaknesses by people of no perspicuity.

Others are surprised that educated people are scattered in society. But I am surprised that some of them can be noticed in society, while others are very careful.

Our first obligation is gratitude toward our Creator. But in order to fulfill this it is needful to begin with people. It would be good to tie all of our attitudes to Him through our involvement with society.

Philosophy dominates over the past and the future, while the present mortifies it.

Some words must be recited with reverence. It is apparent in some cultures to remove your hat when you pronounce the name of God. But among us Russians it is God, faith, fatherland and Russia. All of this anywhere, opportunely and inopportunely, whether an important or vulgar circumstance, is written, sung and talked about and without any shame.

The person standing in the Kremlin and with freezing eyes gazing at the gigantic towers, at the ancient monasteries, at the majestic Moscow River, can only boast of his fatherland and bless Russia, and I will state this boldly, and even though the region has been grievously plundered by nations, even beginning at its birth and alienated from other greatness.

The plow is the foundation of society, the true knot to tie citizens together, the support of laws.

The traveler has many bosses but few friends.

There are people who will not sell their freedom for anything. Such people were created for this world.

There are virtues that pertain to the mind and others that pertain to the heart. Gratitude is the best of virtues, or more correctly stated, the echo of many psychological qualities that pertain to the heart.

There is nothing so boring than to live with a person who has nothing to love: not a dog, not a person, not a horse, not a book.

To live in society, to assume a heavy yoke of obligations that are often useless and vain, and to want to announce the advantages of ambition or self-interest with the desire for credit, is a demand truly vain. The form of your life must strongly and constantly depend on talent, and there will be no doubt of this.

To our benefit, or to our misfortune, perhaps, and who really knows all the paths of Providence? We reside in a sorrowful era where humanity's wisdom is insufficient for the ordinary circle of activity of the plainest citizen. So what type of wisdom can comfort the unfortunate person during these sorrowful eras and what noble heart? One that is sensitive and benevolent, or one who will be satisfied with emaciated rules of philosophy? What wisdom has the strength to provide constant thoughts to a citizen when evil triumphs over innocence and virtue?

To worship virtue and then exchange it, to venerate truth and then not acquire it, is the tearful region of morality that does not rely on the anchor of belief.

Virtue walks right by happiness and malice, throwing a stare of contempt at one and the other.

What kind of officer is not ambitious? Do you not love to be decorated with medals? Then retire! And do not laugh at those who buy them at the cost of their own blood. But what is the reason for such people in the world? It is ambition. Believe me, that this passion is the key of all passions.

When we subject ourselves to fate, this is not blind, but visible, because this is nothing else other than the will of our Creator. He forgives us of our weaknesses. In Him is our strength, but not in some person.

Aleksandr Aleksandrovich Bestuzhev

1797 – 1837

Writer, Political Activist

Aleksandr Bestuzhev was born October 23, 1797, in St Petersburg in a royal family. He was educated while in the military corps and held rank as a staff-captain. After his release from the military he joined the Northern Secret Society, who were involved in the December 1825 rebellion and assassination of Tsar Alexander I. Bestuzhev was arrested for his involvement and sentenced to death, but the sentence was commuted to exile to Yakutsk in Siberia. In 1829 he was moved to the Caucasus by military convoy and impressed back into military service. While there he fought attempting to subdue local tribes and died in battle on June 7, 1837.

His literary accomplishments are many beginning in 1818 with his poetry and continuing through the years of his exile in Siberia and later in the Caucasus. His final volume of Caucasian tales was published in 1836, and which also influenced Mikhail Lermontov in his novels centered in the Caucasus. Most of his compositions were published under the pseudonym Marlinski.

A coward dies a hundred time. A champion dies once, and then very slowly.

A person always prefers what it seems he cannot attain, but when he needs to exert the effort, the will is no longer there.

A squeaking door will not silence with a hammer but with oil

An inescapable danger will make a hero out of a coward, but the same will cause a brave person to become cold-blooded in life and death.

And so in order to speak comprehensively with people, it is necessary to weigh and measure the expression of your feeling with their comprehensions. It is necessary for me to be servile to the rules of our language, to pretend to be fashionable, slither at the feet of etiquette, select the right declensions[7] and consonances, in order to want to express myself with the roar of a lion, a song of some arbitrary wind, or with a silent reproach of the mirror.

During a calamity we fall as if into a ravine suddenly, but when committing crimes we do the same except step by step.

Foresight provides a person at one time the happiness of satisfaction, and at another time the malice of a fantasy.

God knows why when the heart increases its rhythm prudence hides so far in the distance and you will not entice it to return with begging, not with threats. And whatever you say, I do not believe verbose love in novels.

I am not rich. Even though loving luxury, I still have the ability to control my desires because it is easier to tolerate denial of my personal will than someone else's lack of passion. I believe that many have much, but none are satisfied. As a result I firmly believe that wealth consists more in desire than in possession.

---

[7] All Russian nouns are separated into 6 declensions and 3 genders (male, female, neuter), and singular and plural.

Ideas that have outlived their era may long continue walking with a crutch. They can even once or twice appear after death through their agents. But it is difficult for them to again occupy life and progress. They will not entice away all of humanity, or else will just lead astray a few deficient people.

If it is beneath people to be honorable, they display themselves such.

If you spit in their face with saliva made of gold, they will venerate you.

In the book of love the most blank page is the list of mistakes.

It is best to acquire from a friend what people say about you when they laugh at you, or have him at least hint this personally to you.

It is not an embarrassment to sing and retain the first song you learned.

It is obvious that there is no stupidity in the world that intellectual people will not sanctify as their example.

Life is a person's concubine. If she is good to him, he will be her slave. If she is shameful, then he is the master.

Often it is better to build something anew than to try and repair the old.

People are eternally doomed to pursue toys. Childhood should be happy enough a time with them without regrets.

Profound feelings will seldom be exposed, and particularly because they are profound.

Reality is so diverse that there is just no means of measuring it. In the place where the word needs to rhyme with the thought, the harmony is child's play.

Some annoyance is the best means to get a woman to voice her opinion.

The complete absence of every defined activity is intolerable for a person. An animal supposes that all that he has is just to exist, but a person accepts life only based on the possibility that it can be utilized for something.

The one who leaves behind just one bright and novel thought, even though only one useful for humanity's advancement, has not died childless.

The thirst for present credit is the need for love beyond the grave.

There exist people having the ability to naturally speak of the most ordinary things, propose the most immodest questions in the world, and not in the least do anything that seems strange on their lips, but from the first minute of friendship they are ready to disclose every detail about themselves.

There is no more an immaculate, exalted, holy pleasure, than noble feelings and bright thoughts, these sensations to which we abandon ourselves, while entrusting them to others. Then we attach ourselves to them with fatherly love, and indeed, to instill in the human soul an intellectual valor to live, does this not mean but to create and birth it for virtue, and it not this relationship more valuable than a familiar relationship, and more sacred than ties due to blood?

Time exists only for the one who has nothing to do.

To admit to faults is the higher form of courage.

To say this is shameful, but to hide it is sin!

True courage is a man of few words. There is no need for him to advertise himself, since he considers his heroism an obligation, and not a feat.

Valor for the defense of the fatherland is virtuous, but valor in some crime is malicious.

When something is beautiful, is it not because of an absence of flaws?

Where the many do all that they want, everyone tolerates what they do not want.

Whom they do not like for exposing some matter, against him they weave gossip and rumor.

Wine will cause your head to ache. A gambling loss is like a whirlwind exiting your pocket. But a woman will not only impose a headache and empty pocket, but will emaciate the heart.

Without gilded glasses the laws have no eyes.

FADDEI VENEDIKTOVICH BULGARIN

1789 – 1859

Poet, Journalist, Military Hero

Faddei Bulgarin was Polish and was born Jan Tadeusz Krzysztof Bułharyn on June 24, 1789, near Minsk, in the area known at the time as Lithuania. His mother brought him to St Petersburg at any early age and where he acquired his education, 1798-1806, at a military school. The following years he was part of military campaigns against France and Sweden. Once he started writing he was arrested in 1811, for his satire of Grand Prince Konstantine Pavlovich and he was lowered in rank and discharged from the military. He then migrated from Russia to Warsaw and to Paris and then to Prussia where he joined Napoleon's campaign against Russia. He was captured by Russia, but was able to survive further prosecution and migrated to St Petersburg in 1816. There he continued to write poetry and circulated with the poets of the era.

Bulgarin was then suspected of being an accomplice with the Decembrists and was arrested. Due to his Polish background and history of enlistment in Napoleon's army, he was impressed back into Russia's military in 1830 and sent into battle against Poland in 1831. He was released from the military and continued the balance of his life writing.

Bulgarin died September 1, 1859, in Tartu, Estonia.

You will say: are there few people possessing the same manner of thinking and with the same feelings? The matter is that these feelings and thoughts are not worth a crumb. Friendship does not accept feelings and thoughts on a scale, in measure or as a tariff. True friends can dispute between each other, anger at one another, even vex one another, exactly in the manner as we are discontent with ourselves, anger at ourselves and recognize in ourselves our mistakes. To say about a friend, that he is incapable of doing anything stupid, but in this situation he acted foolishly, is the same as saying, I acknowledge that I acted negligently. You will argue, anger and then you will inherently love each other as friends. This is genuine friendship, and friendship is tit-for-tat love. True love does not exist without friendship, and friendship cannot exist without love.

What is called high society can be compared to a fortress. The commander is etiquette. This commander will not allow anyone to enter the fortress if he does not belong to a garrison, but he will capitulate the entire fortress to the first daredevil who will arrive at its steps with a crowd of his timid devotees. Success in high society relative to your mentality is not very difficult, because it depends on the position of the person in society.

One bad review of a composer, and especially a poet, is worse that a bad certificate from the service. A writer is a synonym for a person incapable of doing anything, although we have a custom of placing the writer on the same spot as a comedian, clown and other entertainer. If a writer is bad, he becomes the joke of the crowds; if he is mediocre, he is soon oblivious; if he has a decent talent and an extraordinary gift, then he becomes the object of envy, slander, and persecution, because in particular people are willing to forgive everything, except mental excellence, to which each person seems to have an attraction, and the stupider the greater. The obligation of the writer is to speak the truth, while printed truth pierces the eyes worse than verbal.

A child quickly matures, while a man quickly ages, during misfortune. Only in contentment and lethargy does the young mind weaken and stop in some mundane routine.

Ah! If you would just read my compositions, the meanings hidden in certain verses, and compared them to compositions published in the world before mine, you would be assured that everything of mine is plagiarized.

Beginning at some time, commercial advantages and accounts will often occupy the creators of literature more than the benefit and pleasure of literature for readers.

Foreigners bring to us the thoughts of their masters not to sell to us, but to make it our custom.

Having constant attention on each nation is just as difficult to maintain as the stability of the wind.

It is only our pride that attracts us to the resolution of the secrets of creation that will remain forever impenetrable. Can people really believe sages when each of them is proving an opinion contradictory to the other?

Occasionally we often enjoy a good storyteller, when we are in the mood to listen. But the person who is able to continue the conversation and provide it entertainment is always liked, because he enjoys being both listener and storyteller.

People led solely by their intellect incessantly err in ethical and physical inquiries, and so they must not strive beyond limits that are accessible, not to look incessantly upwards, so you do not break your neck on earth, and not dig a hole for yourself in the ground, to turn yourself into a fossil.

People usually submit themselves more to the influence of their bad qualities and personal advantages, than to the rules of wisdom

So regularly do we in bad circumstances create wise projects that are soon forgotten when catastrophe or danger strikes.

Some live in a consistent state of deception and do not otherwise see objects except as a reflection in the magic mirror of passions.

The intermediary between talent and object is scholarship.

The only item that brings substantial use to our fatherland's economy is when a person can have business outside our borders and is successful to sell our products in foreign countries.

To fulfill your duty due to conscience is normal for the middle class.

We exchange tranquility for disorder, what is firm and solid for what is weak, what is beautiful for what is ugly, and only because this is how fashion changes.

Gavril Romanovich Derzhavin

1743 – 1816

Poet, Political Activist

Gavril Derzhavin was born July 3, 1743 in the village Karmach, Kazan Province, into a middle-class family. His initial schooling was in Kazan, and in 1762 at the age of 19 he joined the military under Empress Catherine II the Great, and then in 1772 he was promoted as an officer.

In was not until 1784, that he began writing and publishing his poetry, but he immediately became famous. Along with writing poetry, Derzhavin continued up the ranks in the government. He was the next great Russian poet after Lomonosov. Derzhavin died July 8, 1816, in his hometown.

A government official more than other citizens must be inspired, motivated and guided by love for the Fatherland. He must live due to his love for the Fatherland, pour it into his subjects, and be such an example in the entire sovereignty.

A true friend of humanity does not shout, does not cry against the laws and established order. But conforming to the latter, it demonstrates as much goodness as is possible, and much goodness always and everywhere is something that can be accomplished if there is only a will.

RUSSIA'S WISDOM

Friendship is not a merit, people do not thank you for it.

Good laws can rectify errors in the soul, but they cannot force a bad heart to be benevolently productive.

Good morals are the reward of an honorable person.

Hope is the most useful of all the soul's passions, as long as it maintains the health through tranquil reflection.

In Russia it seems the laws are only read by the legislators, and are fulfilled only by the stupid.

Live and while living give to others.

News is often nothing else than something of the past you just remembered.

Our youth is presented to us as the brightest and fastest course of a river, while maturity is like a turbulent sea, and old age is a quiet and calm lake.

The best feast occurs with moderation.

The Slavonic-Russian language, according to the witness of most foreign aesthetics, is not in the same class as the ancient Latin or in the efficiency of the Greek, but it transcends all the European languages: the Italian, French and Spanish, and especially the German.

The very best preparation is the defense of your Fatherland.

Too much praise is a joke.

SEMEON EFIMOVICH DESNITZKI

1740 – 1789

Educator, Scholar

Semeon Desnitzki was born about 1740 in the city Nizhin, in Chernigovsk Province, Ukraine. His initial education was at a seminary at Troitzki-Sergeev Monastery, and then 1759-1750 he attended Moscow University, and then transferred to the Petersburg Academy of Sciences. Subsequently he attended the University of Glasgow, Scotland, graduating 1767 in civil and religious law. Returning to Russia he taught law at the Moscow University. Due to his studies abroad, he was able to provide a wider education than other professors.

Desnitzki published books on Russian law during his tenure as professor and he was an excellent orator. In 1781, he was a member of the Masonic Lodge in Moscow. In 1783, Desnitzki was one of the founders of the Russian Academy of Literature, and published an index and history of law in Russia from antiquity to his era. He likewise taught English, having gained a fluency with his studies in Great Britain. He retired from teaching in 1787 due to illness, and died in Moscow on June 15, 1789.

And if any person wants to know – based on the past and the present – by what path and to what magnitude of majesty and ascension that Russia has reached today, then that person can be assured by history that it had similar desires as did the Greeks and Romans to aspire to its prosperity. And in order to happily accomplish this, the nation called on God and people for help.

How he loved is how he sang. He became happy and became quiet.

I know that an intellectual and educated legislator must observe and await the moment and circumstances in order to give to his undertaking firm bedrock and with the least possible doubt. I know that true wisdom consists not in acquisitions, but in foresight of dangers as much as from inconsiderate hurry, and likewise from excessive slowness. In short, to be able to sense the most opportune time, and then skillfully prepare and execute the plan.

It is undoubtable that all true usefulness is inculcated more solidly when the nation is willing to accept it, and not when this is forced upon it.

Meanwhile the human with all the gifts he possesses only appears in his full radiance when we look upon him as though upon a link of an endless chain of genuinely existing entities. Not one person can think or do anything noble as long as he exalts himself due to his noble pride, but he needs to consider himself just an unimportant part of creation.

Not every wealth of every person will attract the heart.

People who spend time in meditation, thought and perception often seem to be superior to others, but they are not actually in reality. Because we, not having any kind of means by which we can measure such talents and place a specific limit to them, are blinded and overwhelmed by them, and often betray ourselves to honoring such gifts in other people, and which we do not understand ourselves, and as a result we magnify them more than they deserve in reality.

The first rule of government is that badness always stands alongside goodness, and goodness walks side by side with badness.

We figure that to deprive a person of possessions or to hinder him in utilizing his things is an obvious crime and that whoever possesses such has the full right to utilize them according to his own arbitrary notion and to exclude others from possessing and utilizing his things.

We still cannot seem to notice any flaw in human nature, and as a result we cannot measure the various types of humanity's successes, ascents and descents.

Nikolai Feodorovich Feodorov

1828/29 – 1903

Futurologist, Librarian, Educator

Nikolai Feodorov was born in Kluchi, Tambov Province, in either 1828 or 1829. He was educated in Odessa, and there began a teaching career that lasted about 20 years. In 1874, he went to work at the Rumyantzevski Museum, Moscow, cataloging all of their artifacts. During these years Feodorov was an avid reader and developed many interesting concepts, most of them eclectic from his self-taught scholarship and the studies of his teaching career. He labeled his concept – the collective matter, but essentially it was Russian cosmism as he explained it. Some if it also dealt with Orthodox theology, and he considered himself a devoted Russian Orthodox, although his concepts were later regarded by Orthodox theologians as heresy.

Feodorov formulated the concept of the cumulative resurrection, the victory over a human's non-existence with their return to life. It order to achieve the consummation of this concept, it was indispensable to defeat animosity and dislike between persons in order to materialize the means for the collective effort of all people to resurrect the dead, and specifically the Russian fathers. He felt that with the utilization of science, it was possible to collect the scattered molecules of a person and recombine them into a living body.

He agreed with the Slavophiles in their definition regarding the significance of the Russian nation, although Feodorov felt they did not adequately explain their goal, as to why they needed a unification of all the strengths and means for their cause. Feodorov was especially pacifist, and his anti-war attitude permeates all his compositions. The writings of Feodorov had a influence on other religious reformers and thinkers in Russia, such as Vl. Solovyov, F. Dostoyevski, and L. Tolstoy.

Feodorov was nicknamed the Moscow Socrates. He died in Moscow on December 15, 1903.

To acknowledge your mortality means to acknowledge each general reason of your private, personal misfortunes. And only this person can be called an intelligent entity and human being, who knows the actual – and common with all other human beings – reason for suffering, and who will take this blind and death-providing strength and transform it into a life-providing goal for the balance of his life, and also with all others.

Only education can create such intelligent entities, and such an education needs to possess the undoubtable right to be obligatory on everyone. Because it will be only due to such an education for humanity to make it a generation having a common concept for all generations. Education is not a luxury, but a necessity. No matter how profound the reasons for mortality, death did not originally exist, it is not an unconditional and unavoidable decree. Blind strength, dependent on an intelligent entity, can be directed by reason.

While feeling the sorrow of the first son of man, sympathy over the father's loss gave birth to a worldwide sorrow over the perishability of everything, over the eventual death of everybody, and then nature first came to the cognizance of its imperfection, and then occurred the birth that installed the beginning of the renovation of the world, the beginning of humanity's epoch, where the world must be recreated by the strengths of the human himself. And without this Son's virtue, without the patrimonial existence, we never could understand the teaching of the Three-in-

One God, the astonishing teaching, and due to its majesty it is hardly fathomable by even the most highest of minds, but is very much felt in heartfelt warmth that is accessible even by a child's comprehension.

The natural and biological is completely opposite to Christianity and even humanity. The natural is consuming; the Christian is a creative process, the reconstruction of its organism with the ingestion of nourishment. The general resurrection in Christianity is comparable to natural increase, that is, the production of previously lived generations. We can say that between the natural and the Christian is this type of relationship, that is, this type of opposition as between the Christian Trinity and the Indian Trimurti, whose revelation so overjoyed the opposers of Christianity, finding in it an amazing similarity with the Christian Trinity, and in reality, a striking similarity – there are 3 and here are 3.

The teaching of the Trinity consists of the path for cumulative effort of the human race. The law of worldwide history not in the sense of knowledge, but in the sense of the direction of a path. The teaching of the inner life of the Three-in-One Entity consists of the revelation of the general matter of the cumulative resurrection, and reveals the true path or the progress of this issue. Our word is the knowledge of the fathers-ancestors and of their nature as the means of life's return. And this knowledge is ours also, as the cumulative of all sons, if the education is common to everybody and the participation in the knowledge of history and nature is obligatory for all without exception. And this word will not just remain as an imagination, as a memorial of the fathers-ancestors, it will not remain as just an artistic portrayal. When knowledge of nature turns death-providing strength into life-providing, then the generation that accomplishes this will have the immortal fathers as its own son, and not mortal sons.

As life progresses and in reality, independently functional persons will be expressed in strife, while unified persons in enslavement, until the time that the unification of the many – in the image of the Three-in-One – will be mental and idealistic. If we were not to permit the separation of activity from thought, the Three-in-One will be for us not just a ideal, but a project, that is, not only a hope, but a command. Only by doing this can we possibly materialize it.

The Divine Essence that within Itself displayed the most perfect image of community, the Essence that is the unification of independent, immortal personalities, who in their entire fullness feeling and comprehending their unity that is inseparable by death, meaning excluding death. This is the Christian idea of God, that is, this means that in the Divine Essence is revealed that very item that is so needed by the human race, for it to become immortal. The Trinity is the church of immortality, and similar to it but from the side of humans there can also be a Church of the Resurrected. In the Trinity there is no reason for death, and in It all the conditions of immortality are contained.

It is only through great, difficult, prolonged labor that we are cleansed from debt, arrive at the resurrection, enter into communion with the Three-in-One, maintaining ourselves independent entities just as He is, immortal individuals, in all fullness feeling and comprehending our unity. And only then we will have the concluding proof of God's existence: we will see Him face to face.

If indeed, the Spirit is unable to present the teaching of the Trinity as an example to our daughters, then the very Trinity will convert into a lifeless, monastic, Platonic concept. The Deity is Son and Daughter, borderless love to the Father who nourishes us.

Orthodoxy is the highest class when compared to Protestantism and Catholicism, or it is the sole true instruction that leads us by a straight path from the liturgy inside the church and Easter to the liturgy outside the church and Easter.

Catholicism is a distortion of Christianity, the revival. It is exchanging the work that achieves the revival with works that do not accomplish revival. [Christianity] merits immortality or a liberation from purgatory. Protestantism does not destroy the distortion, but only exchanges Catholic matters with thought. Religion is a revival, and not a distortion. It is the cult of our ancestors, demanding profound unification, brotherhood.

Not separating Christ's resurrection from our own, from the cumulative resurrection, we must ascribe the guilt of not achieving this resurrection to ourselves, just as with the guilt of banishing Christ from our world. But with his ascension to heaven, we can exactly await his – either merciful or terrible – return to earth as a result of our unification in the matter of the resurrection.

Goodness is to preserve life for the living and return it to those who are losing it and have lost it.

If justification consists in a person becoming similar to Christ as the image of consummate virtue, then we need to understand virtue is a goodness that is not abstract, but a resurrection that is the total expression of love toward the fathers and the community of sons, because Christ is the one who resurrects, and his entire purpose consists in this statement.

Wealth and passion for manufactured toys dooms a person to eternal immaturity, it makes a son and brother – a citizen, needing surveillance and the threat of punishment, leading to diplomatic disputes, to military intervention. Doesn't immaturity consist of subjection to blind evolution, bringing sons to rise against their fathers and in a struggle between brethren?

We must not cause the immortal Entity to depart from our world, leaving the world mortal and imperfect, just as we must not mix God with mythology where blindness and death reign. The difficulty consists in turning nature, the strength of nature, into an instrument of cumulative resurrection and through the cumulative resurrection for us to become a union of immortal entities.

History as a fact is mutual destruction, the annihilation of one another and ourselves, Such plundering and pillage through exploitation and utilization of all external nature, that is, the land, is natural death of culture. History as a fact is always mutual destruction, whether it be in the open as during the eras of barbarism, or hidden, as in the civilized world. Such cruelty causes decimation and along with it more evil.

We see from the preceding that all of life, the past and the present, all that we have done and are doing, in short, proves that history as a fact is mutual destruction, voluntary or involuntary, war, every manner of battle – competition, polemic, dispute – in short, is militarism in it widest sense. Life and history as a project must be reconciliatory or requiring confrontation for unification and for the return of life. The world will then be peaceful, a brotherhood, when the blind strength of nature will be transformed into a directing intelligent will.

A museum is not a collection of things, but an assembly of individuals. Its activity is not confined in the accumulation of dead objects, but in the return of life to the remnants of those who lived in the past, in restoration of the dead through their artifacts to become again living creators.

The dissatisfaction with the present, and distress and despondence regarding the future, is the fatal result of the denial of our birth-related past. From the history of the life and death of our fathers, this is the awesome judgment of history upon those who, swallowed by the moment of the present, do not see 2 infinities surrounding him: the passing and the arriving, and they place themselves higher than those to whom we are obligated in life.

Progress that rejects the fatherland and brotherhood is consummate moral collapse, a denial of the basis of ethical conduct.

The imaginary unity of Islam consists of an unconditional subjection of yourself to the blind power of nature, in which he sees the will of Allah – fatalism. From the positive facet – in holy war, the obligations to be a weapon of destruction for the establishment of their unity. But from the negative facet, in order to be sacrifices of the destructions, not to counteract, but accept illness and death and suffer through them, not to counteract this as though it is something very natural, as part of the living scheme, and not to oppose the destruction. The passions are the same as those part of polygamy. And so in this very manner does this monotheistic religion differentiate itself from those religions that worship both the productive and destructive powers. It is necessary to grasp that paganism and Judeo-Islam are different only in thought, in presentation, in dogma, but are very identical and similar in commands.

Aleksandr Sergeevich Griboyedov

1795 – 1829

Diplomat, Poet, Musical Composer

Aleksandr Griboyedov was born in Moscow on January 4, 1795. He attended Moscow University, graduating in 1810. He then began government service in the Ministry of Foreign Affairs, and in 1818-1821 was secretary to the Russian Diplomatic Embassy in Persia, and then from 1826 he was diplomat in Georgia. Beginning 1828, he was head of the Russian Embassy in Teheran, Iran. On January 30, 1829, the Russian Embassy was attacked by fanatics and Griboyedov was killed in the onslaught.

Griboyedov contributed greatly to the development of Russian literature and theater. As a diplomat he developed Russian cultural ties with Georgia and Armenia.

Adventures can be amazing in the world. But at his age they are all fantasies.

Blessed is the person with beliefs, he will sense warmth in the sun.

RUSSIA'S WISDOM

When I get lost in a crowd, somehow I lose my identity.

Nations have so many affairs to worry about at home that they should have no time to even think about occupying some other nation.

If for some accidental reason some foreigner arrived here, one who knew nothing about Russian history of the entire past century, he of course would conclude from our sharp contradictory trend of morality, that our masters and serfs evolve from 2 different tribes whose customs and ethics still not interwoven.

It is an infantile pleasure for me to hear my verses recited in the theater. Wanting success has only caused me to ruin my own creations as much as possible. Such is the fate of every person who writes for scenes.

It seems any educated person can become a Plato.

The homes are new, but the prejudices are old. But be happy, the years will not destroy them, or fashion or fires.

The more scholarly a person, the more useful he is to the fatherland.

Nikolai Mikhailovich Karamzin

1766 – 1826

Historian

Nikolai Karamzin was born in the village Mikhailovka, Orenburg Province. From the age of 13 he was studying at the Moscow University. In 1781, he entered the military, but the life did not suit him and he was released and settled in Moscow, where he became publisher of the first Russian journal for children.

Karamzin traveled Russia 1789-1790, and visited Kant in Konnigsburg, Prussia. He was in Paris during the French Revolution. Returning to Russia he dedicated his life as a professional writer and journalist, including publishing several almanacs. Karamzin was assigned as a historiographer by Tsar Alexander I, and by 1816, he published the first 8 volumes of his *History of the State of Russia*. The final 3 volumes were published posthumously.

Karamzin died May 22, 1826 in St Petersburg from pneumonia.

A great man proves his greatness though his mistakes. They are difficult or even impossible to erase. Whether they be good ones or bad ones they remain forever.

A legislator must look at things from different sides, and not from one, otherwise, if you divide evil, you just may create more evil.

A person's life is short, but a long time is needed to implement new habits.

A secret weakness is only a weakness. When it is public it is a vice because it deceives others.

A wise ruler finds the ability to increase the motivation toward benevolence in his officials or can at least restrain their drive to do bad.

All wise legislators who were forced to change political statues in reality hoped to depart as little as possible from the old. We presently act completely otherwise: we abandon something, discredit a name, and to accomplish these activities we think of other means.

And glory?... They say that it is the last comfort of a heart ruptured due to lost love. But glory, similar to a rose of love, has its thorns, its deceits and torments. Did it provide many with happiness? The first sound of glory awakens the hydra of envy and profanity, which will pinch at you until you reach your wooden coffin and at your grave it will pour upon you its poison.

Barbaric nations love independence. Intelligent nations love order, but there is no order with autocratic authority.

Be always worthy of freedom, and you will always be free! The heavens are just and will throw into captivity only corrupt nations.

Conspiracies are disasters, they shake the foundation of the state and serve as a dangerous example for the future. If some officials, generals, bodyguards, adopt secretly the authority to annihilate monarchs, or exchange them, what will occur to the autocracy?

Political ploys of the oligarchy have no choice but to quickly turn into ruthlessness, which is the most terrifying of all evil despotism, subjecting every citizen to danger, and the tyrant will proceed to execute a few.

Determination toward inaction decreases willingness toward action.

Every innovation in the state organization is bad and only should be implemented in absolute necessity. Only a specific moment will provide the necessary stability for new laws. We tend to respect more of what was long ago respected and conduct ourselves based on habit.

Everywhere they steal, and who is punished? They await reports, evidence, send senators to investigate, and nothing evolves from it all! Dishonest people betray, while honorable people tolerate this and are silent because they like tranquility. It is not so easy to convict a cleaver thief-judge, especially with the laws the way they are, where the person giving the bribe is no different that the person taking it.

History in some sense is a nation's sacred book, the primary and indispensable. It is a mirror of their existence and activity; a stone plate with their revelations and rules inscribed; the testament of the ancestors bequeathed to posterity. It is supplemented with an explanation of their present and provides an example for the future.

If suddenly the future was revealed to a person, and to the most suitable of all people, then his heart would die from terror and his tongue would freeze at that very minute when he would think to call himself the most happy of all mortals.

It is good and a necessity to learn, but woe to the people and nation which remains a student forever.

It seems to me that for solidarity of existence of the state, it is safer to enslave the people, than to provide them freedom too early. For liberation it is necessary to prepare the person with moral restoration.

Laws that provide deliverance for the people are solely those whose legislation has been long desired by the best minds of the state, and which to add, have been expected by the people.

Let honor and glory be attributed to our language, which is almost not polluted by any foreign inclusions and possesses a natural wealth. It flows like a proud magnificent river – noisy and thundering – and suddenly if need be it calms, murmurs like a gentle stream and sweetly pours into the soul, reflecting all of its facets that are confined only in the high and low pitch of the human voice.

National laws must be derived from its individual comprehensions, ethics, traditions and local conditions.

Nature provides a mind and heart, but education forms them.

Note that cold people in general seem to be great egoists. The mind is active among them more than the heart. The mind always turns them to their individual profit like a magnet to the north.

Nothing of any magnitude can be accomplished if it is for money.

O my dear union of relatives! You proceed consistently as the firmest support of good morals, and if there was any reason for me to envy our ancestors, then of course, it is their attachment to my close associates.

Our life is divided into 2 epochs: the first we traverse in the future, while the second in the past. Up to a certain age, in the pride of our hopes, a person looks ahead with the thought, "There, there destiny awaits me, one of which my heart is worthy." Losses will little annoy him. The future seems to him an unfathomable treasury prepared for his satisfaction. But when the fervency of youth passes, when the insulted self-interest a hundred times involuntarily learns humility, when a hundred times you have been deceived by hope, we finally cease to believe in it. Then with vexation we abandon the future and turn our eyes to the past and want to exchange the lost happiness of flattering expectations with a handful of pleasant memories telling ourselves as a means of comfort, "And we, yes we, were in Arcadia!" Then and then only will we learn to value the present.

Self-designated rulers of peoples are more harmful than personal offenders or delusional sovereigns for civic society. The wisdom of entire ages is necessary for establishment of authority, while one hour of national frenzy will destroy its foundation, and which reflects the people's moral respect of the rank of despots.

So where can I seek tolerance if the very philosophers, the very educators – as they want to be called – display so much hate toward those who do not think just as they do? If I am to consider him a true philosopher, then he should be able to reside with everybody else in the world, whether they like him or whether they disagree with his forms of thinking. It is with noble fervency and without any malice, that he must be able to indicate error in a person's thinking. Tell a person that he is mistaken and why. But do not discredit his opinion and do not tell him he is stupid.

Solitude is acceptable only when its purpose is rest. But incessant solitude is the road to self-elimination.

Statements are for the newspaper; only rules are for the state.

The dignity of a sovereign's rank will not permit him to tolerate his own violation of good conduct. No matter how corrupt people are, inwardly he will not allow any respect of them.

The execution of a guilty person together with the acquitted removes the shame from the execution. Lesser punishments, although useless, are closer to tyranny than the most cruel that have justice as their basis and whose goal is the common welfare.

The national spirit composes the moral potency of the state, just like physical strength is necessary for its solidity. For its security, the state needs not only physical strength, but likewise moral. To sacrifice integrity and virtue is harmful to its morality.

The obligation of the historian or chronicler is to provide an interesting narrative. A well-told independent thought is a gift. The reader needs the former and is grateful for the latter, when his expectation is fulfilled.

The soul that is overly sensitive to the pleasures of passion also feels strongly its displeasures. Paradise and hell are its neighbors. After ecstasy follows either despair or melancholy, which so often open the door to the insane asylum.

The true cosmopolitan is a metaphysical entity or an exceptional extraordinary manifestation to the point that there is no need to speak of him, or praise or condemn him. We are all citizens, the personality of each is tightly woven with the fatherland: when we live it we love ourselves.

The tyrant can often safely reign after tyranny, but never after a wise sovereign.

The tyrant, like any other person, has his predetermined lifetime.

The years of childhood! Who can meditate on them without pleasure! And the older we become, the more pleasant they seem to us.

To love goodness for its personal charms is an effect of the highest morality, an aspect that is rare in the world, otherwise the altars of virtue would never be sanctified. Usually people observe rules of honestly, not as much in the hope of acquiring certain special advantages, as much as because of fear of harm that would occur with an open violation of these rules.

To want what is superfluous, and not to want what is a necessity, are both reprehensible.

True love can be enjoyed without sensual delights, even when its object is hidden beyond the seas. In short, satisfactions due to love are innumerable. Not the tyranny of parents, not the tyranny of fatalism, can remove it from the nice heart.

Two reasons promote conspiracy: common hatred or common disrespect of the sovereign.

We will never become intellectual using foreign educations and glorious using foreign accomplishments.

What is national is infinitesimal compared to humanity as a whole. The primary issue is to be a people, and not Slavs. What is good for people then cannot be bad for Russians, and if the English or Germans develop something useful and advantageous for a person, then likewise for myself, because I am a person also.

When some irreversible evil is done, then it is necessary to think over the matter and take measures, but quietly. Not to sigh, not to beat a drum, since this will just magnify the crime.

Whoever does not respect himself, without doubt will not be respected by others.

Vasili Osipovich Kluchevski

1841 – 1911

Historian, Scholar

Vasili Kluchevski was born January 16, 1841, in the village Voskresenovka, Penzen Province. His father was a parish priest. He entered Moscow University and studied history and philosophy, and after graduating, continued to teach there, and became a professor in 1885, continuing to teach history and philosophy to the end of his life.

Kluchevski was a member of the Imperial St Petersburg Academy of Sciences and president of the Imperial Society of History and Russian Antiquities. He was likewise a mentor for the children of Tsar Alexandr III from 1893-1895.

He is most famous for his 4-volume *Complete Course of Russian History*, published in 1904, as well as several other books on Russian history and philosophy that were used as textbooks in Russian schools.

Kluchevski died in Moscow on May 12, 1911.

A good woman, getting married, promises happiness to herself, the stupid one just waits for it.

A great idea in a bad environment converts into a series of stupidities.

A lawyer is a worm in a cocoon. He life is an alien juridical death. On the basis of the law or at his personal arbitrary discretion he so easily executes a person. Only in the latter situation is the action recognized as a crime, but in the former as a practice of justice.

A man becomes occupied with a woman the way a chemist does his laboratory. He observes in her processes that he does not understand, and which he causes to occur.

A man listens with his ears, a woman – with her eyes. The former in order to understand what is being said to him, the latter – in order to like the person who is speaking to her.

A man loves a woman as much as he can love; a woman loves a man as much as she wants to love. This is why a man usually loves one woman more than she is worth, while a woman wants to love more men than she has the capacity to love.

A virtuous person is not the one who can do good, but the one who is not able to do bad.

A woman is dangerous not when she attacks, but when she falls.

A woman loves to be understood not as a woman, but as a person of the female gender.

A woman's love is that gift that receives its value only when it ceases to be a gift.

Art is a surrogate life, because art loves all, including those shorted in life.

Beautiful women in their old age tend to be very stupid, only because they were very beautiful in their youth.

Beauty is good only when the person does not notice it.

Before demanding that others be worthy of our love, it is necessary to earn their love.

Belief in life after death is a heavy tax on the people who are not able to live to death, since they will cease to live earlier than to reach death.

Do not begin some work if its end is not in your hands.

Earlier, men saw in woman a living source of happiness, for which they forgot the physical enjoyment. Today men see in her a physiological device for physical enjoyment, which only suppresses any type of genuine happiness.

Eloquence is counterfeiting the mind using prose.

Famine is the best educator. It quickly recognizes with whom the education needs to begin and whether to educate the pupil.

Friendship can persevere without love; but love without friendship, never.

Friendship usually serves as a transfer from simple association to enmity.

Gratitude is not the right of the person who is being thanked, but is the obligation of the person who is thanking. To demand gratitude is stupidity. Not to be grateful is mean.

History teachers nothing, but only punishes for not knowing the lessons.

In Russia there are no mediocre talents, no regular artisans, but we have lonely geniuses and millions of utterly worthless people. The geniuses cannot accomplish anything, because they do not have artisans below them, and it is impossible to do anything with the millions because they have no artisans. The geniuses are useless because there are so few of them, while the rest are helpless because there are so many of them.

In science it is necessary to repeat exercises in order to well remember them. In morality it is well to remember mistakes, so not to repeat them.

Instinct is the unconscious mover, but with the will's participation. A robot is a mover without a will and mechanically without conscious.

It is much easier to become a father, than to remain as one.

Life does not consist in living, but in feeling that you are alive.

Mediocre people are usually the most demanding of critics. Not being in a position to accomplish the simplest task that is possible, and not knowing what and how to do it, they demand of others what is completely impossible.

Men marry having high hopes; women marry because of a promise. But since it is easier to fulfill your promise than to justify hopes, we meet disappointed husbands more often than deceived women.

Men see in a woman what they want to make her into, and usually they make her into what she does not want to become.

Only swindlers believe the truth, because they believe in something they do not comprehend.

Our society is an accidental gang of sweet people, living depending on the news reports of the day and aesthetic impressions of the minute.

People imagine they are doing something so they can have the impression they are doing something.

People live first by idolatry and then by ideals, and when ideals become insufficient they idealize the idols.

People seek themselves everywhere else, except not within themselves.

People who are self-centered love authority, people who are ambitious want influence, people who are arrogant seek both, people who are philosophic disdain all of it and all of them.

People who do not have their own mind tend to value a stranger's mind that often conducts itself more intelligently than the person deprived of a mind.

Philanthropy births more requirements than it does eliminate needs.

Russian intelligence is like leaves torn from their tree. They can sorrow over their tree, but the tree will not sorrow over them, since it will grow new leaves.

Sages seek what they do not understand.

Science strives to explain all faults using illnesses, while the moralists state that all illnesses evolve from faults. Soon, to the satisfaction of judges and physicians, criminals will heal and the sick will punish.

Some benevolent act done by an enemy is just as difficult to forget, as to remember some benevolent act done by a friend. For goodness we only repay our enemy with goodness; for evil we take vengeance on both enemy and friend.

Studying history we gain more facts and understand less the meanings of events.

Stupidity is the most precious luxury that only wealthy people can allow themselves to afford.

The administration is a dirty rag to shove into the hole of legislation.

The ancient polytheism is a religion of sensuality without love. Christianity is a religion of love without sensuality. Atheism is a religion without one and the other.

The dissertation is a scientific work having 2 opposing views and not one reader.

The entire daily mundane life of a woman consists of 3 unknowns: Initially she does not know how to acquire a husband, then how to live with a husband, and finally, how to deal with her children.

The entire difference between an intelligent person and stupid one can be summarized in one statement: the former always thinks first and seldom speaks; the latter always speaks and cannot think something over. The former's tongue is always in the sphere of thought; the latter's thought is outside the sphere of the tongue. The former's tongue is a secretary of thoughts, the latter's is its gossiper and betrayer.

The established writers are lamps that during a peaceful era illuminate the path to interpreting passers-by, and upon which during a revolution are hung the ignorant and which break worthless people.

The highest purpose of talent is for your productions to provide people the meaning and value of life.

The historian is an observer, and not a follower.

The undefeatable person is the one who is not afraid to be stupid.

The most joyful laugh is to laugh with those who laugh at you.

The most valuable gift of nature is a joyful, joking and cheerful mind.

The narcissistic person holds other people's opinions of himself higher than his own. And so to be narcissistic means to love yourself more than others and to respect others more than yourself.

The need for reform matures faster than the nations mature for reform. The law of life of the backward governments or countries compared to those advancing is whether they sooner accept the need for reforms and implement them, or do nothing.

The newspaper trains people to meditate on what they do not know, and know what they do not understand.

The only occasion that elderly women display the existence of their mind is when they often depart from it.

The regularity of historical upheavals is inversely proportional to their religious devotion.

The road to truth is not for a few select, but for all the courageous.

The woman who leads her husband astray is considerably less to blame than the husband that leads the woman astray, because it is more difficult for her to become promiscuous, than for the husband to remain virtuous.

The worthy person is not the one without faults, but the one who possesses dignity and integrity.

There are people who have the ability to speak, but do not have the ability to say anything. These are windmills that eternally wave their propellers, but never can seem to fly.

There are people whose entire merit consists in that they have done nothing bad, but nothing good either.

There is a man that all the women love, but not one of them is actually in love with him.

To be happy means not to desire what you cannot receive anyway.

To be happy means to be intelligent.

To be intelligent means not to ask if you know there is no answer.

To live means to be loved. When a person is mentioned as having lived, this means that they were loved much.

When some thinker's mind rotates speedily, the heads of the unthinking public just whirl.

Wives do inspect husbands. Only a few will inspect their hearts; others will inspect their wallets; while the smartest will inspect their teeth.

Women forgive all except one thing – an unpleasant attitude toward her.

Worse of all is to think that you are large enough to fill any sofa you sit in.

Ivan Andreevich Krilov

1769 – 1844

Poet, Librarian, Storyteller

Ivan Krilov was born in Moscow on February 2, 1769. His father was a military officer who worked his way up the ranks on his own merit. His initial education was meager but he moved to St Petersburg and met with other Russian writers and was able in 1789 to start a journal of humor and satire. Empress Catherine the Great initially encouraged his literary effort, but with the French Revolution, the censurers closed his journal, and for the next 10 years, Krilov wandered about the provinces one step ahead of the police. The subsequent Tsars Nicholas I and Alexander II favored Krilov and provided him freedom.

Between 1809 and 1843 he created over 200 fables, penetrated with a democratic undertone, often distinctively satirical, and including all the contemporary vices of the Russian people and their typical traits. Krilov was a member of the Imperial Russian Academy and the Imperial Academy of Sciences, and also dedicated much time to the Imperial Public Library. Other than fables, Krilov also composed some novel-length poems and a comic opera.

Krilov died in St Petersburg on November 21, 1844.

A human's intellect is worth more to be pitied than to be admired.

A person can circumvent something without thinking if only he has a quick tongue.

Although philosophers and scholars speak incessantly of their contempt of credit, of their wisdom and of their intrinsic contentment, however, disregarding all of their eloquently verbose and inflated statements, I can affirmatively say that if they were any less preoccupied with their vanity, then for sure ignorance would be reigning up to now throughout the entirety of humanity.

And even the lowest wheat farmer, fulfilling diligently his obligation for his subsistence, has earned more of the merit of having the appellation of an honorable person, than the proud official and senseless judge.

And so the mistakes of great men are not only able to provide us the feeling of the faults of all people in general, but to also prove the total weakness and inconsistency of human reason.

Every person who considers himself wise has just revealed that one thing about himself that can be called stupid.

Exercises in useless sciences will not serve you in any manner except to deprive you of your present welfare, feeding you a vain hope about the acquisition of a future fantasy bliss. True sages have no need of anything, while self-interested and ambitious sophists grab after everything and feel satisfied in everything.

In all nations it is possible to see the same faults that are totally contrary to benevolent feelings and healthy intellect.

In order to attain success in learning wisdom, it is best to be an observer, and not an active person in those comedies that are played in the world.

In order to become wise and virtuous, the supreme means of doing so is to meditate about the stupidity and strange ethics of people. Investigate diligently the inconsistent human mind, and you will definitely always be on guard so you do not fall into the same faults for which you condemn others.

In order to learn wisdom there is nothing better than to enter into investigation into all humanity's weaknesses. The nonsense of some scatterbrain, the misconduct of an insolent person, and the insanity of ignorance, are worthy to be instructions of a philosopher who desires to utilize his natural talents for gain. True sages during all the ages emerged as such solely due to their contempt and repulsion toward people, in whom they notice their absurd conduct and activities incompatible with intellect.

In our present so-called enlightened ago, people are just as senseless, frivolous, inconsistent, quarrelsome, miserly, arrogant and vain. No matter what supreme intellect might be gifted them, they can never defend themselves from the onslaught of faults.

It is vain to think that as though people were always and at every time the same. I am convinced that weak mortals were never as so foolish, unreasonable, defiled and so worthy of pity than at the present.

It is more proper to call the person who retains a balance between good and bad – honorable, than the person who openly abandons himself to every vice.

It is so ordinary to more severely judge the actions of others then your own personal, and it often occurs that these very faults that are discredited in others and are considered greatly inexcusably are forgivable when pertaining to yourself and it is so easy to find different excuses for your justification.

It is very natural that persons born of such families, those that from ancient times are honored for their most famous rank, are especially more competent than others to accomplish important tasks. They have been raised and educated to do this more than others who have not been accustomed, and it seems they do not even have a sense of obligation to fulfill anything more than necessary.

It is very difficult to notice a wise person until 300 years pass after his death, and this is why many prudent nations initially killed their sages and then later build statues of them.

Many intelligent people affirm that it is immensely more tolerable to be murdered that to be disdained, because death will terminate all tortures, but it is impossible for a person to accustom himself to contempt, and the feeling that this impacts a person – such torturous insult – incessantly increases hour by hour.

People should incessantly meditate over 2 items: first about the shortness of the present life, and second about the endless continuation of the future.

Poverty is the kind of thing that has the best ability to produce philosophers. A person possessing wealth and property seldom wants to teach others moral instruction.

So it is not science that makes people better and prosperous, but honesty and a virtuous conscience. Physics, metaphysics, rhetoric, all of these sciences do not birth true wisdom, because this often occurs with a humble craftsman or with a baker. It is better to honor the tranquil and meek un-education of a poor artist, than the vain and useless rhetoric of an ambitious philosopher and ego-inflated orator.

So what use is philosophy? Nothing at all, except that those stupid people who expend their time in such practices turn completely into idiots.

The one who withdraws is the one who is guilty.

The zeal of a sovereign to promulgate his law has done no less damage to people than any of his other preoccupations.

There are so many royalty who, during their life, do not allow even one day to pass being tormented by ambition – the desire to increase their might – and residing in the fear of perhaps being deprived of the tsar's favor. Can such a life be considered happiness, where the future is nothing but a consistent torment of anxiety and a distrust of all whom you have a obligation to treat respectively, or having to flatter some enemy, not to have even one true friend. And to deal in every matter apprehensively and in alignment with the deceitful tactics of other people?

Think about how we are judged among our friends. To select a friend means to provide to society someone like yourself and to open your heart. Every person would shutter if he would meditate on how important it is to acknowledge someone as your friend. Do you want to be respected? Treat people respectfully.

Vain conceit, the desire to shine using your gifts and be preferred over your contemporaries will never motivate unselfish feelings to materialize, but in place of them it will birth self-interest and envy, although such may be dormant or suppressed, however they are no less cruel. Such passions for the most part serve as the reason of such little respect that scholars ordinarily display one another, because they are always afraid that someone else's credit will reduce their credit and create an obstacle for their advancement toward that immortality that each desires with insatiable hunger.

What type of woman is the most intelligent? The one who will thank you even for a refusal.

MIKHAIL SERGEEVICH LUNIN

1787 – 1845

Political Activist

Mikhail Lunin was born in St Petersburg on December 29, 1787. He was the son of a wealthy landowner in the Tambov-Saratov region, and received an excellent education, learning also the French, English, Latin and Polish languages. By faith he was Catholic.

Lunin enlisted in the military in 1803, and studied and rose in rank, and displayed his bravery during the was of 1812-1814 against the French. However the philosophical attitude of Lunin changed and he resigned from the military in 1815. The following year he joined the Union of Salvation and then later the Northern Secret Society. In 1816, he was part of a group that planned the assassination of Tsar Alexandr I, but they were unable to gather sufficient support. As a result, Lunin left Russia to Paris to escape possible prosecution, but returned in 1817.

In 1822, Lunin reenlisted in the military and became an assistant to then Grand Prince Konstantine Pavlovich. His attitude changed toward his previous associations, although he did exert effort for the emancipation of the serfs and the abolition of the feudal system. Lunin was not a participant in the assassination of Tsar Alexandr I in December 1825, because he was stationed in Poland at the time. However on his return to Russia he was arrested in Warsaw in 1826 and transferred to St Petersburg by military convoy, and confined at the Petro-Pavlovsk Fortress. He was convicted as a participant in the tsar's assassination and sentenced to 15 years at hard labor in Siberia, but it was reduced to 10 years in 1832. Moved from prison to prison he arrived at Yuri, near Irkutsk, Siberia, in 1836.

While in exile, Lunin wrote extensive letters about his political views and had discussions with other inmates and exiles. His letters were discovered and he was again arrested in 1841, and send to the Akatuiskaya Concentration Camp, located beyond Lake Baikal, in eastern Siberia along the border with China. Lunin died on December 3, 1845 at the concentration camp, the official report states it was due to an apoplectic stroke, others claim he was executed.

My life seems to alternate regularly between items not seen which do not understand me, and items that are seen, which I do not understand. Egyptian darkness hides it from my eyes,[8] but I can decipher its beauty.

Epochs that have transpired, unknown, in a secret progression of the nations to the goal of social development, reveal incidences in the activities of their political activists, of whatever genealogy they may be, who must indispensably exit the ordinary ranks and excite the state and peoples, those lethargic due to the continuous influence of fallacious development and prejudice that has be instilled in them over ages. When these people decide to become members of a higher status of the social composition, then their activities are an obligation and the means for the utilization of their mental faculties to pay for these gains that the efforts of the lower classes have gained for them.

In essence, all nations are occupied with solely their own affairs, extra time is either expended on some distant desire, or plainly is

---

[8] Ex 10: 22-23

nothing but a rhetorical exercise, sometimes open, but even then seldom efficient.

Nations and governments do not so easily discard fallacious paths that the interests of political parties or personal desires have imposed.

Nevertheless, it is not proper to magnify the significance of repressive measures. When the government acts without the participation of the people, its circle of moral effect is unavoidably limited, or perhaps even nonexistent.

Positive and immutable conditions need to exist in order for great nations to evolve, and which should not be modified. To become involved in the political construction of a state before social strength is like securing a crown on a building that has no foundation.

Social calamities appear as a warning, they are a foresight provided to kings and nations in order to enlighten them both to what pertains to their mutual circumstances.

The people and state suffer equally, because they estrange themselves from moral authority, which is the only item that can serve as a potent intermediary, in order to conclude and discuss mutual interests.

The people meditate and disregard its profound silence.

The Russian mind can be overshadowed temporarily, but never its national sentiment.

There are 2 guides in Russia: the tongue leads to Kiev, while the pen leads to Schlesselburg.[9]

---

[9] Or, Shlisselburg, a prison inland from Petersburg.

There are 2 types of babblers: some say too much, in order not to say anything; others also say too much, but because they do not know what to say. Some talk in order to hide what they think, others talk in order to hide that they have no thoughts at all.

Times occur when a prosperous course of circumstances present hope for success in the most risky of endeavors.

We are not afraid of death on the battlefield, but we seem to not be able to say a word in the State Council in defense of justice and humanity

We pay, but we have no idea what happens to our money. We do not even know exactly how much we pay, because of the corruption of judges and the bribery among administrative office they take from us at least if not more than the government.

Will we forget the almost most important gift for autocracy: to utilize people according to their abilities? Military leaders, officials, senators, are not born such, nor are those who will support the autocrat. But they are chosen one by one. In order to select them it is necessary to guess who they are. And it is only great people who have the ability to guess who they are.

When people, whose opinion we value, reject the dignities that we possess, we usually become melancholy, as though we have lost them. But when they ascribe to us dignities that we did not even suspect we possessed, we are encouraged and strive to acquire them.

Nikolai Ivanovich Novikov

1744 – 1818

Educator, Journalist, Publisher

Nikolai Novikov was born on his parent's family estate of Tikhvinskoi-Avdotino, near Moscow, on April 27, 1744. In 1755-1760 he studied at a school for the children of the aristocracy that was attached to Moscow University. After graduating he served a short while in the cadet corps, and then from 1767 in a state commission for the education of the general Russian population. At this time Novikov developed his views and which were opposed to the feudal system. After leaving the commission he was editor of some satirical journals, ridiculing the landowners and aristocrats.

Novikov worked at the time to improve Russian culture in the light of the influx of European culture into Russia. Leaving behind the humor, the next journals were of serious content dealing with philosophy and literature. Novikov joined the Masonic Lodge in about 1775 and implemented his utopian ideas into the moral education of young people, those who were deprived of an education due to the feudal system. He started a publishing house in 1779, and printed his own newspapers, and several journals, as well as school textbooks. About 1/3 of all books published during this era came out of Novikov's print shop, including topics such as economy and education, and he also opened bookstores in 16 Russian cities. The income from his books was used to open schools for peasant children.

In 1790, Novikov's mysticism and his spiritual writings were censured by the Russian Orthodox Church, and he was forced to stop publishing books of religious content. In 1792, at the age of 48, Novikov was arrested and without trial was sentenced to 15 years at Schlesselburg Fortress. He was released 4 years later under Tsar Pavel I in 1796 on the first day of his reign as tsar. Novikov left the prison destitute, frail and crippled at the age of 52. He was also ordered to not become involved in any social activism for the balance of his life, and so spent the next 22 years on his family estate solely working with the educational needs of the peasants of the local region, and almost never leaving the area. Novikov died August 12, 1818.

A person who is gifted with an immortal spirit and having the opportunity and capability to utilize such strength to educate, if he will only apply himself in his entire life just as do animals apply themselves, then the mind's ability is not useless to him, and with his endless and inner motivation neither is it harmful and malevolent to him.

A person enters into an altercation with society: if he is more right than it is, then he is a revolutionary; or if society is more right than he is, then he is a criminal and society takes all measures to barricade itself from him.

A person in general does not like truth when it is contrary to his preferences, when it scatters his most precious dreams, when he needs to attain it only at the cost of his hopes and illusions. This is when a person develops hate toward a truth.

And so this thought that the Most Supreme entity constantly meditates about us and worries over us more that any of His other creations should definitely cause us to have a concern for our own selves.

Art and science move forward so slowly that the country where these begin to grow or which accepts them, indispensably must reside for a long time without any change in government. All of this success in the long run we can hope to receive only in such a government that steadfastly persists over many centuries.

As long as he possesses a pure heart, the person at the lowest class can sense truth better than the greatest star with a corrupt heart.

As long as there is money it is easy to acquire respect, but with respect of course you will squander a little money.

Assurance of the greatness of our essence and of the greatness of that which is assigned to us in the future life, naturally motivates us to expand our penetration into the future and compels us to worry about what will occur after we are gone.

But a person who does not consider himself anything, cannot have at the same time any concern for others, and so just reveals the ignominy of his thinking.

Destitute dignified people would just as well be equated with pigs that waste all their life's time and dissolutely roll about in mud. True humans must not squander their life in this manner. If they want to be the world's despots and worthy of honor, then let them be like monarchs worthy of honor who display themselves to their contemporary denizens as fathers of the fatherland and who also think that the more important and more honorable the rank in society it is, the more especially the necessity to serve the fatherland and be useful to it, encompassing purpose.

Even the most disorderly person will not long resist if his delusions become for him proof of his humble manners.

From time immemorial: a sword for the nobleman, a pen for the lawyer, and grammar for the priest, were instituted.

Happiness and the illusion of happiness – are they both not the same?

I am of the same opinion that the weakness of humanity is worthy of compassion, but not of any praise. Many people of weak conscience never will mention the name of a vice. They say that a person's weakness is normal and that this should be covered with empathy. Consequently they have sewn a coat out of empathy to cover vices. But such people of empathy should better be called condoners.

In deliberating his income, the arithmetic taught him only addition.

It is criminal to steal from your brother's pocket and this matter is personal. If you want to steal, then from the king. Thank God that his house is like a bowl overflowing with possessions, so if you steal something, it will not diminish what he possesses.

Do not pay attention to young scoundrels who hate their fatherland, they even ridicule and disdain the virtues of our ancestors.

Learn to know the land and sky so you will have no need of anything, except your own courage.

Nothing is more pleasant or useful and cannot be more worthy in our labors than a tight connection with people and the object of this effort – virtue, prosperity and happiness.

Pride despises all that surrounds it and wants only to possess what carries the appellation of honor. But a noble pride thinks highly itself and only assimilates as much honor for itself relative to its achievements, while also thinking highly of others and from all its heart is prepared to bestow honor on them and ascribing perhaps even more when the truth demands it.

Science in a short time of government grows together with the political establishment. They end up having the same fate and collapse together.

The desire to do good increases the more in us as the more we know and we feel this sensation of strength that excites us to this practice and the beauty of philanthropy. Out of this proceeds an unknown certain inner satisfaction, the first fruit, the first compensation for our virtue.

The most humiliated of virtues in the world needs to be exalted on its majesty throne, while the vile vice and the ruinous objects affecting human nature must be unveiled to the world in all its nakedness. All of these efforts and the intentions mentioned are worthy of all praise, although psychological strengths are not always available to accomplish this.

The most virtuous and reasonable monarch can still err in his decisions. But the Omniscient cannot err, subsequently, we can justly conclude that we have acquired an immense honor and dignity and so we can boast that God has created us – humans – and selected us above all other of His creations.

The people are the first to gather the harvest produced by science; the scholars acquire them considerably later.

The reason for all of humanity's mistakes is ignorance; while the reason for perfection is knowledge.

Time squandered on noticing various inclinations of humanity, no matter how important a fault it might be, is always utilized to your personal gain. By way of this you can learn to hate faults once ascertaining their vileness.

We all seek ourselves in everything. The reasons that motivate us to do this would be weak and ineffective if we – by undertaking something else – were to lose ourselves or the hope of our satisfaction, our happiness and prosperity, from our sight. And so there is nothing that is more pleasant and enticing than ourselves.

We likewise lose all of our aspiration, talent and zeal due to fear. In a servile situation, virtue and knowledge cause suspicion of yourself.

Wealth and popularity does not exactly evolve from human nature, subsequently, the haughtiness of the wealthy or nobility is a humorous pride. Whoever wants to think of himself as highly and boast of some individual dignity must review and investigate himself entirely in other aspects.

Whoever has a rank of excellency must have an excellent mind and excellent knowledge and excellent education. Subsequently any crime this person should commit should also be excellent. So if you receive excellent rewards for your excellent conduct, likewise will your punishment be excellent for your excellent crimes.

To observe the faults of other people is very useful for self-improvement. A personal fault becomes especially repulsive when you see it in another people and you will feel how unpleasant it would be to possess such a fault, and especially if you laugh at him for having this fault, because we love to laugh at everything and everyone, except ourselves and what is ours.

Vladimir Feodorovich Odoyevski

1804 – 1869

Educator, Musician, Publisher

Vladimir Odoyevski was born in Moscow on August 1, 1804. He studied at Moscow University the years 1816-1822, and the years 1823-1825, was president of the society of Wisdom-Lovers that he organized. He went into publishing afterward with almanacs, journals and newspapers. He moved to St Petersburg in 1826, and continued his work there.

From 1846 he was assistant director of the Petersburg Public Library and director of Rumyantzevski museum.[10] From 1861, he was a senator in Moscow. Odoyevski was much involved in organizing charities for the destitute and underprivileged, and publishing literature for distribution to the Russian peasants. He was a great advocate of the government reforms of the 1860's with the abolition of the feudal system and providing rights for the serfs.

But because Odoyevski was in the class of aristocrats, his philosophy was more inclined toward the German idealists. He stopped writing his novels in about 1840, and began a period of spiritual rebirth and growth, and especially due to the influence of the French philosopher-mystic Louis Claude de Saint-Martin, whose writings Odoyevski studied.

---

[10] Nikolai Feodorov, also in this volume, worked there later.

Toward the end of his life, Odoyevski changed his ideology and dedicated his time for Russia's improvement and began adhering to the concepts of the Slavophiles. He was a member of the Russian Musical Society and helped in creating the Petersburg and Moscow conservatories. Odoyevski also composed a series of musical scores.

Odoyevski died in Moscow on February 27, 1869.

A person exchanged the unhappiness of solitude with sufferings of another type, and perhaps even worse. For the salvation of his body he sold the blessedness of his soul to high society as though to an evil spirit.

A person must know not just the past, and forgetting about the future. In the same manner he must not just know the future, forgetting about the present. Knowledge and education solely about the past casts a person into lethargy; knowledge and education solely about the future leads to infinite activity and subsequently harm, because harm in a certain sense is nothing else but the result activity directed toward a goal that is distance from the present moment.

Although to be a constant moralist is flattering for your ambitions, but you will be rather lonesome.

An entire circle of activity is predestined for humanity's mind. Writers and composers belong to all the ages and to all nations, who continue to supplement this circle with expressions of new thoughts and feelings or with the acquisition of yet unknown forms of elegance.

Beautiful is a nation's activity if it is turned to superficial credit, but what is better is if it is turned toward inner effort of self-perfection.

Believe me. All scholars are idiots; all sciences are essentially nonsense. So why do you need agronomy? I suppose it is good where ground is sparse. So why do you need mineralogy, zoology? Do you know the best science? It is truth-ology.

Great and touching is the penance of a sinner, but what is even more exalted is the humility of a great person who, after the accomplishment of some great achievement, disdains himself for not achieving even more.

Humanity is like a rock thrown down from above that is continuously increasing the speed of its motion. For the future generation this is how matters are for the present: they will disassociate from the past to an exceeding degree. Any destruction of our literary accomplishments will assist.

I cannot tolerate the existence of a person who never will contradict anybody, just as with a person who will debate just for the sake of a debate.

I heard said that bad is the absence of good just as cold is the absence of warmth. But if you were to remove warmth from the body, making it cold, to them this signifies that cold is not something that is non-existent, but on the contrary, it is a natural composition of the body.

I heard said that suffering is unavoidable, which means it contradicts that principle in our soul that has allowed us the possibility to imagine existence without suffering.

I reveal a great secret. Listen! All that occurs in society is done for the undefined and undesignated society! It is the orchestra; other people are the scenery. It holds in its hands the authors and musicians and actresses and the heroes and heroines. It fears nothing: not laws, not justice, no conscience. It judges life and death and never changes its verdicts even if they were against common sense. You can easily ascertain the members of this society by the following indications: others play cards, while they watch the card game; others marry, while they attend the wedding; others write books, while they write critiques; others give banquets, while they discuss the quality of the meal; others fight, while they read the results; others dance, while they stand and watch the dancing. The members of this society everywhere and immediately recognize each other not by some special motions, but by the instinct each possesses. And each one, even before he hears the matter from his friend, is already ready to support him.

I would like to hug all the universe in my arms and press all people to my heart. But instead I will just stretch my hands and grab only one cloud.

If fish could write, then they surely would prove and very clearly that birds must not be able to exist since they cannot swim in water.

If the dilemma of life is not yet resolved by humanity, then it is because people still do not fully understand one another, that our language does not convey properly our ideas, such that the listener never actually hears all of what is being said to him, but instead either more or less or to the right or to the left.

If they say that my thoughts were already expressed by someone else, then I can quickly extend my trust to their virtuous character. If I discover that they are new, but unjust, then at least I still have the honor of original acquisition. If they notice that they are old and unjust, then I would be happy for the opportunity to learn something new and depart from the unjust.

If we were to investigate attentively all the misfortunes of the present society, then we will find that the basis of each of them is some type of thought of ancient wisdom, that evolving from the eras of antiquity from among the common classes. If we were to transfer the heroes of antiquity in their entire fullness into our era, they would be the most majestic of criminals, while our criminals would be the heroes of antiquity.

In his elderly years a person accustoms himself to people's injustice, realizing it is an ordinary matter, sometimes bitter, more often humorous, but when in youth when you want to believe all that is exalted and beautiful, people's injustice powerfully devastates and brings upon the soul an inexpressible melancholy. In one respect the youth are to blame because of their inherent goodness and their heart's stature. Unconscionable people never grieve about anything.

In the psychological world poetry is one of those elements without which the tree of life will vanish.

In vain do some fear stupid thoughts. More often than anything society is in pain not because of this malady, but because of an absence of all thinking and especially feelings.

Indeed it is worth delving into the depths of the soul and then each one will find within himself an embryo of all possible crimes.

It is noticeable that 2 or a few people that reside together little by little become similar one to another, not only psychologically, but physically. Not only do their habits become identical, but in many associations even noticeable is the similarity in their facial features. How can this process of adaptation occur? The spirit of one person has an affect on the other.

It seems completely incomprehensible that a certain thing could be found that a certain Someone would install in the world to live and be entrusted to acquire laws for this world and for himself.

Based on this we can only conclude that this world contains no laws for its existence. In every world laws must be completely ready and it is worth finding them.

Literature is the final level of a nation's development. This is a spiritual testament that the nation bequeaths as it draws near to the grave so it does not entirely disappear from the face of the earth.

Look into history, into this cemetery of facts, and you will see what certain words can signify when their meaning does not depend on the inner dignity of a person.

Mathematics leads us to the doors of truth, but it will not open the doors.

My mother was always occupied with continual surveillance of the morality of the region and so she never did watch after me or even after herself.

One of the most vile elements of our national character is the insuperable want to strike at someone's arrogance, and whoever this might be, and even a dead person, and not ever having a special reason to do so, so that he – the dead person – would not be so haughty as the rest.

Only worrying about means for life does not allow life to succeed.

Other than talent, 2 conditions constitute a great artist: self-confidence, that he was born for this artistic vocation, and an equal assurance that every item can be the object of his artistry.

Painters are subject to the deceit of inexperience if they think that they in their pictures are copying nature. The painter, drawing from nature, is just nourished by it, just as some human organ is nourished by the coarse produce of the garden.

Pathetic people! They have assigned names to non-existent things while disregarding the existent. They have closed for themselves the path to truth by using a thousand names, compartments, sub-compartments. It will take half your life just to refute all of this, and half your life you will need just to learn to speak their language!

People will always remain as people as this has been from the beginning of the world. These same passions will remain, these same motivations. From another side, the form of their thoughts and feeling, and especially their physical existence, must significantly change.

Public education produces officials, soldiers, attorneys, tradesmen, but for the poet there is no education. In place of being called a public activist, he possesses the appellation of achiever.

So then this occurs with the member who thinks of doing something in this world, at that minute he is deprived of all advantages integrated into his vocation and he enters into the common group of the defendants and in no manner will he be able to regain any of his previous rights. It is popularly known also that the most important role in this trial is played by those whose reason for existence in this world can definitely never be found.

Speaking is nothing else but to excite in your listener his inner word. If his word in not in harmony with yours, he will not understand you. If his word is holy, yours and even some bad statement will be turned to his benefit. If his word is false, you will impose harm on him even if you have the best intention. It is inarguable that words are corrected by words, but for this to occur the active word must be pure and frank.

Surrounding every thought, every feeling, every word and act, a mesmerized circle is formed to which lesser and weaker thoughts, feelings and acts unwillingly subject themselves.

The matter is that we are all sick with a single sickness: not stretching out our hand. And we somehow are ashamed of this sickness and find it convenient to dump the product of our laziness on destiny. You will not get far with self-oblivion and self-contempt. It is necessary to have in every situation an identified destiny of self-assurance: in the struggle of life, in the struggle with individual thinking. It is necessary to look straight into the eyes of your friend and foe and success and failure and action and inaction.

The most cruel, most obvious tortures we know of are those which a person cannot pass to the next generation. Whoever can describe his sufferings has already discarded half of them from himself.

The only person who can say that there exists limits for humanity's spirit is the one for whom no limits exist.

The principle condition of every knowledge is to know your future, that is, to know what it would be if it was to attain its goal.

The stupid and insane often very logically ascertain matters. However they cannot logically verify their individual situation: the insane as to why he is insane; the stupid as to why he is stupid. Regretfully I myself do not know how any of us can justify himself, whether he is actually in sound mind, that he, for example, does not accept the part as the whole, or the whole as the part, movement as steady and steady as movement.

There are people for whom every failure is a true enjoyment. They rejoice at a typographical error in some expensive publication; a wrong note played by a dignified musician; a grammatical mistake by a talented writer. But when no failures occur, they, according to the goodness of their heart, suppose it is there somewhere anyway. It is sweet to them all the same.

Thoughts develop from gradual organization of the human mind like buds on a tree branch. Sometimes these thoughts are contradistinctive, and for life to progress a struggle exists between these 2 groups of thoughts. People consider them for personal growth, call them true laws of nature and humanity will fight for them and even die for them. Nonetheless for life there is necessary only one struggle between these thoughts, and not completely a triumph of one over the other. What is necessary is to here define some type of balance. As a result not one specific opinion is usually the winner, but what wins is a median between them.

Under every sensation another is hid, one deeper and perhaps more altruistic and under it a third, even more altruistic, and so until you reach the secret human soul where no room is available for external, coarse desires, because time and space do not exist there.

We will note in passing that it is difficult for a person to install their true invitation. If genuine it will tear through all obstacles. Were there many great people, victors, artists, who were born on a bed of roses? Each one of them had to struggle against people's indifference.

What most of all convinces me of my soul's eternity is its expansiveness. Superficially a person appears with his individual character, but the more we penetrate into the depths of the soul the more were are assured that in it resides – like ideas – all virtue, all vices, all desires, all repulsions. And there not one of these elements have the supremacy, but are found in this type of balance as in nature. As a result each person possesses his originality as in poetry.

When we speak, with every word we raise the dust of a thousand thoughts and ideas. When we want to finally provide to a word some defined character, we unwillingly grab some defined association with nature, like a new meaning correlating with our thinking in place of an old meaning. We strive to dress our thoughts in some special clothing that we ourselves cannot create.

With every revelation of science one of humanity's sufferings becomes ameliorated. This it seems is not subject to doubt.

Woe to that nation where people of high integrity die early while the criminals live long. This is a thermometer that indicates a nation's fall. Prophets die.

You are not able to hew apart a spoken word and just the same with the written. There is nothing in the world that can be forgotten or destroyed.

You correctly notice that for happiness only little is needed, and likewise little is also needed for suffering.

VASILI VASILYEVICH ROZANOV

1856 – 1919

Unorthodox Religious Philosopher, Educator

Vasili Rozanov was born in the city Vetluga, Kostroma Province, central Russia, on April 20, 1856. He was originally self-taught and spent a lot of time with personal study at the local library at Simbirsk. In 1872, he moved to Nizhni-Novgorod where he finished his basic education. He then entered Moscow University to study history and philosophy, and graduated in 1882. Over the next several years, 1882-1893, Rozanov taught at public schools in Bryansk, Simbirsk, Vyazma, and other cities of central Russia.

Rozanov's compositions were eclectic and unorthodox in regard to understanding deity, a philosophy that was difficult to understand and fathom, and which to many seemed to be contradictory. He developed themes on the contradistinction between Christ and the world, paganism and Christianity, which in his opinion, expressed the universal fatalism of hopelessness and death. But at the same time, Rozanov states that that a nation cannot exist without established religion and God. The spiritual rebirth must be performed on the field of a correctly understood new Christianity, whose ideals indispensably triumph not only in the other world, but also this material world. Culture, art, family, individualism, must be comprehended and implemented only in the frame of a new religious ideology, as the manifestation of human progress, as an incarnation of deity in a human and in human history. Rozanov attempted to build his philosophic on the deification of the family or tribe. To him the fundamental building block of society and religion was the extended family. Conservative Russian Orthodox prelates felt that Rozanov had gone astray from their fundamental tenets, and some considered him a heretic.

Rozanov viewed the Russian Revolution as a catastrophe, a tragedy for the Russian nation, and a hopeless event in history. The philosophic convictions of Rozanov were viewed critically by the new Soviet state as well as by the new Soviet intelligentsia. In late 1917, he left Moscow and settled in Sergeev Posad, north of Moscow, very much in despair with the future of Russia. He devolved into depression, destitution and hunger in time and died there on February 5, 1919.

A thought is not eternal, a thought is momentary.

In Russia 2 philosophies are prevalent: coercive and progressive, as long as it is coerced.

It is not a major issue to love your homeland when it is prosperous and joyful. We must still love it in particular when it is weak, small, humiliated, and finally dumb, and finally even corrupt. In particular when our *mother* is drunk, lying and all dirty in sin, we must still not walk away from her.

It is not universities who have nourished the present Russian person, but benevolent and uneducated nursemaids.

Love is always exchanging the soul for the body. So when there is nothing to use for exchange, love is extinguished.

Love is not entirely a fire, as it is often defined. Love is air. Without it there is no respiration, and with it breathing is easier. This is all.

Love means, I cannot exist without you. It is difficult without you. I am everywhere lonesome without you.

Only when you are concluding your life do you see that your life was a lesson to which you did not pay attention as a student.

Our heart always needs to be in pain on behalf of someone. This is so strange, but without this, life is empty.

Resurrect, Fatherland! God, why have all of us fled to our kennels? Dust! Only the dust of individual human figures remains, and so where is our nation?

Russian printing and society is not worth having a throat to swallow any of it, even if it was severed into small bits and these pieces were distributed to neighbors and not even for money, but just for a bottle of praise.

The person who lives like trash will be discarded when he dies.

The pain of life is much more a powerful interest of life. This is why religion will always supercede philosophy.

Two Angels sitting on my shoulders: an Angel of laughter and an Angel of tears. And their eternal dispute is my life.

Who loves the Russian people, cannot but also love its Church, because the people and its church are one. And only among Russians it is this way. So what would occur to our land if it did not have the Church? It would become meaningless and freeze over.

Woe to the state that lives in the days of the past, and not in the days of the present. It will delay and postpone, until quickly transpiring events of history leave it far behind.

MIKHAIL MIKHAILOVICH SCHERBATOV

1733 – 1790

Historian, Statesman

Mikhail Scherbatov was born in Moscow on July 22, 1733. He received a private education at home and then entered military service as a cadet, and then continued until retiring in 1767 as a captain. Scherbatov then entered government service that year, and in 1778 he became president of the collegium of state revenue, and senator in 1779, until 1788. At this time he resigned from government service and dedicated himself to science and literature, as well as becoming a representative of the aristocratic opposition to the autocracy, advocating the institution of a constitutional means of government in Russia.

Scherbatov died on December 12, 1790

In 1770, Scherbatov published his multi-volume masterpiece, *History of Russia from Ancient Times*, which also reflected his political views and his philosophy of history. His subsequent history dealt with the decline of morality in Russia and due to the poor government of Imperial Russia under the tsars, but it was not published until 1858 in London. He was a member of the St Petersburg Academy of Sciences beginning from 1776, and a member of the Russian Academy from 1783. (Scherbatov was also maternal grandfather of Peter Chaadaev.)

A person views himself as a weak entity in nature, deprived of natural clothing, who is unable to find sustenance on his own, or to defend himself from wild animals that will attack him, or to deliver himself by flight from danger. So how much majesty and strength does he actually possess?

Although all of us are obligated to know the laws, but not learning their applications and the necessary conformance, no one can become their performer.

But if a person, following the essence of his nature, wants to increase the length of his life, longer than what nature has provided him, if he was to increase beyond the circle that is suppressing him, and with his intellect transverse all ages and all countries, then all will occur relative to his wants. Our creator has given us all of this and all that remains is for us to utilize it.

Does it not seem too early to hastily conjecture about the solidarity of nations, about brotherhood, and will not every compulsive concealment of enmity be just another superficial reconciliation? I believe that national tendencies will lose their offensive character to the extent that they disperse it in an educated society. But this is done so that their education would penetrate the entire depth of the national mass and over a long course of time.

How possible it really is for a person to flatter himself into thinking he can attain a comprehension of higher matters with his own capability of intellect. It is the mistakes of the most prominent of people that can serve as our search for truth.

In all due honesty I can say that if we, having entered later after other nations on the path of education, have nothing more that remains to be done, except to prudently follow the paths of the nations earlier educated, we genuinely among our people and in certain other things had amazing successes and with gigantic steps journeyed to the rectification of our external faults. But at the same time and with much and great speed we ran to the detriment of our morals and attained that point where we have destroyed belief and the divine law in our hearts, the divine sacraments have fallen into contempt, and civil legislation are disdained.

In general the view is that a nation can never be sufficiently educated in any area. Science cannot create common sense, but will help to cleanse it of error.

It seems that megalomania is first of all born in the heart, and most of all in the heart of monarchs.

Let us not flatter ourselves. Although many ages have passed, although the many labors, vigilance and consideration of worthy men who have lived before us have been utilized, there is still much that remains hidden, and it seems almost all of it can be brought to mind in the best manner.

Now gaze into history at the various examples of contentment, those that acquired virtue and those that acquired anxieties incurred due to vices, and compare the beginning and the results of these and others. Is it not the person who reads this with attention and contemplates much that becomes considerably attached to virtue and distanced from vice, and more than the person who solely with his philosophizing wanted to attain all this?

Really, to create a city is not dependant on the sovereign's or government's will, but what is needed is a comfortable region, influx of population and the resident's prosperity.

The person who has abandoned himself completely to his chaotic demands and deifying within his heart his driving passions, meditates little on God's law, and even less about the laws of the country in which he lives. Can such a person be firm, who always collapses at not achieving his objectives and whose stability then departs?

The sovereign must be protected, but not by weapons held by the people who surround him, but by the people's love. If this love does not exist, then no guard of any type will save the sovereign, but will on the contrary provide the means for his own defeat.

Until you give a clear meaning to the words you speak, no matter where you speak, your speech will be dubious and misunderstood.

Where many cities are located, there is both usefulness and harm for the state, because wherever you have a stream of various castes of people, there you will also find a decrease of morality. Farmers are transformed into businessmen, abandoning their primary vocation, corrupting their morals in the process and falling into deception and abandoning their farms. This brings more harm than good to the state.

Who wants to harm others will surely harm himself first using the same items.

Aleksandr Vasilyevich Suvorov

1729 – 1800

Military Hero, Educator

Aleksandr Suvorov was born in Moscow on November 13, 1729, into a military family. From childhood he had an inclination toward military matters, and utilized his father's wealthy library to study artillery, fortifications, and military history. In 1742 entered the cadet corps, and in 1762 into the regular military ranks. In 1768-1772 he fought in Poland where he advanced in his military career, and in 1772 was promoted to General. In 1773-1780, he supervised the forces in the war against Turkey, and was awarded with the title of Count.

The pinnacle of his military career was the suppression of revolt in Poland and the conquest of Warsaw in 1794, and he was then promoted to Field Marshall. He engaged in over 60 battles and won them all. Suvorov died of gangrene in St Petersburg on May 6, 1800.

A good name is a possession of every honorable person, but I also include a good name as a credit to my Fatherland, and all of my activities are inclined to its prosperity.

A proper mood toward another person is to wish him happiness.

An intelligent person can always find a vocation.

Be pure-hearted with your friends, moderate in your needs, and selfless in your actions.

Find a hero of ancient times, observe him, follow after him, attempt to equal him, chase after him, and use him as example, and his glory will also be yours.

Love for the fatherland, embarrassment, and fear of discredit, are means of reducing and restraining many crimes.

Never will personal ambition direct my activities, although it is the passion of people who will quickly pass through life. I forget about myself wherever I need to think about the common welfare. My life has been a school of hard knocks, but my ethics are immaculate and my inherent magnanimity ameliorates my difficulties. My feelings are free to roam, while I personally stand firm.

Pride is a curtain hanging in front of a stupid person. People of a mediocre mind tend to act mean. But the person possessing true dignity possesses exalted feelings that are sheltered by humility.

The conscience is the lamp of the inner and hidden person. It will illuminate the person all on its own and will speak to him with a quiet and silent voice: gently touching the soul, causing it to have feelings, following the person wherever he goes, and not permitting him impunity in any incident.

The intelligent person having a sense of shame will not decline from learning even in his old age, and what he has not been able to learn in his youth.

Vasili Andreevich Zhukovski

1783 – 1852

Poet, Educator

Vasili Zhukovski was born in Mishensk, Tule Province, central Russia, on January 29, 1783. He studied at the Moscow University in 1797-1801. His initial poetry was published in 1797 and which continued to the end of his life. He was conscripted into the military in 1812 in the campaign against Napoleon and his invasion of Russia.

Due to his closeness to the royal family and scholarship, including the military, Zhukovski was hired in 1826 by Tsar Nicholas I to be tutor of the future Tsar Alexandr II.

He died April 12, 1852 and was buried at the Alexandr Nevski Monastery in St Petersburg.

I was walking along the street and stopped in front of a printed announcement that was glued to the wall of a house. It was surrounded by a number of torn old and new fragments that remained from the announcements that were glued at one time or another to the same place. Some were fresh, others were old, a third layer was completely decayed and green from dampness. This is the picture of our world. Everything here is for the passer-by, for the souls of humanity. All, whether in private or social life, societies themselves, ages, empires and nations are nothing else but these announcements for a passer-by. Read it and make use of it. The world exists solely for the souls of humanity. God and soul – here are 2 entities. All else such as the printed announcements glued on poles exist only for a minute.

A person who has full power to make you happy and does not do this, but then proceeds to do the opposite, does he even have the right to be called a human?

All of us error, considering undemanding friendship so much that we would not permit ourselves with strangers. In such effortlessness there often occurs much that is sorrowful. On occasion you will permit yourself to speak with certain carelessness and ease in the presence of many what you should only be saying to yourself in private. Can you call this openness? No! This is plain negligence, verbosity, which only causes your tongue to wag, not worrying whether you will insult someone with what you say or not! And this type of worry is indispensable with friends, more than with strangers.

Family life understood in its full sense is that school where you will learn life in its present form. But not by way of worriless joys, not by way of poetic fantasies, but more with agitations, fears, struggles with yourself, all that lead to your soul's vexation and toward tolerance, from tolerance to belief, and from belief to heartfelt peace.

Illness causes a person to become acquainted with religion – not as a result of the fear of death, but due to the majesty of life. This is a staircase. Our matter is to enter it; every test is a step upward. Each little platform can be called a joy, separating one set of stairs from another. They serve only as a point of rest and transfer to new strengths, for new heights.

Install this as a rule: do not seek any success in society; think only about acquiring the best from others, and not to just display yourself as a good person; it is better to seem lowly and strive to advance, than to seem to be somebody and decline in the process. A genuine worry about your façade and superficiality aspires to gain attention directed only at yourself and deprives you of the possibility of seeing and hearing others, and utilizing yourself for their benefit.

Is not this assurance in the imperishability of earthly items a secret and inherent proof of immortality in a person? Who sorrows over the mortal, sorrows about only himself. Who can be unhappy if he believes in immortality? What he loses in life, which is insignificant in itself, should rejoice over such a loss, because it draws us closer to our great goal!

It is an inherent quality of all people to sin. The difference between people resides in the level of remorse that the soul will impose on them after the sin.

It is more difficult to struggle with a conservative nation that with a conservative throne and ambo. The nation conservative by instinct and so knowing nothing else possesses no ideals outside of existing conditions. The further a nation from the movement of history, the more stubborn it holds to its established forms, to its traditions. It will even accept what is old dressed in new clothing.

Love so that you are loved and be perfectly calm, because nothing will repel misfortune as love will.

Our life is a night under a starry sky. Our soul during its best minutes of existence opens these stars that do not give and cannot give full light, but decorating our sky we become familiar with them, serving at the same time a guide for travelers on earth.

People that travel to God do not arrive on a tour with a guide, but they are pilgrims all the same.

Poetry is God in the holy dreams of our world.

Stop being an epigram, be a poem instead.

Stubbornness is a weakness that has the appearance of strength. It evolves from violating the balance of the union of will and intellect.

The translator of prose is a slave. The translator of poems is a rival.

There is no higher vocation than to be a writer in the contemporary sense. Especially for Russia. A writer who is genius can accomplish more than Peter the Great.

We are united with others due to compassion. Their misfortunes are common with us. We rejoice less than the amount we are sorrowful with others. Misfortune causes another to be more considerate, more honest. In our eyes he is exalted. The more he suffers and struggles, the more considerate we are toward him.

What is envy? It is the injustice, self-interest, which does not tolerate in others what it does not find in yourself. It is the vileness, the desire to discredit all, to level everyone with yourself. What medicine should be provided? The assurance that all is beautiful, even in our worst of enemies, must be beautiful for the noble soul. Do not be joyful over what is sorrowful.

Imperial Russia –

The Political Thinkers

RUSSIA'S WISDOM

IVAN SERGEEVICH AKSAKOV

1823 – 1886

Political Ideologist

Ivan Aksakov born September 26, 1823. He was one of the ideologues of the Slavophiles along with this brother Konstantine Aksakov and A.S. Khomyakov. He completed law school in Petersburg in 1842. In 1849 he was arrested for his participation in the Slavophile movement and shortly after was freed, but he was always under the surveillance of the police, since many considered him the finest journalist of his era. From 1852 and through the end of his life he was editor of several Russian magazines and newspapers. Aksakov was critical of Western rationalism. The dominating ideology of Aksakov was the idea of Russian nationalism, Russian Orthodoxy and community life. One of his efforts was the abolition of Russian royalty as a legal status, but it met with considerable resistance from that group. He was also son-in-law of the poet Feodor Tutchev.

Ivan Aksakov died January 27, 1886, and was buried in Moscow.

The state, of course, is indispensable, but there is no need to believe in it as the sole goal and fullest norm of humanity. The community and personal ideal of humanity consists of something higher than the state, exactly as the conscience and inner veracity consists of something higher than law and external truths.

The Church, interfering in state matters, intervening by having in one hand both a religious sword and a state sword, fails to be the Church and so voluntarily denies its basic religious nature, descending to the level of being a kingdom of this world. So it is with the state, if it thinks to adopt for itself the significance and authority of the Church, it would bring into the Church the element of something completely foreign, alien, and which would limit the infinite religiosity of belief, and externalize and coarsen it. In short, it would distort the very substance of the Church.

Without freedom of conscience the existence of the church is unthinkable, because the reason for the church's existence depends upon a person's religious freedom. Freedom of the human spirit comprises in this manner not only the element of the church, but the very object of its activity. It is understandable that in this element the liberated spirit is very active, and the direction of this spirit can only be religious.

It is impossible not to be struck by the narrow and limited understanding by adherents of the contemporary progress of what they consider the world-wide problem of Christianity – since they dump upon it this responsibility: that in the course of almost 2,000 years it has not installed on earth common prosperity, or they blame it for its impracticality, and that the Christian ideal stands outside of the actual historical life of humanity. But this is the matter, that the Christian ideal is eternal, outside of the conditions of time and place. It does not conform itself to someone's life, but is always above it and will not reconcile itself with it. Christianity eternally will motivate humanity's society and will drive it forward and forward.

Konstantine Sergeevich Aksakov

1817–1860

Political Ideologist

Konstantine Aksakov was born March 29, 1817. From 1832 to 1835 he attended Moscow University, studying philology, and while there became part of the Slavophile circle. Aksakov likewise wrote several volumes on philosophy, history and poetry. He was the older brother of Ivan Aksakov.

Aksakov, like his brother above and the other Slavophiles, felt that Western Christianity had lost its inner veracity, that it had subjected life to the compulsion and jurisdiction of the European domination. Only the Slavic people preserved true Christianity and community life, except that the balance of Russian society was ruined by Tsar Peter I. Aksakov was convinced that Orthodoxy and implementing historical Russian social customs would cause class and national distinctions to vanish. Aksakov also presented a composition to Tsar Alexander II titled *Notes on the Inner Composition of Russia*, where he places blame on the government for despotism and suppression of freedoms.

Aksakov was critical of materialism among the royal and wealthy classes claiming that it led to atheism, instead of bringing the people closer to Orthodoxy.

Aksakov died December 7, 1860, while on vacation at the Ionian Islands, near Greece.

Prior to Christianity, but ready for its acceptance and having a presentiment of its great truths, our nation formed a community life that was then sanctified by the acceptance of Christianity. Having separated itself from state dominion, the Russian nation organized a community life and entrusted the state to provide the nation the possibility of living this community life. Not wanting to govern, our nation wanted to live, it seems, not in one barbarian sense, but in a human sense. Not seeking political freedom, it sought moral freedom, religious freedom, community freedom, a national life within itself.

Outside the nation, outside social life, there can only exist the individual. It is only the individual that can be unlimited relative to the state, only the individual liberates the nation from all interference in the state. Here a sovereign or monarch is unavoidable. Only monarchial authority is unlimited authority. Only in the presence of limited monarchial authority can the nation separate itself from the state and deliver itself from all participation in the state, from every political significance, and so present to itself a moral-social life and a drive to religious freedom. Such a monarchial state needs to deal with the Russian nation.

This view that the Russian person possesses is the view of a free person. Recognizing state limited authority, he retains close to himself his complete independent spirit, conscience and thought.

They say Peter the Great magnified Russia. Exactly so did he deliver it much external majesty, but he attacked its internal integrity with depravity. He brought into its life the seed of destruction and enmity. All the external glorious acts he and his successors performed was with Russia's strength that grew and strengthened in ancient fields, on earlier principles. But now our soldiers that are extracted from our native people are made subject to foreign influences. And so the Petrine state provides victories with the strengths of pre-Petrine Russia. But now these strengths are weakening because the Petrine influence is growing in the nation.

In order for a good statement to turn into a beneficial act, Russia's spirit needs to be raised and established on Russian principles, those that were rejected since the time of Tsar Peter. Russia's external majesty during the era of emperors was definitely brilliant, but external majesty is only solid when it proceeds from inside. It is necessary for the source to be undefiled and not desolate. So now what external brilliance will satisfy as a reward for internal prosperity, for internal harmony? So what external unstable majesty and external unreliable strength can compare with internal solid majesty, with internal reliable strength? External strength can exist as long as the internal exists, although it might be tattered and still intact. If the inside of the tree is rotted, then the external bark, no matter how firm and thick it might be, will not withstand force and at the first wind the tree will collapse, and to everybody's surprise.

Russia has survived long because its internal long-lasting strength has not yet vanished, although constantly weakening and slowly dissipating. We endure because the pre-Petrine Russia has not yet vanished. And so the internal majesty is what must be the primary principle goal of the nation and of course the state.

The contemporary condition of Russia presents an inner dissention covered by an unconscionable lie. The government, and the upper classes along with them, are alienated from the people and seem to be estranged from them. So the people and state stand now on different roads, on different principles. Not only does the government not ask the people for their opinion, but every private individual fears to speak his opinion. The people have no trust of the government, and the government does not trust the people.

MIKHAIL ALEKSANDROVICH BAKUNIN

May 18, 1814 – June 19, 1876

Political Activist

Mikhail Aleksandrovich Bakunin was born May 18, 1814 in the village Pryamukhino, Tver Province, central Russia. He gained a reputation over his lifetime of being a revolutionary, Pan-Slavist, anarchist, a zealous Russian nationalist, and an ideological opponent of Karl Marx.

During the years 1832-1834 he was a close associate of Stankevich and his Slavophile associates, but as time progressed his views expanded more politically. In 1840 he immigrated to Europe where he was a participant in the revolution of 1848-1849 in Prague and Dresden, for which he was twice sentenced to execution. He was exiled back to Russia and was subsequently exiled to Siberia in 1857. In 1861 he was able to escape and returned to Europe to be further part of French revolutionary struggles, including the First Internationale.

Bakunin viewed the state as a historical justification of evil, and which should be replaced by a non-governmental social self-rule based on the principles of freedom, equality, justice and brotherhood. He saw as the biggest problem the necessity of dismantling the state because of its oppression of people. Bakunin's anarchic views were considerably advertised in Russia, Italy, Spain and other countries.

Bakunin died July 1, 1876, in Bern, Switzerland.

And so the question is not whether there will be, or not be, a revolution, but whether its progress will be peaceful or bloody.

Christianity appears as the most genuine typical religion, because it presents itself and displays its nature in all of its fullness, which is the true essence of every religious system, presenting itself as a means of the humiliation, enslavement and destruction of humanity for the sake of holiness.

Despair in your love and in your dignity serves as the best proof of their presence in a person.

Do not squander time doubting yourself, because this is the emptiest effort of all those that a person can devise.

In his youth he was a person not without some brilliance, capable of puzzling weak and nervous people, confusing the immature, and still pushing them out of their ruts. He had a dry and hard nature, an empty mind, and fruitless motivations. He would grasp at a lot, but could never hold to anything, and could not sense a calling to anything, and he did not accept participation in anything.

It is impossible for all humanity to devote itself to science. It would then die of hunger.

On its own merit compulsion is harmful. It produces resentment to the suppressed and punished person. It ruins his character, excites in him vexation toward the prohibiting and punishing faction, leading him into a malevolent altercation with them.

One person's freedom ends when the freedom of another person begins.

Our notorious civilization is nothing else for our country than a source of slavery and destitution.

Social solidarity appears as the first human law; freedom composes the 2nd law of society. Both these laws mutually complement each other and, being distinct from one another, comprise the essence of humanity.

The most important capital of a nation is the moral level of its people.

To leave something that has not been completely or sufficiently discussed signifies to leave a possibility for an incorrect understanding. On the contrary it is necessary to be aware of every ambiguous expression: this requires integrity in scholarship.

What we call the human world does not have another direct creator, other than the human who created it, winning step by step its freedom and human dignity from the external world and from its personal animality.

Vissarion Gregoryevich Belinski

1811 – 1848

Poet, Journalist

Vissarion Belinski was born May 30, 1811 in the Sveaborg, Finland, Fortress, in a physician's family, who served as a doctor for the Baltic float. He attended Moscow University but was expelled in 1832 for failing grades. He became a journalist and joined the circle of Russian philosophic Slavophiles: Stankevich and Bakunin and the Aksakov brothers. After his arrival in Petersburg he work at several magazines as publisher including the publication of many of his own articles. He died of tuberculosis on May 26, 1848, and was buried in St Petersburg.

Belinski had an immense influence on Russian literature, and especially on the next generations of writers and philosophers.

A conviction is precious only if it is truth, and not just because it is ours.

A man with effeminate characteristics is the most poisonous lampoon that can affect a person.

A person first of all appears as a child of his own country, a citizen of his own nation, fervently accepting into his hearts its interests.

A person is only afraid of what he does not know. With knowledge all fear is defeated.

A person knows nothing about himself except for what he sees from the glasses that his volition causes him to wear.

A person must not think that belief is true only because it is old. On the contrary, the longer people live, the more obvious and clear the true law of life becomes to them. To think that we at the present in our own era must believe the same as our grandfathers and forefathers believed is not relevant. This is like thinking that when you grow up that your clothes as a child will still fit you.

A person's youth is a beautiful and elegant spring season, a time of activity and flourishing of strength. It occurs only once in life and will never return.

A wife is not a (*unfit-for-print*), but a friend and companion for our life, and we must the sooner train our minds to love her and even when she becomes an elderly woman. A woman is a mother by definition, according to blood and soul. There is nothing brighter or unselfish than a mother's love. A woman thinks using her heart, while a man loves using his head.

A woman's course of life is to excite in a man his soul's energy, to flame noble passions, to support the sense of obligation, and aspire him to the high and great. This is her summons and it is a great and sacred cause.

Art is the direct reflection of truth, or our meditation in material form.

Blind fanaticism is always the arena of infantile associations.

But the dead reside also among the living, just as the living among the dead.

Creativity due to its essence requires unconditional freedom in the selection of subjects, not only from critics, but from also the artist.

Disdain for the lower ranks of society in our era is not a flaw of the higher classes. On the contrary, it is an illness of the few upstarts who are born of ignorance, those having a lack of sensitivity.

Education is an important matter: it decides the destiny of a person. To educate means not only to feed and nurse, but to provide direction to the heart and mind. But in order to accomplish this, character, scholarship, expertise and her access to all human interests are also required from the side of the mother.

Education only develops the moral strengths of a person, but does not initially provide them. It is the nature of a person that provides them.

Every love is true and beautiful based on its own merit, provided it is in the heart and not in the head.

Fantasy and mysticism are enemies of science, because they are darkness, while science is light.

Feelings of humanism are insulted when people do not respect human dignity in others and it is even more insulted and suffers when a person does not respect his own personal dignity.

How many mothers and fathers there are who in their own way love their children, but consider it a sacred obligation to constantly confirm to them of their responsibility to their parents for their life and clothing and shelter and education! Such parents are unfortunate since they do not guess that they are just depriving themselves of their children in the process.

Humanism[11] is always and everywhere the highest virtue, the highest dignity of a person, because without it a person is only an animal. Being internally an animal, while only externally having the form of a human, is the more repulsive and is contrary to a sound mind.

Humor is often the great intermediary in the matter of differentiating truth from lie.

I cannot fathom the number of petty truths what we must confirm and repeat every day in public!

I do not want prosperity and gifts if I will not first be content on account of each of my relatives – bone of my bones and flesh of my flesh.

I heard said that disharmony is the condition for harmony. Perhaps harmony is very favorable and sweet for music fans, but alas, of course, not for those who are fated to express their participation with the idea of disharmony.

If a selection of love depended on only will and intellect, then love would not be based on feelings and passion. The presence of the element of spontaneity is apparent even in the most intellectual love, because from some relatively worthy individuals one was selected, and this selection is based on an unwilling enticement of the heart.

If there is no full awareness, complete trust, and if even the smallest something is hid, there cannot be any friendship. Friendship, like love, is the dew on a blossomed flower exuding fragrance, but also with sharp thorns.

If you betray a woman's love, she has nothing else remaining in her life and she must collapse and perish under the burden of the catastrophe that has afflicted her or psychologically die for the

---

[11] Or philanthropy

balance of her remaining life, no matter how long she should continue to life. Truly human love can be founded only on a mutual respect of one for another based on human dignity, and not on some capricious feeling and not solely on a heart's passion.

If you want someone to argue with you and understand you in the manner you wish, you must yourself be courteously attentive to your opponent and accept his words and testimonies in the sense that he conveys them to you.

In order to live an enjoyable life there is no need to know your origin and what will occur in the world in the future. Do not think only about what your body wants, but what your soul wants, and then you will have no need to know about your origin or what will occur after death. You will have no need to know this because you will experience complete satisfaction where no questions about the past or the future exist.

In short, the plain, direct, empirical cognizance sees between poetry and philosophy the same type of difference as between vibrant, flaming, iridescent, escalated fantasy and emaciated, cold, arduous, boring intellect.

Inspiration is not the exclusive property of an artist. Without it, the scholar will not get far. Without it the artisan will accomplish little. Inspiration is everywhere, in every work, in every effort. The greatest treasure is a good library.

Intellect and feeling are two strengths that are equally necessary to one another. Each without the other is dead and empty.

Intellect is provided a person so that he would intellectually live, and not only for the reason to notice that he foolishly lives.

It is apparent that a person needs a little more of something other than a healthy mind! It is apparent that at the extreme boundaries fate guards us more than anything.

It is good for a person not to be satisfied with the present progress of activity, but to carry in his soul the ideal of a better existence, who lives and breathes with the one thought of progression and according to the ability and means that nature has granted him, in order to materialize his ideals on earth. Struggle is a condition of life. Life dies when struggle ends. To live means to feel and think, to suffer and prosper; any other life is death.

It is good for those who have the ability to preserve a gracious fire in their hearts, a fervent compassion toward all the great and beautiful in existence, during the winter of their days.

It is good to be educated, a poet, a soldier, a legislator, and others. But what is bad is not to be a man at the same time.

Jealousy without a sufficient basis is an illness of worthless people who do not have respect for themselves, nor for the rights of imposition on a loved one or object. Such is a shallow or menial form of tyranny standing on the level of animal egoism. Jealousy contains the instinct of individualism and domination, but with the purpose of humiliation. It is necessary to acknowledge the right of life and to reject the right of jealousy, stopping its idealization. Jealousy is a person's tyranny over another person. Especially repulsive is a woman's jealousy that transforms her into a fury.

Know that some funny anecdote inserted into a conversation where a specific number of animals are participating, is not funny.

Let everything be done calmly and orderly. Be complimentary and polite everywhere. Then you will gain immense expanse for incorrigible actions, charlatanry and ignorance. Never rebuke someone, never state a formidable word, even if you are right.

Love and respect of parents without doubt is a holy feeling.

Love has its laws of development, it grows like a person's life. It has its extravagant spring, its hot summer, and finally autumn that for some is warm, bright and productive, while for others it is cold, damp and fruitless.

Love is one of the strongest passions drawing a person to all extremes more than any other passions, and it can serve as a touchstone of morality.

Love is so strong that is will materialize the unattainable, triumph over eternally immutable conditions of space and time, over weakness of the flesh, and give a child – lion's strength.

Love kindness and then you will be indispensably useful to your fatherland, and while not even thinking about it or making arrangements.

Love of fatherland must evolve only from love of humanity, as a part of the entire. To love your homeland means to fervently desire to see in it the materialization of the ideals of humanity and to be successful in them to the extent of the strength it possesses.

Love will often err seeing in some beloved object what is not actually there, but often only love opens in it what is beautiful or great, which is inaccessible to observance and to the mind. Love usually is not so much delighted in what is given it, as much as it sorrows over what is not given.

Many people are alive and not living, but still only preparing to live.

Marriage is the materialization of love. Only a ripening soul can fully and truly materialize genuine love. And in this case love sees its supreme reward in its marriage and in the presence of brilliance it will not fade, but immensely extends its aromatic colors just like rays of the sun.

Moral indifference is an illness that especially affects educated people.

No person in life is born prepared, that is, fully informed, but every life is nothing else but an uninterruptible movement of development, constantly forming.

Not to do is not to live. Whoever does not possess the source of life, that is, the source of living activity, whoever does not rely on himself, he is eternally awaiting everything from the outside and incidental.

Of all the human's passions the strongest is narcissism, which once insulted is never forgivable.

One of the highest principles of true morality is confined in respect toward the human dignity in every person, without prejudice. First of all because he is a person, and then because of his personal qualities.

Only labor can make a person prosperous, leading his soul into clarity, harmony and satisfaction with yourself.

Passion is the source of every living productive activity. Passion is poetry and the flower of life. But passion is empty if the heart does not possess goodness.

Patriotism consists not in pompous statements in populated places, but in a fervent sense of love to the fatherland, which has the ability to be expressed without exclamation and is not disclosed only in boasting of your own goodness, but also in a painful enmity toward the bad that is inescapably residing in your fatherland.

People are so stupid that coercion is necessary to lead them to happiness. So what is the blood of a few thousand in comparison with the humiliation and suffering of millions.

Poetry is the highest form of art. Any other art is more or less suppressed and limited in its creative ability. Poetry is expressed in free creative words, which are sound and then pictured, and is clearly defined by spoken articulation. For this reason poetry contains all the elements of other arts.

Society is not like a private person. A person you can insult and slander, but society is above insult and slander.

The ability to always be in a good mood is the most solid basis for happiness in this mundane world. The ability to be creative is a great gift of nature. The act of creativity in the creative soul is a great mystery. A minute of creativity is a minute of great sacred activity.

The ability to write poetry does not mean that you are a poet. All bookstores are filled with proof of this truth.

The difference between a human and animal consists in the human just beginning where an animal already ends.

The greatest, most genuine, most infallible critic is time.

The higher the genius of a poet, the more profound and expansive he understands nature and so with greater success presents it in a mutual tie with our life.

The measure of a woman's dignity can perhaps be the husband that she loves.

The mind departs into talent, into creative fantasy with the person possessing an artistic nature, and so in his compositions, like poetry, they are awesome, immensely smart, but like people are limited and almost stupid.

The mind is a person's spiritual armament.

The more one-sided an opinion, the greater it is accessible for the majority who like what is good to be good, and what is bad to be bad. But yet do not want to hear that perhaps the one and same subject includes what is both good and bad.

The point of departure for moral perfection is first of all material necessity.

There are some women that all it takes is for you to present yourself successful and passionate and they are yours. But there are other women whose attention of a man only causes indifference, coolness and skepticism in them, as a sign of their immense demands on life, or as the result of a turbulent and fully-lived life.

There exists for a person also another great world of life other than the inner world of the heart, and this is the world of historical content and community activism, the great world where thought becomes action and the highest sensation is accomplishment. And good for that person who is not an idle spectator looking at this ocean turbulently carrying him away in life.

There is no doubt that the want to spatter Russian speech with foreign words has no requirement, it is without sufficient basis and is against sound thinking and proper taste. But this does not harm the Russian language and Russian literature, but those who adhere to it. At the opposite extreme, that is, strict purism, it causes consequences as a result of these extremes. The fate of a language cannot depend on something arbitrary from one or another person. Every language has a reliable and trustworthy guardian: this is its individual spirit or genius.

There is nothing easier than to see from a distance objects in the manner that we want to see them, because in this beautiful distance you live completely alien from it, you live within yourself or in a monotonous circle whose mood and weakness are identical with your own.

There is nothing more dangerous than to tie your destiny with the destiny of a woman only because she is young and pretty.

There is nothing more unjust than to measure somebody's individuality using the yardstick of another's individuality, since it is always in some manner different or contrary. Every individuality is true in a greater or lesser measure, while truth of individuality requires calm and impartial research.

There occurs in the life of nations and humanities unfortunate epochs where entire generations are as if brought as a sacrifice on behalf of the subsequent generations. Difficult times pass and goodness arises out of what appeared to be bad.

To deprive art of the right to serve public interests means to not exalt it, but rather humiliate it. This means to deprive it of its very strength of life, that is, the meaning that it now becomes is the subject of some type of sybaritic sweetness, a toy for lazy idle people.

To portray solely the negative facets of life does not mean to entirely slander it, but means to only present one side of it.

We remember this quivering, timid veneration of women where not even one daring thought would enter the mind, but this is not Platonism, this is the first moment of fresh virginal love. This is not the absence of passion, but passion that still fears to express itself. From this moment first love begins, and some want it to remain this way their entire life the way a child rides a stick horse. Love has its own laws of development, its growths, like flowers.

What good is it to me that my genius on earth lives in heaven, while the crowds wallow in the mud? What good it is to me that I understand the idea that I have the assignment to reveal a world of ideas in art, in religion, in history, when I cannot even share it with all those who are supposed to be my brethren of humanity, my associates in Christ, but who are aliens and enemies to me due to their ignorance? What good is it to me, that bliss exists for a few select, while the greater portion does not even suspect its possibility? Let bliss distance itself from me, even if I am one in a thousand to inherit it.

What is artistically acceptable is likewise moral. What is inartistic cannot just be without morality, but at the same time it cannot be immoral.

What is the very best and what is the very worst in each nation is what belongs only to it.

What would be considered life for an animal would be death to a person; what is life to a Goth would be death to a European; what is life to a slave of domestic needs is death to a person of meditation and comprehension.

Who in their youth has not fantasized, not subjected himself to deceit, not chased after hallucinations, and who has not been disenchanted with them, and were not these disenchantments worth the heart's convulsions, grief, apathy, and who has not laughed at them from all their soul?

Who is not a member of his nation is not a member of humanity.

Who is not moving forward is moving backward, there is no such thing as standing still.

Whoever considers himself equally capable of every course of credit is not capable of not even one.

Without love and hate, without sympathy and antipathy, a person is just an illusion. Without passions and contradictions there is no life, no poetry. Just as long as there resides in these passions and contradictions some intellect and humanity, and their results will lead a person to his goal. Without goals there is no activity; without interests there is no goal, and without activity there is no life. The source of interests, goals and activity is the essence of community life.

Yes, we need many, very many among us who have the trait of unselfish love toward truth and strong character, in order to intervene into another's authority, even though this authority is not really there.

You must not reconcile people in matters of conviction using some artificial approach, and not one dignified person will concede his personal opinion for the sake of some reason that lies outside his opinion.

PETER YAKOVLEVICH CHAADAEV

1794 – 1856

Political Philosopher

Peter Chaadaev was born in Moscow on June 7, 1794, into an aristocratic family; his maternal grandfather was the famous historian, M.M. Scherbatov.[12] His parents both died before he was 4, and he was raised by his Scherbatov aunt and uncle in Moscow. His education was at the Moscow University, 1808-1811, and he became friends with Sergei Pushkin, Nikolai Karamzin, and Aleksandr Griboyedov, during this time. After his graduation he was conscripted into the army in the war against Napoleon, but he continued in the military until 1821, when he resigned for refusing to report on soldiers who staged a revolt against the government.

Chaadaev joined the Masons in 1814, and in 1819 the Union of Prosperity, and in 1821, the Secret Northern Society, from which he later disassociated himself. In July 1823, he traveled to England, France, Switzerland, Italy and Germany, returning in 1826. Later that year, Chaadaev was arrested due to suspicion of association with the Decembrists, but after a short confinement he was acquitted and released. He then settled in Moscow to reside, but was always under police surveillance. As a result he isolated himself to write his serious philosophical compositions, and which he continued through the balance of his life. He did not appear in society until 1831.

---

[12] Also in this volume.

His *Philosophical Letters* published in 1836, agitated state officials and even Tsar Nicholas I. Chaadaev was very critical of Russia, feeling it had fallen behind the European nations in every area, that it had nothing to contribute to the world, and should as if start over. Russia was likewise socially backward and deprived of intellectualism. As a result the publishing house was closed by the government, the editor was exiled, and the censurer who approved the letters for publication was forced to retire. The surveillance of Chaadaev increased to the point that he was under house arrest, but this was rescinded the following year under the conditions that he write no more. A local doctor examined him and declared him insane, in order to further discredit Chaadaev. The Slavophiles likewise criticized Chaadaev, since he felt Russia needed to improve by adopting what European nations had to offer in terms of social and government reforms. From another aspect, his letters were a motivation to development of philosophy in Russia.

His future compositions were not published until after his death, and he remained in Moscow leading a life of low profile, but with a steady stream of visitors through his home. Chaadaev never married.

After the Crimean War, not seeing any improvement in Russia, he considered suicide, but later died of tuberculosis in Moscow on April 26, 1856.

A word only echoes in a responsive arena.

A destitute striving for a small portion of prosperity – even though he has nowhere to place it – occurs often cruelly, but never will it be so cruel as cruel as your fathers were, those in particular who made you to be what you are, and who bequeathed to you what you possess.

And so, not to search the interaction between eras, not to eternally work on factual material –will lead to nothing. It is necessary to strive to explain the moral thought of all the historical epochs. It is necessary to strive to exactly define the characteristics of every age according to the laws of practical intellect.

Christian cognizance does not tolerate any blindness and, least of all, other's national prejudice, since it divides peoples more than anything else.

Christian immortality is life without death, but not at all life after death.

Countries are moral entities and precisely to the extent of the distinct individuals that comprise them. Previous ages nurtured them just as people nurture the future years. About us [Russians] can be said, that we compose an exception among the nations. We belong to the one among them that as if does not enter into a connected part of the human race, but exists just in order to teach an important lesson to the world.

Do you sense how truth is engendered within you? No. And falsity? Of course.

For the most part people present themselves to us not as they actually are, but in a manner for us to interpret them as we want. This is because we also accept into our accounts their vanity and their arrogance. But even more we must blame ourselves for all of our failures pertaining to us that are obvious to others.

Glory to God, I always love my fatherland due to its interests, and not in its details.

I did not learn to love my homeland with closed eyes, with a drooped head, with closed lips. I find that a person can be useful for his nation only if he understands it well. I think that the time of blind devotion has passed, that now we first of all are obligated to provide truth to the homeland.

If you decide to act criminally and irresponsibly before death, sorry, you cannot hide your past in your coffin or take it to the grave with you.

In Russia, from stupid measures that are implemented by the government, there exists salvation: stupid observance.

It is amazing how lazy a human's intellect is! To try to deliver yourself from work, which is so necessary for a clear comprehension of the higher world, he will distort this world. He in the process of not working distorts himself and journeys by his own path and which does not lead anywhere.

It is apparent that individuality and freedom exist just to the extent that variation of intellects, moral strengths and comprehensions exist.

It is obvious that earlier events define the future. Such is the law of life. To deny your past means to deprive yourself of a future.

Love of your fatherland is a beautiful thing, but there is something even more beautiful – this is love of truth. Love of the fatherland births heroes, love of truth create sages and benefactors of humanity. Love of homeland divides nations, sustains hatred of other nations and sometimes clothes the land in mourning. Love of truth expands the world of knowledge, creates spiritual consolation, draws people closer to the Deity.

Nonetheless, who does not know how a foreign thought is shoved into our cognizance. How do we subject ourselves to opinions, the convictions of others? Every person who has meditated over this distinctly knows that one mind will subject itself to another and along with this preserves all of its authority, all of its abilities.

Often just one trait successfully grasped will spill more light and more proof than an entire chronicle. And so here is our rule: we will meditate on the facts that are known to us, and we will strive to hold in our minds the larger living images, rather than dead matter.

People think that as soon as they speak one word about the inherent quality for humanity to proceed to perfection, about the progress of the human mind, they feel all has been said and all has been explained. Let us think a little, that a person during all eras did what he felt he had to in order to proceed forward, and never having to return, but during this movement there was always an altercation with nature to force them to the side, yet there was still development and progress.

Our best friend is a powerless enemy. The most evil of our enemies is an envious friend.

Progress of human nature from this point forward has no limit, but others reflect on this concept such that there still remains a boundary that will not allow it to exceed. Even then, as soon as a person is satisfied with some tangible interest, he will no longer move forward, but it will be well at least if he does not withdraw.

Several times this has been observed. As soon as a new idea appears in the public world, immediately all narrow egoisms, all infantile ambitions, all stubborn party line opinions – which seem to ramble about on the surface of society – will throw themselves upon it, overwhelm it, turn it inside out, distort it, and after a minute passes, will grind it into fine particles using all of these factors, and it is carried away to some abstract sphere where it completely vanishes as a fruitless speck of dust.

So what exactly is death? It is none else than that moment in a person's entire existence when he ceases to sense himself in his body, and nothing more.

So what is necessary in order to see clearly? To be able to see through yourself.

Socialism will win not because it is right, but because its opposers are wrong.

The indifference toward life's benefits – some of which we attribute to ourselves as merit – is truly something cynical. One of the primary reasons that progress is so slow among us consists in the absence of every reflection of art in our domestic life.

The majority of evil surfaces particularly because what occurs in the depths of our thinking sharply departs from the indispensability of submission to social standards.

The matter is not to complement memory with facts, there are too many of them already. It is a grave error to think that as if an abundance of facts will secure the credibility of history. A lack of knowledge of history does not necessarily summon a lack of knowledge of facts, but a lack of its comprehension.

The matter is that the significance of nations in humanity is critically defined by its spiritual strength, and that the attention that it excites toward itself depends on their ethical influence on the world, and not on noise that they cause.

The Russian liberal is a senseless gnat maneuvered by only the rays of the sun. This sun is the sun of the west.

The Russian people are a singing people, and not a talking. One thunderous Russian song contains more of Russian life than an entire stack of Russian chronicles and manuscripts.

The true nature of a person provides proof that not one of all entities is capable of infinite enlightenment. At the same time, his supremacy over all other living creation consists in this true nature.

The world has no sympathy to anything profound. It turns its eyes away from great convictions. Profound ideas bore it.

The written word does not fly away as does the spoken word. It places its seal on the intellect. It formidably subjects to itself its indestructibility and prolonged recognition of sacredness. But along with this, codifying the spirit, the word deprives it of movement, it bends it and forces it into narrow frames of composition and chains it in every manner.

There are minds so false, that even if some truth proceeds from them it also becomes false.

There are stupid people so unproductive, that even the sun from a genius is not strong enough to make them productive.

There is a regimen for the soul just as there is for the body, you need to be able to subject the body's regimen to the soul's.

There is nothing easier than to love those whom you love, but it is necessary also to somewhat love those whom you do not love.

There is something in our [Russian] blood that rejects every genuine progress. In short, we lived and presently continue to live for the purpose of teaching some type of great lesson to distant posterity, to those who will learn from it. Until then we insert a blank page into the intellectual order.

This person would have been tolerant if he would have agreed to not know a certain something, but no, he had to know everything.

We have no authority over the past. It is the future that is dependant on us.

We just live in the most limited present, without a past and without a future, in the middle of a flat stagnation. And if we occasionally are agitated, then it is not in expectation or not with the desire of some kind of general welfare, but in the infantile light-mindedness of a child when he stretches and reaches out his hands to some rattle that his nurse shows him.

We live in a country that is pathetically destitute in announcing ideals, that if we do not surround ourselves in our domestic life with a share of poetry and good taste, then it is easy for us to lose every refined feeling, every understanding of elegance.

We need to be delivered from every vain curiosity that destroys and makes our life ugly, and the first action is to uproot the stubborn inclination of the heart to attract novelties and chase after the evils of the day, and then the result of this will be to constantly await greedily what will occur tomorrow. Otherwise you will not acquire peace or prosperity, but only disappointment and rejection.

What use is it for people to be united with the Savior if they are disunited among themselves?

Woe unto that person who would accept some illusion of his vanity or the deception of his mind as some type of extraordinary revelation that liberates him from general responsibility.

Nikolai Gavrilovich Chernishevski

1828 – 1889

Revolutionary, Political Philosopher

Nikolai Chernishevski was born in Saratov, central Russia, on November 12, 1828, into a family of a Russian Orthodox priest. He attended the Saratov Religious Seminary, and then in 1850 graduated in history at the Petersburg University. He worked at several literary journals in St Petersburg. One of his main contributions was regarding land and peasant reforms. He also advocated abolishing the present economic system and replacing it with socialism.

Chernishevski's ideas promoted revolutionary organizations in Russia and as a result in 1862 he was placed in solitary confinement in the Petro-Pavlovsk Fortress in St Petersburg. He continued to write in prison. He was sentenced in 1864 to 7 years hard labor. When he was released he returned to his home in Saratov to live, and he died there on October 17, 1889.

His writings were prohibited from publication in their entirety in Russia until after the revolution of 1905.

A lack of education is not something to boast about. A lack of education is weakness.

A man who is not inspired to fulfill civic duties is nothing more than a entity of the male gender who shaves his beard and mustache.

A patriot is a person who serves his homeland, and his homeland are the people who reside there.

A person must never lose the inclination to better his life.

A person needs to be involved in an activity that he cannot decline, that he cannot postpone. Then a person becomes incomparably firm.

A person's creative activity is empty and useless if it is not inspired by ideas.

A physician's work is really the most productive work: preventing or restoring health. The physician provides society all those strengths that would otherwise perish without his worry.

A walk down Nevski Prospect[13] is not a historical journey.

Accidents in life strike the famous and the unknown equally and impartially, and luck likewise benefits one and the other impartially.

Adolescence is the time of freshness of noble feelings.

All that displays our ideals, goals and objects of our desires and our love, mesmerizes us.

---

[13] Prostitutes would frequent Nevski Prospect in St Petersburg at this time.

Constant movement is reality, because movement is life, while reality and life is one and the same.

Do not judge the moral or mental qualities of a person based on his happiness or unhappiness in life.

Domestic love for the most part is spread among people and for the most part is stable because of its effect on people's lives, and this is the most important and most benevolent of all the good feelings of a person.

Empty and colorless is the life only among colorless people who interpret feelings and necessities while not being capable of having any special feelings and necessities other than the need to paint.

Every educated person feels that the true life is the life of the mind and heart.

Honor is one and the same among women and men, girls, married women, and aged men and women – Do not deceive, Do not steal, Do not drink [alcohol]. A code of honor, in the correct meaning of these words, and pertaining to all people, is only composed from such rules.

If I was to exclude civic motives from the circle of my observations, from the sphere of my activities, what then remains for me to observe? What remains for my participation? All that remains is for me to waste my time with individuals with narrow concerns about their fiscal status, or some flyers to distribute, or amusements.

Intellectual literature delivers people from ignorance, while elegance – from uncouthness and unculturedness.

It is proper to demand more from an intelligent and educated person. If he speaks nonsense, you have the complete right to reprimand him for this, but it would be out of place for you to do this condescendingly, which only airheads have the right to do.

It is unthinkable for beauty and excellence to reside in a person without the inclusion of harmonic development of his organisms and health.

It is well known to each person that if a husband and wife live compatibly and agreeably, then their mutual bound increases every year and finally reaches such a development that they literally cannot live one without the other.

Kindness and intelligence are 2 terms essentially having opposite meanings. Intelligence from the theoretical point of view is kindness from the practical point of view. And on the contrary, what is kindness is definitely intelligent.

Kindness is the supreme level of usefulness, it is the most useful utilization.

Knowledge excites love. The more a person is fluent in some science, the more that love for it develops.

Life is so wide and diverse, that a person can almost always find something to occupy him thoroughly, or to seek something, whatever it is he strongly feels or for which he has a true need.

Love is not a passing display in a person's life pertaining only to the period before marriage, as vulgar persons think. This feeling is living and strengthening every aspect of a married couple's life.

No situation of any type can justify inactivity. It is always possible to do something, even if it is not entirely useless. A person must do what he is capable of doing.

No type of external compulsion can support a person on a high mental or moral level, when he does not want to himself hold to it.

Personal happiness is impossible without the happiness of others.

Progress is the endeavor toward raising a human to the high rank of humanity.

The character of the method must be the same as the character of the goal, only then can the method be brought to its goal. Stupid methods are worth only for stupid goals.

The existence of 2 parties surfaces in every matter: conservative and progressive, both with compatible strengths of custom and desire to better the situation.

The feeling of personal dignity is developed only in the situation of being an independent artisan.

The kind person is the one who does good for others. The evil person is the one who does bad to others. Let us now unite these 2 simple truths and we will have this conclusion: A person is kind when he realizes he must do good to others in order to receive something pleasant in return. A person is bad when he acquires some goodness for himself using force, by inflicting some unpleasantness on others.

The mistakes of people who have a strong mentality are in particular very awesome, because the mistakes can become the thinking of other people.

The more we speak of our dignities, the less others believe in them.

The most pitiful figures are not those people who have a inaccurate manner of thinking, but those who do not have any defined and organized manner of thinking, whose opinions are a collection of disconnected fragments, not glued to each other.

The right to life and happiness is an empty hallucination for the person who has not the means for it.

To betray your country requires extreme decadence of the soul.

To fall every time you trip is fine, as long as you stand back on you feet.

To reject progress is just as stupid as rejecting the law of gravity.

Wealth is an object without which a person can still live happily. But your individual welfare is an object that is indispensable for happiness.

What is primarily needed in domestic life is patience. Love does not continue very long.

Where there is no life, there are no ideas. Where there is no infinite diversity, there is no life.

Work must be relative to a person's strength. He is stupid to accept anything that is beyond his ability.

NIKOLAI ALEKSANDROVICH DOBROLUBOV

1836 – 1861

Philosopher, Political Activist

Nikolai Dobrolubov was born January 24, 1836 in Nizhni-Novgorod into a family of priests. His initial education was at a local seminary, and then he graduated in history. By 1857, Dobrolubov was a regular contributor to various journals

He insisted on the generic association of nature and humans, that matter is the common substance of the entire world. Dobrolubov felt revolution to be the sole means to terminate serfdom (slavery) and the autocracy, and he wrote intensively against the government of the reign of Tsar Nicholas I.

Dobrolubov died of tuberculosis in St Petersburg on November 17, 1861.

We do not know of even one substance in the corporeal world that does not have some type or other of power inherent to it. Likewise it is impossible to imagine some power that is independent of material. Power composes the primal and integral quality of matter and cannot exist separately from it. But the quality of matter cannot be attributed to it, but it can only reside in it. Magnetism can be induced, but it is not acknowledged as substance. It is impossible to create magnetic power without iron or, in general, outside of some substance within which it is located, as one of its primal elementary qualities. So in a person's brain, no matter what its composition, there must exist its special power.

Of course, the entire content of history consists of struggle between aristocracy and democracy. But we would really be understanding it poorly if we thought to limit it solely due to the interests of their posterities. The basis of this struggle has always been hid by another circumstance, one considerably more essential than an abstract theory about genealogy, that is, whether someone should get the inheritance because they are related by blood, or another. The national masses always instinctively, although vaguely, felt what was residing in these people's cognizance, those who were educated and organized. In the eyes of a truly educated person there is no aristocracy or democracy, no noble or serf, no priest or layman, but only people who work or parasite. The elimination of economic parasites and magnification of labor are the constant tendencies of history.

A person can be washed clean and then dressed again in his dirty rags, but nonetheless, somewhere in the most dirty folds of these rags is preserved a feeling and thought. Although unresponsive or unnoticeable, but still a feeling and thought.

Accustoming ourselves to doing everything without second thoughts, without a conviction of whether this is true or good, or else only due to an order, a person becomes indifferent to good and bad, and without his soul's reflection he performs the actions, even if they are opposed to his internal moral sense, but justifying himself by saying, It was an order.

Each person strives to provide for himself as much goodness as possible, and the greatest goodness in the world is to be in love and agreement with all people. How can this goodness be acquired when you sense that you love some people and do not love others? A person needs to learn to love those whom he does not love. A person learns the most difficult skills, learns to read, write, every science and trade. If a person would only learn to love with as much zeal as he learns sciences and trades, he will quickly and easily learn how to love all people and even those who are not friendly to us.

Genuine patriotism as a private display of love toward humanity does not seem to set right with enmity toward distinct nationalities. It develops with special strength in those countries where each individual is presented as having a great possibility to consciously provide a benefit to society and participate in its enterprises.

If it is impossible to see an ideal of moral self-perfection in children, then at least you cannot but agree that they are still incomparably more moral than adults.

If someone has not suffered and not erred, then he has not acquired a sense of value for truth and happiness.

In particular, living and practicing patriotism is distinctive when it excludes every international malice, and the person inspired by such patriotism is ready to labor for all of humanity, and is definitely able to be useful to it.

It is by the level of more or less respect toward labor and the ability to value labor, that the level of a nation's civilization and its relative value can be determined.

It is just as easy to perish in a swamp as it is in the sea, but if the sea is dangerously attractive, then a swamp is dangerously repulsive. It is better to survive a shipwreck, than get stuck in mud.

It is not correct to comprehend health as only the superficial well-being of the body, but it is necessary to understand in general the natural harmonic development of the organism and the correct completeness of all of its corresponding parts.

It is not the person who endures the commands of duties he imposes on himself as some type of heavy yoke or like moral chains that can call himself truly moral, but in particular the person who worries about integrating such demands of duties with the requirements of his inner substance.

Once you have lost a woman's love, you can only blame yourself for not having the ability to preserve this love.

One of the highest dignities of humanity consists in accuracy. Honor and rectitude and active participation in the fate of your close associate are all united in it.

Only labor provides the right to life's enjoyments.

People of the present generation are just actors that have well entered the role of a daily commonplace comedy. They do what the role expects of them, and they do not leave it, regardless of all the insanity, clapping, noise, and whistling of the orchestra.

Proper patriotism for a person is nothing else than the desire to labor for the welfare of your country, and what causes it to produce is the result of nothing else but the desire to do good, as much as possible and even more if this is better.

The feeling of love can be truly good only with the inner harmony of those loved, and only this comprises the principle and pledge of that social prosperity which is promised us. In the future development of humanity, an association of brotherhood and personal equality will reside among people.

The future does not occur to us so clear to us as the past, and it never has as much power over us as does the present.

The person who hates other nations does not even love his own.

The sooner and prompter an impression is expressed, the more often it seems to be just superficial and incidental.

These family and social attitudes can be firm, as long as they flow from inner convictions and are justified by the voluntary and intelligent agreement of all the people that participate in these associations.

We do not seem to attribute any practical significance to the beautiful aspirations of the soul, as long as they remain as only aspirations. Yes, we value only facts and only by their effectiveness do we recognize a person's dignity.

MIKHAIL ALEKSANDROVICH FONVIZIN

1787 – 1854

Military Hero, Political Activist, Promoter of Utopian Socialism

Mikhail Fonvisin was born in Moscow on August 20, 1787. His initial education was at home and then in St Petersburg for middle school, and then Moscow University. Fonvisin joined the military in 1801 and served in the campaign against the French at Austerlitz in 1805 and was awarded the Order of St Anne for bravery in battle. He was promoted to an officer and was in the war against Sweden in 1808·09. Subsequently his military action included the War of 1812 against Napoleon at Vitebsk, Smolensk and Borodino, where he was awarded the Order of St Vladimir and a gold sword for bravery. He continued in the pursuit of Napoleon across Europe, but was taken captive in France, for which he received the Kulm Cross for his accomplishments in the military. After his release from captivity, he continued into France in the rank of military commander, and then in 1820 was promoted to general by Tsar Alexandr I. However the military campaigns took its toll on Fonvisin and he retired from the military in 1822.

Fonvisin became a Mason and joined the lodge in Moscow in 1817. About this time he was introduced into secret societies whose purpose was to overthrow the government of Tsar Alexandr I, including the Union of Salvation and the Secret Northern Society, and he participated in preparation of the revolt in Moscow that occurred in December 1825. He began to develop his political philosophic views at this time with his concept of community or utopian socialism. Much of this include rights for the peasants.

Fonvisin was arrested for revolutionary activities in 1826 and confined at the Petro-Pavlovsk Fortress in St Petersburg. He was sentenced to hard labor in Siberia and exiled in 1827. He was confined in concentration camps in Chita, Eniseisk, Krasnoyarsk and Tobolsk. Finally in 1853, 26 years later, Fonvisin was released and returned to Moscow, however under continued police surveillance. He died the following year on April 30, 1854.

A fire that has no atmosphere will quickly extinguish on its own. Passions are the same. Stubbornly struggling with them, you just irritate them the more. Ignore them and they will diminish on their own.

A flatterer is a creature who does not have a good opinion of others, and neither of himself. All of his aspirations is to first blind some person's mind with adulation, and then manipulate him to be what you want. He is a nighttime thief who will first extinguish the lamp and then begin to steal.

A healthy intellect and the experience of many ages show that just the sovereign's high integrity is needed to form a high integrity in the nation. He holds in his hands a spring attached to them so to turn them in the direction he wants: to virtue or to malice. He judges his people and the people will judge his justice.

A substantial victory on the battlefield, although it brings a certain amount of use to the victors, does not deprive dignity from those defeated if they fulfilled their obligation. But that victory obtained solely due to fear of subsequent events, and which may not even occur, is an irrecoverable loss in the political sense.

A thought flies faster than a bird toward the horizon, and this is natural for it, and it lights the region of the sky with its bright rays of truth, not fearing any kind of obstacle. Coercion can only temporarily stop the effect of common opinion, but no human authority exists to be able to destroy it.

A wife's virtue does not consist in her being on guard over her husband, but to be a participant in his destiny. A virtuous wife must patiently tolerate the stupidity of her husband.

And so what is the difference between the fearlessness of the soldier who risks his life during an attack in line with others, and the fearlessness of the government employee who speaks the truth to the sovereign and who is risking his wrath. The judge who does not fear vendetta, not threats of the powerful, and provides justice to the helpless, is a hero in my eyes.

Are you actually aware that for the amount of lust one person contains all of Siberia is not large enough. Follow nature, you will never be destitute. Follow people's opinions, you will never be wealthy.

Believe me that science residing in a corrupt person is a cruel weapon to commit evil. Education exalts the virtuous soul.

Every authority that is not identified as having the divine qualities of justice and meekness, but produces insult, coercion, tyranny, is an authority not from God, but from people whose misfortunes over time have allowed this. Yielding to force humiliates human dignity.

Everything can be exchanged for virtue, but virtue cannot be replaced by anything.

For the ignorant, every extraordinary item seems to be divine.

Force compels, but justice obligates. Where obligations do not exist, neither does justice.

God Himself in His sole quality of being an omnipotent entity cannot have even the smallest right to demand our submission. But God does have the right to our reverent submission because of His quality of being an all-benevolent entity. Only an entity that is all-benevolent is worthy of submission, but this cannot be compelled by fear.

God is omnipotent for the reason that He cannot do anything other than goodness, and that this impossibility would be an everlasting sign of His perfection He imposed upon Himself, immutable rules of eternal truth, by which He governs the entire universe and which – He being God – cannot Himself violate. A sovereign, who is in the likeness of God, the earthly successor and representative of His authority, cannot in the same manner indicate his potency or dignity in any other way except to legislate in his sovereignty the same type of immutable rules all based on the concept of the common welfare and which he cannot violate himself, or else he will cease to be worthy of being sovereign.

He did not love anybody and was not loved by anybody. The one who loves only himself likewise is not worthy to be loved by anyone else.

I know for sure that I am ashamed of anything I do that is shameful.

If foresight is permitted in politics, then this will result in something worse that plunder. Every person will begin to foresee unforeseen events to their own advantage and interests and they will agitate their neighbor with demands so they will satisfy his foresight.

It is really happiness, if you are happy by yourself?

It is very comforting in human ignorance to count everything as nonsense, everything you do that you do not comprehend.

Nature gave me an acute mind, but did not provide me sound prudence.

No matter how defiled people are, their minds are never as so corrupt as their hearts are corrupt. And we see that those very people who are least of all tied to virtue are often the greatest scholars in virtue. To be exposed is the punishment of a hypocrite and the true reward of an honorable person.

No matter what direction I turn, I see stupidity everywhere.

Philosophers and moralists have used many columns of reams of paper regarding the science of how to life happily. But it is apparent that they did not know the direct path to happiness, because they have themselves never lived in destitution, which is unhappiness. It is true that some of them have earned great wealth, but during their life have conducted themselves otherwise than as they have written. And who knows, maybe they were out of their minds when they taught people such false guides of attaining happiness, so only to utilize the philosopher's stone to their advantage.[14]

Polity is just as clear and plain as mathematics. It in its own essence it is nothing else but precision, accuracy and correctness. The conditions that are concluded with neighbors under the appellations of flyers, unions, compromises, must be founded on just benefits, otherwise they lose their strength, just as a one-sided contract in a civil suit.

Strength and justice are completely different in their essence as well as in their form of operation. Justice demands dignity, talents, virtue. Strength demands prisons, chains, weapons. Tyranny, wherever it might be, is tyranny, and the people's justice

---

[14] Meaning to use philosophic rhetoric as a means of financial gain.

delivers their existence and allows them to continue eternally and steadfastly in every place.

Strength on its own acquires submission with the help of propaganda.

The heart of a wealthy man soon hardens.

The ignorant and uninformed definitely are consoled by deceptions, and devising one delusion after another they increase their polytheism and their rampage against monotheism.

The most superior science of government consists in the ability to get people acclimated to live under a good government. Specific laws are not worth anything in this regard. For legislation to be good a chapter heading stating – Statutes of Decency, needs to be implemented.

The Supreme Authority entrusts to the sovereign the responsibility of the welfare of his subjects.

Truly, once they forcefully uproot prejudice, this is replaced with a root of virtue.

Weak is the soul that is not able to direct the whimsical aspirations of the body. Unfortunate is the body if the soul that governs it is reckless.

Who does not know that all human societies are founded on mutual voluntary obligations that are destroyed as soon as we stop observing them. The obligations between sovereign and subjects is in equally a voluntary manner.

Whoever pronounces "Lord" most of anybody only has the devil on his heart.

Why do all live? It seems to me that here is the limit of questions. Life consists of a goal and means and reason and activity. Life does not attain a goal, but materializes all that is possible, continues all created existence. There is always a need to jump further in order to more fully live, and live even more if this is possible. There is no other goal.

With myself as an example I discovered this truth that an earned rank is no better than a purchased rank.

You can be a great military hero, expand your boundaries using many means of fraud, but people's trust, which is indivisible from virtue, will never return, and the curses on our posterity signify the tyranny sealed by the common repulsion toward his inhumane feats.[15]

---

[15] Referring to Tsar Nicholas I.

FEODOR NIKOLAEVICH GLINKA

1786 – 1880

Military Officer, Poet, Political Activist

Feodor Glinka was born at his family estate in Dukhovschinski County, Smolensk province, eastern Russia. His initial education was at a local military school, and he entered the military with the War of 1805 against the French. He was released from service in 1807, but continued as an officer in a regiment near his home. He traveled Russia at this time: Tver, along the Volga River and Kiev. His first publications were in 1808 and these were his memoirs from his military campaigns.

In 1812 he was again in the military in the campaign against Napoleon's invasion and continued with it until the end of 1814. Returning to Russia, he wrote of his experiences, and this brought Glinka much literary popularity. He continued writing and created a library for soldiers, and was editor of a magazine for the military.

Glinka at this time joined the Union of Salvation that later were the Decembrists. As a result he was arrested in 1826 and confined in the Petro-Pavlovsk Fortress. He was freed later that year, released from military service, and exiled to Petrozavodsk. He was moved to Tver in 1830, and subsequently to Oryol in 1832, and then to Moscow with his freedom in 1835.

He remained in Moscow as a writer until 1853, when he relocated to St Petersburg. His life took a turn at this time toward a serious involvement in religion, and it reflected in his spiritual poems. During the balance of his life, he was deeply involved in mysticism, and his further compositions had no artistic value.

In 1862, Glinka relocated to Tver, spending his time in the archeology of the local region and community affairs. He died in Tver on February 11, 1880.

"What has happened to all your property?" asked Tsar Ivan Vasilyevich of his nobleman Sheremetev at one time.

"Through the hands of the destitute I have transferred it to God," he replied to the tsar. "This is the best use of wealth, a use very worthy of Russian nobles."

A certain person related a beautiful truth. In order to value life, you must value time, because life consists of time.

A joker is like a porcupine. He will prick you even when you joke with him.

A person in the world is like a soldier in a besieged fortress. His personal passions are his domestic enemies; his alien passions are foes from the distance. Often these and others enter into secret conspiracies against him.

A person it seems is barely worthy of the attention of a scattering of a few fast hours of the present and, at the same time on the contrary, with some type of secret satisfaction he loves to revert to the past and lingeringly be consoled with the pleasantries of recollections.

A person's dignity, consisting in the sincere desire of the welfare of others and the constant drive to achieve this, must develop on its own naturally.

A person's heart is like a bright stream of spring water, at the bottom of which hides thick mud. Do not stir the mud and the stream will always be clear, do not agitate the passions and the heart will be calm and life will be tranquil and happy.

A stupid person is like a thorny sagebrush along the road. You walk alongside of it and do not see it and then it catches you.

A wealthy person who has taste is still a person, but a wealthy person who is a philanthropist is an Angel.

All that we have that is extra or excessive belongs to those who are insufficient.

Ambition will never provide those joys that it promises. This is perhaps because it births unattainable desires.

Ancient people knew a human's heart better than we, they knew that it could be comforted and consoled. As a result of this knowledge they guessed better that we did, of what true happiness the society consists.

Belief and life must be displayed by conduct.

But the victory of vice in the presence of the corrupt opinions of all people will never be equated with the victory of virtue. Still no brilliance of any type, no omnipotence of any type, can defend vice from people hating it in secret, and no malice of any type can defend virtue of its final dignity and its respect by noble souls.

By the kind heart of providence it was pleasing to construct a human's heart so that it would always enjoy attention, enjoy a kind word from the person who directs the destiny of society or just his personal affairs. As infants, an extra smile from father or mother will comfort us. As adolescents, one nice word from the teacher will expand to an entire day's satisfaction. As mature adults, the attention of a prudent official secures you on the difficult course of war. While the attention of the sovereign will compel you to sacrifice all of your blood, all of your life's consolations, and throw yourself into the clutches of death with the fire of a young groom soaring toward his bride. It is upon this secret of a human's heart that the authority of government of nations is founded, and this is the only thing that maintains the rule of an autocrat.

Contentment should be an ordinary state of people. Poverty is a social illness, one of the fierce sorrows of a person.

Deeply rooted prejudices separate people from each other like iron walls.

Descending deep into our deliberations, we fantasize that we have already attained the genuine ability to fly as birds. But what has this ability served us? Truly, not for any benefit, not for the prosperity of society, likewise the same pertains to many discoveries of our era. Possessing new elements and gasses, peoples, of course, have not failed in making all of this a field for their disputes and bloody battles.

Do not allow wealth to become a means of boasting. Fate is an empty gift.

During the era of our forefathers, great people lived in small huts. During our era, small people live in immense palaces.

Envy and noble zeal are like 2 individuals having similar features, voice, actions, in short, all of the superficial traits, but they are completely diverse in their heart's qualities. Often one is mistaken for the other in the noise of society and in the darkness of desires. But what is the obvious difference between them? Their effect!

Zeal, having the appearance of dignity, ascends the staircase that it has constructed on its own and aspires to build something like itself in order to attain this height. Envy on the other hand, slithers and undermines the steps by which dignity ascends. "Do not permit me to ever ascend," envy always declares, "rather let the other collapse."

Eternal laws are legislated not for a person, but for humanity. People die, but humanity does not know death.

Every person that gathers to travel to a foreign country worries about the money used there. Preparing to transverse beyond this life and into the future life, you should also worry about the money that is utilized there, and this money is not gold, not jewels, but benevolence.

Every person, whoever he may be, walking along some house and seeing in the corner some burning coals that are ready to burst into flames, has the right and even the responsibility to cry, "Watch out for a fire!" And every person seeing a leak in a boat likewise has the right to scream, "The boat is beginning to leak over here!" Such simple comparisons can be applied to many situations. So why does every person not have the same right, if he notices disorder in the society, to speak directly and openly that he sees this and direct the people's attention to it?

Faults have a glue-type effect. This is why vicious people eternally attach to each other. They are always together, as though one entity. Get near their crowd and stand among them and it will not be easy to detach yourself from them.

For the person who seeks no ambition, but is sensitive and loving toward the beauty of nature, the brilliance of the full moon on a beautiful summer night is more pleasant than the radiance of any crown.

Foreigners, bringing to us their art, likewise bring to us the vices of their country.

Happiness is nowhere to be found if you do not find it in your heart, but it is with us everywhere once we have it.

I have seen much in the world and among people. I have seen pictures of the life of nations, shepherds and hunters, I have seen the nomadic huts of the Kirghiz on the steppes and the villages of the Mongol tribes. Whether it be a hut or a palace, it will not change a person and his passions. Everywhere wealth is respected and power is heeded. But what it is that comforts a person in any place is the comprehension of the Supreme Entity and the name of the Benefactor is known among all the nations of the world. Good and bad, joy and sorrow, alternate like day and night.

I love to watch people who observe the law, ethics and the customs of our forefathers. You will agree my friend that Moses was a great legislator! He was able to fasten the Israelites with shackles of statutes, ceremonies and customs, and all without a sovereign, fatherland and counts. And although they are scattered all over the world, nonetheless they still compose a nation.

If death itself is so unnoticeable an item even as it draws near, then to die, of course, means nothing! When death is awaited then it is horrifying and this fear is born, it seems, more from an alarm in reflecting our life or from eclipsing the conscience. When death is unexpectedly thrust upon you, it should be very easy to accept.

If only a tenth portion of the people would remember the good, relative to as much as they remember the bad, then ingratitude would never exist in the world.

In general the destiny of science has a large similarity to the destiny of nations. These and others evolve from practically nothing. A great nation from one family, important science from one fortunate mind. There is no more strict a gradualness, no more trustworthy a logic, as in the progress and activity of nature.

In our age allow the pen, chisel, paintbrush and musical instrument to turn solely to crediting the virtues and feats of the fatherland. Then who will not be captivated by the pleasantries of these arts and who will not bless the goal to which they incline the nation?

Is it not this way in society that some shallow passion will obscure great virtues? And will not some meaningless capability overshadow great talents?

Is this perhaps the reason we are born, live and act, in order to just disappear after filling the entire sphere of our world with noise and the credit from our work, just like a departing dream or some other imagination after being awaken from sleep? In order after being a soul of the entire world to be transformed into soulless clods of dirt? O, how abysmal will your destiny be. O, person, if you were just born to travel through a valley of sorrows and tears.

Is this precisely an immutable and sorrowful truth, that sharpening the capabilities of the mind dulls the senses of the heart?

It is difficult to cope with people of a bad personality. They interpret everything to their personal advantage.

It is easier for an uneducated person to learn something, than for an educated person to learn it again differently.

It is easier to rid a person of his shadow on a sunny day than to rid society of a vice.

It is interesting to watch how Germans and Russians gamble at cards. The former bet pennies, while the latter dollars. So when the latter lose they complain, but for the former, no big deal. Based on such a trivial pursuit, the character of the nations is determined.

It is not on smooth meadows that flowers of knowledge grow. It is necessary to chop through thorny weeds and step on sharp rocks in order to find them.

It is unforgivable to condescendingly flatter the sovereign, but also unjust to conceal their virtue from the nation.

It seems that this has never yet been seen in the human race, such an inexhaustible drive and such a hurry to live, as at present. Never have people been witness to such fast upheavals and so many marvelous events as during our time. Great events are occurring like waves raised by the storm and rushing one after another.

It was only our mentors – foreigners – and from where only God knows, but according to their own words – from the land of prosperity – they ran headlong to us, to the kingdom of cold, and why? In order to sell us their minds, which eats your eyes like smoke and then vanishes into the atmosphere, and in the process funnel Russian money out of the pockets of our rich.

Judging on the present desire for gold, it seems that people do not fear digging deep into the earth to its very heart as long as they have the hope to find there a golden bottom.

Least of all do we know about what is always with us from the cradle to the grave, always in our chest: least of all do we know about our individual heart. If we only knew why and when and how and the cause for it to rejoice, sorrow or condescends, or enjoy the heavenly inspiration of virtue, or in a whirlwind of desire to drive itself into a foggy sphere of vices. If we only knew all of this, then we would have complete comprehension of ourselves. But, No. The comprehension of yourself, say the ancients sages of previous ages, is an experience, the most difficult of all knowledge in the world.

Life and activity are so tightly woven into each other, just as flame and light. What burns assuredly shines; what lives, then of course, acts.

Lousy hosts always paint the roof in bright colors, not worrying about the supports for the rotting walls.

Love often knocks at the heart's cage, but prudence will not always open it.

Many during their entire life do nothing that is of any importance only because they are always preparing themselves to do something extraordinary, exceptional, amazing!

Many people are like books where only the introduction is interesting enough to read, while the balance, the further you read, the more boring and unbearable it is.

National rulers are convinced due to their experience, that for the defense of the throne and national rights, the status of people has been identified, and for the most part they are those who less than others have utilized the advantages and benefits of national life. Meanwhile the others – these sons of prosperity – thought only of the salvation of their treasures and personal welfare, as the poor crowds ran to the front to deliver the fatherland and to die for it on the battlefield.

Nothing so discloses people's qualities than their vocations.

Often sleeping on a gold bed, a person sees iron dreams.

Only take note of this and you will see that the most brilliant minute of a triumphant action is simultaneously the initiating minute of your ruin. Our grandfathers were personal eyewitnesses to this, and assuredly their grandchildren will also see this at their allotted time, because the orientation of the world is always identical.

Only virtue and wisdom lead a person along the path of moral instruction to that desired height about which people at the bottom know nothing, which seems unattainable to regular souls and to which great souls aspire excitedly.

Desires overwhelm us like waters from a storm; but the dam of good ethics restrains them. Streams of temptation wash the dam, first from the edges, then in the center, and then only one pole remains and even this restrains the charge of turbulent streams. It tears and the waters rush directly at the heart and submerge it. Instructors must repair the old dams, and even better is to redirect the streams to the side using canals.

People possess a tongue that is rich with demands, a tongue that is somewhat worse with desires. But they have completely almost no tongue regarding high spiritual inclinations and relative imperceptible truths with their scattered overtones. What they do have can be compared to nebulous fantastic dreams they are unable to decipher or explain.

Sciences are more than just old books and even perhaps more than the writers themselves. At that time less people read, but they were no less learned and cognizance.

Shameful for us, having defeated the French, to be subject to their fashions and tolerate in our language and literature their foreign words and expressions.

Short and infinitesimal is the existence of a person in this world, but extensive and longevous are its consequences. People come and go, but what they do remains.

Society is similar to a many-stringed musical instrument. It is very difficult to tune and also difficult to keep tuned. Even the smallest string out of tune will cause disharmony.

Some people not having the time to meditate enough on the importance of a minister's or official's function, not developing rules for his own conduct, and not determining sufficiently his own talents and capabilities, will seek popularity and will force themselves into important places in the state. They can be compared with chicks that have not determined if their strength has developed or if their wings have completely grown, and then suddenly fly out of their nest. These and the others will flutter a bit, fly a bit, gravitate down and crash!

Someone once said military strategy will always be a science for the enlightened and only a crude vocation for the ignorant.

Sovereigns live for years, but nations for centuries. All government statutes once confirmed must be similar to trees that every person can water and must care, but which no one is permitted to hew. Then under the trusting shade of such trees planted by wise rulers, the prosperity of the nations will calmly rest.

The defenders of the present age constantly announce that we, hour to hour, are becoming smarter and more educated. Let's believe them and ask, "Are we becoming happier?" So of what does the drive for personal perfection of our generation consist? Should we boast that we have acquired the useless art of flying in hot-air balloons with the ability to bring the entire world to dread, attaining the art of killing up to 100,000 in one day, to burn entire fleets, to access what was previously inaccessible, to traverse regions previously impassable, change our form of government into something of a tragedy?

The half-barbarian tribes that migrate as nomads in the distant steppes do not have magnificent cities and extravagant homes, but as a result they are not familiar with the worries and sorrows that nest in them.

The ingratitude of the nation, the injustice of sovereigns, envy, slander, and intrigues, accompany great people from cradle to grave. Their life is a constant struggle. Where is the reward? In their posterity! In history!

The law is the intermediary between God and the Sovereign, just as the Sovereign is intermediary between the law and the nation.

The laws of nature are firm cliffs, against which the oceans of time vainly strike.

The movement of passions is like the course of a river, as soon as it meets obstacles in its stream it becomes turbulent and noisy.

The regular search for hidden treasure is one of the most ancient stupid endeavors of humanity. In our time true virtues have become the new hidden treasures.

The secret upon which love for the homeland is founded is yet to be explained. I will not attempt to confirm but I will propose a guess. Is not this attachment founded on the memories of childhood, that happy and charming time of our life, and which for no one will ever be returned to us or relived a second time? Nothing can so strongly replace in our heart the loss of that state of innocence where the serene morning of our days was located.

The true lover of science sees an obstacle and is not afraid of it. Spread burning coals on his path and he is ready to walk upon it with bare-footed steps in order to only reach his goal.

The weak are always the spoils of the rich, while the strong seldom become sacrifices of the manipulative. Strength and subtlety divide the dominion over people's fates between themselves.

This is a most just statement, Where there is no greed, there is no poverty. But we can supplement it, Where there is mutual love, there is no greed.

Thoughts of immortality pour an indescribable sweet comfort on the wounds of a heart severed apart from catastrophes.

To gift the very best legislation to a nation, but without correcting first its morality, is just the same as pouring some expensive liquid into a dirty bowl. So how are morals to be improved? During a child's education, and as it becomes older to utilize prudent reprimand. The former will not permit them near vices, while the latter follows to discipline them and banish them from society.

To watch the turbulence of a stormy sea and the passions of a human is often curious, but to abandon yourself arbitrarily to one or the other is always dangerous.

Truly there are so few precious items in the world, and they by the grace of the Supreme are so close to a person, that there is completely no need to have any desire for wings, but all it takes is to stretch your hands in order to get all that is so truly indispensable.

We agree that they have gone astray. But why is it that we, the educated, are not as steadfast in the law that is founded on immutable truths, to the same extent theirs is founded on their errors? This is what should embarrass us! The wealthier the Jew, the more precisely and inviolately he fulfills even the most minute customs. Among us, on the contrary, our wealth tramples the statues of our beliefs and the customs of our forefathers with its golden feet.

We would not know the sweet medicine of healing it if were not for the bitter sorrow of illness.

What does each person seek? What do all people seek? Happiness! But you cannot seek for it where it cannot be found. Paths of terror will not ascend to happiness.

What is a constitution? An immutable state statute guiding the government and protecting the rights of the people.

When some ancient persons did some charity, they never hid their name, but they sought some manner to loudly announce it to the people and to their posterity. But we need to accept the fact that it is only the Christian teaching that compels us to contribute so that the right hand does not know what the left hand is doing.

When we are overwhelmed with some passion our eyes become microscopes and even the most infinitesimal of objects seem to appear immense.

Who is truly free? The person who does not condescend to personal passions and other's lusts.

Woe to that person whom war causes to become inhuman.

Timofei Nikolaevich Granovski

1813 – 1855

Historian

Timofei Granovski was born in Oryol, central Russia, on March 9, 1813. His mother came from a wealthy Ukrainian family which provided means for all her children. Up to the age of 13, Granovski was home schooled, where he was taught the French and English languages. Later he attended private school in Moscow, 1826-1828, and then returned home. In 1831-1832 he served at the Ministry of Internal Affairs. This work did not attract Granovski, so he entered St Petersburg University to study law, and finished in 1835, and then went to work in a library.

Granovski went to Berlin to study German philosophy, and then returned to Russia in 1839. He taught history at the Moscow University, specializing in the European Middle Ages.

He died October 4, 1855 in Moscow, due to illness. He was only 42 years of age.

One philosopher said that death is the great equalizer. These words can be applied to our science. With every historical crime it provides historical circumstances that ameliorate the guilt of the criminal, whoever he may be, an entire nation or a private individual. Let us be permitted to say that a person is not a historian if he is incapable to bring a living feeling of love toward associate into past events and to recognize a brother in a foreign nation separated from him by several centuries. During the most shameful periods of the life of humanity there have also been redemptive areas, visible to us even from a distance of several centuries, and at the bottom of the most sinful heart – as judged by their contemporaries – hides some type of feeling, but only one that is better and immaculate. Such a view can serve to the detriment of a severe sentence of justice. This does not demand justification, but explanation, to turn directly to the people involved, and not to the sentence provided as judgment for their actions.

And how can a nation that views itself as the center of the universe, and alienates itself from other nations, attain significance in world history?

And where should we seek the explanation of every contemporary perfection and flaw, if not in historical development?

Every attempt to install a sharp line of demarcation between unavoidable events due to logic and due to accident will only cause significant errors in evaluation and will more or less possess nothing more than a character of arbitrary incidence.

In every epoch when society divides into 2 factions, among the fanatical contenders there will arise a middle and balanced group, to which from the one side bold people will join, those not having extreme inclinations, and from the other side weak people who are not capable of any energetic persuasion.

Of course, not nations, not their leaders, ascertain their conduct in the light of the textbooks of general history and do not seek in them direction for their own actions. Nonetheless, it is impossible to deny the popular historical intent among the masses, more or less developed on the basis of preserved tradition about the past.

Prejudice is shameful and especially if it is bought with some type of bribe or promise. But prejudice that evolves from conviction, whether it has a real basis or not, is not only not reprehensible in history, but even provides some interest for people.

Science in its conclusion, according to its customs, is compelling. But meanwhile it does not satisfy and leaves some type of psychological needs unexplained and unanswered.

The human is impatient. He thinks that with the fall of one immediately another that is better will begin. But history is not in a hurry. Destroying one system of order, it provides time for its ruins to decay, and the destroyers of the former system will never at all see with their eyes that goal to which they progressed.

The general law does not gaze into a person's soul before it is legislated, woe to that society that does gaze into it.

We cannot watch the past except from the point of view of the present. In the accomplished destiny of our fathers do we predominantly seek explanation of what personally pertains to us.

When some type or other ancient institution is subject to danger from the influence of new ideas, it will collapse relatively soon and will concede its place. But if it earlier contained some type or other life-possessing principle, it will revive its strength for battle against these new principles.

What nation does not consider itself the best, the most ethical in all the world?

Konstantine Dmitrievich Kavelin

1818 – 1885

Historian, Lawyer, Sociologist

Konstantine Kavelin was born in St Petersburg on November 4, 1818. His initial schooling was at home, and then in 1835 he entered Moscow University to study history and philosophy, but then changed to study law, and graduated in 1839. During this era he became friends with the Aksakov brothers who were dedicated Slavophiles. However after graduation Kavelin's attitude changed to being a Westerner.

In 1842, Kavelin entered government service in the Ministry of Justice, and became part of the circle of Westerners. But he left government service in 1844 and become a professor of law at Moscow University. At this time he began writing for various Russian journals on the topics of Russian history and the history of Russian law, but only until 1848 when he relocated to St Petersburg and began teaching law at Petersburg University.

His involvement with government polity began 1855 with his articles on the liberation of the serfs and abolition of the feudal system. As a result, Kavelin was estranged from the royal family, and in 1861 was forced to leave the university. He traveled abroad for about 3 years, and when he returned he worked at the Ministry of Finances. Kavelin was not allowed to teach again until 1877, and then became professor of law at the Military-War Academy in St Petersburg, where he taught to the end of his life.

He again associated with the Slavophiles in the later years of his life. Kavelin died in St Petersburg on May 3, 1885.

A person should not estrange himself from ideas and questions as though from his shadow. They change along with him, and seem for a while to calm and then as though die, in order to again appear in a new view and with new strength.

A very few trouble themselves with the question, that maybe there is something hidden behind the cloak of tradition, something not accepted, something not developed by science and which stands outsides its sphere, beyond its threshold, but meanwhile comprises the living need of people. But many and very many sense this, and this sensation is expressed negatively in the dissatisfaction with science, knowledge that cannot seem to define it; and expressed positively in tenacity, which causes tradition to be held as an anchor of salvation.

All that occurs within the bounds of our foresight or intention is what we call indispensable. But what we were unable to envision or what does not reside as part of our intention, but meanwhile still occurs, we count this accidental.

Every person deep in his soul knows that he conceives either good and does it or stupidity. He carries this feeling of good and bad in himself. But ask what is good and what is bad, and no one will answer you properly on this question. If you should orient this question to apply to one or another specific attitude, action, occupation, then even the most uneducated and vague person will not have it difficult to answer.

In the dust of polemics and struggle, the contentious and irritating disputes with an opponent, we easily, and unfortunately, all too often migrate from determination to personal altercation, suspecting malice in the good conscience of alien opinions, dragging entire directions of debate under a moral microscope and sentencing them to anathema. No view of any type on its own is moral or immoral. It is only more or less agreeable with objective correctness and truth, and this is what needs to be explained.

It is not only difficult for our children, but even for us, to presently reflect on the original mode of life of just our nearest ancestors.

It seems that European customs usually serve as the basis of our social ideals, but our ethical ideals have been transferred to us almost entirely from the program of the Slavophiles.

Only in science do we have interaction with what is common or fatal or immutable. But in the life of reality, we on the contrary are occupied with special, conditional, movable and changeable items.

Our Russian arguments are infected from their very beginning, because we seldom argue against what the other person is saying, but almost always against what it is he is thinking, against his supposed or assumed intention and the thoughts at the back of his mind. We are eternally on guard, eternally holding a rock in our pocket.

Outside of people there is no falsity, no truth, and science in vain attempts to discover that truth exists independently on its own.

Perfection in the Christian sense is possible only outside the world and its deceits.

Religious aspirations can become aggressive, megalomaniac and exclusive even just from that minute when from matters of conviction and personal conscience they migrate into doctrine, become an issue of the mind, science, criticism, when people of identical persuasion transform into a secular society following secular goals.

ALEKSEI STEPANOVICH KHOMYAKOV

1804 – 1860

Philosopher, Military Hero, Poet

Aleksei Khomyakov was born in Moscow on May 5, 1804, into an ancient aristocratic family. His initial education was at home, and then at Moscow University, where in 1821 he graduated in mathematics and science. In 1822 he joined the military and was shipped to Astrakhan, but only for a year, and then he relocated to St Petersburg, and left the military in 1825, to travel Europe. Khomyakov was back into the military in the year 1828-1829 with war against Turkey, and again left the military to return to his home. Khomyakov again traveled in 1847, visiting Germany.

His next efforts lead to becoming ideological leader of the Slavophiles In 1839, he proposed the principles of the Slavophile ideology in his first book. Khomyakov formulated the idea of conciliarity: the religious tie that must unite members of the Church in love and truth. The preservation of the conciliar principle in the life of the Russian nation – the ancient Slavic institute of community as its analogy – served for Khomyakov the theoretical foundation to deduce the worldwide historical significance of the Russian nation. Khomyakov later improved the Slavophile concept together with I.V. Kireev, Yu.F. Samarin and K.S. Aksakov. He considered the monarchy of Imperial Russian the sole means of effective government rule of Russia, and that socialism and capitalism were on the same negative level and evolving from Western decadence. He also promoted Russian Orthodoxy as important to resolving any of Russia's religious conflicts.

Khomyakov considered the source of reality to be the willing intellect. He developed the concept of the all-encompassing knowledge or living knowledge, where he realized the fullness of spiritual experience.

Khomyakov died in the process of assisting peasants during a cholera epidemic on September 23, 1860, in Ryazan province.

All the attributes of the Church, those internal as well as those external, are understood only through it and only by those whom grace has summoned to be its members. For aliens and the un-summoned, they are not understood. External changes in ceremony seem to the un-summoned a change in the spirit that is displayed in the ceremony, as for example, during the transfer of the Old Testament Church into the New Testament, or the attack of ceremonies and ecclesiastical postures from the time of the apostles. The Church and its members know the inner significance of the faith as a whole and the immutability of its spirit, which is God's Spirit.

An enslaved nation absorbs many evil principles. The soul fails under the heaviness of the burdens that bind the body and cannot develop thoughts that are truly humanist. But a government such as this is a worse mentor than slavery, and the deep corruption of the victors takes vengeance for the misfortunes of the defeated.

Every person seeking proof of ecclesiastical truth either displays his doubt and excludes himself from the Church by doing this, or gives himself the impression of doubting and so at the same time preserves hope to eventually prove truth and reach the truth of God. Human weakness becomes obvious in the weakness of wanting proof.

History summons Russia to become the forefront of worldwide enlightenment. It provides Russia the right to do this due to its principles that encompass every facet and completeness.

It seems that everyone just like ourselves wants matters to just take care of themselves, for life to progress for us with the income from labor and education without any effort on our part in manual labor. And so we hide behind the income of others, the logic of events that are supposed to work for us.

Many truths, and perhaps even the most important truths, those which are given only for the study of humanity, are transmitted from one to another outside of logical manners, some with just a hint that will then waken hidden strengths within the soul. Science would be dead if it was to reject the rational truth only because it does not appear in the form of a syllogism.

Misfortune – what a horrible school! Of course, a person who has endured much becomes very tolerant, but this is the result of his soul being pummeled, weakened. A person deteriorates and becomes apprehensive from his experiences. He loses that assurance in tomorrow, without which it is impossible to do anything. He becomes complacent, because he adapts to horrible thoughts. Finally he fears misfortune, that is, he fears to have to again feel anew the series of pressing sufferings, the series of missed heartbeats, which his memory will never dissipate should even storms force it.

Societies collapse not from some type of strong shaking, or from the result of some type of struggle. They collapse just as do some old trees that have lost all their life-supporting sap and will soon be unable to withstand a powerful storm. They die as old people die, as a traditional saying states: tired of life. Only a blind person is mentally permitted to as if not see this historical inevitability.

We know that when one of us goes astray, he falls alone, but no one is saved on his own. The one who is saved is saved in the

Church as its member and in union with all its other members. If a person believes, he is part of the communion of faith. Does he love? He is in communion of love. Does he pray? He is in the communion of prayer. For this reason no one can rely on his prayer alone, and every person praying, asks the entire Church for intercession, but not as if he is doubting in the intercession of the one intercessor Christ, but in assurance that the entire Church always prays for all its members.

When all falsity of teaching disappears, there will be no reason to again utilize the appellation of Orthodoxy, because pseudo-Christianity will no longer exist. When the Church expands, or when the fullness of the nations enter into it, then local appellations will disappear, because the Church will not be tied with some place and will not preserve the legacy of pagan pride, but it will call itself the sole, holy, conciliar and apostolic, knowing that the entire world belongs to it, and that no locality will have any type of significance. But for the time being the appellation of Orthodox will serve to represent God's name according to His inexpressible will.

You cannot force yourself to love. And if there is something that you do not like, this does not mean that you have not love in you, but only that there is a certain something in you that interferes with love. You can rotate a bottle and shake it as hard as you want, but as long as the cork is in it nothing will spill out until you remove the cork. So it is with love. Your soul is full of love, but this love cannot be displayed until your sins are removed in order to allow it passage. Free your soul from whatever is obstructing it and you will love everyone and even him whom you called your enemy and have hated.

Nikolai Fillipovich Pavlov

1803 – 1864

Cultural Activist, Actor

Nikolai Pavlov was born in the village Penka, Tambov Province, central Russia, on September 7, 1803. His father was Vladimir Mikhailovich Grushetzki, and because the son was illegitimate he took his mother's family name.

Pavlov completed acting school in Moscow in 1821 and for a while was an actor. He continued his education at Moscow University in literature. The balance of his life was spent dedicated to Russian theater, art and literature. He died in Moscow on March 29, 1864.

A person at the minute he is drunk is happy for everybody, and accepts everybody in his warm location.

Ambition does not lead to benevolence: the higher the rank, the more lonesome it is, and the more plague-ridden people that are placed near us with whom you should not be involved.

If a man enjoys humiliating a woman to his level, the woman still will always exalt him over herself and over the entire world.

In general a person does not want to explain some new manifestation as some natural occurrence. Everything needs to be a miracle.

It is difficult to take vengeance on a woman. She defends herself with her weakness or scatterbrain, or does not even sense what is occurring.

There is no muscle so strong in nature that would continue the life of dying love.

They called me a genius, but so complacently that it was apparent no one wanted to be in my place.

They exalted me to heaven, but so sincerely, so offensively, the way a person exalts everything that he envies, the way he is happy to attain ecstasy from the person he considers beneath himself.

The need to satisfy initial wants does not place anybody in a position of complete dependence. A person living on scraps will never thank another for a piece of bread. He will accept a piece of bread as a annoying debt on your part as the observance of the Christian command.

We would cease being afraid of wild animals if they would be able to speak at least a little.

This is not subject to doubt that every stick has 2 ends and that one end is opposite the other, that one is not the other, although the stick is one and the same. All of what exists in the world is composed of the same type of 2 contradistinctions. You agree that although love and hate are one and the same feeling, although love composes one end of passion while hate the other end. Their activity and self-interest are also contrary to the point that they are usually considered as 2 different things.

They just proceeded by as ordinary people – they were and then they were not. This is the book of their existence.

But foresight, having colored nature with an eloquent diversity, distinguished every creation with special traits, because the human everywhere is equally worthy of attention, because in the life of each person, whoever he may be, however he should pass his allotted time, we incur either feeling or statement or incident, which causes the head – the one accustomed to meditation – to surface. Observe intently the peaceful tenants of earth, to the last of its people, in it you will find food for the spirit undergoing its test exactly like with a person who, before the eyes of the entire world, is carried along on the waves of life from one edge to the other, and which will toss him to the heights of immortal happiness or throw him into the abyss of immortal devastation.

A strong character will often surface in a tight circle, under the roof of someone's house; a bizarre incident will select occasionally an unexpected sacrifice, and its instructive strokes fall without witnesses, in the midst of a tranquil domestic existence, just as lightning strikes some traveler who is caught in a storm in some desolate and unpopulated steppe.

When the soul carries within it a great sorrow, when a person is not getting along with you in order to reconcile with the past, in order to rest your disagreement, this person needs a valley and mountains and sea and warm fresh air. He needs it so the grief will not turn into bitterness, into despair, so he will not become hostile.

Osip Ivanovich Senkovski

1800 – 1858

Orientalist, Polyglot, Journalist

Osip Senkovski was born Jozef Julian Sekowski in the city Antagonk, Lithuania, on March 19, 1800, into an ancient Polish aristocratic family. He studied in Volinsk University, where he became interested in the Orient, and so began learning Arabic, Hebrew and other eastern languages. At the same time, Senkovski utilized his knowledge of Russian and his developing literary talent to publish several humorous articles.

In 1819, he was assigned to the Russian Embassy in Constantinople, Turkey, and then he traveled in Syria, continuing his study of Arabic. Then it was Egypt in 1821, and then he returned to Russia. The state utilized his knowledge of Eastern languages by assigning him as a translator in the Ministry of Foreign Affairs.

In 1828, Senkovski taught Eastern languages at the Petersburg University, until the end of his career, and he continued to write articles dealing with the Middle East and Orient.

Senkovski died in St Petersburg on March 4, 1858.

A professionally educated or elegant conversation consists particularly with every person speaking about himself, but in a manner so others do not notice this

All philanthropists will agree on the axiom that it is cruel and inhuman to kill an entity just like yourself who would steal and eat someone else's ox or horse, and doing this act in separate instances, while at the same time these eloquent philanthropists, inflating the budget of military institutions, all uniformly and in unison will state that it is a humane, excellent and praiseworthy act to suddenly kill thirty or forty thousand of the same entities on some battlefield.

And so what is society? People? And what people? Society is a gathering of individual ideas of that relative epoch. People consist of persons, and a person consists of his own ideas. Every person expresses himself only with some type of idea that serves as his simple environment and which provides his head for rent for that specific interval. He is its slave and weapon. He is firm in this idea. His capabilities, thoughts and feeling surround his idea, as does himself with all of his ethical existence. In society there does not exist an individual person because a person of society is always the incarnation of some type of idea.

Aspiration, inspiration and whim have ceased to be principles of conduct. People now think in terms of their collective. They move as a collective, and love and hate each other, and fight in terms of a collective.

But time heals all sorrows, applying to it the ointment of salvation, which is forgetting.

Eternity! This is the simple absence of any measurement.

Even a lot of nothings with one conniving charlatan at the forefront will compose an immense sum.

Everybody praised him. All wished him prosperity, successes, wealth, but none moved from their place to help him construct for himself a decent existence on earth.

How lonesome it is to govern with prudence when having to deal with people's stupidities.

I am a librarian, I do not tolerate stupidity. I only bring all of it into order and systematically organize it.

I am convinced that the sun's radiance was created only in order to be able to see beauty.

I hate charlatans, these sinners who want to inflate their character. It is so much better to associate with honorable sinners.

If you were able to possess even one small particle of this all-encompassing and immutable wisdom from before the beginning of time, that which governs nature, preserves and develops it, then tell us, what good would you think of or would you do for the benefit of nature that would add to it some important and invisible part?

In the world there do exist heavy, immovable, iron-bodied people who call themselves founders, who would want all satisfactions to evolve from one, long, undivided piece, like an Alexandrian column, and not be subject to fragmentation.

It is apparent that humanity, due to the manner it is created, that no manner what direction you turn it, nevertheless it will not observe laws precisely.

It is better to watch the sorrow of a virtue than the joy of some vice.

Money taken is seldom returned with pleasure, even from a stranger.

Now after acquiring a telescope even a bat will not hide in the air from the astronomers.

Often enough the mind has been forced to feign stupidity in order for a person to be able to listen to himself.

People are great masters in the various subtleties of politeness. However many historical figures have proven their gratitude by dooming the residents of entire cities to the sword and the desolation of entire provinces.

People have lost their mind and heart when they no longer can like and treasure such a valuable item as a penny.

So seldom do we grasp happiness, since it passes by so quickly.

The fear of death resides not in a person's soul, but in his physical part. He acts only as long as his corporeal strengths have the overwhelming force and subject the spiritual principles of existence to its use. It is solely the body that fears death, because death threatens him with destruction, and as soon as sickness and exhaustion deprive his corporeal substance of its awesome autocracy, which people call the voice of nature, and the spirit no longer incurs any further contradiction, the body's destruction becomes for us as an insignificant alien object.

The human is a special creature, the only one in all of nature, whose primary amusement consists in comforting himself with the stupidities of his species.

The primary difficulty of life, believe me, evolves solely from people wearing clothes that are alien to their nature. If each of us would only wear clothes that were compatible with our vocation or our culture.

The sages of ancient times said that a mechanism always operates easier and better than the people who operate them.

The souls of stupid people punished for their inactivity or incapability are sent to work and to be educated by the heads of industrious scholars, where they are shackled to a piece of ambiguous ancient text with the obligation to derive some meaning from it and explain it in a proper manner.

The time has already passed when a person lived 80 years as the entirely of one life and thought one long thought that encompassed 18 volumes. Now our life, mind and heart is composed of small, scattered, loose fragments and it is considerably better, more diverse, more pleasant to the eyes, and even less expensive. We think in fragments, we exist in fragments and are scattered in fragments.

The very circumstance that the law is violated clearly proves that it does result in some observance, that is still has some affect, and people still keep it in view.

There are people whose self-interest and ambition is so immense, so inflated, a pride that is so colossal, that they block the entire horizon in every direction with their person. Every word expelled into the air incessantly falls back on them like a bullet in a wall, and creates a void in their vanity.

There exists some very pleasant sins, for which it is worth dragging the body on its bones for some known number of years.

There is no difference of any kind between death and sleep, except that a person does not awaken from death. Sweetness that you feel as you fall asleep is particularly the result of the submergence of the spirit into complete oblivion and inactivity, into death.

Truly you did not know that the immaculate and straight mind is the greatest poison in nature? The mind must never be utilized otherwise except separated and dissolved. It is necessary to divide it in half or in thirds with stupidity or with hypocrisy or with foam, but the very best is with egoism. Or else easily mix it into some nastiness, although it can also be dissolved into ridicule. Then it will be very acceptable, tasteful, kind and worth something.

We have attempted to govern people using all possible means, and in no manner have we been able to satisfy them. We have governed them with humility, then they become disorderly. We utilize magnanimity with them, they respond with ingratitude. We run to wisdom, they fill us full of hot air. We legislate laws, they just hang them on hooks. We turn to use severity, they start to complain and threaten us with rebellion.

What is called great truths are harmful only when they crawl into the head.

When the nation reaches such a high level of intellectual perfection, that it can speak all the day long intellectually about nobody and nothing, only then is it worthy of the appellation of a true educated nation.

Whenever a stupid person died, you can be completely assured that within one and-a-half seconds another will be born in his place. There has not yet been a census of intelligent people because there are many charlatans among them.

Whoever bribes justice never complains enough on the insufficiency of justice in the world.

What should cause a person to be aspiring and fervent, should also train him to have great self-control.

Nikolai Vasilyevich Shelgunov

1824 – 1891

Revolutionary Activist, Botanist

Nikolai Shelgunov was born in St Petersburg on December 4, 1824, into an aristocratic family. In 1841, he completed studies at the Forestry Institute, and then served in the forestry division of the Ministry of State Property. Toward the end of the 1850s, he became a professor at the Forestry Institute and wrote several books on the topic.

Shelgunov left the institute and became involved in anti-government political activism, writing several articles on the corruption of the Imperial Government and his advocacy of socialism. He traveled to London in 1858-1859. On his return he again taught at the institute but only until 1862. He again began working with Russian journals writing articles that conflicted with the political policies of the Imperial Government. That year he was arrested and incarcerated in Schlesselburg Fortress, where he sat for 2 years. In 1864, Shelgunov was exiled to the Vologda province, where he wandered for the next 5 years from city to city as a mendicant, losing his health and property. In between he still wrote revolutionary articles.

In 1869, Shelgunov was released from his exile but was not allowed to return to St Petersburg, so he went to Kaluga, and then in 1874 to Novgorod, and subsequently to Vyborg (today in Finland), and finally back to St Petersburg. But in 1883, he was sent back to Vyborg.

Shelgunov terminated his political involvement at this time, and his compositions to the end of his life were focused on morality and ethics, and his reflections on Russian life were subsequently published and became popular. He died in St Petersburg on April 12, 1891.

Many thousands of anti-government activists attended his funeral, many of them the future social-democrats of Russia, all to display their support of the efforts of Shelgunov.

A fiery character is always a malevolent character. And the more a person is aspiring and fiery, the more he must train himself and develop self-control.

A person who cannot seem to define his destiny is just a coward, one who does not want to have a destiny, an idler. While the person who is not capable of having a destiny is just stupid.

Adolescence with its noble enthusiasm, with its turbulent aspiration to honor, virtue, to social justice, is one of the greatest strengths of progress.

All that is weak constantly hides behind a nebulous and transcendental romanticism, fantasizing of life beyond the grave., It sees the soul anchor of salvation of humanity from political destitution in the moral self-perfection of the individual.

Childhood is that great interval of life when the foundation for your entire future moral basis as an adult is built.

Courage normally walks along side a soft character, and a courageous person more than others is capable of magnanimity.

Duty is tightly interwoven with rectitude. A person first of all else has the duty of being right in his words and activities. He speaks and does only what he should, how he should and when he should.

Falsity is included in diminution as well as in exaggeration, in hiding as well as distorting the truth, in pretending agreement with an alien opinion, in just making a gesture of a promise but not meaning it. We do not have the intention of accomplishing any of this, yet face the indecision of saying the truth when saying it becomes our duty.

Feelings are the mind's colors. Without them our minds would be dry, lifeless contours, but not pictures.

Genius summons amazement, but character motivates respect. Geniuses act on the mind, people who have character act on the conscience. And if people have veneration for the former, they are followers of the latter.

Genuine and better politeness is the one founded on sincerity. It must be inspired by the heart, it mush be full of pleasure and display a readiness to assist in the happiness of a close associate.

Happiness is created from individual satisfactions of our aspirations and desires. Like flowers that we notice and gather, it is scattered along the path of life. But as every person walks his own road, so the flowers that he gathers are those that grow alongside his road. For this reason, each person has his own happiness.

Having a conviction is mental wholesomeness, a complex unity of the complete soul with a precise, defined resonance. A conviction is something yet uncompleted, something inflexible, firm, immutable.

If a person has organized his entire character, then his word will never be different than his conduct, and here is where the essence of rectitude is confined.

Life is happy only when a person can fully and freely utilize his strengths in diverse and wide directions, and the fullest and most comprehensive life is the happiest life. And the comprehensive life is always a social one.

Only inspiration having integrity, only passion that is honorable, will create humanity's majesty. Where such passion is suppressed, do not expect to find there a person or a citizen.

Our heroism stumbles, but not in feats of military bravery, but only in feats of civil courage.

The problem of being close to your countrymen is not for the landlord to become a serf, but on the contrary, for every serf to become a landowner.

Imperial Russia –

The Religious Thinkers

Ambrose Optinski

1812 – 1891

Russian Orthodox Monk and Monastery Father Superior

Ambrose was born Aleksandr Mikhailovich Grenkov on November 21, 1812, in a small village in Tambov Province, central Russia. His father was a deacon at the local Orthodox parish, although for the most part he was raised by his grandfather who was an Orthodox parish priest.

In 1825, Aleksandr entered the Tambov Religious school and then from 1830 to 1836 he studied at the Tambov Seminary, where he studied Greek, Hebrew, French, Tatar (Mongol) and Slavic. He become ill during his final year and promised to become a monk. Graduating from Tambov Seminary, Aleksandr became a teacher at Lipitzski Religious school until 1839. He became ill again and remembered his promise should he become well. After his health was restored Aleksandr went to Optinski Monastery, arriving October 8, 1839, and became a postulant the following year. In November 1842, Aleksandr took vows as a monk and accepted the name of Ambrose. In 1860, *staretz* Macarius died, and Ambrose took over responsibility of Optinski Monastery as *staretz* or Father Superior. Ambrose died October 10, 1891.

It is not without good reason that the earthly life is called a valley of sorrow. It is the subjected and destitute who weep, while the officials and wealthy just sigh. There is not one on earth who is without sorrow and grief. Reflecting on all of this, we will turn with our minds and hearts to the all-benevolent God, who to this time nourishes us and provides us with all our necessities. We will unload all our sorrows on the Lord.

Evil has always run ahead, but not overcome. Among the number of the selected students of Christ our Savior was his betrayer. But those who opposed the truth received their deserved compensation, while others cannot be harmed no matter how hard you try.

We reside in a valley of sorrow. For this reason at times we will have the opportunity to dance, while other times to weep. Let us at least comfort ourselves with the thought that this valley of sorrow is temporal. All will fly by, all will run by, like a shadow. Like an echo, and then will arrive eternity, one constant, immutable, endless and – just for us the blessed – bright. We will hope that the Lord according to His infinite kind heart will not deprive us of His mercy.

It is not proper to fulfill in any manner the will of psychological enemies that torment you with every influence and propositions. This entire mental battle, an entangling web, evolves from this subjection to malicious influences, those to which you may ascribe significance or trust, and instead of disdaining them and calling against them the help of God. The primary reason for your mental battle is your high opinion of yourself, and which is obvious to everybody.

When people are vexing you, do not ever say, "Why or How come? This is nowhere to be found in Scripture." There on the contrary is said, "If someone strikes you on the right cheek, turn to him the other." Indeed it is not easy for someone to strike you on the right cheek, so we should understand this as follows: If someone is to slander you or somehow discredit you, although you are innocent, then this means – striking you on the right cheek. Do not complain, but tolerate this abuse patiently, which is to provide the left cheek.

You complain about your difficult life. But comfort is provided in Scripture with the words, "Every person will receive his reward relative to his work." But we do incur many difficulties and often suffer depression. But our self-esteem likes consolation, and expanse and rest and would like to easily inherit Christ's Kingdom, and while on the cross he prayed for those who were crucified alongside him. All of this we forget and so go into depression often.

Sorrow is a precious dowry for our Groom. If someone loves Jesus, he will strive with all his strengths to accumulate a greater dowry and so display his love for him all the more, the immaculate, supra-loving, precious Jesus. And he rejoices even more if the dowry is drawn in the carriage of his beloved bride. The dowry is our sorrows and pains, and the Lord Jesus loves such persons.

To life in a simple hut, but not to live contritely, will not bring benefit to you. It is better for the weak soul and body to reside in a comfortable cell and be contrite, while blaming and censuring yourself for such a comfortable and large cell. There are only a few and those with a strong body who can endure an austere life, who can endure cold and hunger and wetness and lack of freedom without harming themselves.

Pyotr Semeonovich Avsenev

(Archimandrite Theofan)

1810 – 1852

Russian Orthodox Prelate

Pyotr Semeonovich Avsenev was born 1810 in the village of Moskovski, Voronezh Province, central Russia, the son of a parish priest. He received his education at the local religion school and then a religious seminary. In 1829, he entered Kiev Religious Academy, where he concentrated his studies on German philosophy and language, finishing in 1835. He remained at the academy to teach German history and literature. The following year Avsenev become professor of philosophy, and in 1836 was invited to teach at the University of St Vladimir (today known as the Kiev National University).

In 1844, Avsenev quit his post at the university and took vows as a monk with the name Theofan. In 1846, Theofan was promoted to rank of archimandrite of Kiev University. The following years were concentrated more on theology than previous. In 1851, Theofan was promoted to being ambassador of the Russian Orthodox Church at the Vatican, Rome. Arriving in Rome, he passed away shortly after on March 31, 1852.

A topic of especial interest to Avsenev were aspects of the religious life in dreams, visions, clairvoyance and related supernatural phenomenon. As a result he developed a plan of the soul's history, including questions of its evolution, growth and state after physical death. Avsenev while in Rome displayed considerable patriotic attitude toward Russia and defense of the Russian Orthodox Church.

Russia in relationship to the west is a contradiction. In the west you have small sovereignties separated one from another due to natural elements. As a result in the west the sovereignties possess a principle of individualism in individuality. In Russia it is the opposite as we see a blending of the tribes that are uniformly spread over its expanse. Among us develops the thought that the various tribes must blend into one large nation. The Russian character is a universal character. Constant intercourse of Russia with the east brought into our character oriental elements. But from the other side, Russians attempt to have empathy with the west; they live and adapt all that they see good in the west. Many of their superior traits are compatible with this universal Russian character and are here noticeable. Among these traits those that merit special attention are our unusual endurance, magnanimity, charity, virtue and open character, while possessing the absence of passionate vexation and violence.

In relationship to dogma our denomination agrees with Catholicism, but we alienate ourselves from Catholic pomposity and insist more on spirit and thought. Our legislation is based on the primary principle of equality of rights of all members of society and their absolute submission to the monarch. In the East a despot rules; in the West there is almost no single supreme authority. In between despotism and constitutional liberty is the location of our autocracy. We Russians in a philosophical sense do not distinguish ourselves in an independent-originality. We cannot plant ourselves in German dialectical speculation, which field our spirit does not accept. But from another side purely empirical philosophy, like the English have, will not be forced on us. It is easy to guess that our philosophy will have a character that is preeminently religious in nature, because religion is deeply inculcated into our spirit and has entered into our essence.

What we call God is what we see in heaven and in each person. Look at the winter sky at night and you will see stars, stars, stars and more stars, and there is no end to them. And when you think that each of these stars is many, many times larger than the earth upon which we live, and that beyond these stars that we see there are even more hundreds, thousands, millions of the same and even larger stars, and that there is no end to stars and no end to the sky, then you will realize that something that we cannot comprehend exists. When we look at ourselves and see within ourselves what we call ourselves – our soul, when we see within ourselves that something which we cannot comprehend, but which we know more firmly than anything else, and through this we recognize all the exists, and then we see that something in our soul that is more incomprehensible and greater than what we see in the sky. This something that we see in the sky and what we recognize within ourselves – in our own soul – we call God.

To live completely in silence, without any cares, not in the least worrying about the responsibilities of your cell or other needs – such a matter is beyond our capability. When we see that the former holy fathers, and our contemporary, worried over their food, each to some extent, and although worrying little and maybe callously, but they still worried. So much should we, the weak and inconsiderate, humble ourselves and worry over our flesh in such circumstances.

IGNATI BRYANCHANINOV

1807 – 1867

Russian Orthodox Prelate, Theologian

Dmitri Aleksandrovich Bryanchaninov, later known as Bishop Ignati, was born February 5, 1807 in the village Pokrovskoi, Vologda Province, northern Russia. Even as a child Dmitri had an inclination toward the Russian Orthodox Christianity and solitude. However, in 1822, at the insistence of his father, he entered the Military Engineering School, which he completed in 1826. He had a brilliant future ahead of him but made a decision to enter the priesthood. His father felt otherwise and sent him to work at the Daugavpils Fortress, in Latvia. There he became critically ill and was released on November 6, 1827. He immediately entered the Aleksandro-Svirski Monastery, near St Petersburg, and then after a year went to the Ploshanskaya Hermitage, near Bryansk. In 1829, Dmitri relocated to the Svenski Monastery, also near Bryansk, and then to Optinski Monastery, arriving 1830.

In 1831, Dmitri took vows as a monk with the new name of Ignati, and was soon promoted to father superior of the Penshemski Lopotov Monastery, in Vologda province. In 1833 he became father superior of the Troitzi-Sergeev Hermitage near St Petersburg. Due to illness, Fr. Ignati left his hermitage in 1847 for a year and then returned. He started to codify his religious convictions about this time and had them published.

Fr. Ignati was promoted to Bishop of the Caucasus and Black Sea in 1857, arriving in Stavropol in 1858 to take his new responsibilities. He likewise continued to write articles dealing with monasticism, theology and other religious topics. Illness in 1861 forced Fr. Ignati to retire and he went to the Nikolo-Babayevski Monastery in Kostroma Province, where he spent the balance of his life in monastic contemplation and seclusion.

Fr. Ignati died April 30, 1867 at the Nikolo-Babayevski Monastery.

The Holy Spirit acts on its own authority like God. It arrives at the time to a humble and contrite person, when this person does not expect its arrival. It suddenly transforms the mind, transforms the heart. With its effectiveness it encompasses the person's entire will and all capabilities, while the person has no ability to grasp or even meditate on the effects that are being executed in him. When grace is manifested in him, it does not indicate something usual or sensual, but secretly instructs him in matters that he earlier did not visualize and did not even imagine.

Contrary to this is the demonic manifestation that always presents freedom to a person to ascertain such an event, whether to accept or deny it.

Our existence is derived from God, and our restoration, and all our natural qualities, all capabilities – both religious and corporeal. We are in debt to God, yet we are unable to pay this debt! Having this view of ourselves, we form ourselves for the condition of our spirit to be opposite to the opinion of our era, for our condition to be conforming to what the Lord called destitution of spirit, as He commanded us to have and which condition He blessed.

Lord, gift us to see our personal sins so our mind – so attracted entirely to the attention of our personal mistakes – would cease to see the mistakes of our associates and in this manner would see all the good in our associates. Gift to our heart the ability to abandon this fatalistic care for the flaws of our associate, while uniting all of our cares into one care for the attainment of the commanded purity and holiness that you have prepared for us. Gift us, who have been wearing defiled spiritual garments, to again make them white: they have already been washed by the water of baptism and now need the washing of water of tears due to their defilement. Gift us to see in the light of your grace the many and diverse maladies that reside within us, which suppress the spiritual movements in our heart and which then lead into it movements of our flesh and blood that are so hostile to God's kingdom. Gift us the great gift of repentance that precedes and births the great gift of the cognizance of our sins. Protect us with these great gifts from the abyss of self-deception that reveals itself in our soul due to not noticing and not understanding its sinfulness. This is born from actions of promiscuity and vanity that our soul does not notice and does not understand. Preserve us on our path by us using these great gifts and allow us to attain you who have summoned us, those who recognize themselves as sinners and who recognize themselves as being distant from righteousness. Let us bring words of praise eternally in bliss unto you the sole true God, the redeemer of the captives, the savior of the perishing. Amen.

Sacred spirits declined from association with human, just as those who are unworthy of such an association – the fallen spirits – have drawn us into their apostasy, integrating with us. And in order to more comfortably restrain us in the captivity, they strive to build these chains for us that are unnoticeable to us. If they reveal themselves then they reveal themselves in order to strengthen their dominion over us. All of us who are found in this slavery to sin need to know that association with the holy Angels is alien to us, the reason being our estrangement from them due to our apostasy. What is inherent to us, based on the same reason, is association with the rejected spirits, to whose regiment we belong in soul. Holy Angels appear only to holy people who have been restored to a holy life and so have association with God and his Angels.

Humans must out of necessity be satisfied with that experience of evil with which they struggle during the interim of their short earthly life. Their bad intentions are categorically destroyed at that moment when they out of necessity leave the course of earthly life, their presence now demanded at the divine judgment and in eternity.

Demons on the contrary are destined and assigned to reside on earth to the end of time, having begun at the time of their conclusive apostasy. Every person can easily imagine the amount of experience in the creation of evil that they have acquired over the course of such a long interim, with their abilities and during constant intention of imposing harm, and not at all diverted by any influenced good aspiration or inclination.

A contrite person is incapable of having malice and hate. He has no enemies. If another human causes him harm or insult, he sees in that human an instrument of justice or divine providence.

A naturally benevolent and good-intentioned person has no need to present himself as such. On the contrary, who loves sin, whose will is in sin, he needs a façade. Simplicity breeds belief. It is impossible to draw near to God except through simplicity.

A person guided by secular wisdom in no manner can properly judge his personal inner state, nor can he do the same for his associates. He judges himself and others relative to how he imagines himself and how he imagines his associates based on superficial aspects, according to physical conclusions, and this is erroneous. And this is why God's word quite assuredly calls him a hypocrite. It is worth noticing that once a person ascends to spiritual intellect the faults and errors of his associates begin to seem very unimportant, since they have been redeemed by the

Savior and have been healed by repentance, and it is these same errors and faults that seemed to be immensely greater and important.

All of us are weak. The observance of Christ's law consists in carrying each other's burdens in a magnanimous, loving and contrite manner.

An attentive prayer requires self-denial, but very few decide on the course of self-denial.

An unbeliever does not see divine providence. He thinks that his destiny depends on the cleverness of his mental faculties. Confining all goodness into solely temporal pleasures, striving exclusively for them, he creates evil — mentally, verbally, and actually.

Analytic minds cannot imagine existence of the mind without analysis — looking at things plainly and clearly. Seeing the strength of the mind, they ascribe it to a higher level of analysis — they recognize a profound, refined and contemplated subtlety in places that no other would look. They look with penetrating simplicity at all that is subject to humanity's investigation.

And for me it is more than enough for me to acknowledge that I am sinful. Such knowledge is enough for me. He touched me, my hardened heart, just as Moses did the rock with his staff, and out of my heart flowed a living stream of tears. I prefer my wail before my Lord above all secular wisdom, and my sin before me is to blame. My sin was the primary object and forced me to spiritual contemplation.

At present any book that deals with any religious subject is already labeled as spiritual. At present, whoever is in this race, is indisputably spiritual. Who conducts himself contently and reverently, is spiritual to the highest degree! But the Holy Scripture does not teach this. Only those books in the exact meaning of the word – spiritual – can be called this, and it is those books written by the inspiration of the Holy Spirit.

Better not to ask something of God if this is something you do not actually need. Devote yourself completely to His will with your self-denial.

Bodily accomplishment is weak against sin; mental accomplishment is worthless. Strong is the accomplishment of belief! This is the reliable tool of victory.

But if you think that you love God, but in your heart resides an unpleasant mood even to one person, then you reside in a sorrowful self-deception.

Christ, who descended to earth for the sinful, and not for the righteous, remains to this time invisible, but yet in full substance among people, performing great signs and healing. According to his promise, he will reside among us to the end of time.

Cognizance of your sin and the repentance that is born of sin is an activity not having any end on earth. The cognizance of sin motivates repentance. Repentance is proceeded by cleansing. The gradually cleansed eye of the minds begins to review such faults and detriments throughout the entire human substance, which it earlier, while residing in its gloom, completely did not notice.

Counsel does not automatically include the conditions for its indispensable fulfillment, it can be done, or cannot be done. The counselor has no responsibility for his counsel if he provided it in the fear of God and prudence, and not arbitrarily, if this was insisted and asked for the counsel. Likewise the person receiving counsel is not obligated to it. It is up to him after meditating and ascertaining its effects to decide whether to fulfill or not fulfill the counsel he has received.

Criminals incarcerated in prisons are not allowed to be mediators on behalf of other criminals. The Lord is love, and we are unable to fathom the extent that He desires the salvation of all. Let us suppose our salvation is this love, and everyone's, but from our side we will strive what is dependant on us, our cleansing.

Demonic attractions excite corporeal desires and engender illnesses, and those regular human methods of healing have no effect.

Demons do not know the future that is known only to the sole God and His intellectual creatures to whom God was well pleased to reveal the future. But just as reasoning and experienced people can foresee and guess at events that may just well occur – based on events that have occurred in the past or are presently occurring – so can the cunning and much experience evil spirits occasionally suppose with assurance and foretell the future.

Demons, having access to our souls even while we are vigilant, also have access when we are asleep. Having succeeded in self-conceit, demons begin to appear in the form of angels of light, in the form of martyrs and saints, even in the form of the Theotokos and Christ Himself, accommodating them and promising them heavenly crowns. In this manner they raise self-conceit and pride to the heights.

Display honor to your associate as to an image of God. This honor residing in your soul is invisible to others and is obvious only to your conscience. Your activity should be conforming to your psychological mood. Display honor to your associate, not making any distinction due to ago, gender or rank, and gradually holy love will begin to appear in your heart. The reason for this love is not flesh and blood or the inclinations of your feelings, but God. Those deprived of the credit of Christianity are not deprived of another glory and the one they received at their creation: God's image.

Divine benevolence must not be rejected, even though some or many may utilize it for malevolence.

Does not death witness as it overwhelms and continually defeats all of humanity that we are created for eternity, that on earth we are just short-termed and temporal migrants, and that due to this reason our worries about eternity must be primary and the greatest of our worry, and the worries of the earth must be very minor!

Dreams sent by God possess an overwhelming conviction. This conviction is understood by God's saints, while it is inaccessible to those who still persist in struggle with their desires.

Due to sin I banished paradise from my heart. Now I am here having mixed good and evil, here having a fierce struggle between good and evil, here is the altercation of innumerable passions, here is torment, the taste of the future torment of hell. In vain do I blame my forefathers for imparting sin to me. Yet I am liberated from the captivity of sin by the Redeemer and now collapse back into sin not due to force but arbitrarily.

Every contemplation of heaven, if it is not accompanied by repentance evolving from the soul's depths, is dead and not sincere.

Every era has its assigned sufferings. To our era was given only minor sufferings.

For a successful entrance into the world of spirits an education of God's law is indispensable while time is opportune. Particularly it is for this education that a certain interval of time has been assigned by God to every person for his passage through this earth.

God gifts what is His to a person, and these people make each other their own people, temporarily according to the flesh, forever according to the spirit, and only when God's good will is to give this gift of Himself to a person.

God redeemed the human. The freedom to either submit either to God or to the devil is presented to the redeemed person. But the devil is allowed access to a person in order for this freedom to be utilized without compulsion.

God's son, having accepted humanity, became a human in every respect, and he transforms his brethren, also offspring of humanity, to become offspring of God.

Have freedom in your life, knowing that God's rules were legislated for people, and not people created for the rules.

Having heard of the death of some close associate, do not abandon yourself to inconsolable wail, to which the world regularly abandons itself, testifying that their hope is only in the flesh.

Having taught yourself only the literal understanding immediately births pride and a high opinion of yourself; this alienates a person from God. Having provided yourself a superficial knowledge of God, this in essence is nothing more than a complete lack of knowledge of Him and a rejection of Him in His true essence. Preaching such a belief you can drown in unbelief.

Having this opinion of yourself, that you are morally solid, you will never cleanse yourself of sin. Having this opinion of yourself, that you are filled with grace, never will you receive grace. Having this opinion of yourself, that you are holy, you will never attain holiness.

His first arrival was arrival as Redeemer. His second arrival will be arrival as Judge to demand an account from humanity for humanity's conduct pertaining to God's divine redemption gifted them.

His voice gathered in this darkness and shadow of death is comforting and consoling for the Christian, progressing and consummating our earthly journey, traveling to heaven.

Humanity never desires to declare itself as a proponent of evil, although it is immersed in evil. It constantly aspires to declare itself virtuous.

Humility is heavenly life on earth.

I would not advise you to dwell deep into the details and specifics of your sinful qualities. Gather them all into one pot of repentance and throw it into the abyss of God's kind heart. A constant or detailed recollection of all your sins accomplished during your secular life will further throw you into despondency, perplexity and confusion.

If a person suffer apostasy, is defeated, gone astray, deceived, sinning before God, let him not submit to despair or melancholy. Be condescending to yourself, do not condemn yourself. If you are defeated, then run to God with repentance and your defeat will be forgiven, otherwise the sin of your guilt will further ruin you.

If fallen spirits do not exist, then the incarnation of God has no reason, no purpose.

If the saints reprimanded the sinning and criminal, then they reprimanded by God's command, due to their responsibility, by inspiration of the Holy Spirit, and not by inspiration of their passions and demons. Whoever decides to arbitrarily reprimand brother or sister or state something to him, he clearly discloses and proves that he considered himself more prudence and more benevolent than the person he is reprimanding, that he is acting due to the drive of his desire and by deception of demonic thoughts.

If you have the need to converse with yourself, do not heap upon yourself flattery, but reproach. Bitter medicines are useful to us in our fallen state. Who flatters themselves has already accepted their compensation here on earth – and just self-deception, praise and a love of the world that is enmity toward God. There is nothing for him to await in the eternity except condemnation.

If you prepare yourself ahead of time for sorrow, you will notice it ameliorated. If you reject comfort, it will still comfort those who are worthy of it.

If you want to be a faithful and zealous child of the Orthodox Church, then work to attain this by the observance of the Evangelic commands pertaining to your close associate. Do not be bold enough to rebuke him! Do not be bold enough to teach him! Do not be bold enough to condemn and discredit him! Such behavior is not faith, but insane zeal, conceit, pride.

In essence, what we see and call death is only the separation of the soul from the body, but before all it is for those already dead their departure from the true life of God.

In order to battle the enemy, it is absolutely necessary to see him. Without seeing the spirits the battle against them has no field.

It is better to acknowledge your ignorance than to state something harming someone's soul.

It is impossible to draw near to God without temptations. The untempted virtue, the holy fathers said, is not a virtue! If you see some person who is magnified from among the Orthodox benevolent, but he lives without any temptations and succeeds in secular matters, know that his virtue, his orthodoxy is not accepted of God.

It is pleasing to God for our autonomy to be tested, the direction it is inclined.

It is very ineffective to read the commands of the New Testament only for pleasure and be impressed with the high standard morality that is there contained. Pitifully, many are just satisfied with this.

Love toward associate is a road leading to love toward God, because it is Christ's good will to secretly clothe God in each of our associates as He did in Christ. Do not think, beloved brother, that the command to love associate was always so close to our fallen heart. The command is spiritual, but our hearts consist of flesh and blood. The command is new, but our heart is obsolete.

Love toward God is fully spiritual. What is born of the spirit is spirit. What is born of flesh is flesh. Corporeal love that is born of flesh and blood has it own qualities of substance and decay. It is inconsistent, alterable; its fire is totally dependent on the material substance. Hearing from the Scripture that our God is a fire, that love is a fire, and feeling within ourselves the fire of natural love, do not think that this fire is one and the same. No! These fires are hostile to one another and will consume one another.

May the all-benevolent God gift us a manner to passage the earthly life so that we would during the time assigned us sever association with the spirits of the fallen, and enter into association with the spirits of the saints. So that we, accomplishing this, and after having unclothed the body, will be added to the spirits of the saints, and not to the spirits of the rejected.

My heart is agreeable to be kind-hearted as long as my blood is flowing; but for Christ to be kind-hearted according to his own command led him to crucifixion.

Natural love will acquire for its loved one only the earthly; it does not think about the heavenly. It struggles against heaven and the Holy Spirit because it exists under the authority of the evil one, the unclean and ruining spirit.

Not one human has remained immortal on earth. But meanwhile we live as if we are immortal. The thought of death and eternity slips away from us, becoming for us something completely alien. This is a clear witness the human race resides in apostasy. Our souls are bound by some type of gloom, by some type of irremovable shackles of self-deception by which the world and time restrain us in captivity and enslavement.

One sensation of all the heart's sensations during its fallen state can be its utilization in invisible divine services: sorrow over sins, over sinfulness, over fall, over your ruin, all of this the process of wailing, repentance, breaking of the spirit. With the sensation of repentance all other sensations are silent.

Ordinarily it seems people's punishments sprout from their violation of God's law and going astray from them.

Others discover that solitude is the closest means to spiritual success, while others say that it is love toward associates that leads to spiritual success. My heart more prefers the latter, because love toward associate is the obligatory debt of every person. As far as silence is concerned, only a few are capable.

Our virtues must indispensably contain some impurities of uncleanness that evolve from our weaknesses. We must not demand from our soul, from our heart, more than they are able to provide.

People that are vain and with a high opinion of themselves live to teach and instruct. Do not worry about the worth of their advice. They do not imagine that they can impose on some associate an incurable wound due to stupid advice that is accepted with unconditional assurance by some inexperienced novitiate whose blood is heated.

People who arbitrarily follow the inspiration of their heart, conducting themselves autonomously, do not cease in this state to be instruments, blind instruments of divine providence, according to the endless wisdom and omnipotence of this providence.

Pertaining to the rules of prayer, know that this is for you, and you are not for [the prayer], but this is for the Lord. So have this freedom with discernment. Add more when you are weak; subtract some when you are strong. Be moderate and careful in one and the other.

Prayer shines in the reflection of the drops of tears we shed, just as the colorful rainbow is reflected in the drops of rain. The rainbow being a reflection of the symbol of peace between God and people.

Preserve yourself in profound peace and reject all that violates peace as incorrect, even though they may appear to have a superficial aspect of right and proper.

Pride is a reliable indication of an empty person, a slave of passions, a sign that Christ's teaching has not found a means to access his soul.

Repentance fulfills on its own the shortcomings of a person's virtue, and allows a person to adopt the virtues of the Redeemer! God provided us repentance as assistance to our weaknesses.

Struggling with passions is extraordinarily useful. It brings a person closer to meekness of spirit.

Suffering will end when life ends.

Take a look: vanity, flattery, insensitivity are slithering in front of you! When they achieve their goal, they will laugh at you and abandon you at their first occasion. Do not ever devote your generosity toward some self-interest.

When sorrow exchanges places with comfort, and comfort with sorrows, this births belief in God and callousness to the world.

The Book of Psalms is the supreme spiritual book. There is no need to accept it literally. A literal comprehension of Scripture kills the soul.

The constant sinful life is constant denial of Christ, if not performed even in word and thought.

The desire to see spirits, curiously learn something about them and from them, is an indication of the greatest stupidity, as well as complete lack of moral knowledge and the active traditions of the Orthodox Church. The knowledge of spirits is acquired entirely by means other than an inexperienced and careless researcher supposes. Open communication with spirits for the inexperienced is either the greatest disaster or will serve as the source for the greatest disaster.

The devil is ready to increase our healthy mind by ten-fold and increase by a thousand-fold our practical information, as long as he can steal from us the knowledge of the cross by which a person will stand on the right side of God.

The devil strives to disperse our gazes, so that eternity will escape from our gazes.

The first command given by the Savor of the world to all of humanity without reservation is the command of repentance. This command encompasses, includes, locates within itself the balance of commands. The most terrifying act to do to yourself is to reject repentance! The terrifying coldness, ruthlessness toward yourself, is the result of neglecting repentance. The person cruel to himself cannot be but cruel to others. The person kind-hearted to himself with the acceptance of repentance becomes merciful to both himself and associates. The primary sign of pride is a cold attitude toward close associates and abandoning the ecclesiastical confession.

The fundamental quality of all visions sent of God consists of they bringing humility and contriteness to the soul, filling it with a fear of God, the cognizance of our sinfulness and meaninglessness. On the other hand, visions that cause us to thrust ourselves arbitrarily into opposition to God's will only lead us to conceit and arrogance, into having a high opinion of ourselves. Our only joy then becomes the satisfaction of our vanity and ambition and self-interests.

The most dangerous form of prayer consists in a petitioner creating dreams or pictures with the ability of his imagination, adapting them obviously from the Sacred Scriptures but essentially from his own personal state, from his fall, from his sinfulness, from his self-deception. With such pictures he flatters his own opinion, his vanity, his arrogance, his pride, only deceiving himself. The dreamer, from the first step on the path of petition, departs from the sphere of truth and enters the sphere of falsity, into the sphere of Satan, and arbitrarily submits to the influence of Satan.

The number of the hairs of our head are known by God. Not even one forgotten bird falls outside the will of God its creator. So is it possible for temptation to approach without His will?

The offering pleasant unto God is a contrite heart, a broken spirit. In His anger God repels the offering brought with self-reliance, with a proud opinion of oneself.

The person who believes in dreams is like chasing after your shadow and the person who attempts it will catch it.

The qualities of the new person must be all new. No obsolete quality of any type should remain in him.

The soul, wherever it might be residing, if it is not defeated by insensitivity, everywhere feels a need for God's word. At the same time the temptation to fall presses on it and tightens

The source of allure is pride and its fruit is abundant pride.

The spiritual vision of spirits is accomplished by the mind and heart. The heart rebukes evil spirits. The mind is insufficient to do this, since it is unable to differentiate with solely its personal strengths the apparitions of truth from the apparitions of falsity that are concealed by an apparition of truth.

There is no agreement of any type between the Evangelic definition of goodness and that goodness of fallen human nature. The goodness of our fallen nature is intermixed with bad, and so inherently this goodness can be transformed into something bad, just as delicious and healthy food can become poisonous when it is mixed with poison.

Think about this, that if we must provide an answer for every expletive we say, how much more strenuous will it be to answer for God's word spoken for the purpose of vanity and incited by self-interest.

This item is established, that for human souls one place of residence is pre-assigned, the identical consolation and the identical penalty as with Angels, and this serves as an indication that souls in essence in all areas are similar to Angels.

Those infected with a high opinion of their dignity, especially regarding their holiness, are capable of and prepared to produce all violence, all hypocrisy, guile, deceit and every malice.

Those long unread books collected on shelves become infiltrated with dust and ruined from mildew. A person who takes such a book meets with great difficulty in attempting to read it. So is my conscience. Long not being reinvestigated, it opens only with great difficulty. Having opened it, I do not find the satisfaction I was awaiting. Only ripe sins appear sufficiently clear. The small type of the words, and so many of them, are almost blurred and it is difficult to decipher their original form.

Those people who demand from their associates a complete estrangement of faults have a faulty understanding of this subject.

To recognize on your own any and every good deed of yours is nothing more than a state of self-deception. This state of self-deception serves as the basis of demonic allure. The fallen angel residing in the false, proud understanding of Christianity finds a refuge, to this understanding he comfortably grafts in his deception, and by means of deception it subjects a person to its authority, casting him into what is called demonic allure.

True humility is unnatural to corporeal contemplation. Humility belongs to a religious intellect.

Various colors and objects of the tangible world as if do not exist for a blind person. So it is with those blinded by sin; the spiritual world and spirits likewise do not exist. Our ignorance of something does not in any manner serve as an indication of its non-existence.

We strive to recognize our sins and wash them with tears of repentance before that time, that awesome time when any repentance will only torment us, rather than heal us.

We will die for natural love toward associate and will live again with a new love, a love that is in God.

John of Kronshtadt

1829 – 1908

Russian Orthodox Priest and Philanthropist

Especially venerated among the Russian prelates and mystics of the 19th century was John Ilyich Sergeev of Kronshtadt. He was born October 18, 1829, in Archangelsk Province, northern Russian, to a peasant family that was involved in the local Russian Orthodox parish church. His father wanted John to become part of the clergy, and sent him to seminary in Archangelsk. Later, John attended the Petersburg Religious Academy from 1851–1855, and upon graduation was appointed to the Morskoi (Naval) Cathedral in Kronshtadt, the Imperial Naval Base at St Petersburg.

He ministered at the same church for the next 26 years. Thousands upon thousands from all over Russia flocked to his church to listen to his sermons and watch him perform liturgy and recite prayers. The parishioners were mesmerized, believing that Fr. John took their prayers during liturgy and delivered them directly to God. Pilgrims asked him regularly for his counsel and blessing, and opened their hearts to him.

John of Kronshtadt's ministry was focused on philanthropy, assisting the needy of St Petersburg. He opened work houses for the unemployed, schools for children, a dining hall with meals at inexpensive prices, an orphanage, a shelter for abused women and abandoned children. Much work at his parish was dedicated to helping men with alcohol addiction.

Fr. John died December 20, 1908.

Among people who aspire to maintain a religious life, there occurs a very subtle and very difficult war through their thoughts every moment of life – it is a spiritual battle. Every moment you must have your eyes wide open at all about you, in order to notice any thoughts entering your soul from the devil's influence and then repel them. Such people should also have a heart that is always aflame with faith, humility, love. If it is otherwise it is so easy for diabolic guile to settle within you, or create unbelief or less belief, and this will lead to doing wrong, from which it will be difficult to cleanse yourself.

Due to a lack of attention you have fallen into the devil's captivity, and due to your ingratitude and pride. Strive to free yourself from this prison with the help of the all-powerful warrior, Lord Jesus Christ, who has defeated our common enemy and foe. As a result all divine strength is provided you. Look upon the example of the struggles of the Apostles, saints, martyrs and all the prelates and imitate them, and they will always help those who call upon them in faith.

Having Christ in your heart, fear that you do not lose him, but keep him in rest in your heart. To bitterly begin some words, it will be difficult and will cost you many bitter tears to again exert the effort to attach yourself to him after your fall. With all your strength hold fast to Christ, keep him and do not loose your holy boldness in his presence.

I am a human and in me the mercy, truth and justice of God operate without interruption. God at one time will pardon and comfort, and at another time will punish and humiliate me with sorrows for my inner and corporal movements against Him. But the world is filled with people just like me. This means that the

Lord displays his mercy, truth and justice in them, just as He does in me. He operates all in all.

If the Lord was not a lover of humanity and long patient, then would He tolerate from us such immense wrongs, would He have been incarnated, have suffered and died for you, provided you His immaculate body and blood, upon which the Angels gaze in fear and trepidation? Would He have started to deliver you from sins and from spiritual death an infinite number of times? But now His entire life He tolerates from us this innumerable amount of wrongs and just waits for our attention toward Him. Glorify His love and long-patience. Imagine how matters would be without Him, without his salvation. Just terror and agitation would envelope the soul, and the unrepentant sinners will receive God's wrath on the day of the wrath and revelation of the just judgment of God.

Just as a soul encompasses the entirety of its body, so God encompasses the entire universe, all world is encompassed by God. The soul fills the entire body, and the Spirit of the Lord fills all the world, Pr 1:7. However the soul is limited by the body, but the Spirit of the Lord is not limited by the world and is not restrained in the world, as the soul is in the body.

Prayer is the ascension of the mind and heart to God. Based on this it is obvious that prayer cannot be effective if a person's mind and heart are firmly connected to something corporeal, for example, money or honor, or some passion still retained in the person's heart: hate or envy of others, because passion regularly binds the heart, while God wants to expand it and provide it true freedom.

Regarding the remission of sins of others, pray such as you pray about the remission of your own errors when they, imposing sorrow and suppression upon your soul, motivate you with pain and illness, grieving the heart. And so with tears beseech God for His pardon, and pray at the same time about the salvation of others as you do for yourself. If you will attain this and train yourself to do this as a habit, then you will receive from the Lord an abundance of spiritual gifts, the gifts of the Holy Spirit, which loves the soul, having compassion on the salvation of others, because He, the holiest Spirit, in every manner wants to save all of us, as long as we do not oppose Him. Do not harden your hearts. The Spirit intercedes for us in sighs that cannot be expressed.

Separate within yourself the life-providing Spirit from the death-dealing spirit that is strangling your soul. When your soul possesses good thoughts, matters will go well and easy for you. When you have calm and joy upon your heart, then a spirit of goodness resides within you, the Holy Spirit. But when malicious thoughts or malicious motions evolve from your heart, then is this is bad and difficult. When a person is internally agitated, then he possesses an evil spirit, a malicious spirit.

Tears have the power to cleanse the defilement of our hearts, and suffering is likewise applied, because through suffering the sinful expanse of the heart is compressed, and this compression of the heart makes the tears flow easier.

The enemy entices using corporeal beauty and a minute's happiness. The enemy repulses and considers as nothing what evolves from God, the source of spiritual and eternal beauty. And you also are to desire the eternal spiritual beauty – God, who created all beauty. Ascend from the decaying and temporal and stinking to the imperishable, the eternally fragrant and miraculously fragrant bodies of the saints, those alive yet after their death. God, in Your captivity resides humanity, and take into captivity all of the sins we are possible of committing, those that blind the mind and hearts of people.

The heavenly kingdom – consisting of holiness, purity, restraint, prayer, prudence, love toward God and associate – is acquired by effort, that is, the effort of the grace-filled assistance of God and your individual zeal, and the person utilizing such effort will acquire it. The flesh opposes the spirit, that is, every virtue, so we would not do what we want, but for the sake of God and the salvation of the soul and the welfare of our close associates an opposition of every evil, every desire of the flesh and lust is required. So we need to adopt every virtue by such effort.

The human spirit is capable of great wealth. Only meditate from your heart on God, only desire a fervent union with God, and He is immediately with you. And not any walls of a house, not any rivets of a prison gate, not mountains, not abysses can serve as an obstacle. The boldness of a conversation of the creation with its creator, reverently standing in His presence, is food for the soul, it is air and light to nourish it. The creator is the soul's warmth, cleansing of sins, the easy yoke of Christ, his light burden.

The world, as the composition of the living, wise God, is full of life. Everywhere in all is life and wisdom, in everything we see the expression of His mind, and in the whole, so in its parts. This is a genuine book though which we cannot gain knowledge of God. Before the world evolved, only the one living, infinite God existed. When the world was summoned out of nothing into existence, God, of course, did not become limited, but all fullness of life and infinity remained with Him. But this fullness of life and infinity was expressed in His creation, the living and organic, an immeasurable amount and all gifted with life.

What is this history of the human race? History is the fall and then the rise, history is the wavering of humanity's thoughts, family and social life, and the history of the fall of kingdoms and nations or individual cities and establishments. So what picture will our time present? A picture of the fall of all societies. Where is the reason for such a weakness of minds, conditions, establishments, expressly gathered to establish an unstable government and as there are among them others unstable as in the past? Where is the reason for the darkness, weakness and fall? In unbelief, in apostasy from God, from God's wise commands, in reliance upon your blind intellect, in following your passions. And in fact, it is without God, without God's intellect, without God's law, and without God's church which is the pillar and confirmation of the truth, and without all of which societies cannot stand firm and establishments cannot have a strong foundation, and as a result they all eventually collapse. As it states, "Without me you cannot do anything."

When you are on the path to God you will meet obstacles placed by the devil: doubt and unbelief, and likewise malice in your heart toward others who have earned unconditional honor and love, and also other desires. Do not be agitated by them, but know that they are just smoke and the stench of the enemy, and all will move over for you by the work of the Lord Jesus Christ.

When I am with you Lord, I rely on victory. The Lord cannot but be victorious.

Who considers himself prepared to accept grace, who considers himself worthy of God, who awaits and requests His secret arrival, who says that he is ready to accept, hear and see the Lord, is only deceiving himself, he is only flattering himself. Such a person has attained such a high cliff of pride and his fall is into a dark ravine of destruction.

Why do we need to study the teachings of the holy fathers? Because, having studied them, we are able to recognize our own passions and weaknesses, and know whom our struggle is against. So we can utilize the same weapons to proceed in this war against our enemies.

VICTOR DMITRIEVICH KUDRYAVTZOV-PLATONOV

1828 – 1891

Religious Philosopher

Victor Kudryavtzov was born in Kuderev parish, Pskov province, central Russia, on October 9, 1828. His father was a chaplain in the Russian army. Traveling about the country with his parents, Kudryavtzov studied at several seminaries: in Warsaw, Poland; Volinsk, Lithuania; and Mogilyov and Chernigov, Ukraine.

In 1848 he entered Moscow Religious Academy and displayed himself as an exceptional student. He caught the eye of Russian Orthodox Metropolitan Platonov and who subsidized the young student. As a result, Victor attached the prelate's name to his own out of respect. He graduated from the seminary in 1854, and became a professor of theology. He continued at the seminary and taught Biblical history, Greek language, and metaphysics. In 1860, he transferred to the Imperial Moscow University where he taught the history of philosophy and logic through the end of his career.

Occupied with religious philosophy, Kudryavtzov hoped to reach the goal of understanding the secrets of the universe through reason. One of the chief topics was the basis of God's existence. Kudryavtzov was the creator of the system known as transcendental monism. He also authored several works on gnoseology, where he develops his concept of ideal knowledge, presenting it as a direct contemplation of supra-sensation or super-sensitivity. He also provides an analysis of the basic currents of religion during his era and investigates the various proofs of God's existence.

In January 1891, his wife died, and he was unable to endure the loss, and he died later in the year on December 3, 1891.

Just as a person cannot live in this world without food, light, air, and etc, these external conditions of his corporeal existence, so also in the spiritual life he cannot live without truth, without goodness. The initial source of this is unconditional truth and unconditional goodness. And truth and goodness is not something fabricated or created by some person, but it is true and genuine – and objective – existence in the genuinely existing Supreme Entity. The truth and goodness in a person is only his reflection of the rays of a higher light, a reflection more or less strong and clear, according to the measure of purity of the person himself and his capability and moral strength to accept the rays of this light and provide life to his spiritual-moral existence.

The influence of philosophy, of course, will seem to be insignificant if we will have in view only a limited number of philosopher-specialists or an insignificant quantity of readers of books of philosophic content. But it is another matter if we turn our attention to that indirect influence that indicates philosophy to be a means of those philosophic elements that enter into the sphere of every scientific specialist and from those, as we have seen, who cannot deny even one point of science, having the strength of their deep-rooted philosophic knowledge.

Fundamental philosophic ideas and concepts are not something continually being revealed anew. Confined deep in a person's mind, they are intrinsic to each one, their essence known from a long time back, and they can only be unveiled, explained and proven though study.

All the processes of humanity's religious development can essentially be called a search for the absolute consummation. God is a total-consummate substance: complete thought that penetrates and permeates all religions, the eternal kernel of truth that is maintained inside the shell of all possibilities, or sometimes at least with imperfect propositions.

Mysticism can only state what is somewhat supra-sensitive, but it cannot state anything pertaining to what is reality, because every definition of some quality or attribute of an object already is the region of distinguishing deliberation, of which mysticism does not want to know.

I heard said that religious ideas first appeared and were confirmed at the time when many people were still very undeveloped and untaught, when every mental contrivance that seemed to attract some attention was accepted as belief. But in particular this very supposed lack of development would have served as an obstacle for the expansion of religious ideas if it was really no more than a contrivance. The more mentally undeveloped and superficial the person, the greater the difficulty for him to believe in the existence of what is not plainly shown to him or something he cannot experience.

That awesome displays of nature excite fear in a person, this is true. But in what manner fear is here united to veneration, that is, religious attitude to the object of fear, is decisively unexplainable. Even animals sense fear during threatening displays of nature, and even stronger than does a human. But why does such fear not transmit into them and create in them some veneration, as it does in religion?

So where will we find this common mind of nature, this higher thought, that is directing everything according to the law of harmony and order? Or are we supposed to recognize the entire world as some type of conscious-intellectual creature, as an external shell of innumerable diverse objects, and suppose its displays to be the world's soul, just as did some ancient philosophers. Or, if we were to abandon this presentation of an unripened growth of philosophy, we must allow this intellect and this mind to direct all the individual displays of the world to one goal, which is the mind and intellect of the divine God, who governs the world with His providence.

In order for us, in our life, to walk the narrow and difficult path of virtue, we must be convinced that this path will lead us to a higher goal of our existence – perfection and bliss. But is a similar type of conviction possible with the deliberation that the Creator of this world does not turn any attention to us, that He has installed us and subjected our private life to the will of incidences, that His gaze is turned not on us, but only on the fixed pattern of the world and history? So then why should we worry about self-perfection, virtue, struggling with vices, of our efforts will not only remain without assistance, but will pass completely unnoticed before God's eyes?

A person's alienation and departure from God could not summon a comparable alienation of God from the person and his complete abandonment to some arbitrary fate. On the contrary, the more a person departs from God, the more that God according to His goodness will strive to draw closer to him and seek the perishing person by virtue of His supreme love toward him. The more and more the alienation of a person from God only summons His greater attraction to the person until it reaches that moment of limitation, when his intense and extreme alienation from God summons finally the most supreme act of Divine love to be as close to the human as possible – the incarnation of God.

From this point it is apparent that parallel with the natural religious development, there must proceed another form of religious cognizance, where the objective facet will appear as the chief defining principle. The development of religious life will be dependent on the special and prime activity of the Deity, God Himself is revealed in religion as its primary guide and teacher. This will be a supernatural or revelatory religion.

Indeed, if God created the world initially, primordially, by the free act of His omnipotent will and provided nature with known laws, then of course, He has the equal authority to change these laws, if He should feel it necessary for some higher purpose. If they tell us that these laws are immutable and constant, then we must note that this immutability and constancy is not absolute, even though it evolves from the indispensability of the divine nature, which would be the composition of these manifestations. Their constancy is dependant on the free will of God.

Macarius Optinski

1788 – 1860

Russian Orthodox Monk and Monastery *Staretz*

Macarius was born Mikhail Nikolaevich Ivanov on November 20, 1788. His family were aristocrats from the Orlov Province, central Russia. He received a basic education, but at age 14 went to work as a bookkeeper at the Lvov district treasury. He returned to Orlov in 1806 after his father's death. In 1810, he went on a pilgrimage to a local hermitage about 30 miles from home. Once arriving he made the decision to remain and in December 1810 he took vows as a monk and accepted the name Melchizedek. In March 1815 he was promoted and accepted the new name of Macarius. He remained there until 1834 when he moved to the Optinski Monastery.

In 1839, Macarius became *staretz*, or Father Superior, of Optinski Monastery and he remained there through the balance of his life. He died September 7, 1860.

All of life is a marvelous mystery known only to the one God. There are no such things in life as accidents or blind circumstances; all is the result of God's forethought. We do not know the significance of one or the other circumstances, in front of us are a large numbers of caskets, but no keys.

Because our minds and hearts are not cleansed and are unable to clearly view the mysterious meanings of Sacred Scripture, they at least need to be humbled and God is strong to send us the illumination of true intellect.

Before worrying about perishing by cholera, we should about the sins that burden us, because the scythe of death will mow the person as grass, and even without cholera. And so place all your hopes on the Lord God, without whose will even birds do not die, much less a human.

Each person is in need of the fire of tribulation and temptation and experience in patience. You look at things from the point of how God's providence is concerned over our salvation: to one it is more, and to another less incidences leading to patience and instruction is required. While for some other the time has not yet arrived.

Eat all that is served you without doubt to God's glory. And along with this place a guard over your lips to curb profanity, expletives and discredit. This is more important than a fast.

Every evil occurs due to a lack of self-restraint. Fasting motivates a person to prayer, and which is especially odious to the enemy. People come to me for counsel and for confession. Among other things I counsel them to observe the holy fasts. All of them agree, but when the matter deals with actually keeping a fast, they do not want or cannot or some other excuse. The enemy is agitating them to not observe the holy fasts.

God wants our salvation and organizes it in a manner incomprehensible to us. Abandon yourself to God's will and you will acquire peace for your sorrowful soul and heart.

If a person will not be deprived of the Lord's compensation for just a bowl of cold water, then how much more of God's mercy will you be worthy of for your participation in some benevolence. Studying the books of the holy fathers is a drink, not tangible, but living, instructing and saving a person.

No matter what book you will pick up, even if is the best of all authors, but after you read it several times, you will become bored with it. But the Gospel, the more that you read it, the more you will receive comfort and every good sensation.

Profound meaning is hidden in the Gospel, which is gradually explained to a person who attentively reads Scripture. And by comprehending the inexhaustible depth of its contents, we can acknowledge the divine origin of these books, because it is also possible to differentiate the compositions of human hands from the direct inspiration of God.

Read the holy Gospel, penetrate into it using your spirit, make it the rule of your life, the book upon your altar. In every conduct and daily question, act in agreement with the Gospel's instruction. This is the sole light of your life.

Reading the books of the holy fathers, comprehend the passions you possess, and how to oppose them and how to uproot them, depending on God's help to accomplish this.

The constant sorrows sent by God to humanity are a portent of God's special providence regarding humans.

Utilize food to God's glory, what can strengthen your corporeal substance, in the manner that the ecclesiastical statutes have instituted the proper time for meat and meatless food.[16] Do not listen to those who counsel you to do the contrary – not to eat and drink at all. According to the teaching of the holy fathers, we must not be mortifiers of our body, but mortifiers of the passions of our body: pride and vanity, promiscuity, greed, anger, envy, insult,

---

[16] Wednesday and Friday are considered meatless days in Russian Orthodoxy.

malice toward associates, and others. In their place we must plant in ourselves: love, meekness, humility, kindness, patience, and other Christian virtues, all strengthened by prayer.

We should not believe in premonitions. There are no premonitions of any type. The Lord guides us with His providence, and I will not depend on some bird's chirp, or some assumed day, or something else. Who believes superstitions only finds it difficult on his soul. But on the contrary, who considers himself dependant only on God's providence, he will have joy in his soul.

Who does not possess consolation and patiently endures all assigned him, he can hope in its entirety that there, that is, in the future life, he will receive consolation, one that is great and indescribable. Take courage and be strong and hope on the assistance and mercy of God.

You think that the Lord punishes us for our sins. Perhaps. And perhaps for the testing of our faith, and maybe for one or another reason. Nonetheless, whatever it might be, it is your concern. We need to view the temporal punishments that affect us as God's grace and love toward us. Because the All-kind Lord wants to use temporal sorrows to deliver us from the eternal horrors of torment, and to meditate on this is awesome.

SERAPHIM SAROVSKI

July 19, 1759 – January 2, 1833

Russian Orthodox Monk and Mystic

Seraphim of Sarov was born July 19, 1759, as Prokhor Moshnin, in Kursk, Russia, along the northern Ukraine border, in the family of a middle-income merchant. At the age of 20 he abandoned his family home and went first to Kiev, and then walked to Sarov Monastery, in Nizhni-Novgorod province, where he was accepted as a postulant in 1778. After 6 years, in 1786, he was tonsured as a monk and became hieromonk. He declined becoming the subsequent abbot and in 1794 departed into the forest, where he began his period of fasting, silence and seclusion at a secluded hut. He returned to Sarov Monastery as an elder, accepting visitors and providing counsel. During this period he had many visions.

Seraphim died January 2, 1833.

It is necessary to equip yourself with God's word, because God's word is the bread of Angels and sustains the soul that hungers for God. More than all you must exert effort in reciting the New Testament and Psalms while standing. This will provide your mind's illumination and which will change gradually into a divine mind. It is necessary to train yourself to do this, so your soul will as if swim in God's law, which guiding you will direct your life. Very useful is to occupy yourself with reciting God's word alone and to read the entire Bible carefully. As a result of you doing this, God will not leave you or cease providing you with His mercy, but will fill you with the gift of knowledge. When a person equips his soul with God's word then his mental faculties will be fluent in knowing what is good and what is bad.

Prayer, fasting, vigils and all other Christian virtues, as good as they are on their own, however are not in their entirety the goal of our Christian life. They serve as an indispensable means for us to attain this goal. The true goal of our Christian life consists in acquiring God's Holy Spirit. Fasting and vigils and prayers and charity and every benevolent effort we do for the sake of Christ are means by which we can acquire God's Holy Spirit.

What is the reason we discredit other brethren? Because we do not attempt to comprehend ourselves. Whoever is occupied with comprehending himself does not have the time to notice anything about others. Ascertain yourself and cease discrediting others. Condemn some malicious conduct, but not the person committing the act. We must first consider ourselves sinners, and be cautious of any bad act that we might do since it will be our own, and have compassion on the poor conduct of others. The devil hates this since he is the great deceiver. My joy, I beseech you, is to acquire a peaceful spirit, and then a thousand souls that surround you will be saved.

A saint is a sinner who made the decision to rectify his life.

Acquire peace in your soul, and thousands surrounding you will be saved.

Be pleasing to the Lord God, and should the person be tested with the infliction of some illness, then He will provide him strength for endurance.

Buy a brush, buy a bloom, and more often sweep your cell, because as your cell is swept clean, so will your soul be swept clean.

Depart from sin and your illnesses will depart, because they are imposed on us due to sin.

Humility can subject the entire world.

If a person knew that the Lord prepared him for His heavenly kingdom, he would be prepared to sit his whole life in a hole with insects.

If the concept of family is destroyed, then governments will collapse and nations will become depraved.

In order to escape condemnation, you must pay attention to yourself. Do not accept strange influences from others and be dead to all the world.

It is better for us to disdain what is not ours, that is, the temporal and transitory; and rather want what is ours, that is, the imperishable and immortal.

It is necessary to strive by using all means available to preserve psychological peace and not to agitate insult or irritation from others. To do this it is necessary, and however possible, to restrain yourself from anger and by means of attention to guard your mind from indecent exposures.

Judge yourself, so the Lord does not judge you.

Let there be thousands who live with you in peace, but of the thousands only reveal your secret to one.

Out of joy a person can contribute something very appropriate, but from inner miserliness – nothing.

The true goal of our Christian life consists in obtaining the Holy Spirit.

The world lies in evil, we need to know of this, remember this, and defeat it to the extent we possibly can.

Virginity is the supreme virtue, a state of being equal to the Angels, and it can stand on its own merit relative to all other virtues.

We must condescend in our souls to its weaknesses and imperfections and endure its shortcomings, just as we endure the shortcomings of our associates, but we are not to become lazy, and rather continually motivate ourselves to do better.

When a person accepts something divine, then he rejoices in his heart. But when it is diabolic, then he is confused.

When a person is suffering a large insufficiency in items he requires for his body, then it is difficult to overcome melancholy. But this, of course, only pertains to weak souls.

When a person strives to possess a contrite heart and undisturbed and peaceful meditation, then all the traps of the enemy become ineffective. Where there is peace of mind, there the Lord God Himself resides. Peace is His residence.

GRIGORI SAVVICH SKOVORODA

1722 · 1794

Christian Humanist, Nomad, Educator, Musician, Poet

Grigori Skovoroda was born December 3, 1722. He entered the Kievo-Brethren Academy in September 1738 at the ago of 16. Not including a 2-year interruption he spent a total of 10 years at the Kiev Academy.

In 1742, the 20-year old Skovoroda was enlisted to sing at the elegant royal court of Empress Elizabeth Petrovna. He did not remain in St Petersburg long and in 1744, returned to the academy. He continued to have an excellent singing voice his entire life.

At the Kievo-Brethren School at age 22 Skovoroda zealously tackled Hebrew, Greek and Latin, mastering them over the next 6 years. He also intensely studied rhetoric, philosophy, metaphysics, mathematics, natural science and theology. Later he learned to speak German and Italian. During this time he translated Greek and Latin philosophers into Ukrainian.

Skovoroda graduated from the school and decided to travel, about 1750. Skovoroda started his travels through central Europe as a philosophic nomad. All he took with him was a staff and a small purse hanging from his neck with the least of personal necessities. He traveled on foot though Poland, Prussia, Germany, Italy and the intervening countries and where he could with at the least expense. Now it was 1759 and Skovoroda was hired to teach at the Kharkov Seminary until 1769.

The final period of his life – from 1769 to his death in 1794 – was his period of mendicancy, an ascetic severance from all the normal comforts of human continuance and also his teaching career. Skovoroda at age 46 transformed himself into a nomad, without possessions and entirely dependant on the will of God, meaning, the kindness and hospitality of Ukrainian and Russian villagers. He traveled on foot through Ukraine and southern Russia, and writing his version of Christian humanism, fables, songs, and philosophic narratives, in the intervals at his various temporary residences.

Skovoroda passed away in a small village in north-east Ukraine, on the morning of October 29, 1794. He was 2 months short of 72.

Gratitude to the blessed God because He has made easy what is necessary, and difficult what is unnecessary.

There is nothing sweeter for a person and nothing more needful than happiness, and there is nothing easier to acquire than this. Gratitude to the blessed God. God's Kingdom is within us. Happiness in the heart, the heart in love, love in the eternal law.

This is continuous fine weather and a sun that never sets which enlightens the abyss of the darkness of the heart. Gratitude to the blessed God.

What would occur if happiness, so needed and so loved by all, was dependent on place, on time, on flesh and blood? I will say it more clearly: What would occur if God was to confine happiness in America or on the Canary Islands or in Asian Jerusalem or in the chambers of a king or during the age of Solomon or in wealth or in the desert or in rank or in science or in health? Then our happiness would be meager. Who can travel to these places? How can all be born during the same era? How can we all fit in one rank and file? What type of happiness is this if founded on the sand of someone's flesh, or in limited space and time, or on a mortal person? Is this not difficult? Yes. Difficult and impossible. Gratitude to the blessed God because He has made the difficult unnecessary.

Do you want to be fortunate at present? Do not seek happiness across the sea, do not ask it of a person, do not journey throughout the planet, do not ramble yard to yard, do not drag yourself across the earth, do not worry over Jerusalem. With gold you can buy a village, an item difficult to find, something you could not find and live without, but happiness as an indispensable necessity is everywhere free and gifted always.

The air and sun are always with you, everywhere and free. All that flees away from you, know that it is someone else's and do not consider it yours. All of this is alien and superfluous. What are your needs? For this reason it is difficult. If it was undependable it would never have parted from you. Gratitude to the blessed God.

Happiness is not from heaven, nor does it depend on the earth. Say together with David, "What do I have in heaven? And what do I want from you on earth?"[17]

What is required of you? That which is very easy. But what is it that is easy? O, my friend, all that is difficult is hard and bitter and evil and false. There is something easy. That my friend is what is needful. What is needful? Only one item is needful. One thing only is necessary for you, one thing only that is good and easy; all the rest is labor and illness.

We have measured the earth, sun, stars, depths of the oceans, and crawled into the depths of the earth for gold, viewed the moon for rivers and mountains, discovered new stars and know their magnitude, filled canyons, and built ingenious machines. Hardly a day passes if something new is not thought of. What are we not capable of doing? What are we unable to do? But there is something, and it is the most important, that nonetheless escapes us. What this is we ourselves cannot identify. We are just like a child: he senses that something is not right, but why it is not right he cannot identify.

---

[17] Ps 73:25

Many wander about Jerusalem, the Jordan, Bethlehem, the mountains of Carmel, on Tabor, the hills of Sinai and Athens, smell the regions between the Tigris and Euphrates Rivers. Here he is, of course, they think, "Here, here! Here is Christ! Here! We have found him." They cry to others, "Here is Christ." "I know," cried the Angel, "the crucified Jesus is the Christ. He is not here. No!" Many seek him at the highest reaches of the earth, in majestic homes, with ceremonial pillars, and other places. Many seek with their mouth wide open viewing the clear blue starry outer space, the sun, the moon, the entire Copernican universe. "He is not here!" They seek him in long prayers and liturgies, in fasts, in sacred rites. They seek him in money, in a hundred-year healthy life, in a physical resurrection, in a physical healing of the eyes. "He is not here!" What is the problem? So where is he? Of course he is here. If we were to orate our sermons, learn all the prophetic mysteries, relocated mountains, resurrect the dead, distribute our possessions, torture our bodies with bitter cold, and etc, but the Angel appearing as lightning only cries to them, "He is not here." Of course, he is nowhere to be found if he is not here. So what? Of course my friend, for you he is not here. You do not know him and so cannot see him. Take off your shoes with Moses and discard your stupid Here. Yes! On behalf of the Angel I say to you, "You will find him in the blink of an eye."

The unfortunate scribe, he read the prophets, sought a man and tripped over a corpse and fell over him. Christ is not in the kingdom of corpses. He always lives and that is where to seek him. If, first, you do not seek inside yourself, it is useless to seek in other places.

Always, in every age and among all people, his voice has echoed in the heart of each person who did not extinguish within himself the spark of Divinity through carnal passion. Satan sowed 7 evil deeds in the hearts of people, instigating their evil desires. The motivation to materialize these desires enslaves our flesh and suffocates the Divine fire. On the contrary, once defeating the flesh, the spirit ascends from servile obedience of nature to a ruling nature, to its initial birth and to its beginningless beginning. Having cleansed itself in this contact, the soul is discharged from the bodily earth and the earthly body from tight confines flies as spirit in freedom. The inner spirit exists, but all external items that are accessible to the senses are a passing shadow, a stream of water changing without interruption. Our residence in the world is the journey of a pilgrim, the journey of the generation of Israel to the Promised Land. The generation of Israel, the descendents of Abraham, who first saw truth through a bodily vestment, are those people who have recognized the spirit in themselves, or, recognized something. Such people are seldom met, less than a white raven; they are to be sought with the lamp of Diogenes. To their number belongs all who recognize the truth, regardless of what faith or nationality they adhere to.

Soul, benefit and beauty resides in all of our deeds and conversations, and without it all is dead and vile. All of us are born without it, although for it. Who is more naturally inclined and willing towards it, he is more noble and shaper; and who has greater participation with it, he is the more genuine, but it is not the assistant who inwardly senses the bliss or satisfaction. Those set apart depend on it alone in developing thought for the human race. It is the most beautiful face of God, which he, at some time sealing it upon our souls, turns us from wild and ugly monsters or deformed humans that are wild beasts, towards companionship and into testifiable, communal people, valuable, passive, temperate, magnanimous and equitable.

You want to acquire as much gratification for your body as possible. But will your body live very long? To worry about goodness for the body is just like a person building a home for himself on ice. What type of joy can exist in such a life, what type of tranquility? Do you not sense danger continually, that sooner or later the ice will melt and sooner or later the time will come for you to depart from your mortal body. Move your home to some stable field, and work for what will not die: improve your soul, free yourself from sins, deceits and superstitions.

This most blessed nature or spirit keeps the entire world in movement, just like the ingenuity of the mechanism of a mechanical clock on a tower. The existence of all creation follows the consideration of the Father. He Himself enlivens, feeds, arranges, repairs, protects and according to His own will, which is called the general law or statute, and then He returns it to its original coarse material or soil, which we call death.

For this reason the intelligent antiquity equated it with mathematics or geometry, because it could always be arranged proportionately or measured, or molded into various figures, for example: grass, trees, animals and all else. While the Jewish sages compared him to a potter?[18] This is common providence because it pertains to the welfare of all creatures.

Just as there are few who presently comprehend God, so it is not surprising that in antiquity they often venerated objects as God, which was a common error, and for this reason their entire worship service was ludicrous.

However, during all these ages the peoples still believed in a secret someone and were in agreement on this matter, and it was a power effusing everywhere and possessing all.

For this reason to honor and remember Him throughout the entire earthly sphere, buildings were publicly dedicated, just as at present all of this everywhere continues. And although for example the subject may in error display veneration to the personal attendant instead of the master, but no one seems to debate the matter that he has a sovereign over him, whom perhaps he has never seen in public. His subject is every nation, and everyone likewise recognizes their enslavement in His presence. This type of faith is common and simple.

---

[18] Rom 9:21

The law of God resides forever, while the traditions of people are local and temporal. The law of God is the tree of Paradise, while tradition is its shadow.

The law of God is the fruit of life, while tradition are the leaves. The law of God is God in the heart of a person, while tradition is the leaf of a fig tree, often covering a viper. The door of the temple of God is the law of God, while tradition is the front porch connected to the temple. As far as the entrance to the altar and as far as the tail from the head, so is the distance of tradition from the law of God.

The condition of a clean heart opposes the abyss. It is a calm breath in the soul and the wind of winnowing, the Holy Spirit. It is like a beautiful garden, soft winds, fragrant flowers and fulfilled consolations, where the imperishable tree of life flowers.

And these are its fruits: wishing the best for another, gentleness, a good disposition, meekness, sincerity, assurance, safety, satisfaction, encouragement, and other inalienable traits.

Whoever has such a soul, peace be upon him and mercy, courage, and eternal joy upon the head of this true Christian.

It is not the person who strives to look into His secrets that is faithful to the Sovereign, but the person who fervently fulfills His will.

This eternal wisdom of God continues its speech without ceasing throughout all ages and nations. And it is none other than the ubiquitous nature of the invisible face of God and the living word secretly thundering secretly inside all of us. But we do not want to hear its counsel: some because of deafness, but the majority because of unfortunate obstinacy, because of dependence on a poor upbringing.

Among the Jews, wise individuals called prophets fulfilled with most profound danger what was commanded them, listening intently to this immaterial voice. It is the beginning and end of all prophetic books: all written in them is from it, through it and for it. For this reason it received several names. It is called the image of God, glory, light, word, counsel, resurrection, life, path, rectitude, peace, fate, justification, grace, truth, power of God, name of God, will of God, rock of faith, Kingdom of God, and others. The very first Christians called it Christ, that is, King, because it alone directs the entire state, all inhabitants and every person individually to eternal and temporal prosperity. And besides, during antiquity all that was supreme and primary was venerated as royal.

Fear of death falls upon every person in their old age. It is necessary to prepare for this at a opportune time early in life as a weapon against the enemy, to develop a peaceful attitude of the will toward this event. Such a psychological peace is prepared at a distance from the event, quietly in a secret conclave of heart where it grows and increases with a feeling of goodness. This feeling is a crown of life.

I do not plow, I do not sow, I do not buy, I do not war, I reject every sorrow caused by livelihood. So what do I do? This is what. Always blessing the Lord, I sing to his resurrection. I learn gratitude, my friend. This is my work. I learn to be content with all that proceeds from the providence of God and given to me for my life. The ungrateful will is the key to infernal torment; the grateful heart is the paradise of sweetness. O, my friend. Learn of gratitude while sitting at home, walking the road, when falling asleep and when waking. Accept and convert all you have into goodness and contentment. And never attribute error to God for any of your experiences. Rejoice always, be thankful for all, pray.

We are all here yet we are unable to find ourselves. What an amazing thing! A person lives in the world many years and cannot notice on his own when he senses himself better than all else. If this person would only notice this it would be clear to him what true goodness is. It would become clear to him that matters are well with him only when love toward people resides in his soul. It is apparent we meditate little when alone and even to this time do not realize this. We have distorted our mind and do not strive to recognize the one item that we need. If we would only just for a moment stop the course of our vain life and take a good look within ourselves we would know what our goodness consists of. Our body is weak, unclean, mortal, but in it there is hid a treasure, the immortal spirit of god. It is worth it for us to recognize this spirit within ourselves and we will begin to love people, and if we begin to love people then we will receive all that our heart desires and we will be fortunate.

If wealth possesses what poverty does not, then rectify the situation. But satisfaction in poverty is not always with wealth. If a certain region has less produce, there the air is much healthier. Where there is less cranberry and bilberry, the is also less scurvy; where there are less doctors, there are less ill; where there is less gold, there are less luxuries; where there is less science, there is less stupidity; where there is less laws, there is less criminals; where there is less weapons, there is less wars; where there are less cooks, there is less bad cooking; where there is less honor, there is less respect; where there is less sweetness, there are less cavities; where there is less glory, there is less disrespect; where there are less friends, there are less enemies; where there is health, there is also less dissipation.

"Why do you ask about My name?" said God to Moses. "If there is something behind somebody that moves you can see what always was, is and will be, and then you know Me. My name is the same as My essence. I and the existing. I am what is. Who wants to know My name knows nothing about Me."

Among the ancients this power was called: world-wide intellect, nature, life, eternity. Among Christians this power is called spirit, Father, Lord, mind, truth. The visible changing world is as if a shadow of this power. As God is eternal so is the visible world – its shadow – also eternal. But the visible world is only a shadow. Only the invisible power – God – truly exists.

Due to diverse natural inclinations the path of life is diverse. However the end can be the same for all: honor, peace and life.

Even if you are beyond the sea it is bad to be without God, but for the wise person the entire world is his fatherland. For him it is everywhere and always well. He does not reap goodness in various places, but carries it within himself. This goodness serves as a sun for him at all times and his treasure in all regions.

Happiness is yours and the world is yours and paradise is yours and God resides within you. And watch to make sure your God is always with you and then you will be with Him.

If some statement tries to pass itself off as God's law, and not needing love, all of this is a human concept, and not God's law.

If someone falls into a pit or a well, he should not think about how difficult it will be to get out, but how to get out.

It is better for an intelligent and magnanimous person to have love and honor, than for a thousand of stupid people to have the same.

It is not a good situation for us when we know much that is extraneous, but do not what is most needful: ourselves. We do not know what it is that resides within us. If we knew and remembered what resides in each of us, then our life would be completely different.

Light and darkness, decay and eternity, belief and violation – the entire world is composed of what one needs from another. If you are darkness, be darkness, but the son of light should be light.

Many who do not have the strength to do something on their own are not believed by others should they claim some accomplishment.

The world tried to catch me but could not.

They say that observing the law of God is difficult. This is not true. The law of life does not require anything from us, except love toward associate. And love is not difficult, but joyous.

What good it is to know the manner that some activity is accomplished if you are not involved in it directly? It is easy to discover, but difficult to apply. Science and adaptation is one and the same. It does not live in discovery but in accomplishment.

Whoever does not love a serf must learn to live in simplicity and destitution.

Whoever is angry at the weather or harvest is also angry at God Himself who implements all.

Whoever was born to be amused with eternity, for him it is pleasant to live in fields, forests and gardens, rather than in mountains.

VLADIMIR SERGEEVICH SOLOVYOV

1853 – 1900

Religious Philosopher, Theologian, Educator

Vladimir Solovyov was born in Moscow on January 16, 1853. He was the son of famous historian Sergei Mikhailovich Solovyov and brother of historical-fiction writer Vsevolod Solovyov. He completed his studies in history and philology at Moscow University in 1873, and then in 1877 became a member of the Ministry of National Education. He received his doctorate in philosophy in 1880 and started to lecture at St Petersburg University.

His initial books on religious philosophy began in 1874, with the *Crisis of Western Philosophy*; in 1880, *A Criticism of Abstract Principles*; in 1881, *Reading on Divine-Humanity*; and his masterpiece on morality and ethics, *Justification of the Good*. Solovyov was a dedicated Russian Orthodox his entire life, although in the 1880s he published a series of papers about the idea of uniting the Eastern and Western branches of Christianity (Orthodox and Catholic) under the leadership of the Roman Pontiff. As a result of this, Solovyov was subject to stern criticism by the Slavophiles and Orthodox conservatives.

The basis of his religious philosophy was his concept of the unity of universal existence, known as all-in-oneness. Solovyov died in Moscow on July 31, 1900.

A person is a social entity, and the higher issue of his life, the concluding goal of his efforts, lie not in his personal destiny, but in the social destinies of all humanity.

A person needs to be moral on his own volition, but in order to accomplish this he must also to a certain extent be immoral on his own volition.

All that we call evil in a moral sense: violence, slavery, annihilation of one entity by another, all of this is the worldwide law, the law of nature, and which only continues to exist because creation struggles against and destroys each other.

Altruism is the freedom of the spirit from the tie to material goods.

Always, when people altruistically serve some kind of high interest and entirely devote themselves to it, they at the same time, and even outside of their volition, attain other useful results.

Asceticism, as introduced as the principle of self-discipline, is the struggle with the flesh in order to strengthen the spirit and inspire the body.

Christianity is the revelation of the perfect God in imperfect humans.

Contemporary religion is a very pathetic thing. Personally speaking, religion is not at all a governing principle, as the center of religion gravitation. But what is called religion is now your personal mood, your personal taste.

Enjoyment is nothing else but the condition of the will that has attained its goal, whatever this will might be and whatever its goal might be.

If true prosperity is the composition of stable satisfaction, then any person can be truly prosperous if he finds satisfaction in the place from which no one can steal, that is, within himself.

Justice is not just simply equality, but equality in the fulfillment of your obligation.

Justice in a moral sense is a certain ability to limit yourself, it is a limit of your pretensions on the infringement of others' rights. Justice appears in this manner as a certain sacrifice, a self-denial.

Poverty, once it passes a predetermine boundary, when it becomes repulsive and forces a person to dedicate all his time and all his strengths to mechanical work, such poverty contradicts human dignity and so is incompatible with genuine social morality.

Sexual passion deceives the human heart with the illusion of love. This is not love, only, apparently something similar to love. Love is when 2 lives are tied together as one essence and internally indivisible, but natural passion only strives to attain this, but will never attain it, because its means are only something external, separate from both accomplices and can be for them completely foreign and even malevolent. Malice and animosity in our inherent nature is fully real, while love in it is an illusion.

The dilemma of justice does not completely reside in the question, If the world lying in evil will convert into God's kingdom? But whether until that time it will completely convert into hell.

The disappointed and despairing suicidal person became disappointed and despaired not in life's meaning, but in exactly the opposite, in his reliance on the lack of meaning in life.

The essence of justice consists in the balance of 2 moral interests: personal freedom and the general welfare.

The idea of a nation is not what it thinks about itself in the interval, but what God thinks of it over eternity.

The inherent fundamental and root reason for all activities of humanity, those small and great, private and historical-worldwide, is the human will.

The meaning of society is to provide security to each of its members, not only materially, but with a worthy existence.

The moral obligation of genuine patriotism is to serve the nation within humanity, and to serve humanity within the nation.

The moral significance of marriage consists in a woman ceasing to be an instrument of natural attraction, and now recognized as a creation that is absolutely valuable on its own merit, as an indispensable consummation of the individual person for his true wholeness.

The quality of government workers depends on the quality of that society from which they evolve and, subsequently, the best and most reliable method of improvement is to present a first-class educated society.

They compare a nation with a plant growing, they speak of the roots of feudalism, of the depth of the field. They forget that the plant, in order for it to produce flowers and fruit, must not only be held by the roots in the soil, but to rise above the soil, it must be open for external outside influences, for dew and rain, for the unrestrained wind and the sun's rays.

To utilize violence to materialize justice means to admit that justice is powerless.

True belief cannot exist without appropriate conduct. Whoever truly believes will indispensably conduct himself such.

Two desires that are close to one another are like 2 invisible wings that raise the human soul over the balance of nature: the desire for immortality and the desire for justice.

Veneration is touching the higher ideal as an actual substance that is summoning an aspiration to a genuine change in yourself in the sense of drawing close to a higher self-perfection.

War is always a direct means for the external, and an indirect means for the internal, unification of humanity. Reason prohibits us from discarding this weapon as long as it is needed, but the conscience obligates us to strive to cause it to cease being needed.

War on its face value is the temporal suspension of the correct attitude between quarrelling nations, and their more or less complete return to the natural state of struggle of the basic powers.

Whoever wants to accept some external authority as their meaning of life will end by accepting some nonsense of his personal volition as his meaning of life.

What we consider the best in our heart we must not disclose arbitrarily, because we need to keep it safe from visible and invisible enemies. All of our treasure must be preserved in the inner chambers of the heart. Do not disclose the secrets of your heart to everyone.

THEOPHAN THE RECLUSE

1815 – 1894

Russian Orthodox Prelate, Ambassador, Mystic

Theophan was born Georgi Vasilyevich Govorov on January 10, 1815. His entire family was connected with the priesthood of the Russian Orthodox Church. He studied at the Livenski Religious Seminary, then at the Orlovski Religious Seminary, and then at the Kiev Religious Seminary. He took vows as a monk in 1841 with the name of Theophan and soon became a teacher of Latin at the Kiev Seminary, but moved to Novgorod to teach there in 1842, and then to the Aleksandr-Nevski Monastery in 1846. In 1847, Theophan moved to Jerusalem as part of the Russian Mission, but then returned in 1854 to St Petersburg. In 1859, Theophan was ordained as Bishop of Tambov Diocese and then in 1863 as Bishop of Vladimir Diocese.

All the moving and responsibilities caused Theophan to decide to become a recluse at the Visha Monastery in Tambov. So in 1872, he became a hermit to the end of his life, 22 years later. He died January 6, 1894.

A person should not say that the Father was at the beginning and then the Son was born and the Holy Spirit emanated from them. But that there only is the Father and is the Son and is the Holy Spirit. As the Father is without beginning, so are They with the Father born and emanated without a beginning. The Son is born without a beginning, the Holy Spirit proceeds without a beginning. So is the form of he existence of the true God, that in Him the Father was without a beginning and without birth and without emanation, but the Son was born and the Holy Spirit proceeds.

God is entirely unfathomable: the substance of God, His Tri-hypostatic nature, the divine qualities, and His effects. The initial sound thought of the mind regarding God is to acknowledge the various facets of his unfathomable being, and with a steadfast conviction in His existence, all-perfection and all-effectiveness in general in His creation and especially in humans. The latter is something a person cannot but confess. It is a supreme act of the mind to aspire to comprehend Him who is beyond comprehension, and this drive is a reliable expression of a person's humble and reverent worship of God.

God is without a beginning. He is immutable, immeasurable, so also is the Son and likewise the Holy Spirit. God is omnipresent, omniscient, omnipotent, all-benevolent, all-just, and likewise is the Son and the Holy Spirit. God is the creator and contemplator, and likewise is the Son and the Holy Spirit. Having such an understanding of the Son and Holy Spirit, who is bold enough to fuse them into a single hypostasis of the Father? They have a common substance, one and the same for all, but each hypostasis is separate.

God is unapproachable. But just as without knowledge of God it is impossible to be human, and who is predestined for communion with God, and since it is so, in order to ascend to this state consciously and intellectually, then it was God's good will to reveal Himself to humanity, to the extent they are able to understand,

and even the amount that was disclosed still contains much that is unfathomable. The amount revealed is as much as needed for them to profess belief in attaining their final goal. Gratitude to the Lord!

So much of this can be viewed, but only as a weak glimmer of light, as though in a fog, but all of this knowledge is provided us for God to sufficiently guide a person to his predestination. In all respects it is a lamp shining in a dark place.

The highest ranks of the holy church in its primary and institutional organization are the holy apostles, and these ranks are supplemented and at the present are introduced by the holy Church through the holy fathers by the inspiration of the Holy Spirit and guidance of the Lord our Savior, who is the head of the Church. So if you have rejected all of this or will reject it, then you have become or will become an enemy of God, and your deliberations will not be in accord with God's, and so your conduct will be against God's will.

The enemy has forced many off the path, influencing them, that God needs to be served only spiritually and that the external needs to be discarded. It is true that God needs to be served spiritually, but in order to approach this spiritual worship, we need first to exercise the eternal, and so, having attained the spiritual, and if God should grant this to someone, to support, enliven and strengthen this spiritual worship indispensably together with the ostensive.

Should children be first introduced into the spiritual? Let them first learn to worship God ostensively, and when they grow a bit more, then learn to worship Him also spiritually. But having learned to also worship God spiritually, they will not discard the ostensive, because it is similar to putting logs into a furnace, it warms and fires the inner spiritual. This is the order that we have in the church of God.

All the saints of God conducted themselves in this manner, as we notice in their biographies. Do you want to discover salvation just as they did? Then imitate them in this matter. Maintain and fulfill all that is contained in the Church. But just do not stop here, but ascend higher, to the spiritual, all your attention turn toward the edification of the Spirit, or on the inner life, so that you are always with God in your heart. If you will conduct yourself so, then the matter will become real.

What is important of everything ostensive in the Church is to emphasize and place as special and supreme of all – the other of the 7 divine sacraments that were installed by the Lord and Savior for the believer's communion of divine grace. In the Church of God, the word of God containing the truth revealed by God, and the divine sacraments that communicate grace, just as important as the pupil of your eye, and so value them just as you would value the pupil of your eye. All the other ecclesiastical ranks, although also sacred and must be reverently honored, but none of them can proceed in comparison with the 7 sacred sacraments. These sacraments, although visible, contain and communicate divine grace, and divine grace cannot be received circumventing them, and subsequently, discovering salvation. All the other ecclesiastical ranks promote motivation to receive this grace, but they do not direct communicate it. Impress this upon your mind more firmly.

Whoever alienates himself from the sacred sacraments is without grace, and so does not possess the Holy Spirit. And who does not possess the Holy Sprit is not Christ's, and if you are not Christ's, then you are not God's.

The strength of grace penetrates inwardly and here restores the divine order in all of its beauty, it heals the disorder, and so orients our strengths and parts in a direction away from our self and to God, to worship Him and increase our benevolence.

As God the Son, of the same substance as the Father, uniting in Himself both deity and humanity, is one with Him as the Son of Man. He became in this manner the mediator, uniting within himself fallen humanity with God. All believers, by the strength of the sacraments he instituted, become one with him, and through him and in him unite with God, and with his communion, a living and essential one, we are predestined to be His people.

The creation, not possessing existence on its own account, but which was summoned into existence from nothing, yet cannot continue existence on its own, but hangs over the abyss of oblivion, and which at any moment is ready to swallow it. It is the omnipotent will of the Tri-hypostasis God – who summoned it into existence – who holds it over this abyss. God wanted, and creation appeared, and creation continues to reproduce because God wants it to continue its existence. The continuation of creation's existence is an inherent part of its nature. God's will of the continuation of creation's existence is the basis of its life, all is founded upon it.

Truth is hidden in the parables for the person having the kernel or the foresight of truth to understand it, while another will not ascertain anything in it, and because the orientation of his mind, rule of his life and his heart's inclination, is in a different direction and filled with mundane and secular matters.

The true life in Jesus Christ is depicted in the Gospel, in the conduct and words of our Lord Jesus Christ. Read it, heed it and learn to live in Christ, imitating his conduct and following his teaching. The holy Church guides you to this work, proposing a daily reading of a passage from the Gospel. Each day is dedicating to studying an excerpt, from either what the Lord did or what he taught. Observe this and Christ will mentally form within you, and then it will be your responsibility to reflect him in your life.

The Golden Age of Russian Literature

VLADIMIR IVANOVICH DAL

1801 – 1872

Lexicographer, Writer, Ethnographer

Vladimir Dal was actually Danish, but he was born and lived in Russia his entire life and considered himself Russian. He was born November 22, 1801, in Lugansk, Ukraine, into a doctor's family. He studied in St Petersburg, and then attended medical school and graduated. Dal initially went into government service at the Ministry of Internal Affairs in Novgorod, working there 10 years. He left the ministry in 1859 and moved to Moscow.

Dal started writing in 1829 with publications of his stories of country Russian life, using the penname of the Cossack of Lugansk. His continued writing and in 1838 was selected as a member of the Petersburg Academy of Sciences. His magnum opus was his 4-volume *Interpretive Dictionary of the Living Language of Great Russia*, an accomplishment incomparable in the history of Russian lexicography and intensely utilized to the present. Dal likewise gathered and published volumes on native Russian aphorisms.

He joined the Russian Orthodox Church instead of his native Lutheran and composed several books about religious life in the Russian countryside.

Dal died in Moscow on October 4, 1872.

A Russian person cannot be happy in solitude, he needs the participation of those surrounding him. Without them he cannot be happy.

As much as I may know, there is nothing better than our Russian nation, and there is no more truthful a manner to deal with it than to be truthful.

I hope we will never reach that point where we feed our Russian language food from an alien language.

Just as a ruble is comprised of kopeks, so is knowledge comprised of the study of bits of literature.

Language is the labor of entire successive generations.

Little credit is to be gained with an attitude of greed.

Old people tell you, "Be careful." These old people lie, they are just envious of you.

Only a considerate and talented nation can preserve the majestic tranquility of mood and humor in any, and in the most difficult of, circumstances. Proverbs, maxims, jokes, are born in the wombs of the national masses when they speak of a healthy and strong organism.

Patriotism as the goal and result of patriotic inculcation of the young is the display of love toward homeland, native land, and fatherland.

Socialism and communism, based on the merit of their teaching, are inherent enemies of all government order.

The instructor must himself be what he wants his student to become.

They interpret and interpret even more, and reach no conclusion.

To die today is terrifying, but at some other time is nothing.

Why does this occur in the world? Why do matters end this way? That the innocent will answer for the guilty. It seems the shameless and irresponsible person is exalted, while the meek and the well-intended and quiet person, and who is incapable of telling even the simplest and ignorable lie, becomes the victim.

A friend has concern for a friend, but God's concern is for all.

A person can recognize God only in himself. Until you find Him in yourself, your will not find Him anywhere.

After shearing, the Lord still provides warmth for the sheep.

Every person's concern is for himself, but God's concern is for all.

God has much room for the virtuous.

God is not in power, but in truth.

God is not like your brother, He will help you sooner.

God loves those who have love.

God possesses much mercy. With mercy God is not crippled.

God provides sustenance, and no one see Him.

God to his people is more than a father to his children

God's dew provides God's land moisture.

God's gives the day, God gives the food.

God's shores run lengthwise and across.

God's water travels across God's ground.

If you place your hope on God, you will not collapse.

If you travel with God, you will reach goodness.

It is not due to our sins that God is merciful.

People speak differently about God, but all feel and understand Him the same.

The Lord's power is consummated in weakness.

The person walks, but God leads.

There is no God for the person who does not know God in himself.

To live is to serve God. God is in little and God is in much.

What God loves will not perish.

Whoever loves God will receive much goodness.

FEODOR MIKHAILOVICH DOSTOYEVSKI

1821 – 1881

Classical Author

Feodor Dostoyevski was born in Moscow on October 30, 1821. In 1837, he and his brother Mikhail moved to St Petersburg to attend engineering school. After graduating he served in the St Petersburg city engineering department, but begin writing short stories in his spare time. In 1844, he quit his job and dedicated himself full time to writing.

In 1847, Dostoyevski began associating with Belinski and his circle of Slavophiles, and he was arrested that year as a participant in the circle of Petrashevski, a group of progressive intellectuals that Tsar Nicholas I felt threatening to his government. Dostoyevski spent 8 months in prison at the Petro-Pavlovsk Fortress, and was sentenced to death, but the sentence was commuted to hard labor in Siberia, where he was exiled from 1850 to 1859. He was then released and allowed to return to St Petersburg. Dostoyevski's major novels begin at this time.

In 1861, he and his brother Mikhail began to publish several literary journals, which contained many of Dostoyevski's works. In 1867, Dostoyevski married and he and his bride went to Germany to honeymoon, residing also in Switzerland and Italy, except that they were in Europe for 4 years.

Dostoyevski's works are heavily infiltrated with St Petersburg life, since this was his home. He researched human nature by means of investigating it in various situations, reflected in all his novels, and gave a ruthless analysis of Russian life by exposing the conditions of the unethical situation of the nation. Yet Dostoyevski insisted on the predestination of Russia as the savior of humanity. His deep religious convictions likewise surface in his books, especially the influence of Orthodoxy on the life of peasant Russians.

Dostoyevski continued to write until his death January 29, 1881. He was not even 60 years of age.

If a person was to distort the Christian belief, by uniting it with the goals of the present world, then suddenly the entirety of the meaning of Christianity will be lost. The mind must absolutely fall into disbelief, and in place of the great Christ the ideal of constructing a new tower of Babylon will materialize. The high vision of Christianity for humanity will be reduced to the view of a herd of animals, and under the guise of socialist love toward humanity an unmasked contempt toward true Christianity will appear.

Nature as I understand it, proclaims to me of some type of harmony existing in it as a whole. Humanity's comprehension of this created form is a proclamation of religion. It says to me that although I fully know that I cannot and never will participate in this harmony as a whole, and that I will not understand it completely, what it signifies, but I nonetheless must submit to this proclamation, I must humble myself to it, accept suffering for the sake of the harmony as a whole, and agree to live.

The real – created – world is terminal, the ethereal world is eternal. If 2 parallel lines were to cross, all the laws of this world would terminate. But in infinity they do meet, and infinity is undoubtable, because if infinity did not exist then we would not have a temporal world. But if infinity does exist, then so does God, and so does another world based on other laws than the real – created – world.

Here it seems we have a contradiction: If life is so abundant, that is, beyond the earthly and the immortal, then what is the reason to value the earthly life so much? The resolution in particular is opposite, because only with belief in his immortality does a person aspire to his intellectual goal on earth. Without a conviction in his immortality, and even if it is just sensed as an imperceptible concern, a person's ties with the earth are slowly torn, becoming thinner and decaying. Losing this higher meaning of life will eventually lead to suicide.

Much on earth is hid from us, but in place of this we are gifted a secret, hidden feeling of our living tie with another world, with a world that is celestial and higher. Yes, the roots of our thoughts and feelings are not here, but in other worlds. This is why philosophers say that the essential objects should not be attained here on earth.

Beauty – this is an awesome and terrifying thing! Awesome because it is indefinable, but there is no reason to define it, because God is the one who created this enigma. Here the shores merge, here all contradictions live together. I, brother, am very uneducated, but I have thought over this much. Awesome are its many secrets! They are just too many enigmas that overload a person in the world. Decipher it as much as you can and crawl dry out of water. Beauty! I cannot bear such a thing, that here is something higher than a person's heart and with a supreme mind, that begins with the ideal of the Madonna, and ends with the ideal of Sodom. It is wide, clumsy, and excessively wide, but I need to narrow it. The devil knows what this is. This is it! What the mind imagines as shameful, the heart entirely as beauty. It is terrifying that beauty is not only awesome but a clandestine thing. Here the devil and God struggle, and the battlefield is people's hearts.

I do not want and cannot believe that evil is the normal condition of people. But it seems that they all just laugh at this belief of mine. How can they not believe me? I have seen truth – it is not in vain that I have acquired a mind. I saw it and its living image filled my soul forever. I saw it in such an overflowing fullness that I cannot believe it cannot reside among people. How can I relieve myself of it? I will condescend, of course, even several times, and I will speak likewise, perhaps, with foreign words, but not for long. This living image that I saw will reside with me and always direct me and correct me.

But eventually we will adapt to science. All of this will occur, perhaps then, when we will no longer be on this world. We cannot even guess what will then be, but know that it will not be so bad. It is the destiny for our generation to attain this honor of the first step and the first word.

My friend, to love people as they are is impossible. But yet we must. And so be nice to them while restraining your feelings, biting your tongue and closing your eyes (the latter is indispensable). Tolerate the bad that evolves from them, not becoming irritated at them to the extent possible, remembering that you also are human. It seems that you can be strict with them but only if you have even a little bit more reasonable means to do this. People by their inherent nature are contrite and will condescend due to fear. Do not do this to them and do not cease to disdain manipulation. Be able to have contempt for them if they do something vile, even if their goodness attempts to cover it. My dear person, I tell you this only after determining myself. We can all see this in ourselves, the honorable and dishonorable.

Strongly developing your personality, fully assured in your right to be an individual, not possessing any fear of any sort, no one being able to do anything against you as a result of your individualism, meaning that that there is no greater utilization of your life than to give it all to everyone, so that others would also be exactly the same type of self-controlled and prosperous individual. This is the law of nature and the normal person is drawn in this direction. But there exists just one strand, just one thin thread, that holds you together, and it will easily break if you should fall into some mechanism, and everything you have will immediately shatter and ruin. To still have such a calamity occur with such an accident is nothing but an infinitesimal incident in utilizing your personal abilities.

I repeat and I strongly repeat: All people who react in a spontaneous manner, both male and female activists, are stupid and limited. How to explain this? This is how: As a result of their limited ability and shortsightedness, they accept their second-rate reasons – as first rate. In this manner they quickly and easily convince others that they have found the immutable basis for their effort, and then they rest in their discovery. To them this is the most important. But in order to begin to be effective, it is necessary to be completely tranquil ahead of time and not to have any doubts remaining.

This was one of those people with the most noble and prudent heart of all and who even were embarrassed to suppose that someone else committed something bad. They quickly attired their close associates in every virtue, would rejoice at the success of some stranger, would live in such a manner constantly in an ideal world, but with every failure they would first of all blame themselves.

Suppose that this is you who wants to personally raise the building of human fate with the goal at the finale to prosper people, to give them in the end peace and tranquility. But to accomplish this it is indispensable and unavoidable to motivate just that tiny creation, that child within your breast beating with a hammer, and on his displayed tears to found this building, and so on these conditions you would agree to become the architect.

There is no worry that is so uninterruptible and so tormenting for a person than for him, now remaining free, to find as soon as possible someone to admire. But the person seeks to admire something that is indisputable, and so indisputable that all people would be willing to immediately agree on a uniform admiration. So this necessity of society to admire is the primary torment of every person individually and of the entirety of humanity from the beginning of time.

This is why we have a mind, in order to attain what we want. You think you do not need to walk miles, but only to continue a hundred steps, all the better, all the closer to the goal if you are directed toward the goal. And if you want to absolutely reach the goal by taking just one large step, then this in my opinion is not at all feasible. This is even called avoidance.

A cultured and decent person cannot be conceited without an unlimited insistence directed toward himself and without holding himself in contempt at any minute to the point of hate.

A person in general very and very much loves to be insulted.

A person is an entity that can adjust to anything, and I think that this is his best quality.

A person needs to be exceptionally in love with himself in order to write about himself without embarrassment.

A stupid person is always satisfied with what he says, and he will always state more than the necessary. He loves the extra baggage.

But alienation and eccentric behavior will sooner harm than give a right to attention, especially when all are striving to unite parts and find even some kind of common interpretation in some regular stupid person.

Destitute people are capricious. This is how nature conceived them.

For weak and empty characters accustomed to constant subjection and deciding to finally go insane and protest is unrealistic, on the contrary, you must be firm and consistent, always possessing the characteristics of having firmness and consistency.

Humanity always as a whole has aspired to build itself to become worldwide without reservations. There have been many great nations with great histories, but the higher these nations ascended, the more unhappy they were. Because there was always some stronger nation that would see the need to gain the victory over them and incorporate them into their own.

Humble yourself, prideful person, and first of all break your pride. Humble yourself, idle person, and first of all labor in the field of your native land.

I constantly counted myself smarter than all the others that surrounded me, and often – and will you believe this – I actually convinced myself of it.

I cry, Give me a person so I can love him. Then they shove some Orthodox saint at me! So how am I to love some saint?

I do not have the right to criticize others because I am unable to suffer as they do, and in order to become a critic of others, it is necessary to suffer your way to the pedestal.

I do not need monuments! Erect me a monument in your hearts, and any more than this is not needed, not needed, not needed.

I heard said that those who stand in a high place only drag themselves down, and down into an abyss. I think that many suicides and murders have occurred only because the person took a revolver in his hands.

In reality a person likes to see his best friend humiliated in his presence. The greater part of friendship is founded on such humiliation. And this is already old stuff and known to be an axiom to all intelligent people.

In the world are people who know every hidden secret! Sitting between them, listening, and yet you yourself know that you understand nothing, but it is so interesting to your heart. And why? Because here you find something to do, mentally perplexing, and some joy.

It is amazing how many arbitrary thoughts freely scatter in the mind when the person particularly is entirely agitated by some colossal news, and this it seems should suppress other feelings and disperse all superfluous thoughts, and especially trivial ones. While the trivial on the contrary seem to want to climb in.

It is not enough to refute an idea, it is best to exchange it with something beautiful of equal strength.

It is not just some odd fellow who is not always private and isolated, and perhaps it does occur that he carries within himself a guilt in his heart, while on the contrary the balance of people of his epoch are all blown in different directions by some wind, and for some interval sever themselves from him.

It seems that many powerful people have a natural need of this type, to find someone or something to venerate. It is often very difficult for a strong person to deal with his own strength.

It will not be any worse for us if our best petitions were fulfilled. Well, let's try it out. Provide for me, for example, an example, something more independent. Untie someone's hands, expand his circle of activity, weaken oversight, and we will – I guarantee you this – we will immediately request to return to oversight.

Just annihilate in humanity the belief in its immortality, and immediately not only will love emaciate, but also will every living strength that would otherwise continue world life. If this is not enough, then nothing will be considered immoral, and everything will be permitted.

Love includes a voluntary gift from the one who is loved to the other for the right to tyrannize him.

Money of course is a despotic potency, but at the same time it is a supreme equity, and this is its primary strength. Money equalizes all inequality.

Nonetheless, your boots will force you to deal with reality, even with the brightest aspiration toward some ideal.

People can be beautiful and happy, never losing the ability to live in the world. I do not want to and cannot believe that evil is a normal composition of people.

Simplicity in essence is supreme subtlety.

So do you notice this, that if a palace is not available, but only a chicken coop and rain begins, perhaps I will crawl into the chicken coop so not to get wet, but nonetheless I will not accept a chicken coop as a palace, even though I am grateful that it sheltered me from the rain.

Suppose for example I am able to intensely suffer, but another it seems cannot ever suffer to the extent that I suffer, and because he is someone else and not I, and beyond this, seldom does a person agree to recognize another as a martyr, as though this is a rank.

The condescending spirit exiting oppression will itself then oppress.

The intellect only knows what it has succeeded to know, while the human nature acts as a unified entity, all that is in it, the conscious and the unconscious, and even though it might be harmful, it still lives. What we do learn is our comfort, so why should we not search more?

The nature of a human will not tolerate blasphemy and in the final end will itself accomplish vendetta for it.

The principle matter is to love others as you do yourself. This is what is important and all that is needed. Nothing can equal it. Then you will immediately determine how to build yourself.

The secret of human existence is not in just figuring how to live, but in figuring for what to live.

The snake of literary self-interest stings often deeply and incurably, especially people who are useless and stupid.

There is nothing is the world more difficult than truthfulness, and nothing easier than flattery. If in a person's truthfulness there is just one flavorful implication of falsity, then some dissonance will immediately occur, and subsequently a scandal. If in flattery everything to the final note is false, then it is pleasant and is satisfactory to listen, and even with crude satisfaction, but nonetheless satisfaction. And no matter how crude the flattery, at least and for sure half of it will seem to be correct.

There is only one independent desire that a person needs, and at whatever the cost of the independence is whatever will be brought to him.

They think to develop justly, but having rejected Christ, they end in this manner, flooding the world with blood, because bloodshed will summon more bloodshed, and the person who utilizes a weapon will die by a weapon.

They thought that others were giving them pennies for free, but no. They were being paid for displaying themselves as destitute persons.

Times of prosperity do not fall from heaven. We create them. It is contained in our heart.

To solely love prosperity even to the point of embarrassment can occur.

Tranquility and even death is worth more to a person than an unreserved choice as to what is good and bad.

Two times two regardless of my will is still four. So it is with anybody's will.

Unhappiness is an infectious disease. The unhappy and melancholy need to distance themselves from each other so they will not infect each other even more.

We take account for our benefits even in the most magnanimous, even in the most unselfish actions we accomplish, and take account for them inconspicuously, involuntarily. Of course, almost all of them deceive and convince themselves that they are acting solely out of goodwill.

What remains inside is immeasurably more than what exits as words. Your notion, although it might be a bad one, as long as it with you, is always deeper, but when expressed in words, it is ridiculous and disgraceful.

Afanasi Afanasivich Fet

1820 – 1892

Poet, Judge

For the first 14 years of his life and the last 19 years, Afanasi Fet went by his original family name of Shenshin. He was born November 23, 1820, in the village Novosyolka, Orlov Province, central Russia. His schooling in the years 1835 to 1837 were in Estonia, at which time he began to write poetry. In 1838, he entered Moscow University, initially in law and then changed to history and philosophy, attending until 1844. His poetry was regularly published in Russian journals.

In 1845, Fet was conscripted into the military and by the following years was an officer, yet at the same time writing and publishing his poetry. In 1858, Fet was released from the military and he settled to live in Moscow. In 1867, Fet was assigned the responsibility of being a judicial magistrate, the first step in the judicial system, which he served for 11 years. Subsequently he continued to write poetry.

Fet as Afanasi Shenshin died of heart disease in Moscow on November 21, 1892.

RUSSIA'S WISDOM

Every object has a thousand boundaries, but only art has an arbitrary limit – love.

Every person has the type of wife that he needs.

I have to admit that in all worldwide and psychological questions, we most willingly turn to poets. To do this requires considerable preparatory work in order to precisely present the question only such so that the poet can provide in just a few verses his best explanation.

Instinct in your selection is infallible. It is impossible to think of a more apparent and touching convergence than the convergence of lips between 2 people.

Two worlds dominate since the beginning of time, each one right during its existence: one encompasses a person, the other encompasses my soul and life.

We fear not those who, while correctly understanding our words, will chide us, but sooner those who, while not understanding what was said, are able to praise us.

Whoever is not in a position of throwing themselves down head first from the 7th floor with unswerving belief that he will float through the air, he is not a lyricist.

You can run to whatever dialectics that interests you, but a egg still contains not only a future hen or rooster, but a infinite generation of their posterity. In other words, a solid protective shell contains an unlimited generation of bird posterity.

NIKOLAI VASILYEVICH GOGOL

1809 – 1852

Classical Writer

Nikolai Gogol was born March 20, 1809 in the village Bolshiye Sorochintsi, central Ukraine, from an ancient Ukrainian Cossack family. He attended higher education in Nizhyn, northern Ukraine, in the years 1821-1828. After finishing school he moved to St Petersburg, where he attempted to get into acting and writing. His initial compositions were a failure, but by 1830, his short stories were published and were attracting popularity.

From 1836, Gogol travelled and lived in Germany, Switzerland, France, and Italy. Gogol's ideology changed when he was traveling and writing, and he began to think very highly of himself, feeling some superior providence was guiding him. He began to reprimand people of their vices and look widely at life and his need to achieve self-perfection, and that this could only be achived with serious religious depth and convictions. Illnesses then affected Gogol and which only increased his religious mood. He was disenchanted with the mundane and shallow life of Russian aristocracy, and suddenly felt that his past work did not fulfill the divine expectations that his goal should be. In 1847 he wrote an apology of his beliefs and convictions, and where Russia had failed and his series of recommendations for Russia's restoration. The result was only the contempt of his friends and business associates toward him, and this only increased his illness and internal pain and depression.

Gogol died February 21, 1852, not even 43 years of age.

For us seeking improvement, divine literature is in some sense the eternal repetition of the feat of love. Humanity from every area, from all ends of the world, sorrowing from its failures, cries to its creator. And those having resided in the darkness of paganism and deprived of the cognizance and knowledge of God must realize that order and organization can be implemented in the world only through Him who in a harmonious manner commanded the world that He created to be put into motion. Distressed creation called to its creator and it awaited enlightenment from the lips of the creator Himself. Weeping they all summoned the Entity responsible for their existence, and these cries were heard strongest from the lips of His elect and prophets. They earlier sensed and guessed that if the Creator was to present Himself directly to humanity, He would present Himself in no other form than as an image of His creation, created after His image and likeness. The incarnation of God on earth was presented to everyone according to the extent that each of them was cleansed and able to comprehend Deity. But this was clearly spoken only by the prophets of the nation selected of God. And His most unblemished incarnation through the immaculate virgin was foretold even by gentiles, but clearly spoken of only by the prophets.

Their cries were heard: he appeared in the world, the world that he created. Among us he appeared, and one just like us in the form of a human, just as they earlier sensed, just as they earlier heard while residing in the gloomy darkness of paganism. But it was not in the form that that they expected him to present himself to their defiled comprehension: not in arrogant brilliance and majesty, not as a punisher of crimes, not as a judge who arrived to destroy some and reward others. No! His appearance was accomplished in a manner that only those who were God's could understand.

No one can be saved without love toward God, and love toward God you do not have. You will not find it in a monastery, because those who go to a monastery are those whom God has already called to go there. Without God's will you cannot begin to love Him. Yes, and how can you love someone whom you have not seen? What prayers and efforts will you use to petition Him for his love? Watch, how many good and beautiful people are there in the world, who fervently attempt to attain this love and hear only callousness and cold emptiness in their souls. It is difficult to love someone whom you have not seen. Only Christ brought and proclaimed to us the secret that in love toward our brethren we receive love toward God. It is worth so much to love them in the manner that Christ ordered us, and the summation will be love toward God Himself. Go into the world and first acquire love toward brethren.

For the Christian there is no final class in the course. He is eternally a disciple and to his grave. But usually and naturally the course of a person attains full development of his mind at about 30 years of age. From 30 to 40, some advancement is made relative to the strength of his faculties. Beyond this point nothing seems to want to advance within him, and all that he now accomplished is not only not any better than before, but even weaker and colder than before. But none of this applies for the Christian, and where other limits exist in the process of self-perfection, for him this is only a beginning. The most capable and most gifted of people seem to decline once they pass 40: they lose memory, become tired easily and lose physical strength. Categorize all the philosophers and genius of the highest order in the world, and the better part of them were effective only until they reached full maturity, then they have reached the limit of their mental development, and in old age return to a infantile mind.

But reviewing the final years of the life of the saints, you will notice that their mental and religious faculties were further strengthened relative to their proximity to decrepitude and death. Even from among those who by nature did not receive any brilliant gifts and were considered plain and stupid all their life, in their old age became eloquent and talented. Why is this? Because within them there always resided this aspiration of strength which usually only resides within a person when he is a young adult, when he sees before him accomplishments he needs to achieve and so acquire his reward though applause, imagining the distant rainbow and which only deceives him. But all of this fades away.

But the eternally distance shines ahead of the Christian, and he sees eternal accomplishments. He, like an adolescent, hungers for life's battle. He has struggles to win and battlefields to enter, as he looks upon himself constantly noticing his shortcomings and faults which lead him into new battles to overcome. As a result of this, all his strengths cannot decrease or weaken, but are energized constantly. His aspiration is applause in heaven and this adds greater motivation to his purpose. This is the reason why the Christian proceeds forward, when others slide backward, and why his faculties develop likewise as he motions ahead.

I consider it my obligation to now tell you a departing word: do not allow any kind of event to agitate you, whatever might occur around you. Each person must handle his own affairs, pray in quietness. This is the only manner for a community to excel, when each individual person will concentrate on himself and live as a Christian, serving God with the means that are provided him, and striving to have a good influence on a small circle of people that surround him. All will then fall into order, a correct attitude among people will develop on its own, limits will be established applicable to everybody. And humanity will move forward.

My friend, may God preserve you from bias, because the result of bias is that a person produces malevolence, whether in literature, service, family, society, in short, everyplace. The biased person is self-confident; the biased person is bold; the biased person arms everyone against him; the biased person cannot be able to find some middle ground. Observe prudently each thing and remember that it can have 2 completely opposite sides and one of which may not be revealed to you until the proper time.

A people can attain their happiness when they observe in a holy manner the customs of their antiquity, their simple ethics and their independence.

A person is always verbose when a secret sweetness in his breast is confined.

A person's nature, and especially a Russian's, contains a marvelous quality. As soon as he notices that another to some extent begins to lean toward him or show some condescension, then he is just about ready to ask for forgiveness. A person never wants to be first to yield, but as soon as one decides to attempt this magnanimous act, the other eagerly proceeds to as if jump ahead of his magnanimity.

A sage is always great in his own thoughts and ignorant in life's trivial pursuits.

A writer only has one teacher – it is his readers.

Anger anyplace is out of place, and even if you should be right, because this will just obscure the matter and confuse him.

But a human is a strange entity: he is embitter strongly due to the bad mood of those whom he could not respect, and on account of whom he responded sharply, reprimanding their vanity and superficiality. This all the more was vexing for him, that having deciphered the matter clearly, part of the problem was due to himself.

But a joke played on a person is feared even by the person who fears nothing else in the world.

But in place of having to severely judge your past, it is much better to be relentless to your present involvements.

But the exalted and beautiful can evolve often from the most lowly and contemptible life or is summoned by an impact of those innumerable incidences that have such diverse characteristics, which constantly color our human life and whose acknowledgement seldom provides distraction from the life of some sage.

But the mind and taste of a person present a strange aspect. Before attaining truth, it will make as many detours as it will make tangents or dead-ends, and will then be surprised at its perplexity.

Even honest and decent people have disagreement among themselves; it is only among crooks that we see something that appears to be friendship and unity at the time when one of them is severely prosecuted.

Even if you have the occasion to become angry at someone or other, become angry at yourself at the same time, even if for no other reason than that you are able to get angry at another.

Every person contains a personal inner work; every person accomplishes within the soul their personal agenda, and which often will disincline him from participation in social matters. And in no way is it possible to demand that another sacrifice himself and his individual goal for some type of thought that we admire or some goal of ours to which we prefer to aspire ourselves.

Everything can be distorted and everything can be applied a bad meaning. A person has the capability to do this. It is necessary for us to look at a thing and its basis for what it is, and not judge it based on the caricature that others have imposed on it, but on its own merit.

Genius is like a terrible rich person before whom all the world and all treasures are nothing.

He is smart but only because the magazine's latest issue was on the stands. But if a book is late, there is nothing in his head.

Honor is foremost when reprimanding. It is the supreme gift of God to a person .

Humor is an important matter. It does not remove life, or opinion, but is the guilty party in their presence.

If a person ruins some matter so important to the land by using a useless social custom, it is obvious he does not love his land.

If for example you were to say that in one city one government official has an alcohol problem, then all government officials will be insulted, but another completely different official might just say, "How can this be? I have a relative of this category of government official, and he is an excellent person. How can this be said, that we have a government official with an alcohol problem?" It is as though just one can ruin the entire class! And such vexation decisively extends to all classes.

If his mind does not visualize it, then for him it does not exist. He has even forgotten that the mind proceeds first when all the moral strengths in a person proceed forward, and it stands motionless and even moves backward when its moral strengths do not increase. He has even forgotten that not all the facets of the mind reside in one person. Another person can see particularly that side of things which he cannot see, and he seems to know what he cannot know. But he does not accept this and so whatever he cannot see himself is just a lie to him.

In general arguments are things of the type to which smart and elderly people for the meanwhile should not cling. Let the young people cry themselves out well first, this is their matter.

In order to cause a picture to radiate, much psychological warmth is required, taken from a contemptible life and transmitted into a pearl of creativity.

In short it is a rare trait for a person when he acquires so much love for goodness that he decides to sacrifice on its behalf his ambition and self-interest, and all of the trivialities that so easily irritate his egoism, and to impose on himself an immutable principle: to serve his country and not himself.

In the literary world there is not death, but nonetheless the deceased still intervene into our affairs and act effectively with us just as do the living.

It is better many times over to be agitated at what is within us than at what is outside and surrounding us.

It is sufficient to gain in our associations with people a certain smoothness of character and condescension, in order to impose on them the inability to notice our faults.

It is through sufferings and sorrows that we are assigned to obtain crumbs of wisdom, and those not found in books.

It is worth only to more intently concentrate on the present, the future will suddenly arrive all on its own.

Many of us in the past and at present, especially among the young, have started to brag beyond what they should of Russian valor, and they do not think at all instead about rooting and nourishing this within themselves. Their purpose is to display this as a show and tell Europe, "Look, you Germans. We are better than you." Such boasting will ruin everything. It just irritates others and causes harm to the braggart.

Melancholy is a genuine temptation of the spirit of darkness that attacks us, knowing how difficult it is to fight a person. Depression is contrary to God. It is the result of insufficient love on our part to God. Depression births despair which is psychological suicide, the most horrible of all malice that a person can accomplish, because it severs all paths to salvation.

No, this is not a dream. This is that fatal irrefutable edge between recollection and hope.

Often it is not until society or the entire generation displays the total depth of its present abomination that it is possible for them to aspire toward what is beautiful. And it is not until the path and road to it are shown clearly like a bright day for everyone that it is possible to even speak of the exalted and beautiful.

Our age is so menial, desires are so scattered in every direction, that in no manner can we concentrate in our mind on one subject of some sort, and as a result we unwillingly chop up all of our compositions into pieces and into attractive toys.

Our earthly life must not even for one minute be calm. We are summoned to the world for battle, and not a holiday celebration. When we attain the victory then we will celebrate in this world.

People will have no respect for you until you first place yourself at their service.

Poetic thoughts are more accessible to every person than poetic sounds, or better said, poetic poetry.

So what will happen to our world should music ever leave us?

Strive only that all will be honorable at the top, and then all at the bottom will be honorable on its own.

The beginning, root and confirmation of all is love toward God. But we have this beginning as the end, and we love all that is in the interval more than God.

The higher the truth, the greater necessity to be careful with it, otherwise it suddenly will turn to some common notion, and common notions are hardly respected. Atheists have not caused so much damage as the damage that hypocrites have caused or those plainly unqualified to preach God, boldly proclaiming His name using their unsanctified mouth.

The mind develops even faster when it proposes to itself a great and poetic question.

The public masses, representing the nation, are very strange in their desires. The public mass is similar in such a situation to a woman who orders an artist to draw a portrait of her that is exactly her. But woe to that artist if he is unable to hide all of her blemishes.

The tone of the question establishes the tone of the answer. Pompously convey your question and your will receive a pompous answer. Simply state your question and your will receive a simple answer.

There are no knots tighter than comradeship! Father loves his child, mother loves her child, child loves father and mother. But it does not stop here, the pet also loves the child. But it is only the human who can develop a relationship based on the soul and not just on blood. Related by soul is superior to every blood relationship.

There is no deprivation that will not have as a subsequent result a change, as a witness that not even for a short time will the Creator abandon the person. The heart will not remain empty even for a minute and it cannot exist without some type of feeling.

Those who are always acting in an antagonistic spirit are always excessively overwhelmed by their own position and in this enthusiastic impulse hold only to one rule: to contradict all that previously was effective.

True nationalism consists not in a description of a sarafan, but in the very spirit of the people. A poet perhaps can be nationalistic when he describes in full the world outside his own, but sees it using the eyes of his nationalism, the eyes of his people. When he feels and speaks such as his fellow countryman feel and speak, it is as though they feel and speak the same.

We are so astonishingly constructed, our nerves are so strangely interconnected, that only something suddenly deafening, glaring from first sight, will impose on us immediate agitation.

We are summoned to this world not to destroy and ruin, but to be like God Himself and direct all things to goodness, and even what people have already damaged and turned into some bad purpose.

We need to be cautious of arguments just as of fire, no matter how powerfully they will verbally attack us. Regardless of the wrong opinion they will throw at us, we must not all irritate them in return or prove them wrong. It is better to be silent and internally withdraw, then weigh all that was said and ascertain his situation with cold blood. But do not speak your determination if you feel that you will not be able to particularly relay your message to the person with whom you are speaking, or if you feel you cannot state this cold-bloodily and unpretentiously. Truly what is stated in anger will irritate and not mitigate.

We need toleration. Without it nothing will be left for art. All generations are good, when they are good in their generation.

We see only the obstacles, not noticing that they are our steps as we ascend.

What a person needs to do is suffer a little, then you will be able to understand the situation of others who have suffered and you will almost know what to say to them.

What do people want? They hunger for eternal bliss, endless happiness, yet one minute of grief is sufficient for them to act like children, and to destroy buildings that have taken so long to construct.

What has the greatest effect on the imagination cannot be soon knocked out of the head.

What is more insane, what even seems more funny to me, are people who exalt poets, as though they were officials, and using pathetic epithets, calling them first-class. It is as though poets are a plant, or lifeless minerals that require a system to hold them in their head.

Whatever you say, the sounds of the soul and heart expressed in words have several times more diversity that musical sounds.

Where is that person who would have the ability to tell us in our native Russian language this omnipotent word – Forward? Who, knowing all our strengths and qualities and the depth of our entire nature, in one magical motion could speed the life of a Russian person to some height.

One of my close associates that considered me genuinely valuable raised a monument on my behalf, but also has raised one on his own behalf in the process, a steadfast foundation in life's actions, an encouragement and refreshment of all who surround him.

You and I not too long ago deliberated about all the obligations of any and all types in our government. Reviewing each within its legitimate boundaries, we find that they particularly are what they should be, all of them to the last are as though created from

On-high for us with the purpose of us having to answer for all the demands of our government's existence, and all of them were created for this purpose, and not because of their attempt to cross or expand the limits of their obligations or even to go beyond their limits. If only every person, even the honorable and intellectual, would strive to ascend even one step in responsibility and above his mundane position.

You can never love the entire world if you cannot first love those who stand closest to you and have the opportunity to embitter you.

You very well know that to add a new official in order to limit the first official in his graft and embezzlement means to have 2 thieves and embezzlers in the place of one. Yes in general, the bureaucracy is limited, and even the smallest bureaucracy. A person must not be restrained by another person; the following year you will discover the need to have to restrain the new person that you installed to restrain the first, and then the installation of a person to restrain the previous will have no end. It is necessary to show trust to an honorable person, otherwise no honesty will ever exist.

Ivan Aleksandrovich Goncharov

1812 – 1891

Classical Author

Ivan Goncharov was born in Simbirsk, central Russia, on June 6, 1812. He completed Moscow University in 1834 and returned to his native city, becoming secretary-governor. After a year he moved to St Petersburg, where he pursued his career in writing, publishing several successful novels. In 1852 he traveled on a ship around the world, and this led him to further writing of his experiences.

Goncharov died in St Petersburg on September 15, 1891, of pneumonia.

A phenomenon transferred in its entirety from life into some artistic production always loses its genuineness of reality and does not become artistic truth. It will be produced incorrectly, and even improbably.

An official has a boss, but not a fatherland. The official considers his chancellery or department his fatherland.

Beauty of stupidity is not beauty. Gaze into a stupid beautiful woman. Stare deeply into every facial characteristic and into her smile. Little by little her features – her beauty – will be transformed into penetrating ugliness.

But I have become convinced that to read and hear the tales of dangerous journeys is much more terrifying than to actually experience them. I also heard said that is more horrible for witnesses to watch a person die, than it is for the person himself to die.

Debt is a demon that can in no way be expelled except with money.

Foresight and premonition of future steps in life are provided in general to perspicacious and observant minds, and to women especially, often without experience, but whose precedents serve as instinct for subtle minds.

Friendship does not need to be a slave or a domineer. Friendship likes equality.

Great love is not indivisible from great mind. The width of mind is comparable to the depth of heart. As a result great hearts attain the extreme pinnacles of humanity, since they are great minds.

Has life in the world become more comfortable now that more comforts are available?

Here, as in the balance of the world, exists a provincial custom to pass off your regular dishes as royal tableware.

I am just like a forgotten grenade lying in some field with my fuse. If you do not touch it, it will rust and diffuse on its own. But if you will push it, throw it, beat with a stick, it will explode and penetrate the body of the person who agitated it.

Ideas that strive to swallow all others and appropriate dominion over minds seem to me quite repulsive. It is like authority that wants to subject all people under its yoke along with their activities and rights.

If an ugly person needs much moral integrity so not to stab himself in the eye due to his ugliness, then a beautiful person needs even more to subject himself to humility because of beauty. Woe to beauty. A mind needs much strength so not to know about this!

If this should even occur – according to Christ's words – to have one flock and one shepherd, then perhaps – as the cosmopolitans dream – then at some time all nationalities will merge into one human family. So let it be. But to attain this goal, all nationalities are to work with all their strength, and for each of them to contribute of their specialties, all the best they have, and to bring this into a common treasury encompassing all humanity.

If you are not able to directly, openly and even precisely say to your friend all that you think of him, his actions, or listen from him the same such truths about yourself, this means that you do not genuinely believe one another, do not understand and do not respect one another.

It is impossible to live on earth without sacrifice, effort and deprivation. Life is not a garden where only flowers grow.

It was not for a good reason that even among the ancients the indispensable prerequisite for a complete education was considered travel. But among us it has become luxury and entertainment.

Liberal women have their own understandings of love, virtue, shame, and they courageously bear the thorns of their faults.

Life for yourself and about yourself is not life, but a passive state. Life requires words and activities and struggle.

Methods of creativity is not something you will learn by instruction. Every creator has his own methods. Such a person can only imitate higher methods, but this is of no value to him. In the work of a creative spirit he must develop his own, and not investigate others.

More that anything, it is a person's language that determines of what nationality a person is a member. The diversity of language will never allow a complete or intimate or sincere connection.

No toleration of any type, no condescension resides in a person when his aesthetic feeling is insulted.

Old truths will never shutter in the present of new ones. It will take this new or correct or reasonable burden on its shoulders. Only the sick and unnecessary fear to enter forward steps ahead.

Desire is cruel and potent. It does not submit to a person's imagination and dictates, but on the contrary, subjects people to its unexpected whims.

Desire, like a tiger, will allow you to sit on it, but then it will growl and grit its teeth.

Pride, human dignity, right to respect, integrity and ambition: if you were to remove these flowers from the garland that adorns a human, he will become almost an object.

Serious art, as with all serious matters, demand life's entire devotion.

Smart women like it when foolish things are done for them, especially costly. Only that the majority of such women do not like the person doing this to them, but some other.

Talent is a precious quality: it cannot lie.

The crowds compassionately look at someone fallen and shames itself due to its silence.

The masses can be guides of freedom, but they cannot be its protectors. Even then, guides are like shipping canals that transfer cargo from place to place, but they do not know of what the cargo consists. So it is with the masses or with democracy, they can implement with equal advantage for themselves either severe despotism or the most extreme liberty.

The mind is the same everywhere. Intelligent people possess certain typical traits, just as do all stupid people, regardless of their different nationality, clothing, language, religion, even opinion of life.

The source of knowledge is inexhaustible. What successes that humanity can acquire on this path, upon which all peoples will stop to seek, find and grasp.

The work of a true genius is not destroyed by the fire of passion, but only comes to a stop. And when the fire passes, it proceeds forward, slowly and barely, but moving nonetheless. Even in just the person's soul, independent of art, there smolders another creation, there resides another living thirst, other than a corporeal, another strength, other than the strength of physical force.

Tomfoolery is fun when a person naively fools around, distracting and joking with others. But when he laughs at himself and at others due to habit, with forethought, then it becomes clumsy and deliberate.

Wisdom is the consummation of truths developed by the mind, observance and experience and applied to life. This is a harmony of ideas with life.

Wisdom does not consist in knowing much. We will never be able to know everything. Wisdom consists not in how to know more, but in knowing what information is the most important, what is less important, and what is least important. Wisdom in our domestic and sundry affairs, it seems to me, consists not in figuring what needs to be done, as much as figuring what needs to be done first and then what later.

Yes, women are everything. They are often the obvious, often the hidden, motive of all humanity's activities. Their presence, respiration, or better said, the female atmosphere, provides light and fruit of life.

You need to agree that history and moral education are 2 things that are overly contradictory, that it is impossible to transform one into the other. If people conducted themselves in a moral manner, history would not exist in the world, and only morality would. And on the contrary, if people conducted themselves based on history, morality would be a science completely irrelevant. I feel it is sufficient for us to conduct ourselves based on history.

Mikhail Yuryevich Lermontov

1814 – 1841

Poet, Classical Writer, Military Officer

Mikhail Lermontov was born in Moscow on October 3, 1814. He studied at Moscow University, 1830-1832, but was expelled due to violating their discipline. He then transferred to a military school in St Petersburg, from which he graduated 1834, and he remained in the military as an officer, but wrote poetry in his spare time. Because of a poem he composed regarding Aleksandr Pushkin in 1837, Lermontov was tried by a military court and he was subsequently exiled to the Caucasus. In 1838 he returned to St Petersburg, but again in 1840 was transferred back. He was killed in a duel in Pyatigorsk, on July 15, 1841.

His novels centered in the Caucasus reflect the civilian pathos and fatalism of the era following the suppression of freedoms in Russia under Tsar Nicholas I. His most famous personage was Pechorin in *Hero of Our Time*, an intelligent and gifted person who is unable to advance in Imperial Russia, and is continually disenchanted with the progress of his life. He also reflected Lermontov's personal state. The fact that Lermontov was willing to risk his life in a duel at the age of 26, also reflects the people's attitude of the era toward the value of their life.

All that is for us in the world is a secret, and who thinks to be able to guess what is in a stranger's heart or all the details of their best friend's life, is making a bitter mistake. In every heart, in every life, a feeling has run through it, an incident has flown by it, ones that no one can reveal to another, and some of them are very important, and some usually provide a secret direction to feelings and incidents.

This might be cruel but needs to be accepted, that the purest and most immaculate love is half mixed with self-interest.

I notice in passing that a good tune reigns only where you will not hear anything better. But alas! My friends! Because of this you will there hear little.

My mother would tell me that a 17 year-old girl has just as much common sense as a 25 year-old man.

Our public is similar to the provincial official[19] who, having overheard the conversation of 2 diplomats who are members of 2 competing royal families, remains convinced that each of them is deceiving his government in the use of some mutual gentle friendship.

It is popularly known that in nature, contradictory reasons often cause the same effects.

The history of any person's soul, and even the most menial soul, is just as interesting and just as useful as the history of an entire nation.

---

[19] An official not from a major city, but from an outlying province of Russian.

The insidious immodesty of a true friend is understood by all.

The portrait is nice, but the original is vile!

We always excuse what we know.

Wealth is not happiness! Nonetheless it is closer to it than destitution. There is nothing more tasteless than to be satisfied with your fate residing in a shack and with a bowl of porridge.

When the fatherland forgets the memorial names of its deliverers, then as a result the past no longer exists for us. Such a nation is pitiful.

Mikhail Vasilyevich Lomonosov

1711 – 1765

Scholar, Encyclopedist, Scientist

Mikhail Lomonosov was born in the village Mishaninski, Archangel Province, northern Russia, on November 8, 1711. The village is today known as Lomonosova. He was the first Russian scientist of worldwide renown, an encyclopedist, chemist, physicist, geographer, geologist, metallurgist and astronomer. He founded the principle of the preservation of matter and energy, and the basics of electricity for Russian technicians. In addition to his technical contributions, Lomonosov was also a poet, historian and educator, all of which was used to improve and define a modern Russian literary language.

Lomonosov began higher education in Moscow in 1730, and then studied in St Petersburg, and later in Germany. In 1745, he was the first member of the Petersburg Academy of Sciences and in 1748 founded the first chemical laboratory associated with the Academy of Sciences. It was due to the initiative of Lomonosov that the Moscow University was founded and which later was named after him. Lomonosov also pressed the government to take possession of Siberia and the northern coast of Russia. In his spare time, he created mosaics.

Lomonosov died in St Petersburg on April 4, 1765, living only to 53.

A small person on a mountain is still small; a giant is large even in a hole.

Authors who write using nebulous and ambiguous terms only unconsciously display their ignorance or else deliberately hide it. They write vaguely about what they vaguely understand.

Charles V, Holy Roman Emperor, stated that a person speaks with God in Spanish, with his friends in French, with his enemies in German, and proper to speak with women in Italian. But if he would have been familiar with the Russian language, then of course he would have added to speak Russian when speaking courteously and decently with all the others, because he would have found in Russian the beauty of the Spanish, liveliness of the French, firmness of the German, grace of the Italian, and the wealth and strength of the Greek and Latin languages for depiction and brevity.

Even the highest algebra is a pathetic weapon in areas of morality.

For our general benefit and especially for development of science in the fatherland, I will not incite or defend sin since it is a detriment to our fathers.

For the most part let the journalist adopt the attitude that for him there is nothing more shameful than to steal from any of his associates recently expounded thoughts and conclusions and to claim them as his own, as though he was the one who stated them based on his own deliberations.

If you were to exert effort and do something good, then your effort will pass away but the good will remain. But if you do something bad and enjoy it, then the enjoyment will pass away but the bad will remain.

In order to be in the position to state sincere and just conclusions and opinions, it is necessary to banish from your mind every prejudice, every preconception, and not demand that the authors – whom we are choosing to put on trial – to servilely subject themselves to the intents that are being demanded of them. But rather to act oppositely and not regard them as genuine enemies against whom we have been summoned to wage open war.

Inexhaustible effort will overcome all obstacles.

It is an important matter to utilize temporal and transient efforts to provide immortality to multitudes of people, to preserve the credit due to praiseworthy activities, and to leave activities of the past as a legacy for the future generation and for profound eternity, and to unite those whose nature has been changed after a long period of time.

Love is strong like lightning, but penetrates without thunder, and even its most powerful strikes are pleasant.

Science and experience are only means by which to gather material for the intellect.

Science is a clear comprehension of truth, illumination of the mind, an undefiled joy of life, laud of youth, support of old age, builder of cities and regiments, strength of success in failure, the decoration of happiness, and everywhere a trusting and inseparable traveling companion.

Stupidity is that myth of the whale who holds up the world.[20]

---

[20] Russian tale similar to Atlas holding the world on its shoulders, except it is a whale.

That which pertains to magazines, their responsibility consists in providing clear and reliable short explanations of the content of recently published compositions. The goal and use of the summaries consists in faster advertisement throughout the republic of the scholarship and knowledge of books.

The person who attains old age will suffer illness resulting from living in luxury as a young man. The best path is to distance yourself from luxuries while young.

There exists no ignorance that could not provide so many questions that even the most intelligent person could not resolve.

To notice mistakes is worth little. To provide something better is what the cultured and worthy person can provide.

ALEKSANDR NIKOLAEVICH OSTROVSKI

1823 – 1886

Dramatist, Theater Activist

Aleksandr Ostrovski was born in Moscow on March 31, 1823. He became familiar early with Russian literature due to his father's immense library and felt an inclination to write, even though the father felt he should become a lawyer. In 1835, Ostrovski entered a private Moscow school, and then in 1840, he entered Moscow University to study law, but he left in 1843 after an altercation with a professor. He then went to work as a recorder in the judicial system until 1851.

By 1846, Ostrovski had written several scenes for plays, but none succeeded. It was not until 1850 that his plays gained popularity, but at the same time they were considered revolutionary and Ostrovski was placed under surveillance by Tsar Nicholas I, that same year. The surveillance was not terminated until 1861 by order of Tsar Alexandr II.

Beginning in 1853, Ostrovski wrote a new play each year for the next 30 years. In 1856, he also started to contribute articles to journals, and dedicated effort toward the education of the peasants in the Volga River valley as far as Nizhni-Novgorod. Ostrovski provided Russia an important and vital contribution to the development and progress of theater and was awarded in 1863 with the Uvarov Prize[21] and was selected as correspondent of the

Petersburg Academy of Sciences. An artistic circle was also organized by Ostrovski in 1866, to provide a entrance into the arts for many talented artists.

Ostrovski organized the Society of Russian Dramatic Writers and Opera Composers in 1874, and he became its president until his death. As a result of his contributions, in 1883 Tsar Alexandr III assigned Ostrovski a state payment of 3,000 rubles a years for his retirement until his death. His intensive and dedicated efforts had an exhaustive effect on Ostrovski's health and it began to decline about this time. Ostrovski died at his family estate Schelekov, Kostroma Province, on June 2, 1886. He was only 63.

We must love people, but not to interfere in their personal affairs. In order to interfere into a person's affairs you must know them, but for some reason to know them is not given to me. As long as I do not have the ability to ascertain who speaks truth and who manipulates, it is best for me not to get involved. But if you begin some inquiry into people, then willingly or unwillingly they will fool you, because every person wants to justify themselves, to somehow dump their guilt on someone else, and to somehow display themselves in a better state.

A duel? Why? The 2 of us have this type of duel, a constant one between us, an uninterruptible struggle. I enlighten and you corrupt.

A strange entity is the human. In his youth he is given passions in order to impose on himself all sorts of stupidity to ruin his entire life. Then in his elderly years common sense is give him in order to repent during his remaining years.

---

[21] Named after S.S. Uvarov, president of the Academy of Sciences, since 1818.

And crocodiles weep, but nonetheless will still swallow an entire calf.

Destitution is not frightful due to deprivations or deficiencies, but because it forces a person into a lower social circle where the people have no intellect, no honor, no morals, and only vices, prejudices and superstitions.

Do you know that when you are very embittered, it is not necessary to restrain yourself. You should either weep, or fight, or quickly share with someone your sorrow. Or else you will begin to think and think and you will imagine that there is no greater sorrow than yours in the world and so you have no further reason to live. Whether your condition is healthy we cannot ascertain since it is the soul that is depressed, and various terrors and misfortunes are tied to you, but only by strings.

Having put on a military uniform, it is difficult to exchange it for a sports coat.

I know this sincere simplicity. It consists of not knowing what should be known, and in knowing what should not be known. It is necessary to be profoundly unethical in order to reconcile with such simplicity.

I read the biography of Plutarch. For me this is very strange, why these people are considered great. I have noticed all of his traits in myself, but I have just never had the opportunity to write my own biography.

If a weak person should pick up another weak person, he will use his strength in just picking him up and not have any left to carry him anywhere.

If it is shameful to state something, so this means it is shameful to want and do the same.

Insensitive hearts always intervene not into their own affairs, but climb with their advice where they were never asked.

Many books are written for enjoyment of readers, and you read it and put it away. But people do not live by books, but by their parent's instructions.

Money is also more expensive than friends.

Not knowing the conditions surrounding the need for a question, it is impossible to know how to answer.

Of course there occurs such happy natures that even to very old age they preserve the ability to easily fly from one flower to the next in an astonishing manner.

So what does this matter have in comparison with eternity? And I was almost ready to say – a salted pickle.

There does exist a love that nature itself will impress upon a woman. There is no need to respond to this love; this love knows the secret. And then another love exists, based on affection and evolving from instinct, which is called infatuation. This love is a purely superficial display, it is what terrifyingly scares a man.

The person who says, "Let me do something horribly bad to you," for him no difference exists between a honorable act and dishonorable act until he is beaten.

There is nothing else worth guarding if first you do not guard yourself.

To be a bit more fashionable for us means to be a bit more colorful.

We have male and female peasants, and if they like someone very much, they said, "I have feelings for him." And this is true, if you like someone you have feelings toward them.

What is better: shame or need? Shame, they say, soon passes, but need eternally pokes at you and never will allow you rest.

Without money it is not easy to live as an example. What a worry not to have money! Only if a person is satisfied, he has all he needs. If now we have too much money, this means we must live exactly in the same manner as other wealthy people live, or else every other will have the right to criticize us. And this is so difficult to tolerate, especially an elderly person.

You must not blame the public, because the public is never to blame. This is just a social opinion and it is a joke to complain about it. Somehow you need to earn the public's favor.

Aleksandr Sergeevich Pushkin

1799 – 1837

Classical Poet and Novelist

Aleksandr Pushkin was born in St Petersburg on May 26, 1799. He attended private school in Tsarskoi Selo, beginning 1811. He was able to escape the effects of the war of 1812-1814 while secluded at school.

His first poems of note are dated 1813, at the age of 14. Apart from literature, Pushkin improved the literary form of the Russian language, next since Lomonosov almost 100 years earlier. He is responsible for standardizing the Russian language, especially with the influx of French with the era of Catherine the Great.

Pushkin's novels and poetry encompassed every area of Russian life, including many fables and tales. At the same time, many of them reflected his personal motives, his liberal political convictions. Pushkin was much opposed to the tyranny of the Russian state. As a result he was suppressed and exiled from St Petersburg in 1820-1824 to Ekaterinoslav, the Caucasus, the Crimea, Odessa, and later to the village Mikhailovski, Pskov province, in 1824-1826, which was the family estate, and he was isolated there. However, in all his places of exile, Pushkin continued to write. He returned to Moscow to live for a while, and then to St Petersburg in 1831.

Pushkin died from wounds inflicted on him by Georges Charles d'Anthès, a French subject who was serving in the Russian military, during a duel, on January 29, 1837, in St Petersburg. He was only 37 years of age.

"This is not something new, this was already stated," is one of the most usual accusations of critics. But if all has already been said, all understanding expressed and repeated in the course of centuries, so what will follow next? Is it that humanity's spirit is unable to conceive anything else new? No! But there is also no need to slander him. The mind is inexhaustible in reflections of comprehension just as the tongue is inexhaustible in combining words. All words are located in a lexicon, but books that appear every minute are not the same as a reprinted lexicon. An isolated thought never can present anything new. Thoughts can be diverse to the extent of infinity.

A certain person rightly noticed that naiveté is a congenital quality of the French people. On the contrary a distinctive feature of Russian ethos is some type of joyful mental deceit.

A foreign language is not spread by swords and fires, but with overwhelming abundance and excellence.

A moral axiom or aphorism becomes amazingly useful in those situation when we cannot seem to figure something else to say on our own to justify ourselves.

A repeated concise term eventually becomes nonsense.

A scholar without natural talent is similar to a poor Mullah, who tore pages from the Quran and ate them, thinking this is the manner of filling himself with the spirit of Islam.

Although I am earnestly tied to the Sovereign, I am far from celebrating all that I see around myself. As an author people irritate me as though I have prejudices. I am insulted, but I swear honorable, that for nothing in this world would I even exchange my fatherland or have any other history, except the history of our forefathers, the ones that God provided us.

An educated person occupied with his affairs, immersed in his meditations, does not have the time to reveal himself in society and acquire a habit of vain sophistication just like the idle residents of high society. We must be condescending to his ingenuous rudeness, pledge of conscientiousness and love of truth. Pedantism has its good side. He is only confused and repulsive when the shallow-minds and ignorance of others rear its ugly head.

But Europe has always had an attitude of ignorance of Russia as well as ingratitude. Russian higher society has noticed that Europe is nothing but one family.

Do not allow God to see a Russian revolt, it is so senseless and ruthless.

Ecstasy excludes tranquility, an indispensable condition of beauty. Ecstasy does not guess at mental strengths. Ecstasy is short, inconsistent, and subsequently does not have the strength to materialize true great accomplishment. Ecstasy is the intense condition of a soul's reflection. Inspiration can occur without ecstasy, but ecstasy without inspiration does not exist.

Every item in the world is the end of previous items and a means for all in the future. And so every person can in some form say to himself, "All the world pertains to me."

Every line of a great writer remains valuable for posterity. We with curiosity investigate autographs, even though they are nothing else but a fragment from a used notebook or a note to a tailor regarding a bill to be paid.

For a person to compose his memoirs is self-deceiving as well as pleasant. No one loves you and no one knows you as much as you do. The subject matter is inexhaustible, but difficult. It is possible not to lie, but to be sincere is next to impossible. The pen will often just stop, like running from a crevasse. The effort is knowing that some stranger only wants to read it complacently. For people to judge it and disdain it is easy, but to disdain your personal evaluation is impossible.

For the most part people are conceited, inconsiderate, thoughtless, ignorant, stubborn. But this is an old truth which nonetheless is not a bad one to repeat. They seldom tolerate a contradiction; never do they forgive disrespect; they are easily attracted by pompous statements and willingly repeat every rumor. And to add to this, they cannot seem to detach themselves from any of this.

Genius and malice are 2 incompatible things.

However there are people who love themselves with such delight, they surprise their own genius with such excitement, they think of their prosperity with such humility, think about their dissatisfactions with such compassion, that the egoism they possess is so mixed with the side of enthusiasm and sensationalism.

Humanity's mind, using a simple and popular expression, is not a prophet, but a guesser. It sees the general progress of things and can conclude profound suppositions from just one item, and which are often justified by time, but it is impossible to foresee accidents – the potent and instantaneous weapon of providence.

I cannot but notice that from the time of the ascension upon the throne of the house of Romanoff our government has always been on the forefront on the course of education and information. But the people seem to lethargically follow after it, and often not even willingly.

I heard said that misfortune is a good school. And perhaps it is. But happiness is the best university. It supplements the education of the soul, making it capable of what is good and beautiful.

In our relationships with foreigners we have no pride and no shame. I, of course, disdain my fatherland from head to toe, but it vexes me if some foreigner should share the same feeling with me.

Inspiration is the mood of the soul towards the earnest receipt of some impression and imagination and their understanding, resulting in their explanation. Inspiration is needed in geometry just as in poetry.

Inspiration is the soul's inclination to the most subtle and acute acceptance of an impression that subsequently leads to a fast deliberation of understanding and which promotes explanation of that impression. Inspiration is needed in poetry just as in geometry.

Is there an assigned epoch as the destiny for every nation where the galaxy of genius suddenly appears, shines, and then disappears?

It is fine not to award your critics with an answer when the attack is purely literary and harms only the sales of the discredited book. But out of respect to yourself you should not abandon the matter without attending to the insulting persons and slanders. At the present and unfortunately this occurs way too often. The public does not deserve disrespect if a response is not provided.

It is not the glory of the ancestors that we boast of, but the rank of some uncle or the balls our female cousin attended. Note that disrespect to ancestors is the first sign of incivility and unethical conduct.

It is possible for a literary language to be completely the same as the conversational? No, and because the conversational language is improved every minute by expressions that are engendered in conversation, but we must not repulse those inclusions that have been acquired in the course of centuries. To write solely in the conversational language means not to know the language.

Loneliness is one of the properties of a thinking entity.

Malice without proof of justification leaves almost eternal traces.

Nothing so inflames love than an approving notice from some stranger. Love is blind and – not trusting even itself – hurriedly grabs for every support.

One of our popular writers was asked why he never responded to criticism. He replied, "Critics do not understand me, and I do not understand my critics. And if this is the case, then the public does not understand either."

Poetry exists as the exclusive passion of only a few, those who are born with an inclination toward poetry. It will encompass and swallow all observances, all strengths, all impressions on his life.

Precision and brevity are the primary qualities of prose. It requires thinking and more thinking. Without this any brilliant expression serves to no purpose.

Russians are lazy and have no sense of curiosity.

Since long into the past the motto of every Russian was – the worse the better.

Skepticism in every situation is only the first step of mental advancement.

The better and more stable changes are those that occur with one improvement of ethic and morality, and not as a result of coercive political upheavals, so terrifying for humanity.

The crowds greedily read confessions and personal notes, because in their insensitivity they rejoice over the humiliation of some high person, over the weaknesses of strong people. The crowds are in ecstasy with the revelation of some vile conduct. "He is small, just as we are; he is vile, just as we are." Such scoundrels lie. It is the crowds that are small and vile.

The dependence of family life makes a person more moral. The dependence that we impose on ourselves due to ambition or self-interest only humiliates us.

The devil guessed that I would be born in Russia since I had a soul and talent.

The first sign of an intelligent person, from the first gaze know with whom you have matters and not to display your bling.

The happy person is the one who lives carefully in the world.

The mind seeks wealth, but the heart does not find it.

The more we are cold, calculating, discrete, the less we subject ourselves to be made a fool. Egoism can be repulsive, but it is not ludicrous, it is a lack of prudence.

The person who has no need of the protection of powerful people values them with kindness and hospitality, because this is something he does not need from them.

There are 2 types of stupidity: one evolves from a lack of feelings and thoughts that can be converted into words; the other from an abundance of feelings and thoughts and an insufficient amount of words to express them.

This is how it must be in every situation. The government opens a road, private people find it better and very comfortable to utilize.

Those who initiate impossible upheavals for us are either young and do not know our people, or are callous and insensitive individuals for whom someone else's head is a dime and their neck is a penny.

Time changes a person in the physical manner as well in his psychological attitude. An adult man with sighs or with smiles will reject fantasies that would agitate a young person. Immature thoughts, as with an immature body, always possesses something strange and humorous. A stupid person does not change, because time will not bring him development, and experience does not exist for him.

To be flaunted is good; to be content is better by double.

To boast of the credit of your ancestors is not only possible but a necessity. To not respect them is shameful timidity. It is a selfless thought that grandchildren will be respected for the name that we bestow upon them. Is not this the most noble hope of the human heart?

To seek for inspiration always seemed to me a funny and stupid silliness. Inspiration is not something to seek, it must find the poet on its own.

True taste consists not in some unaccountable rejection of some word or other, or changing your mind, but in a feeling of balance and identification.

Usually the value of health is only felt after illness. Disagreeing lovers likewise make reconciliation the more pleasurable.

We are compassionate toward the unfortunate due to having the identical original ego. We essentially see that we are not alone to be unfortunate. Only an especially noble and selfless soul can sense happiness at the same time. But happiness is a great *perhaps*, just as speaking about paradise or eternity.

What does aristocracy of breeding and wealth signify in comparison with the aristocracy of authorship talent? No wealth of any type can buy out the influence of national thought. No authority of any type, no government of any type can withstand the all-annihilating effectiveness of the printing press. Have respect for the class of writers, but at the same time do not allow them to entirely overwhelm you.

What shall we conclude from this? That genius has its weaknesses and this comforts mediocrity, but this sorrows noble hearts reminding them of the imperfection of humanity, that the genuine place of the writer is his study cabinet and that finally only independence and self-respect can raise us above life's trivialities and over the storms of faith.

Mikhail Evgrafovich Saltikov-Schedrin

1826 – 1889

Classical Writer, Statesman

Mikhail Saltikov wrote under the pen name of Nikolai Schedrin. He was born in the village Spas-Yugol, Tver Province, central Russia, on January 15, 1826, of an ancient aristocratic family. Saltikov received an excellent private education at home, and at age 10 was accepted into a private school in Moscow, and then in 1838, he went to a private school at Tsarskoi Selo, near St Petersburg. Here he started to compose poetry.

His poetry had a strong socialist inclination and this turned the attention of state authorities toward him. The French Revolution of 1848 especially had an influence on him. So that year Saltikov was exiled to the city Vyatka for promulgating ideas and concepts that were destructive for Russia and due to his influence from events in Western Europe. During his 8 years in Vyatka, he became involved in politics and so became an official in the provincial government, and he also had the opportunity to experience the manner of life of the peasants and the provincial aristocracy.

At the end of 1855, after the death of Nicholas I, the restriction was rescinded and Saltikov was allowed to live wherever he wanted, and so he returned to St Petersburg and continued composing literature. At the same time, in 1856-1858, he worked at the Ministry of Internal Affairs, and was involved in reforms leading to the abolition of the feudal system and providing rights for the serfs.

The years 1858-1862, he served as vice-governor of Ryazan and Tver Provinces, but then retired from government service in 1863 and moved to St Petersburg. There he became editor of a literary journal, but only in 1864, and then returned to government service, now as treasury director for several cities in central Russia: Penza, Tule, Ryazan. But in 1868, Saltikov was back in St Petersburg as editor of another literary journal. He traveled Europe the years 1875-1880, and in Paris he met with Turgenev. Returning to Russia his subsequent novels were poor quality, and as a result of the anger that had developed within Saltikov at the condition of Russia and the lack of government involvement to improve the population's living conditions.

Saltikov died in St Petersburg on April 28, 1889.

When we have the opinion that there are no limits to our happiness, that wise laws do not pertain to us, and we are not subject to the actions of stupid people, then the laws of the middle-way come to our help. Their role includes the responsibility to remind living people that there is no respiring entity in the world that has not had some law pertaining to it at one time or another.

If you should see that a higher person is at fault, then keep in view that he will always have an excuse, "It was due to my vocation that I did this, and it was just an experience." And all will be forgiven him, because he has long forgiven himself for committing all of this. But he will never forgive you for bringing this up to the attention of officials or authorities or for reminding him of his mistake.

A cat gazes from a distance at a piece of fat in a trap and just as the experience of previous days proves that she should not see this piece, then from a natural attitude she begins to hate it. But alas! The motive for this hate is fraudulent. It is not the fat that it hates but the fate that will occur and so the fat is distanced from the cat. In vain does the cat attempt to forget about the fat, in vain turning away from it, and so the cat starts to lick its paws and catch gnats with its teeth and other distractions. The fat is one of those items not to love if it is not accessible.

Alas! The ancient wisdom bequeathed such a multitude of aphorisms that of them, rock by rock, an entire indestructible wall was erected. Each of these aphorisms is structured on the bones of individuals, sealed by blood, having for itself a complete legend of sacrificial devotion, protest, wail, death. Each of them strikes with extreme diversity using some kind of arbitrary accuracy that is hidden by tradition. As you gaze into these aphorisms deeper you will assuredly see at their bottom an entire martyrology.

Although in the Russian Empire the number of laws are more than excessive, but all of them are dispersed over various topics, and very hopefully the majority of them have been consumed in earlier fires.

And then there were people who suspected that the turbulent transfer from unrestrained cannibalism to the lesser unrestrained liberalism was presented to them as not completely natural.

Can you really call success the vocation you successfully accomplished, and only because you were to be punished if you did not?

Do not attempt to move some obstacle, but rather attempt to occupy it.

Do we not see that the most educated nations count themselves especially happy on Sundays and holidays, that is, when officials free themselves from writing laws.

Even the most profound diversity of thought cannot interfere with people doing one and the same thing, even if authority needs to be imposed.

Freedom from the obligation to think is the most beloved seasoning without which an entire person's life is nothing else other than a valley of sorrows.

I cannot imagine that the subject official did not have some type or other question.

I do not discredit repentance, but find that nonetheless it is better to conduct yourself in such a manner that there is never a reason for repentance.

I think that our former bribery (and with satisfaction I utilize the word – bribery – and I can even truthfully believe that no one will even take a quarter at the present) has shown a very significant contribution. Bribery has arranged an abundance of friendship and created simple associations. It has demolished obstacles and reduced distances. It has curbed bureaucratic indifference and made accessible the heart of the official to resolve shallow miseries

I was thinking if it seems to be proper to place a shot of vodka in front of some Russian's eyes, proper to open the door to some saloon, so that he would immediately lose his bearings, forget about his sorrows, and about scholarship, and even about the sacred obligation to be sober, and consistently abandon shepherding the herd of cows which was entrusted to his care! No!

Something seems to not be right here. It is only people who discredit the Russian people who have conjured this up, or at least those activists against our present system.

If a person thought to prove his right to life by means of suicide, did he prove very much?

If anybody by time he reaches 20 years of age has not wanted and has not aspired toward the general revitalization, it is very difficult to say about him if he has ever had a heart capable of empathy and compassion.

In general elderly people squander their time, intermingling with young people. Alas! As much as they may strive to pass themselves as having a youthful approach, but nonetheless in the end, their morals will interfere.

In order to love your homeland, there is no demand to know in detail its geographic boundaries.

In what manner can we prove that the elder's point of view is correct rather than the young person's. Where do we find support for our elder other than personally experience prudence, to which the young person will normally have a negligent attitude due to arrogance? Does youth have the right to assert itself so loftily to ancient wisdom? Of course it does not, but this is how it is, whether it does or it doesn't. If this is the attitude of youth there is nothing you can do.

It is necessary to be very tolerant with an official. Only in the extreme situation when you are totally without doubt that the official is having a difficult time on account of a subject of some preceding conversation can you help him, and by inserting some type of casual thought. But this needs to be done in such a manner that the general will not for a minute doubt that this thought was not personally his.

It is not feudal rights that are so pitiful, but what is pitiful is that these laws – and disregarding its abolition – still reside in our hearts. Departing from it only superficially, we have not improved within ourselves any courage, which consists of the first sign of liberation from this web, or obtained new views on life, or any more demanding inclination against, but we have simply pacified ourselves on the sole formal recognition of the facts of its abolition.

It will never seem to any administration that clearly understands the benefit of some enterprise that this benefit can be unclear or doubtful for someone. Finally, every administrator manipulates so that another would extend their trust to him. But what is the best manner to express this trust, if it is not an impeccable observance of what you do not understand?

Knowing your good heart, I very much remember how difficult it must have been for you to accuse everybody. But if your government wants this, then what can you do, my friend, except accuse!

Many think that if a person has the ability to unnoticeably pull a handkerchief from the pocket of whomever is standing next to him, then this is as though sufficient to verify his reputation as a pickpocket or a politician.

No useful occupation is senseless if it, time to time, is freshened at dinner with champagne and oysters.

Not separatism, not socialism can interfere with writing reports, circulars, documents and opinions.

Of course, some details have changed, but have details at some time actually composed something of substance? Today they have one view, tomorrow they will have another. If the principle basis of life is steadfast, then there is nothing easier than to provide details of one or another form, whatever you want.

People ordinarily begin at the point where they joke in reference to the creation of the world, but they conclude by not acknowledging authority.

Persistent repetition aloud of the first nonsense that pops out can destroy every pleasant thought.

Presently there are many dangers, but the principle danger is the stupid habit of utilizing smart words in conversation. It is absolutely necessary to abandon this habit and strive to speak in a manner that is simpler, especially in saloons and brothels. Let us take for example just the word *association*. Essentially it has entered literary custom to the point that it does not scare anybody. But saloons and brothels still adhere to an academic lexicon into which this word has not yet entered. So if you were to there utter words similar to association, irrigation, aberration, it is all the same: the sexual and harmful connotation they will still understand, meaning that you are propagating a revolution.

Reform attempts in a beneficial manner unite with the smell of raw vodka and have a benevolent attitude toward fraud, which proves that fraud is strong and it is so strong that it is impossible to deal with it.

Reforms are unavoidable, but no less unavoidable than are punctuation marks, or to say this in other words, once one reform is instituted, then this is enough, time to place a period.

Right now people are so weak, that even in the sight of a hundred-dollar bill they loose control of their emotions. So what will occur when they see an entire million in the fog?

So in essence what is Petersburg? It is not Moscow's son, with only this specialty, that it has a window frame directed toward Europe, but carved by a censurer's scissors.

Such measures taken, such as hand shaking, a giddy smile and in general a humble acknowledgement, are felt as though they are spontaneous and do not leave any apparent or expressible traces in history.

The attitude of the masses to a popular idea is the sole measurement by which you can judge the level of their vitality.

The entire difference between a healthy person and a mentally ill consists in the former installing an obvious border between the ideal and the real, while the latter does not recognize any type of distinction between them in this sense.

The less educated a person, the more stubborn he is in his undertakings and once having thought of some type of accomplishment, sooner or later he will achieve it.

The political arena converts exceptionally easy into an arena for the resolution of the question – In what situation is it most advantageous? Of course, the reasonable question is avoided – For whom is it most advantageous. The result of such an arrangement of things surfaces, of course, not as a triumph of the state, but a triumph of cunning people. It is not the devotion of the country, not talent, and not mental ability, that provides a guarantee of success, but shrewdness, ruthlessness, and betrayal.

There are expressions that are liked only because they are secretly tempting, although their inner meaning always remains undecipherable.

There is no debate that people can be given and even should be given the opportunity to eat of the fruit of the knowledge of good and evil, except that this fruit should be held firmly by the hand and so that at any time you can withdraw it from excessively drooling lips.

There is nothing for some official that is more burdensome than for him to see that there is a limit to his fervency.

This is not part of a Russian person's nature, to pass his years and not insult anyone. It seems that if you do not insult someone, then this means that you are cowardly and pathetic, that altercation means nothing to you.

This is why if we meet a person who, speaking of life, drapes himself in the mantle of scholarly, educated and social interests and assures us that he has never been so happy and has never lived such a full life, as he researches the questions of the arrival of the Varangians or of the gravesite of Prince Pozharski,[22] then we cannot truthfully say that this person either intentionally or unconsciously is hiding his present feelings.

This sufficiently often occurs with people who at one time were close to us and then for some long interval departed, and then again they meet. And suddenly it seems that not only do they have nothing about which to talk, but now they are annoyed with one another.

Very often young people initially only play a role, but then they are enticed into the reality and acquire bad habits.

We should not be serious over every matter. We should also not deprive ourselves of humor at the proper time. This is what oils our life. When the wheels squeak take and oil them.

Well I heard this asked regularly, is it possible to attain our ideal in life in such a circumstance, where not only we but every other has the right to proclaim their desire to live? I cannot live in the same place where every other has the same right as I do to live.

---

[22] Dmitri Mikhailovich Pozharski, entered Moscow at the conclusion of the Time of Troubles, 1712. Debate still ranges whether he was buried at the Kazan Cathedral in Red Square or at the Spaso-Efimiev Monastery in Suzdal.

Sorry, master, I cannot tolerate it when I see some loafer wandering near me who is surviving off others' charitable attitude.

What is the state? Some confuse it with the fatherland; others with the law; a third with punishment of criminals; a fourth – and the immense majority – with authority.

Whenever you feel that law imposes an obstacle on you, then, having removed something from the table, place it under you. And then all of this that is now no longer seen will ameliorate much of your activity.

Within a person resides some type of nebulous instinct of self-preservation, which increases his susceptibility of every surrounding motion and to allow dealing with it.

You are assiduous, young man! And this I cannot deny of you! But you are excessively assiduous, and this contains a fault in the presence of which even complete inactivity is presented as a quality far from useless.

Vladimir Aleksandrovich Sollogub

1813 – 1882

Classical Writer

Vladimir Sollogub was born in St Petersburg on August 8, 1813; he was actually from a Lithuanian-Polish aristocratic family, although he always considered himself Russian.

His parents wanted him to have a diplomatic career and in 1829 he attended Dorpat University (today known as Tartu, Estonia), and graduated in 1833. He entered Russian government service at the Ministry of Foreign Affairs at the Vienna, Austria office, and then returned to Russia to work at the Ministry of Internal Affairs in the Caucasus region. In 1870, he became president of the commission for the improvement of prisons in Moscow. He sided with Belinski in his political views as a Slavophile and often attended their circle.

But Sollogub was never a great success in his government service, and did not consider his inherited wealth as a benefit. He was always preoccupied with his literary efforts. He also supported many of the arts through his wife who was a singer and musician.

Although Sollogub died in Hamburg, Germany, on July 5, 1882, his body was returned to Russia and buried in Moscow.

At the present, just about anything can be counterfeited, even art. A spark falling from the sky is small, and it will not light a fire in every heart, it will not illuminate every soul, but it will provide the mechanism to each person, whoever has at least a hand and a will. We will live to that point when art becomes a trade. Soon enough it will become lower than a trade. Only a few have the ability to distinguish the genuine from the forged.

Constant sorrow and uninterruptible happiness both lead to indifference. Despair becomes a habit of life and imposes some type of premature death for the soul.

Egoism is such a blemish that always finds for itself an appropriate individual and who is not just an excuse.

Every narrative of a persons' heart for the greater part is nothing else than a narrative unfinished.

Fiction will never become strange unless occasionally it will present real life to us.

I want to live and move, and not stand in one spot and feel time just passing through me.

Loving souls, once deceived, do not condescend, but transfer only the excess of their heavenly fire to a person more worthy.

There are words that we utilize during our entire life while not understanding them, and then suddenly we do, and just that one word causes us to fall, and then over a cliff and all is destroyed.

We like to discredit others in order to excuse ourselves. But perhaps what is faulty in us should also be excusable in others.

We often discredit the Germans because they always seem to find a warm spot in our holy Russia and attain in particular what we are aspiring. But are we not to blame for this ourselves? They are stubborn, while we neglect the situation. They labor incessantly and inexhaustibly, while we are ready to squander our entire flame on one impulse and spend the balance of our life in lethargy. What is amazing is how they interfere with our civil life, create obstacles for us on our paths, and then take our places right under our eyes, and all of what is so close to our hearts.

When an inspiration flies into us, do not express it in words. Lifeless words little affect the living soul. One thing, perhaps, music, as something between the soul and the word, between sky and ground, can express in a weak tint a portion of the inexpressible ecstasy that even only once in life will dawn upon each person from above.

LEO NIKOLAEVICH TOLSTOY

1828 – 1910

Classical Author, Religious Philosopher

Leo Tolstoy was born October 28, 1828, at his family estate Yasnaya Polyana, near Tule, central Russia. He was shuffled family to family because of the death of both his parents when he was young. The family lived in Moscow for a while, until Tolstoy was 8, and then returned to Tule. He entered Kazan University, but was unable to finish his courses, and returned home in 1847, there studying philosophy on his own. In 1851, he moved to the Caucasus region and joined the army, where he fought local barbaric tribes. During his time here Tolstoy began his literary career with several short stories of his childhood and adolescence. He was then transferred to the Crimea with the war in 1854, and then migrated to St Petersburg the following year.

Now released from the military, Tolstoy became involved with a circle of writers and began writing for local journals, his career as a serious classical author begins at this time. Spring and summer of 1857, Tolstoy traveled Europe, and then back to St Petersburg. In 1860, he returned to Yasnaya Polyana and dedicated himself to the education of the peasant children and opening schools for them, including creating textbooks. In the subsequent years, Tolstoy penned his *War and Peace* and several of the novels for which he is most famous. But his rise to popularity had a deleterious effect on him. His study of philosophy, his effort to improve the life of the serfs and their children on his estate, and the negative psychological effects that war had on him, drove Tolstoy to reevaluate his life and to discover life's meaning and purpose. Then Tolstoy turned to a study of the New Testament, and especially the Gospels, and he turned his life toward a different and better direction.

From about 1880, his studies and compositions were concentrated on a pristine Christianity, one that was without rites and theology, but emphasized conduct and morality. His future novels now had an ethical basis to them, especially *Resurrection*. Tolstoy introduced a new form of Christian humanism to resolve the problems of humanity, and especially to terminate war. His book, *The Kingdom of God within You*, was the materialization of Tolstoy's concept of Christian pacifism and non-violence.

Tolstoy's new writings placed him in direct conflict with the Russian Orthodox Church, and he was excommunicated on February 20, 1901. The strain that Tolstoy endured as a result of his new religious philosophy over the next several years forced him to leave home for a period of recuperation. After visiting his sister – she was a nun – at her convent, Leo Tolstoy died at the Astapovo train station of pneumonia on November 7, 1910.

Among the innumerable quantity of thoughts and dreams, without any evidence of having entered the mind and imagination, there are a few that leave in them a deep and impacting furrow, such that often, not remembering the essence of the thought, you remember that there was something nice in your head, you feel traces of the thought and then strive to again replicate it.

Conceit is an attitude that is most incompatible with true sorrow and along with this, this attitude is so firmly integrated into a person's nature that very seldom will the greatest misfortune banish it. Conceit during sorrow is expressed by the desire to display yourself either sorrowful or unfortunate or firm. And these basic desires – which we do not recognize ourselves as having, but which almost never will leave us, even in the worst of sorrows – will exhaust us of our strength, dignity and sincerity.

Do not believe that this life is just a migration into the other world and that it will be well for us only there. This is not true. We must do well here in this world. And in order for it to be well for us here in this world, we need to live in the manner that He wants, the One who sent us into this world.

Eternal despair, labor, struggle and deprivation are all unavoidable conditions from which you should not even try to escape even for a second. Struggle and labor based on love is what we call happiness. But honor founded on a love solely of yourself is unhappiness.

Every person knowing to the most infinitesimal detail all the complexity of the conditions that surround him, subconsciously supposes that the complexity of these conditions and the difficulty of their explanation is only his personal and accidental speculation, but no way does he think that others are also surrounded by the same complexity of their personal conditions, just as he is.

It so often occurs that for years you see your family through the one and same fallacious veil of etiquette, while the true attitudes of the family members remain a secret to you. I even notice that the more beautiful this veil the less penetrating it is, and so the more cruel the true attitudes that are being hidden from you. Often it is not so painful to beat your head against the doorjambs with all your strength until you reach exhaustion and that point of finally breaking the veil. And this exhausted and painful place occurs in almost every family.

Some people, when they meet some opponent, and notice whatever type of success he has attained, are ready to immediately deny him all the good in him and see only the possible bad in him. Some people act on the contrary and more than anything want to find in this successful opponent those qualities that allowed him to overcome obstacles, and want to find in him – even if should cause pain in their own heart – only that which is good.

There are 2 sides of life in every person: the personal life that is the more free the more it is inclined to its interests; and the elemental life, the crowded, where a person inescapably observes all the laws that are ascribed to him. A person consciously lives for himself, but unconsciously serves as a tool for the attainment of historical and collective goals. An accomplished action cannot be reverted and its effects, coincident with time with the millions of actions of other people, receives historical significance. The higher a person stands on the social ladder, the more a person is tied to great people, the more authority a person has over other people, so the more apparent is the predetermination and inescapability of each of his actions.

War is so unjust and ugly that all who wage it must try to stifle the voice of conscience within themselves.

We have not only in criticism, but in literature, even plainly in society, an opinion established that you can be agitated, bitter and bad as long as it is in a nice manner. But I find this to be very vile. A person who is bitter or bad is not in a normal state. On the contrary, only a loving person is in a normal state to do what is good and clearly see and think.

"War is not friendship, but the most vile matter occurring in life; and we ought to understand this and not play at war.
　"But what is war? What is needed for success in warfare? What are the morality of the military? The goal of war is murder; the weapons of war are spying, treachery, and their encouragement, the annihilation of a country's residents, pillaging

them or stealing to provide the army's provision, and fraud and falsehood are termed military strategy. The morality of the military class is the absence of freedom, that is, discipline, idleness, ignorance, cruelty, depravity, and drunkenness. And in spite of all this it is the highest vocation, respected by everyone. All the kings... wear military uniforms, and he who kills the most people receives the highest reward.

"They will meet, as we will meet tomorrow, to murder one another; they will kill and maim tens of thousands, and then have thanksgiving services for having killed so many people – whose number is even exaggerated – and they announce a victory, supposing that the more people killed is the greater the achievement."[23]

I believe in the God that I understand, as a spirit, as love, as the fundamental principle of all. I believe that He is in me, and I am in Him. That God, who is recognized by the person in whom He resides, is the desire for benevolence for all that exists; He is the beginning of all life, and He is love. I believe that the will of God is most clearly of all expressed in the teachings of the person Christ.

God descended on earth, the Son of God, one of 3 persons of the Holy Trinity and materialized as a human and he redeemed the sin of Adam. But we have been trained to think that this God must have said something mysteriously enigmatic, something that is so difficult to understand that it can only be understood with the help of belief and grace. But now suddenly the words of God have become so plain, so clear, so intellectual. God plainly says, "Do not do harm one to another and no more harm will exist." Can

---

[23] Tolstoy, Leo, *War and Peace*, Volume 3, Part 2, chapter 25. Tolstoy reflects on the role of the soldier using Andrei Bolkhonski as his mouthpiece to his friend Pierre Bezukhov on the eve of the battle at Borodino

the revelation of God really be so simple? Is God the only one to have said this? It seems to us that we already know this, because it is so simple.

Yesterday[24] a conversation regarding divinity and faith led me to recognize an immense concept, the materialization of which I felt myself capable of dedicating my life to. This thought was the basis for a new religion, one that would be pertinent to the development of humanity. It would be the religion of Christ, but purged of theology and sacraments; a practical religion that would not promise a future bliss, but provide bliss on earth. It seemed to me that the only manner to bring this concept to fulfillment would be the effort of successive generations consciously working toward this goal. One generation will bequeath this concept to the next and at some time, either fanaticism or intelligence will bring it to its materialization. To act consciously to unify people with this religion is the thought that I feel will drive me.

What motivates me to do what I am doing is not greed or credit or worldly recognition, but the fear of not fulfilling that which is required of me by Him who sent me into this world, and every hour I await my return to Him. So I am convinced that I will not find a resolution to my question and amelioration of my suffering in existing denominations. I reached such despair that I drew to suicide, but then my salvation arrived. My salvation consisted in the fact that since childhood, I retained a vague notion that the Gospel contains the answer to my question. I sensed truth in this teaching, the Gospel, disregarding all the distortion to which it has been subjected in the teaching of the Christian Church. And I, as my final attempt, rejecting every interpretation of Evangelical teaching, began to read the Gospel and delve into its concepts. And the more I delved into the concepts of this book, the more that something new was unveiled to me, something unlike that which Christian churches taught, but it was the resolution to the question that my life sought for. And finally this answer became

---

[24] March 4, 1855, while Tolstoy was in the military serving at the front during the Crimean War.

completely clear. And this answer was not just only clear, but also doubtless.

If I believe in God, then there is nothing to ask about what will result from my obedience to God, because I know that God is love, and nothing but goodness can evolve from it. The true law of life is so simple, obvious and understandable, that there is no manner for anybody to justible their poor quality life by apologizing that they do not know this law. If people live contrary to the law of true life, they can only do one thing: deny their intelligence. And this is exactly what they do. When a person acknowledges true belief, what occurs to him is the same as with a person who lights a lamp in a dark room. All becomes visible and joy enters the person's soul.

Love provides people goodness, because it unites a person with God. Christ disclosed to people that eternity is not just the future, but that what is eternal is invisible and resides in us right now in our life, that we become eternal when we unite with God as a spirit, in Whom all live and move. We attain this eternity not through prayers, sacraments or rites, but only through love.

Recently I was at Optina Pustin,[25] and saw there people burning with sincere love toward God and people, and in addition, considering it an absolute necessity to stand in church for several hours daily, take communion, bless and be blessed, and then paralyze within themselves the active strength of love. How can I hate such superstitious people?

One item that is definitely fact and doubtless is what Christ said when dying, "Into your hands I provide my spirit." Namely that dying I proceed to the same place that I originated. And if I believe this, that I originated from rational love, then I joyfully return to it, knowing that all will be well with me. And I am not

---

[25] A Russian Orthodox monastery in the city Kozelsk, Kaluga Province, in central Russia. Ambrose Optinski (also in this volume) was Father Superior at this time.

only not distressed, but I rejoice at the migration that is ahead of me.

Everywhere many times Christ says that the person who will not take the cross, who will not deny everything, that is, whoever is not prepared for all the consequences that result from fulfilling the rule regarding not resisting harm, cannot be his student. Jesus says to his disciples, 'Be mendicant, be prepared, do not resist harm, accept persecution, suffering and death.' He prepared himself for suffering and death, not resisting harm, and so scolded Peter who was concerned for him, and he himself died while forbidding resistance to harm and not changing his teaching. All his initial students fulfilled this principle of not resisting harm and their entire life passed as mendicants, in persecutions, and never did they compensate harm for harm.

In vain do people say that the Christian teaching applies only to personal salvation, and does not apply to questions of society and the state. This is only a bold and merely verbal confirmation of what is so obviously incorrect, and which collapses at the first serious thought regarding it.

My personal life has been interwoven with the government, but the government demands from me unchristian activities, those that are directly against the commandments of Christ. The law of God or the law of people? It stands directly before those who now want to be Christians, just as it stood before me.

The law of Christ with its teaching of love, humility, self-denial, always earlier touched my heart and drew me to it. But from every facet in history and in my contemporary surroundings, and in my life, I saw a contradictory law that was against my heart, my conscience, my intellect, that was being impressed on my animal instinct. I felt that if I was to accept the law of Christ, I would remain alone and matters will become bad for me, and I will incur persecution and sorrow, those very things that Jesus said would occur. If I accept the law of people, and everybody will approve of me, I will be content and secure, and this will sharpen my mind and I would approve all of the service I provided, and this will rest my conscience. I would laugh and rejoice, just as Christ said. I felt this and so I did not delve deep into the significance of the law of Christ, and strove to understand it in such a manner so it would not annoy me as I lived the life of an animal. But it was impossible to understand it in this manner, and so I did not understand it at all.

Now the teaching of Christ, as I now perceive it, has another and different significance: it is the installation of the kingdom of God on earth and dependant on us. The fulfillment of the teaching of Christ expressed in these 5 commands installs this kingdom of God. The Kingdom of God is the peace of all peoples among themselves. Peace among people is the supreme attainable benefit for people on earth. So was the Kingdom of God presented to all the Hebrew prophets. And so it has been presented and is presented to the heart of every person. All prophecy promises peace to people.

The entire teaching of Christ consists in providing the Kingdom of God as peace to people. In the Sermon on the Mount, in the conversation with Nicodemus, in the letters of the apostles, in all of his instruction he speaks only of what it is that divides people and interferes with their institution of peace and entrance into the Kingdom of God. All the parables are solely descriptions of what the Kingdom of God is and that by loving the brethren and being in peace with them a person can enter it. It is worth it for people to believe the teaching of Christ and fulfill it, and peace will be installed on earth, but not the type of peace that is installed by people, which is temporal and incidental, but a peace that is universal, unassailable and eternal.

With the fulfillment of these commands the life of people will become what every person's heart seeks and wants. All people will become brethren and each will always be in peace with others, enjoying all the benefits of peace during the period of life that God assigns to them. They will beat their swords into plows and their spears into pruning shears. The Kingdom of God, the kingdom of peace, as all the prophets promised will materialize.

The commands of peace given by Christ are simple, clear and foresee all possible incidences of discord and can prevent them, and in this manner the Kingdom of God on earth will materialize. It seems that Christ is definitely the Messiah. He fulfilled what was promised regarding him. But we do not fulfill what people have eternally wanted, what we have prayed for and continue to pray for.

I believe the teaching of Christ and this is what my belief consists of. I believe that my welfare on earth is only possible when all people will fulfill the teaching of Christ. I believe that the fulfillment of this teaching is possible, easy and joyful.

I believe that my earlier life according to the teaching of the world was torture; and that only a life according to the teaching of Christ provides me goodness in this world, which the Father of life has ordained for me.

I believe that this teaching provides goodness for all humanity, saves me from inevitable ruin and gives me here a greater goodness. For this reason, it is impossible for me not to fulfill it.

Love provides goodness to a person not as its consequences, but in the practice of love itself, and this provides him a goodness that is completely independent from the manner other people conduct themselves and what generally occurs in the superficial world. Love provides goodness in this manner: a loving person unites with God and not only desires nothing for himself, but wants to distribute all that he possesses, even his own life, to others. In such a devotion to God does this person find goodness. And so whatever other people may do, all what may occur in the world, this cannot have any influence on his actions. Love is devotion to God, to do what God wants, and God is love, that is, wanting goodness for everybody. As a result, He does not want any person to perish when fulfilling His law.

A loving person, and even if he is alone among non-loving people, will not perish. And even if he does perish among people as Jesus died on the cross, then even his death will be a joy to him and become significant to others, and it will not be hopeless and futile as is the death of secular people. And if a person who does not devote himself to love uses the excuse, "Because not everybody will do this and that person will remain alone," this is wrong and bad. This attitude can be compared to a person who needs to work in order to feed himself and his family, but decides not to work because other people are not working.

Yes, dear friends, let us dedicate our life to increasing love in ourselves and permit the world to continue going as it wants to, that is, in the manner that fate has assigned it. Let us conduct ourselves so and believe that we will receive a greater goodness for ourselves if we always do goodness to people, and what it is that we want to do. Know that this is so simple and easy and joyful. Only love every person; not loving only those who love you, but all people, especially those who hate you just as Christ taught, and life will become an incessant joy. And all questions which lost people will vainly attempt to resolve by using violence, are not only resolved but cease to exist. "And we know that we have passed from death into life if we love the brethren. He who does not love his brother does not possess eternal life. Only he who loves his brother possesses eternal life that resides in him."

Only try this, dear friends, and you will see that the teaching of love – not in word, but in action – is so close to you and so understandable and so necessary a matter.

I am not telling you to be perfect, because self-perfection contains something personal that gratifies ambition. I am telling you to do what God wants to be done, that God who gave us life; to display what He has instilled in us, which is just like Himself: the principle to live according to God.

Believe yourself and live in this manner, harnessing all your strength to accomplish one matter: to display God in yourself. And you will be able to do all that you can for your own goodness and for the goodness of the entire world.

I write what I am writing only because I stand at the edge of the coffin and cannot any more be silent, knowing the one thing that can liberate people of the Christian world from these horrible bodily sufferings and especially from this spiritual distortion by which they all more and more defile themselves.

In our time it cannot but be clear for all thinking people that people's lives – and not only Russian people but all the nations of the Christian world – cannot continue in the manner that it has with their misery and their ever increasing needs, and the luxury of the wealthy with their struggle of all against all: the revolutionaries against the government, the government against the revolutionaries, the enslaved nations against the enslavers, the struggle within the government itself, the west against the east with their ever increasing weapons only consuming the strength of the nation, with their luxury and their moral corruption. And if it does not change it will inevitably become more miserable and even more miserable.

The means of deliverance from this miserable situation – and the means are not fantastic, not artificial, but the most natural – consists in the peoples of the Christian world adopting an understanding of life and the guidance of life evolving from it that is compatible with the present maturity of humanity, the one that was disclosed to them 19 centuries ago, and this is the Christian teaching in its true meaning.

99% of all crimes that blemish humanity evolve due to the influence of alcohol one way or another.

A cowardly friend is more dangerous than an enemy, because the enemy you fear, while the friend you rely on.

A ideal is a guiding star. Without it there is no firm direction, and if there is no firm direction there is no life.

A person can serve to making better community life only to the extent that he in his own life fulfills the demands of his conscience.

A person must always be happy. If your happiness ends, the seek and resolve the mistake you made.

A person must exert the effort to restrain himself from words that are contrary to love towards associate and contrary to the person's acknowledgement of the divine rule residing within him. This includes the effort to restrain oneself from thoughts contrary to love toward associates and the person's acknowledgement of the divine rule residing within him.

A person needs to believe in the possibility of happiness in order to be happy.

A person only has an affect on others when his personal life reflects his convictions.

A person ruins his stomach and complains at dinner. So it is with people who are dissatisfied with life. We do not have any right to be dissatisfied with this life. If it seems to us that we are dissatisfied with it, then this only means that we have a basis to be dissatisfied with ourselves.

A person with nothing to do always has many helpers.

A person's mind resides independently from the heart and often instills in it thoughts that sorrow feelings, that are not understandable and cruel to it.

A person's true strength consists not in upheavals, but in an infallible tranquility.

A proud person causes a bark of ice to grow over him. There is no entrance for any other feeling through this bark.

A question not resolved by diplomacy is even less resolved by gunpowder and blood.

A slave who is content with his state is twice a slave, because he is not just a body in slavery, but his soul is in slavery also.

A summons to a vocation can be recognized and proven only through sacrifice, which will provide the student or artist rest or prosperity so he can devote himself to his vocation.

Aesthetics is an expression of ethics. Art expresses those feelings that the artist experiences. If the feelings are good, then his art is good and exalted. And on the contrary, if the artist is an immoral person, then his art will be immoral.

All feelings of a high quality are united with some type of undefined grief.

All happy families are similar one to another. Every unhappy family is unhappy in its own way.[26]

All moral education of children leads to a good example. Live right or at least strive to life right and according to the measure of your success in your good life you will educate children properly.

All of life is only a drive and gradual approach to perfection, which is unreachable, because it is perfection.

All of our misfortunes are the result of us selling our soul for a bowl of lentil soup[27] of corporeal joys.

---

[26] This is the first line to *Anna Karenina*.
[27] The reference is to Esau selling his birthright to Jacob for a bowl of soup, Gen 25:33-34.

All of people's disasters occur not as a result of they not doing what they needed to do, as much as from doing what they should not have done.

All people occupied with truly an important manner are always simple, because they do not have the time to think of superfluous activities.

All people of the world have an identical right to the utilization of the natural resources of the world and the identical right to respect them.

All the aspirations of people, all their motivations to life are only an aspiration to an increase of freedom. Wealth – poverty, glory – oblivion, authority – subjection, strength – weakness, work – leisure, food – famine, are all just greater or smaller levels of freedom.

An expansive nature is not just one characteristic of a Russian person. He is inexhaustive and unfathomable, a person of extreme possibilities.

An exposed lie is just as valuable an acquisition for the welfare of humanity as is a clearly expressed truth.

An undoubtable condition of happiness is work. First, it needs to be work that you love and do voluntarily. Second, the work needs to be corporeal, creating an appetite and a firm and restful sleep.

Belief is understanding life's meaning and the recognition of obligations that evolve from this understanding.

Benevolence is the eternal and supreme goal of our life. No matter how we understand benevolence, our life is nothing else but this aspiration to benevolence.

Books containing other people's speeches do not suppress independent and creative thought, but actually summon creative thinking.

Both of you be cautious, pay attention to your mutual attitudes more than to anything else, so that some habit of irritation or alienation will not creek in. It is not an easy matter to become one soul and one body. You need to work at it. But the reward for this effort is great. I know one principle manner as the means to do this: do not forget one minute about your marital love, do not squander your love by acting like just ordinary people. In order to have attitudes of a husband with his wife, and not that you should forget to also have such attitudes toward strangers and close associates, keep the love between you. This is your consolidation.

But it is difficult for a dissatisfied person not to reproach someone else, and it seems that who is closest to you of all is what dissatisfies you the most.

Charity consists not only in material assistance, as much as spiritual support of your close associate. Spiritual support first of all consists in not discrediting your close associate and respecting his human dignity.

Criticism is only productive when it, after concluding that something is bad or wrong, will also state what is good and right to replace it.

Digging into our soul we often dig up what was lying there not noticed.

Dissatisfaction on its own face value is an unavoidable condition of an intellectual life. Only this dissatisfaction motivates us to work on ourselves.

Do not ever despair when you are in a struggle. Do not consider a struggle a precedent of some future something to happen. This is life: difficult and painful, but true life.

Do not swim or row if you do not know where you are swimming or rowing. And do not spend your life and effort not knowing why.

Do only what spiritually stimulates you, and be assured that in this manner you will be most of all useful to society

Do something benevolent in secret and worry should someone discover it, and you will learn the joys of doing benevolence. Your knowledge of a benevolent life without people's approval is the best reward of a benevolent life.

Each person has self-interest, and all and whatever a person does evolves from self-interest. This attitude of self-interest is the conviction that I am better and smarter than all other people.

Effort is an indispensable condition of moral perfection.

Even if a crowd is an accumulation of good people, the close proximity of just their animal and vile facets will express the weakness and cruelty of human nature.

Every majestic act is done in particular under the conditions of inconspicuousness, humility, simplicity.

Every person knows that he must not do what will disconnect him from people, but rather do what will unite him with them.

Every person wants to change humanity, but no one seems to think enough about how to change himself.

Every thought is wrong and it is also right. It is wrong because it is one-sided due to the person's impossibility to encompass all truth, and it is right because of its expression of one side of a person's convictions.

Family attitudes are complex for an ethical person, for someone unethical, everything is smooth.

For the most part it seems that you argue with fervency only because you cannot in any manner understand what your opponent is particularly trying to prove.

Genuine depravity is particularly when you free yourself from all moral attitudes toward a woman and only deal with her in physical intercourse.

Goodness for the soul has the same affect as health for the body. It is not noticeable when you possess it, it provides success in every effort.

Happiness does not consist in always doing what you want, but in always wanting to do what you can.

Happiness, happiness, the irrecoverable interval of childhood. How can we not love it, how can we not cherish our memories of it! Such memories freshen, ennoble my soul and serve for me the source of better consolations.

Have a goal for your entire life, a goal for a special time, a goal for the year, for the month, for the week, for the day, and for the hour, and for the minute, and sacrifice the lower goals in favor of the higher.

He possessed the ability to understand art and truly, with a taste to be able to imitate art, and then he thought that he had that same endowment as needed to be an artist.

Human life is full of corporeal sufferings, at every second it can be horrible disrupted. In order for life not to become just a big cruel joke, it must have a meaning, one that will not cause the meaning of life to be destroyed, not due to its sufferings, not due to its longevity, or its temporality.

I find it uneasy to look into the eyes of 3 categories of people: those who are considerable worse than I am; those who are considerable better than I am; and those with whom we mutually will not waste our time speaking to each other.

I heard said that it is not necessary to love yourself. But without love of yourself, there would not be life. The matter is what to love about yourself, and this is your soul and your body.

I often hear people brag about the immaculacy of their souls, and only because they possess a short memory.

I often heard young people say, "I do not want to live by some alien philosophy. I will think of all of this myself." But why should you rethink what has already been thought? Take what was already conceived and proceed further using it. This is the strength of humanity.

If a person did not possess feeling of want, he would not be a person. The reason for every activity is want.

If a person is solely a corporeal entity, then death is the conclusion of something that is worthless anyway and there is no reason to sorrow over it. If a person is a spiritual entity and the soul is only temporal in the body, then death is only a change.

If in place of divine authority another type of strength was to arise, then it is necessary to describe of what this new strength consists. Because particularly in this very strength the entire interest in history is confined.

If life does not present itself as an immense joy, then this is because your mind is incorrectly oriented.

If reason does not indicate to you your place in the world and your significance, then know that what is to blame is not the incorrect arrangement of the world, and not your mind, but the incorrect direction that you have given it.

If the goal of a marriage is having a family, then the man who has many wives will perhaps find much satisfaction, but not in any circumstance will he have a family.

If the strength of unethical people lies in their consolidation, then for moral people to be strong they must do the same.

If we were to suppose that the course of humanity can be governed by reason, then the possibility of life will be destroyed.

If you are doing something, then do it well. If you cannot or if you do not want to do it well, then it is best not to do it at all.

If you should ask, "Why does evil exist?" I answer with a question, "Why does life exist?" Evil exists so life will. Life appears as a liberation from evil.

If you want to live calmly and contently, then separate from everything you can live without.

In an unethical society, all acquisitions that increase the authority of humans over nature is not only not benevolent, but undoubtedly is obviously malevolent.

In any attachment there exists 2 sides: one is to love, the other is to permit someone to love you. One kisses, while the other presents his cheek.

In moments of indecision you must act quickly and strive to take the first step, although it might be superfluous.

In order to accomplish something great, all the efforts of your soul need to be concentrated on that specific item.

In order to accomplish something in family life, what is unavoidable is either complete contention between the spouses, or loving agreement. When the attitude between the spouses are undefined and there is not one or the other, no matter of any type will ever be accomplished.

In order to be happy only one item is needed – love, and love with self-sacrifice, to love all and everyone, to throw to every side a web of love, and to accept whoever is caught in it.

In order to be happy, it is necessary to constantly strive to grasp such happiness and understand it. It depends not on circumstances, but on yourself.

In order to live honorably, you need to strain, stumble, struggle, err, begin and discard, and again begin and again discard, and eternally struggle and suffer deprivation.

In our associations we notice 2 sorts of people. Some obviously conduct themselves with you just as they would with anybody else. Whether they are pleasant or not is a matter of taste, but they are not dangerous. Others are afraid of insulting you, embittering or annoying you or even complementing you. They speak without pretensions, very attentive to you and often flatter. For the most part these people are pleasant. Fear them! With such people occurs the most unusual transformations into an opposite character: from being polite to becoming mean, from a flatterer to an insulter, from good to bad.

In youth all strengths of the soul are directed to the future and this future accepts such diverse, vivacious and enchanting forms under the influence of hope based not on the experience of the past, but on the imagined possibility of happiness, that solely understood and shared fantasies of future happiness compose now the true happiness of this age.

Integrity is the extreme measure of virtue, to which every person is obligated. Higher than it is the level of perfection, lower is the level of moral corruption.

It always seems to us that they like us because we are good. But we never do guess that the ones that like us are those who are good.

It always takes efforts to accomplish some good work, but when this effort is repeated several times, then the work becomes a habit.

It is better to know less than you can, then to know more than you need. Do not fear a lack of information, but fear the extraneous, the overwhelming knowledge that you acquire only as your ambition.

It is easier to yield to yourself than to condescend to others. And there is no situation where a person cannot find some type of happiness.

It is not embarrassing and not harmful not to know something. We are not able to know everything, but it is embarrassing to pretend that we know something when we don't.

It is well known that a person has a capability to delve completely into one subject, and whichever one seems to him the most useless. And it is well known that there exists no useless subject that would – with sufficient concentration of attention turned toward it – not inflate to fill eternity.

It seems that once a person touches nature, all the bad in his heart should vanish. This is the direct expression of goodness and beauty.

It seems that the most important, interesting thoughts are particularly those that we in no case will ever tell another.

It seems to me that just one smile contains all that is called – the beauty of the face. If a smile adds to the attraction of the face, then the face is beautiful. If is does not change it, then it is ordinary. If it ruins it, then the smile is facetious.

It was delightful for me to exchange this deteriorating feeling of accustomed devotion for a fresh feeling of love filled with mystery and uncertainty. Beyond this, at one and the same type to stop loving and then start loving again, meaning to love 2 times more than before

Kindness is such an indispensable seasoning for everything. The best qualities without kindness are not worth anything, and the worst of vices are easily forgiven with its inclusion.

Let people's approval be the result of your actions and not your goal.

Life only contains one happiness that is never doubted, and this is to live for another.

Love cannot be harmful, but always beneficial, and never a wolf of egoism or conceit clothed in a sheep's wool.

Love is the rule by which to observe all other rules.

Love is the strength of life.

Love is the substance of life, but not a life of nonsense, suffering and ruin, but a life of blessing that is endless.

Love is the truest and supreme virtue that resolves all of life's contradictions, and not only destroys any fear of death, but attracts a person to sacrificing his existence on behalf of others.

Love terminates death's negativity and turns it into an empty hallucination. It turns life from nonsense into something sensible, and from misfortune will create prosperity.

Malice, as with love, is not a chemical substance, but is organic, like yeast or fermentation. Just a little will ferment all.

Melancholy and a bad disposition are not only annoying for the surrounding individuals, but also infectious.

Most men expect a dignity from their wife of which they are not worthy.

Most of our hot arguments occur only as a result us not being to understand in any manner what particularly our interlocutor is trying to prove.

Mutual love between people is the fundamental law of community life. It is true that a person cannot force himself to love in the same manner that he can force himself to work, but this does not conclude that it is possible to deal with people without love, especially if something is required of them. If you do not feel love toward people, sit quietly.

No activity of any type can be stable if it does not have a basis in an individual's own personal interest.

No matter how strange, the most solid and secure convictions are often the most superficial. Profound convictions are always mobile.

No matter how uncomfortable anger is for others, it is the most difficult for the person causing it and having to experience it. Whatever begins in anger, ends in embarrassment.

Often humility is divined as weakness and indecision, but when experience proves to people that they have erred, then all of a sudden humility is now attractive, it is now regarded as strength and respect of character.

Once some matter is resolved by using violence, the violence will never terminate.

One mathematician told me that the accomplishment is not in revealing truths, but in their search.

One of the 2: either war is insanity, or else people make it an insanity, meaning they are themselves not a sane creation, which is what seems to be the case.

One of the first conditions that is recognized by everybody for happiness is to have such a life where the tie between the human and nature is not violated, that is, life under the open sky, in direct sunlight, with clean air: a communion with the soil, plants and animals.

One of the most common deceptions that leads to the greatest disasters is the deceit of the words, "Everybody does this."

One of the most surprising deceptions is that a person's happiness consists in doing nothing.

Only people who are capable of strong love can endure intense pain. But this demand to love serves as a reaction to sorrow for them and heals them. As a result the moral nature of the human is even more fervent than the corporeal nature. Sorrow will never kill.

Our enemies can be more useful to us than our friends, since friends will often forgive us of our weaknesses, but it is only our enemies that will regularly notice them. Do not disdain discredit by your enemies.

People are divided into 2 categories: some think first and then act and speak; others act and speak first, and then think about what they have done.

People assure themselves and others that they are occupied with the welfare of the nation, but they are actually occupied with the building of [Orthodox] churches and motivated solely by selfish conceit.

People who concede that war is not only inevitable, but is useful and so is desirable, such people are repulsive and terrifying as a result of their moral degradation.

Perhaps what I said belongs to one of those evil truths that unconsciously hide in the soul of each person, and which must not be related in order not to harm him. Just like the residue at the bottom of a wine bottle, it is best not to shake it so not to ruin the wine.

Philanthropy and altruism are only good when it is a sacrifice. It is only when the beneficiary receives a gift under this circumstance that it is a spiritual gift.

Powerful people who are effective are always plain.

Pride is not entirely the same as a cognizance of human dignity. Pride increases relative to external success, but the cognizance of your human dignity, on the contrary, increases relative to your external humility.

Really, people presently living on the necks of others do not themselves understand that they should not. But they will not get off willingly, but will just wait until they are removed and then crushed.

Respect was conjured by someone in order to cover that empty spot where love should be located.

Secrecy is not an indication of wisdom. The more wise a person, the easier the movement of the tongue that expresses his thoughts.

She died without regret and reservation, and so accomplished the best and greatest deed in this life.

Simplicity is an indispensable condition of beauty.

Simplicity is the primary condition of moral beauty. In order for the readers to identify with the hero, they need to be able to recognize in him their own weaknesses, as well as virtues. Virtues are possible, weaknesses are unavoidable.

Slander, a false and bad opinion of another, and which he cannot rectify, is the best school to learn to respond with kindness.

So here they are, the Russian character: it seems a plain person, but should a severe disaster arrive, immense strength will arise in him, the human beauty.

So many recollections of past events surface when you strive to resurrect in your imagination the characteristics of a loved one, but you only see them vaguely through these recollections, like through tears. These are tears of reflection.

So many thoughts can be contained at the same time and especially in an empty head.

Sometimes labor is unnecessary, vain, impatient, irritating, annoying to others, or causes the attention of others on yourself.

Such labor is much worse than idleness. Genuine labor is always quiet, consistent and unnoticed.

The accomplishments of a person whose direction is to attain only personal benefit are a complete rejection of human purpose.

The aesthetic and the ethical are 2 arms of he same lever. To the extent that one side is lengthened and unloaded, to the same extent the other side is shortened and loaded. As soon as a person loses his moral sense, then he becomes more inclined toward the aesthetic and less to the ethical.

The anxieties of bashful people occur as a result of their ignorance of opinions that others have about them. But as soon as these opinions are clearly expressed, and whatever they are, the anxiety is curbed.

The battle will be won by the person who firmly decides to win it.

The best person is the one who lives by other people's feelings and by his own convictions. The worst sort of person is the one who lives by other people's convictions and his individual feelings. From the different combinations of these 4 bases, the motives of activity of different people can be determines. People who live only by their feelings are beasts.

The business of a critic is to interpret the compositions of great writers: to select the best of them from the large quantity of rubbish that is composed by us all. What pertains to criticism is that often the greater number of great writers become small, while those who think they are profound become shallow, and those who consider themselves wise are now stupid.

The capability of remembering the past and to imagine for yourself a future is provided us only in order to more reliably resolve the action of the present, while being guided by our reflections of one and the other.

The conscience is the highest law of all living existence, which each person recognizes in himself, not only with the cognizance of the rights of all of existence, but also love toward it.

The correct path is to adopt what your predecessors have done and then go further.

The difference between tangible and mental poisons is that the majority of tangible poisons are repulsive to the taste, while mental poisons unfortunately are often attractive.

The drive for self-perfection is a natural quality of a person because he can never be completely satisfied with himself.

The education of children is the only self-sacrifice that nobody assists as much as the children being taught.

The enlightened person is the one who knows the purpose of their life.

The greater portion of people's conduct occurs not due to deliberation, or even due to feelings, but due to unconscious imitation, due to influence.

The hero of my short stories always was, is, and will be a beautiful person. Truly.

The heroic exit, as I understand it, for a [Russian Orthodox] priest, for example, is when he gathers his parishioners, walks to their presence in front of his ambo and, instead of performing ecclesiastical rites and the veneration of icons, bows as low as the floor to the people, and asks them for their forgiveness for leading them astray.

The higher a person raises himself in his personal opinion, the less reliable the state he is in. The higher you place yourself in the presence of people, the lower you become in their opinion.

The ideal wife, in my opinion, is the one who bears children, feeds and raises a large number of children, is capable of working for people, and who has adopted her own personal ideology. But in order to adopt for yourself a higher ideology, it seems to me, there is no need to take courses at a school, but only to read the Gospel and not close the eyes, ears, and especially, the heart.

The integrity of a wise person consists in three items: first is to himself do what he advises others to do; second is to never act against decency; and third is to patiently tolerate the weaknesses of people who surround him.

The king is history's slave. History, which is the unconscious and fatalistic process of humanity, is utilized every minute by kings for their own behalf as an instrument for their individual goals.

The landlord was, just as are all people, an independently and privately thinking person, difficult to understanding other's thoughts and especially passionate toward his own.

The level of a person's integrity is an index of the level of his moral perfection. Integrity is a method of measuring morality.

The man accepting more of an active participation in life's daily battle does not entirely devote himself to love and he cannot remember every single matter or is he equally concerned on every issue, except for what is all-consuming, dealing with his individual desire in life's daily battle.

The more a person is content with himself, the less it takes for him to be content.

The more difficult and heavy the circumstances, the more necessary the firmness, action and decisiveness, and the more harmful the apathy.

The more that a person contributes to others, and the less he requires for himself, the better he is. The less he contributes to others and the more he requires for himself, the worse he is.

The more we become accustomed to little items, the less that deprivation threatens us.

The most common and widespread reasons for lies is the desire to deceive not people, but yourself.

The most harmful lie is a subtle lie, complex and clothed in triumph and majesty, and this is usually how lies of religion are introduced.

The most horrifying consequent of alcoholic beverages is that wine deadens a person's intellect and conscience. As a result of drinking wine, people become more uncouth, stupid and malicious.

The most pathetic slave is the person who abandons also his intellect to slavery by accepting as truth what his intellect does not comprehend.

The most precise expression of life's meaning can be this one: the world is in motion and advances in the process. The human's duty is to participate in this motion, submit to it and work together with it for its effectiveness.

The most reliable sign of veracity is simplicity and clarity. A lie is always complex, elaborate and verbose.

The movement for the benefit of humanity is accomplished not with executioners, but with martyrs.

The necessity for an education lies on each person. The nation likes and seeks education, just as it likes and seek air to breathe.

The opinion that we conclude at our first impression of a person often changes more or less soon. But until that time when this change of opinion occurs, it is always either very good or very bad to make such a judgment about a person.

The person of the future is already here among us.

The person who ascertains his significance will recognize his dignity in the process.

The person who ceases to drink and smoke acquires a mental clarity and tranquil composure, which from this new and reliable facet will illuminate all the surprises of life for him.

The primary difference between true belief and false is that a person with false belief wants God to be benevolent towards him for his offerings and gifts. With true belief, a person wants only one item, to learn to please God.

The primary exercise of philosophy of all ages consists particularly in finding that indispensable tie that exists between personal and common interest.

The purpose of education can be summarized easily. If you want to live well, then you need to be educated. But it seems that people want to just tell others to do this and to educate others.

The significance of intellect is the revelation of truth, and so a great and ruinous deception is the use of intellect to hide or distort truth.

The smarter and kinder a person, the more he will notice this goodness in other people.

The student is the one who has read much from books; the educated is the one who has adopted all of the most widespread knowledge and customs of his era; the enlightened is the one who understands the meaning of his life.

The substance of any belief consists in the meaning that it will provide to life, and one that is not destroyed by death.

The understanding of beauty does not coincide with goodness, and is the sooner contradictory to it. Goodness for the most part coincides with a victory over desires.

The voice of conscience can be differentiated from all other psychological motivations by the fact that it always requires something useless and intangible, but beautiful and attainable only with our personal effort.

The woman knows that our brother always lies about his superior feelings. All he needs is a body and so he will forgive all vile conduct, but some ugly, tasteless, bad color of a suit he will never forgive.

There are no such conditions to which a person could not accustom himself, and especially if he sees that all who surround him reside in the same manner.

There are only 2 sources of people's vices: idleness and superstition; and there are only 2 virtues: activity and intellect.

There are people who reside in a state of melancholy or irritation and yet they enjoy being in this state, and even brag about it. But what is the difference, because as soon as you release the reins from the horse that you are riding downhill, you can still whip him.

There exist 2 desires whose fulfillment can comprise a person's true happiness: to be useful and to have a tranquil conscience.

There is a side of dreams that is better than reality, and there is a side of reality that is better than dreams. Complete happiness would be a union of one and the other.

There is a side to fantasy that is better than reality, and reality has a side that is better than fantasy. Complete happiness would be the combination of one and the other.

There is no need to try to convince people who think otherwise by using arguments. You need to first shift their feelings and then make them feel they are right if they agree with you.

There is no such thing as a great person as far as a lackey is concerned, because a lackey has his own understanding of greatness.

There is nothing like work that cultivates a person. Without work a person cannot preserve his human dignity.

There is only one means to put an end to evil – to do good to evil people.

Think correctly and your thought will ripen into benevolent activities.

This is one undoubtable sign that divides people's actions into good and bad: if it increases actions of love and unity of people – it is good; if it causes animosity and separation – it is bad.

Time is an infinite movement, without even one moment of rest, and this concept cannot be fathomed otherwise.

To be able to have control of yourself is the greatest personal ability. But when you are a slave to your desires, this is the most terrible slavery.

To be ashamed in the presence of people is a good sensation, but it is best of all to be ashamed of yourself.

True compassion only begins when you place yourself in the stead of the sufferer, experiencing his suffering in its true intensity.

True love is not love for just one individual, but a psychological state of preparation of love for all.

True love on its own senses so much holiness, innocence, strength, motivation and self-confidence, that there does not exist crime, obstacles, or any mundane facets of its life.

War is murder. And no matter how many people gather together in order to accomplish such an event, and no matter what it is they call themselves, murder is still the worst of all sins in the world.

We can look at one and the same object tragically and cause it to torment us, or look at it simply and ever joyfully.

We have become stupid because for evermore we have closed to ourselves the true significance of every science – learning those entrances through which walked all the great minds of humanity to explain truth. From the time that history began its record, excellent minds have appeared who made humanity what it is. Such supreme mental giants are scattered over the millennia of history.

What has always been important and will be is that benevolence is needed not just for a specific person, but for all people.

What is important is not the amount of knowledge, but its quality. It is possible to know a lot, but not know what is needful.

When a person is young, all strengths are directed toward the future, and this future accepts such diverse, living and mesmerizing forms under the influence of hope, one that is founded not on the experience of the past, but on the imagined possibility of happiness, that some understood and divided fantasies of future happiness already compose the happiness of that maturity.

Where labor is converted into creativity, naturally and even physiologically the fear of death disappears.

Why go over people's heads with your statements when so much still remains to be said that is solid and basic truth.

Will at any time the newness, and the worriless need for love, and strength of belief that we possessed during childhood return? What period in our life could be better than when the 2 best virtues – innocent joy and immeasurable requirement of love – were the sole excitements in life?

You must not propose the question to yourself whether to marry, but propose the effort of wanting to live properly. And when the time arrives and circumstances are such, and you have no reason not to marry, you will not err.

IVAN SERGEEVICH TURGENEV

1818 – 1883

Classical Author

Ivan Turgenev was born in Oryol on September 9, 1818. He was originally home-schooled by tutors, but then attended school in Moscow, where he especially concentrated on learning German literature and philosophy. Then he attended St Petersburg University, studying philology and began writing poetry and plays. In 1838, Turgenev went to Berlin University, Germany, to study philosophy, returning in 1841, and getting a job at the Ministry of Internal Affairs. His first efforts were distributing circulars where he proposed changes in the Russian economic system, and to ameliorate the plight of Russian serfs and peasants, and abolish the feudal system.

In 1847, Turgenev left Russia for Paris, and where he continued to write about Russian peasant life. They were published in 1852 as *Notes of a Hunter*. He returned to Russia in 1850 but was forced to exile to his hometown in 1852 because of his obituary for Nikolai Gogol, that the government censures felt inappropriate, but only for a year. He then returned to St Petersburg, but under government surveillance, until Tsar Alexandr II ascended the throne in 1855. That year Turgenev again left for Paris and returning to Russia in 1858, and continuing to write his novels and short stories.

During these years Turgenev joined the political philosophy of the Slavophiles and became part of their effort against the westernization of Russia. He again visited Germany and France in the succeeding years, returning to Russia in 1879, and spent the balance of his life circulating with other Russian authors, but then returned to Paris in 1882. He died outside of Paris on September 3, 1883.

A foreign country will teach you to love your fatherland. Travel abroad and inspect the foreigners and you will return with more of a Russian heart.

A good student sees the mistakes of his teacher, but he honorably keeps silent regarding them. Because these mistakes serve him to his use and instruct him on the proper path.

A person learns very late in life, and only after many experiences, and after watching the actual collapse or weakness of his colleague, that he should have had compassion on him and helped him. And not to do such with any underlying self-gratification due to the kindness and effort, but on the contrary, with all humility and natural understanding. Guilt is almost unavoidable in such circumstances.

A person wanting to sacrifice himself, but who first decided to count and weigh all the consequences, all the probable benefits of his action, is hardly capable of sacrificing himself to begin with.

A strong person does not need happiness.

A woman who is 27 years old, a wife and mother, should not pretend to be an adolescent, otherwise her life will be vain.

All in the world – and the good and the bad – is provided to a person not according to his merits, but as the result of some unknown and illogical laws.

Ancient peoples called their gods – jealous. So why should we not think that a certain destiny of a humorous nature must unavoidably be introduced to the actions, to the very character of people, who are summoned to this great new work, like tribute, as a propitiatory sacrifice of jealous gods?

As life is presently progressing there is only one item that will unexpectedly occur and so we spend a lot of time to be able to deal with it when it occurs.

As soon as 10 Russians congregate, immediately their questions arise about the significance, about the future of Russia. Here, by the way, they insert the decay of the west, how it surpasses us in every point, but the west is still decay! We know how to curse them, but our opinion of them is respectable.

Attempt to tell young people that you cannot provide them the complete truth because you do not possess it yourself, young people will not want to listen to you at all.

Based on their education they are not sorcerers, but fortune tellers.

Beauty does not need to live eternally in order to be eternal. Just one moment is sufficient.

But at the first occasion I will be active, that is, speak and write what I think and feel, deducting that inactivity is a crime that others cover by claiming limits to their obligations. I am not a policeman on guard, however if there is a crime being committed on the street outside my window, should I not run to help and alarm if needs be the entire city in order to save the victim? But when the attack is against a healthy mind, holy morality and –

more than this – religion itself, then how can I not intervene due to my convictions or my obligation?

But nature does not deal with logic, with our human logic. It has its own that we do not understand and will not recognize until that time when it – like a wheel – will finally pass us.

Catechisms are necessary, as long as they are positive dogmas that will affirm the Biblical concept of infinity. Yet we still have none that are good, although in other regions they are a later appearance. As a result the [Orthodox] Church's guards have forbidden entrance into the Bible without guides, meaning, commentaries and preachers.

Comforting others, people for the most part want to quickly separate from the unpleasant feeling of involuntary egoistic compassion.

Considering this objectively, who will arbitrarily depart from the customs of his predecessors, with those joys that he enjoyed as a child?

Cosmopolitanism is nonsense. The cosmopolitan is worthless and worse than worthless. Outside of nationalism there is no art, no truth, no life, nothing at all. Without physiognomy there is not even an ideal person, only a mundane face is possible without physiognomy.

Devoting themselves to moving forward, people are very inclined to forget their point of departure.

Did you notice that a person who ordinarily is scattered in the circle of subjects is never scatterbrain in the company of officials?

Do not deceive yourself to another person, since you are not living his life on earth.

Do we really need to think that some flaws in a person – self-assurance for example or levity – are indispensable because it allows a woman to cling to them? Or does love fear perfection, to the extent perfection is possible on earth, as though it is something strange or frightening to it.

Do you know the difference between a mistake made by our brother and a mistake made by a woman? This is it: the man can for example say that 2 times 2 is not 4, but 5 or 3-1/2. But the woman will say that 2 times 2 is a stearin candle.[28]

Each of us often remembers events of the past, with regret or with compassion, or just because we have nothing else to do. But to cast a cold and clear gaze at his entire earlier life – in the manner a passer-by walking along the top of a mountain turns and looks back at the field he has just crossed – can only be done when his faculties are intact. But then a secret coldness will grasp the person's heart when he does this the first time in his life.

Each one of us only has ourselves to blame that we live. And there is even no great thinker, no such benefactor of humanity, who can claim that he has the right to live. What is important is what we contribute to the world.

Every thought is like dough: it needs to be kneaded well to make anything out of it.

From long ago the monarchic government was considered equal to the patriarchal, and this comparison was proper for all monarchs, as many as, among other items, did not have any difference between them in the form of the government's activity or the means of keeping the rights of the people secure. The father is the head of the family, whether it is composed of children or adolescents or just people and those elderly and experienced. For his care of children the father is obligated to foresee all, accept all

---

[28] Comment in Turgenev's *Rudin*, 1856, by the misogynist Pigasov, his display of a woman's lack of logic.

with caution, in short, to think and act on their behalf. Guiding adolescents, just knowledge of their primary needs and utilities is not sufficient enough. You must have capability and directing and retaining their minds, ascertaining their inclinations, desires that compose a special category of needs, and be able to design your own reactions relative to theirs, while at the same time covering your own inefficiencies. When children grow into maturity, then their opinions will have an indispensable influence on the father's actions, and the dependence of such children can be called only a dependence of honor toward them.

Gaze at these trees, at this sky. Beauty and life breeze from every direction. And poetry is found wherever beauty and life.

Happiness is not attained by war. But we must not forget that it is not happiness, but human dignity that is the chief goal in life.

Here we will define the significance or essence of true education. It is the knowledge of your rights and your obligations.

Humility consists in us not just feeling our personal worth, not just providing others what we are obligated, but that we would be condescending to good intentions. Or else we can raise the fallen, or encourage those who open to us their zeal and love toward goodness, while at the same time being burdened with heavy chains and not in a position to cast them. Humility and modesty walk side by side.

Humility will vanquish and defeat arrogance. But do not forget, the feeling of victory will create its own form of arrogance.

I love Russia, I love poetry, but I also love humanity, I love truth above all else. It is not permitted to write about Russia in any other language than Russian.

I would like the universities to turn more attention to utilitarian subjects, to the essential and indispensable, and discard what has outlived its use. But professors do not want to depart from what they know and what has cost them so much to acquire.

If a person knows and says that he is destitute and senses this within himself, then something special must also reside within him, some type of personal vanity.

If you want to irritate well or even damage your opponent, then criticize him for some fault or vice that he knows that you have.

In one item I am convinced: It is not time for us to become Protestant. Otherwise we will even sooner cook the simple minds.

It seems to me that a journalist should not be excessively taken away by what is presently considered the spirit of the era, and to use it alone to evaluate present compositions.

It seems to me that not all have a right to accuse the simple Russian people of excessive inclination to alcoholism. If a German commoner is not drunk, it is because of his finances and not because of any restraint, this is the reason. But for the most part a German peasant has a need only of wine when he wants to be more happy than he regularly is. The Russian for the most part drinks due to sorrow. The saloon for him is the sole enchanted palace that transfers him from a bitter existence to that land of joy where he will not see his master hovering over him or the police captain. He drinks from the river of oblivion.

Life is not a game and not an amusement, life is not even pleasure. Life is a difficult effort. Renunciation, renunciation of what is constant, this is its secret meaning, its solution. Not the fulfillment of thoughts and dreams, no matter how exalted they may be, but the fulfillment of obligation. This is about what a person worries. Unless you place upon yourself chains, the iron chains of obligation, you cannot reach your goal, the end of the course, without failing. But while we are young we think, The freer we are the better all is and the further we will get.

Life will only not deceive the person who concentrates on it, and not expect anything from it, but will calmly accept its few gifts and calmly utilize them.

Love at any age has its turmoil.

Love letters are read usually only by 2 individuals, because for the third person they would be unbearable to read if not hilarious.

Masses of people always end in the same manner that they proceed after such individuals, blindly believing in those the masses earlier ridiculed, even cursed and prosecuted, but who, not fearing their prosecution or curses or even fearing their ridicule, proceed steadfastly forward, penetrating a spiritual gaze at the goal that only they can see, seeking, falling, rising, and finally finding. Only the one whose heart is leading him will find it.

Nature is not a temple, but a workshop, and the person in it is a worker.

No place does time fly as fast as in Russia. In prison, they say, it flies even faster.

Nonetheless, like any other young person I was not deprived of that silent, inner unrest that usually ends very peacefully and prosperously, but only after resolving a dozen or so rough poems.

Nothing can be worse and more insulting than happiness arriving far too late.

O, I am aware likewise of this ability to say to another the most unpleasant things but in a most inoffensive manner. In place of this it is better to say to him right to his face, "You, brother, are stupid." It is also worth it to notice this but state it differently and with a cheerful smile, "It seems that both of us are stupid."

Often we do not understand our past. So how can we answer for the future? We cannot place chains on the future.

Often when we want to be liked by another person we will inflate what we have for friends when we are in a conversation with him, almost never suspecting that we are boasting about ourselves by doing this.

Our life does not depend on ourselves, but yet each of us does have one anchor from which we will never tear ourselves loose, unless we really want to: the feeling of debt.

Philosophic deceitfully woven webs and nonsense can never be affixed to the Russian mind. This is because he has an exceptionally healthy mind. But we should not suppose that anything that is called philosophy will attack every honorable intention toward truth and toward comprehension.

Russia can do well without any of us, but none of us will ever fare well without Russia. Woe to the person who thinks he will fare well without it, and twice the woe to the person who actually does succeed without Russia.

Secular people do not just discard, but plainly trash a person, considering him unnecessary, just like a pair of gloves after a ball, or like a candy wrapper after you remove the candy.

So how can philosophy – the science of sciences – be nationalized? If this is the case then mathematics will want to be nationalized. We have suffered sufficient miseries from a nationalized religion, from the Roman church, from the Anglican church, from the Russian God. Should not philosophy be universal, just as with religion? Its truths must belong to all everyone. Cosmopolitanism must be an inseparable part of its character.

So how can we apply a Christian tenet to a judicial code where the chapter about property is complete opposed to the Evangelic rule:

Give all to the poor? Or how can we correlate in the criminal justice system the level of punishment with the other Christian command: Turn the right cheek to him who strikes you on the left? If laws are supposed to be in agreement with the texts of our Christian teaching, then the administration of finances will demand the same. Then where will this lead us? No, civil laws are for citizens; the law of Christ is for people. It acts from above and penetrates all, and arranges all for the sake of the sake of the higher citizenship. But we must not impose it on secular justice, because it is a gift of heaven and must live and act in people's hearts, and subsequently through them in courts and on rulers.

So who is it that said that only truth is real? Falsity is just as alive as truth, and if not more.

Some young people have actually discovered Russian science. For us, 2 times 2 is also 4, but it is expressed in a more agile fashion.

Stupid addictions are always stronger than love of goodness and truth in a person's heart, whether he be a citizen or a slave.

The autocrat seeing himself raised to such a height will never consider it any honor to have to descend in order to attend to the significance of the silence of his subjects.

The best pledge, the best guarantee for all activities of humanity is vociferation. Evil, once it is in the open, loses a lot of its strength.

The forward guard, you know, very easily can become the rear guard. The entire matter is the change in direction.

The only nation that has a history is the one worthy of it. Providence, it seems, preserves history only for those who attach their charity to the common contribution for the welfare of humanity. Those that plainly ruin, not renewing the land, disappear from its face without memory.

The only people that remain misunderstood are either those who themselves do not know what they want, or those who care less if they are understood.

The Russian peasant with mother's milk sucks into himself the feeling of his slavery, the thought that all for which he has worked, and all that he has acquired with his blood and his sweat, all that he ever could possibly have, his boss has the right to take it away whenever he wants. The Russian peasant fears to even appear wealthy, lest he bring upon himself new taxes.

There is nothing more difficult to comprehend than something stupidly done.

This attitude of our servitude is so much deeply implanted in us that we will not depart from it very soon. It seems that we need a boss for every matter and everywhere. For the most part this boss is a living subject, what we would define as acquiring voluntary authority over us. As a result we just subscribe ourselves to enslavement.

This is of what the majority of great poetic compositions consist: the immorality of life is what inspires the genius of these creators. Our view of them is just as our view of life in general, and they can be eternally diverse and even contradictory and at the same time identically correct.

This is the flaw of the most part of travelers: they always love to occupy themselves in their compositions, rather than their subject when describing their journeys. It is as though the reader needs to know where the author found a good diner, a quiet inn, where a nice looking waitress glanced at him and smiled. For me this is not understandable how they can be so open with the public how they occupy themselves in so much of the text, or other busybody matters, where it seems they should be concentrating on the travel experience and locations.

To interfere with evil is one means for us to do some good.

To preserve a young heart to your old age, as some say, is difficult as well as almost humorous. The one who did not squander belief in goodness, consistency of the will, desire and activity, can still be content.

To tolerate persecution from an entire unstable nation is considerably more bearable than from one person.

Unjust and incorrect discredit in the lips of people whom you love is bitter.

We can talk fervently, excitedly, overwhelmingly, about everything in the world, but with an appetite we can only talk about ourselves.

What can be more pleasant than to listen to some impartial foreigner recollect your ancestors, narrating the history of your state, your fatherland, and from some very advantageous side.

What is it we dream about so much? About our happiness? No reason to think about it. It will never arrive so why chase after it! It is like health, when you do not notice it, you have it.

Whatever the attack that strikes a person, his first comfort is to consume the other person, and forgive me for such a crude expression.

When a person whom we have loved for a long while begins to change or change himself, then we will long debate with what is only obvious to us, and we will wait long hoping this is not the reality. How difficult it is to say, "This is just a hallucination, friend, forgive me." And what will surface in your place, not even the grave and not oblivion, but something worse.

When you argue with a person more intelligent than you, he will win. But out of your defeat you can still derive some benefit.

Who knows the number of posterity that each living person will leave behind on earth, those who are destined to be born only after his death? Who can say what mysterious chain binds a person's destiny with his children's destiny, his posterity, and how his aspirations will reflect on them, or if they will blame him for his faults that had a bad affect on them? All of us must humble ourselves and bow our heads in the presence of the unknowable.

With great diligence we study ourselves and then imagine that we know others.

You do know that if the life of the best person is portrayed in such colors where nothing is added to it to embellish him, the result will be terrifying! But then this would only discredit the person.

You explain some matter to a woman, based on your convictions, but she will not be content until she thinks of some type of menial incidental reason as to why you said what you did, and not something else.

You said what was on your mind, but not at the proper time. But the other did not say what was on his mind, and it was the proper time. Subsequently he was right, but you remain with the comforts of your personal conscience.

FEODOR IVANOVICH TUTCHEV

1803 – 1873

Poet, Diplomat

Feodor Tutchev was born July 15, 1873 in the village Ovstug, Orlov Province, central Russia, into an aristocratic family. At age 16, he entered Moscow University, and that same year he published his first poetry. He complete his education in history and philology, and then entered state diplomatic service. In the years 1822-1837 he was at the Russian Embassy in Munich, Bavaria, and 1837-1839, in Turin, Italy. During these years he continued to write poetry. In 1844, Tutchev returned to Russia, and became an official at the Ministry of Internal Affairs.

His first large volume of poetry was not published until 1854, and it was greeted with great success. His subject matter was Russian life and events, culture and landscape, and so was attractive to the general population. Tutchev viewed love as a tragedy and a fatal inclination. After 1860, Tutchev's compositions were more political, based his many years of service in the imperial government.

Tutchev died July 15, 1873, in Tsarskoi Selo, near St Petersburg.

A fatal law that has almost never been altered has existed in the history of humanity's societies. Great crises, great conflicts occur regularly not when criminality reaches its limits, when it reigns and governs using weapons of power and ruthlessness. No! Upheaval explodes for the most part during the first timid attempt of returning to goodness, during the first sincere, perhaps, but uncertain and unprepared feeble effort toward indispensable restoration.

Alas! The most exempt of all forms of responsibilities appears to be the exemption from stupidity.

Alas! Scripture is a horrible evil. It is as though a second fall due to sin, but now of the destitute intellect, as though the victory of matter and not spirit.

Among certain persons in defined circumstances it is totally natural to develop a specific repulsion to everything that can possibly be viewed as public opinion, and which they are in no position to maintain. And even if public opinion does not just impose on them some discomfort, but on the contrary, supports it and serves it in its entirety, and even carries it on its back, they take advantage of it by saddling it in order to beat it on its legs.

As with society, so with the individual person, the first condition of progress is self-cognizance.

Do we not forget that truth needs to have a positive foundation, that every positive science adopts its strength from philosophy, that prose is indivisible from philosophy.

Every person is born to be happy, but in order to recognize your happiness, your soul is destined to struggle with the contradictions of the world.

Every person at his defined maturity becomes for a short interval a lyric poet. He just needs to untangle his tongue.

Have you not said somewhere, "Much is beautiful in my life except for happiness." Your entire religion and your entire outlook consists in this statement.

I am a living example of that fatal – but at the same time an ethical and logical – aspect of the inherent ability for every vice to possess a punishment proper for it.

In order for poetry to flower, it must have roots in the ground.

In the world there is nothing more humorous and less meritorious to some people than destiny, despite its imaginary facelessness.

Just as I never took government service seriously, it is right that government service in turn likewise laughed right at me.

No matter how hard the government strives, what feelings, even the most benevolent, most magnanimous, and most generous that it could ever achieve, but if it ceases to be representative and the materialization of the national interests of the country, if it will only personify the politics of personal ambitions, then it will never merit either gratitude or the respect of countries abroad.

Of course, between stupid things and the true interests of the authorities, not one shred of solidarity exists, but what does exist is complete inefficiency.

One of the most pitiful inclinations that is noticed among us is the inclination to approach all questions from their most menial and vile side, the need to penetrate the mansion from its back door. This is a thousand time worse than ignorance. Such an inclination exposes and always will expose the inherent malice of such people.

Right now it seems no type of genuine progress can be attained without struggle. This is the reason for the animosity that

Europeans display toward us, but yet it may also be a tremendous merit that it is in a position to display toward us.

The fear of society's opinion of you is stronger than actual evidence against you.

The impressions of childhood become younger proportionately to a person getting older.

There exists for every wrong direction a fatal unavoidability of bringing our self to some suicidal absurdity, and not just due to what we say, but due to what we do.

Such types of people exist who feel they are metals[29] among humanity, as much as they seem themselves to be the direct handicraft and inspiration of the Great Artist and as much as they distinguish themselves from regular stampings of low denomination coins.

We can never be superfluous or excessive enough in details when pertaining to beloved individuals.

With the years a person's dependence grows, until finally on one beautiful morning he does not appear nailed to one place like a tree to the ground.

---

[29] Meaning an award.

Pyotr Andreevich Vyazemski

1792 – 1878

Poet, Historian, Translator

Pyotr Vyazemski was born in Moscow on July 12, 1792. When his father died at an early age, Vyazemski inherited a vast fortune, and because much of it was from ancient times held by his aristocratic family. This also allowed him to circulate in the aristocratic circles of Moscow and St Petersburg. Joining government service, he was station in Warsaw, Poland for a while.

At the same time his repulsion for the autocratic government of Russia grew. Even though he had this wealth and prestige, it was due to his ancestors and not what he earned on his own, and at the same time he saw the sufferings of the common Russian. Vyazemski wrote a petition to Tsar Alexandr I in 1820 about the liberation of the serfs and abolition of patrimonial property. As a result he was relieved of his government position and forced to live in isolation and under state surveillance. By 1830, he reconciled with the new Tsar Nicholas I and again entered government service, and rose to a high rank in the imperial government.

In 1841, he became a member of the St Petersburg Academy of Sciences, and in 1866, he co-founded and was first president to the Russian Historical Society. During his life, Vyazemski was a close associate and regular correspondent with Aleksandr Pushkin.

Vyazemski died in Baden-Baden, Germany, on November 10, 1878.

The destiny of great men whose credit exists as an inherent part of the nation depends often on a small number of people, and sometimes on just one person. Is this not because gratitude is so meager to expediently explain and especially slow? While envy on the contrary is rich in means, ingenious and never slothful? And often the former interrupts with its intervening silence only when its later voice can vainly echo over the dust of the gentle heart, now extinguished in dejection and awaiting its creative summons, as a new life-provider of new strength and hope!

The names of good rulers, if extraordinary events do not raise them to a higher lever, with which they can act effectively and directly with the destiny of the state and prepare for themselves a place in the history of the nation, must be satisfied with a temporal use of their abilities and the credit they derive from this. The names of good rulers are always preserved and immortalized by enlightened nations as the best of their legacies, as integral property never to be removed.

The credit of writers, a sacred pledge, entrusted as a national pride, can be destroyed only together with the nation if it is destroyed. It can also be humiliated by corruption of the state, or under the burden of personal dissolution, the apostasy from the ancestors' greatness.

Nationalism is a feeling of freedom that is congenital. We love our homeland, nation to which we belong, which is ours and it considers us its own. According to the law of nature by which we love ourselves and our families and parents and brothers and sisters. But to instill this feeling into a system or instruction or law will only stifle it, and the result is patriotism that only leads the people to vile activities. The effects of patriotism engendered in the minds of people implement their special interests and not those of the nation.

A person, although somewhat belonging to a social activity on one or another course, is subject with his good and bad qualities to social justice. It is his legacy and possession.

A so clear trait of the Russian mind is a guile humor. But our wit is not inclusive like the French wit whose plays on words or subtle expressions of their mind is more artistic. The best Russian jokes can only serve as an amusement.

Ancient idols temples do not last forever, and their gilded items soon fade. The religious sincerity of their devotees cools. Later a new edifice is built for the residence of some new idol.

Blood demands blood. Blood spilt in the name of the law or by excitation of desires likewise cries for vengeance because a person cannot have the right of his associate's life. The law can deprive freedom, because it can also gift it at the same time. But life is exempt from its domain. Death is a mystery: not one mortal has been able to ascertain it. So how can we arrange something that we lack in knowledge?

Credit provided to some unworthy person only reflects the unworthiness of the bragger.

First of all we are people, and then a member of earth's population, that is, regional residents. Whatever you do a person is found within every fellow countryman in whatever region you reside.

For the intelligent person who recognizes his dignity, there is nothing more nauseous and insulting than praise that is out of place and clumsy.

Having a preference for or against something is its own form of intoxication. It obscures or distorts the bright and healthy intellect and sober prudence.

I would have wanted credit, but in order to embellish my father's grave and my son's cradle with it.

In general, and with very rare exceptions, novelties in literary composition are an indication of either vanity, pursuing empty distinctions, or else what is almost an indication of philosophic rhetoric, so as not to plainly write stupidity. The more prudent approach is to maintain the custom, and even if it is not completely correct.

In the theater you can disdain the contemptible and laugh at the stupidity to what extent you want, since you see it all yourself in front of your eyes. Having left the theater, proper and decent people seek what is good and best for the same characters, regardless of the impressions left on them during the scenes.

In women we see the triumph of strength over weakness. Women direct us, dominate us, but how? With their weaknesses, with which they attract us and mesmerize us.

It is impossible to imitate beauty; it is impossible to steal it or adopt it. On the contrary, the writer's flaws pass from hand to hand in the possession of his timid imitators.

It is pathetic that malice has assigned a faulty meaning to the word – liberal. According to present understanding, a liberal is a person who utilizes his freedom of thought. Of course, many unselfish people magnanimously deny themselves this right of utilizing this freedom, and like the sage who only knew that he knew nothing, they only think that it is better not to think.

It is possible to get bored of contentment and enjoying ambition, but what exalted heart will not cease beating with the excitement and fervency of youth with sacred thoughts of putting life to a good use?

It is possible to steal a brilliant thought, a cheerful expression. But the fervency of someone's soul, the secret of controlling the feelings of other person's hearts, cannot be stolen.

Love of nationalism is a feeling, but I do not accept it as a system. I hate exclusiveness, not only incontestable and imperative, but also conditional and ambiguous.

Magazines and newspapers are the source of water with its uninterruptedly movement of drop after drop striking a rock or the head of the reader who has placed it under its erosive effect.

Manipulation is the mind of little minds. A lion destroys, a fox is cunning.

Not all can be or must be expressed with the poetic language. A verse is capricious and whimsical; it retains nothing and endures nothing. A thought can be correct and even brilliant, but when restrained by rhyme it loses its value and provides nothing to the poem.

People's love toward their king is born from trustworthiness, and trustworthiness from success.

Perfection is an unattainable goal, but the effort of self-perfection is no less an obligation and quality of humanity's nature.

Seldom does this occur, that a talent will stand right on the road directly from the first step. Such a road you place before you with mature strength. Usually it reaches for and drags you a while following the traces remaining from your predecessors.

So people very willingly denounce their associate using prepared epithets. This may comfort their soul: they are not blaming, but only exchanging blame. Perhaps it will return to them.

The mind of a human knows rest and inactivity, but the mind of humanity is always working and its movements are aggressive.

The weak individual's heart lives and keeps warm as a result of others' approvals. His own personal approval is not always sufficient for him, and the soul becomes cold with silent complacency. And any distant glory is a deception since it cannot be a benefactor providing present happiness.

The words – present and future, have a conditional and inconsistent meaning. Everything that is present was at some time the future and this future will turn into the past. Something old can be discarded to the side and forgotten, but this is still not sufficient proof that it has become obsolete, it has just gone out of use. It is this way so questions can surface.

To love art is a secret that is gifted either by nature or by stealing by stubborn force. In either situation it is worthy of respect and envy. Nonetheless, few provide art the tribute that it deserves.

Truly an honorable person has the obligation to be useful to society in every area and in every circumstance, as long as he is in the position to be able to show people such philanthropy.

We have many among us who do not comprehend indirect or subtle complements. They only can accept solid and loud applause.

We love to go forward and indiscriminately. Hard drinking for a Russian is not only a physically illness, but a moral. We do almost everything when drinking, the stupid and the good. We sleep it off and become sober, we do not answer for what we said or what we did in our delirium.

What is love for our fatherland during our life? It is spite toward the present situation.

What kind of love is here? They will ask. When is love futile? Ask for the resolution of this riddle from the One who built the human's heart. Why do we love with kindness, or with passion for our unworthy brother, son, for whom we are often red with embarrassment? Essentially this quality is not only in the physical faculty, but in the moral; not only in the positive sense, but also in the abstract attitude that has an effect on us like the strength from some type of talisman.

Without having a complete education, a person needs to possess an immense indestructible store of psychological strength in order not to subject themselves to the destructive strength of circumstances always intending to level natural strengths and restrain the crowds of noble ambitious men in ranks, those who want to burst from the ordinary and mundane environment.

THE SILVER AGE OF RUSSIAN LITERATURE

LEONID NIKOLAEVICH ANDREEV

1871 – 1919

Poet, Political Activist

Leonid Andreev was born September 9, 1871, in Oryol, central Russia, into a financially secure family. He studied law at Moscow University. From 1897, he published articles in Moscow newspapers. It was the famous Russian author Maxim Gorki who took notice of Andreev's literary talents and invited him to join a circle of other Russian authors who were involved with a book publishing enterprise. In 1908, Andreev married and moved to Finland, although near the Russian border, where he continued to write short stories. During the year 1914 and before WW1, the Andreevs traveled Europe, and had 2 sons (one of them was Daniel Andreev who returned to Russia).

After the October Revolution, Andreev remained in Finland and vehemently wrote against the Communist occupation of Russia, which took a told on his health. His life ended in destitution and an eventually a premature death of heart failure on December 9, 1919, only 48 years old. In 1957 his crypt was moved to St Petersburg (Leningrad) and reburied there.

Compassion is a great and philanthropic feeling, and people – even the lowest of people – are worthy of it. But it is necessary that they be people and not just wax figures to possess this.

Even the most insignificant chance of authority easily whirls any undeveloped mind.

Every person is a distinct world possessing its own laws and goals, with its personal joys and sorrows. Every person is likewise an illusion that appears for a moment and disappears, oblivious to the world.

Falsity on its face value is the most extensive and most vile form of enslavement to which a person can commit himself in this life.

For a regular person who did not accomplish anything in life, all of his sorrows end with his death. With a writer, often his sorrows only begin with his death. If during his life the writer was able to insult a number of others, then after his death it is their chance to insult him, if it is their desire. And there is no way for the writer to defend himself. With respect to his vocation, the writer should write as though he can respect every line that proceeds from under his pen, whether he will personally sign his work or not, or whether he will be paid much or little or awarded for his work or not.

For the murderer or the criminal, the most terrifying is not the police, not the courts, but he himself, his nerves which are able to protest against the balance of his body that has sustained itself on his known tragedies.

If a person was destined to become divine, then his throne would be a book.

If people truly understood themselves, then more than mountains, more that all the world's marvels and beauties, they would be impressed by their ability to think.

Love is what you have toward a country cursed of God, where tardiness seems to be the law, where not one train arrives on schedule, and the railway station officials in their red hats are all stupid or plain idiots, and even the guards have gone out of their minds due to bewilderment. Greetings and kisses are always late; one train is too early and another is too late; all the clocks lie about the time of arrivals and departures. It is like a circle of drunk dancing ghosts, some running in a circle, others chase after them grabbing the air with their stretched hands. All in the world arrives too late, but only love has the ability to turn one minute's tardiness into a bottomless eternity of separation.

Money will not resolve any injustice of nature, but only make it worse. Money is the freedom that traverses the world which slaves mint for their masters. The person never having money thinks that it can provide him love, and the person never having been loved by a woman thinks that money can provide him happiness.

Moral instincts are instilled so deeply that it is only with a certain departure from normal conditions that a complete liberation from them is possible.

More boldness is needed for life than for death. Struggle is the joy of life.

Of all that is amazing and unfathomable is what makes life precious. The most amazing and unfathomable is the human mind. Divinity resides in it, and also the pledge of immortality, and potent strength that knows no barricades.

People who are called good are called this because they have an ability to hide their conduct and thoughts from others. But if such a person is cuddled, toyed and questioned manipulatively, then out of him will flow every lie, vice and disgrace just like puss from an infected sore.

Pious people are unable to distinguish counterfeit from genuine. Only counterfeiters are able to do this.

Silence is the natural state of a person, when he intensely believes in certain words himself and loves them terribly. Life is never what we expect of it.

There does exist in the world women who are smart, good and talented, but a logical woman is something the world has not yet seen and will never see. When a woman falls in love she become irresponsible.

There is so much darkness in life, and talents are so needed to light its path. So each of us needs to cherish each of them like a precious diamond.

To live is a terrifying exercise for a person who has no money, health or will. It is only to enemies that a person is in debt. Only wealth provides freedom.

When you are moving forward, you should often look behind you, otherwise you will forget your origin and also your destination in the process.

Arkadi Timofeevich Averchenko

1881 – 1925

Author, Satirist, Theatrical Critic

Arkadi Averchenko was born March 18, 1881 in Sebastopol, on the Black Sea, Ukraine, into a middle class business family. He was unable to acquire any decent education his entire life due to his poor vision, but was able to compensate for it with his natural inquisitiveness and self-education. He went to work at age 15 at the railway station in Sebastopol, but for only a year, and his literary talents began about this life with his comic and ironic compositions. In 1897 and for 4 years he worked in Donbass in the office at the mines, and then in 1900 moved to Kharkov also in office work. His publications became more popular about this time.

Beginning in 1906 he became editor of some satirical magazines, and he move to St Petersburg in 1908 and continued to write humor and satire for local magazines. Twice he traveled to Europe, in 1911 and 1912.

After the Revolution, the magazine offices were closed, and he returned to Sebastopol in 1919, there again working as a journalist. When the Communists invaded Crimea, Averchenko migrated to Constantinople, and then in 1921 to Paris. Now his satires were of the new Soviet system. Averchenko moved about Europe, to Sophia, Belgrade, and Prague, which became his final home. He had surgery to restore the loss of his vision over the years, and soon after he became ill and died in Prague of a ruptured aorta on March 12, 1925.

During the Middle Ages the progressive development of culture was measured only by the number of sorcerers that were burned to death in the city squares, and the experiments to convert living people into cats, wolves and dogs (experiments that brought such scholars of this era to complete disappointment). The newer history takes a different path, a more enlightened road. True, sorcerers still continued to be burned at the stake, but they did this without any type of inspiration or elevation, with the sole goal of filling – even with some type or other of distraction – the gaping vacancy in their motivated minds and souls.

Evenings it is possible to develop smart and attractive plans, whatever you like, but in the morning all you want to do is sleep.

I have passed 2 hours and 47 minutes with you almost entirely unnoticed.

It is difficult to comprehend Chinese and women.

It was not until after the Roman Empire fell that everyone began to respect it.

My uncle's wealth is directly proportional to the distance that separates him from all of his nephews.

O, omnipotent concept of time! Be 3 times blessed. You are the best doctor and the best medicine, because no assistants of the medical laboratory can close, can secure so well the deep and open wounds as you can, eternally progressing, gray and wise.

The world is clandestine and nebulous. The world is beautiful and attractive and at the same time it is awesome, and in particular its mystery and enigma.

We incur such strange and unexplainable events in our life that are not subject to the most attentive analysis and before which we stand as in front of a magic curtain, hiding behind it a complete series of amazing miracles and mysteries.

When you live long with a person, you will not notice the primary and essential attitudes he has toward you. What is noticeable are only the details that comprise what is essential.

While in the company of people who have had too much to drink, a psychological moment will arise when everyone is deathly bored with each other, and each person wants to leave, to run from their drunken friends, go home, take a bath, cleanse yourself from the stench and dirt of the restaurant, from the tobacco soot, change clothes and lie in a clean fresh bed under a thick comfortable blanket. But usually this moment just slides by everybody. Each thinks that his exit will fatally insult, impoverish the others, and so every person stands in their spot, not knowing what else to do, what else to talk about, just waiting for someone else to take the first step into the dark silent midnight.

Maksim Alekseevich Antonovich

1835 – 1918

Philosopher, Writer

Maksim Antonovich was born April 27, 1835 in the city Belopolye, Kharkov Province, Ukraine. Son of a Orthodox deacon, he completed his initial education at the religious school at Kharkov Seminary in 1855, and then continued studies at Petersburg Religious Academy until 1859. When he completed Petersburg Religious Academy he refused an ecclesiastical career. From 1862 and until its closure in 1866 he was an editor at the magazine *Contemporary*. In his philosophical articles he defended materialism and the position of contemporary natural sciences. At the same time he was an official at the Ministry of War. From 1866 to 1868, Antonovich traveled Europe. Returning to Russia he again worked at several magazines and translated philosophy into Russian.

His talents also reached into mathematics, which he used while at the Ministry of War. He moved to Romania in 1881, and then return to Russia in 1908, to work at the State Bank, until his death, November 14, 1918, in Petrograd.

The world as a material object having a special extent must have a beginning and end in time and space. This, according to our perceptions, is an essential quality of all matter. But our mind, or better said, fantasy, is not satisfied by such a response, and so questions are further and unrelentingly presented us. What existed before the manifestation of the world and what is it that exists beyond the end of its boundaries? So really is there nothing in both one and the other circumstance? So really, is some nonexistence to be found beyond its boundaries, some type of fathomless emptiness, without extent and limits? What is the distinction between the border of the world and the emptiness of nonexistence that is beyond it, the void? And what would occur if some type or any type of object from the sphere of existence entered into this emptiness? In short, our thought process rejects the ability to perceive a beginning and end, to place existence and nonexistence side by side, and so the world must be eternal according to the concept of time and eternal according to spatial expanse. Otherwise we would not be able to perceive it.

These questions and answers are such a web and abyss from which the mind can in no manner liberate itself otherwise except by means of heroic practical severing of the knot. This antinomy and other parallels prove only on its own the old philosophic cliché that in our mind there is nothing that has existed in our senses or has passed through them, that is, that our entire mental activity is arranged only from materials accessible by the senses, that all of our abstract understandings, laws, ideas are only volatile sensual perceptions extracted from them. We see that separate objects have a beginning and an end, and from similar impressions there is arranged a common understanding of finitude. But from another side, we nowhere and never have seen the actual end, and only the contrary, we everywhere observed that what is beyond end of one object, table, home, or city, is followed by the beginning of other objects, fields, or neighboring house. And from similar impressions of uninterruptible attachments of objects we form an image of a general perception of eternity. Accordingly when an object appears that evolves from the limits of our sensual perception, then we can attach to it both these equally-experienced and equally-strong understandings of finiteness and infinity. Subsequently, the question of applying one or the other understanding to the specify situation is completely fruitless and vain, since there can be brought to some use of one or the other completely identical theoretical bases particularly as a result of what we saw in the experience of the same quantity of parts of finiteness and infinity.

This very item is applied also to the evolution of the world in the process of time: we see at every step the emergence of new objects, the birth of new individuals. And the more that we convince ourselves in these situations that all evolves from something, then an emergence from nothing seems to us impossible. We can with the same theoretical rule orient both these abstract concepts to the question of the beginning of the world in time. In practical terms the question of the world's limits can be resolved in this manner, that since we have not seen the end of the world, and science with all its perfected instruments and capabilities have not reached the point of doing this, so here we have a practical basis to consider the world infinite and limitless.

ALEKSANDR ALEKSANDROVICH BLOK

1880 –1921

Poet

Blok was born on November 16, 1880 in Petersburg in a family of professors of law. His poetic gift appeared early in his childhood. Even at the age of 5, he wrote his first poems. In 1906 he completed courses in philology at Petersburg University. During the years 1901-1902, he wrote 80 poems dedicated to his future wife, L.M. Mendeleeva. Blok's first poems were published in 1903 in the magazine, *New Path* and he continued to write and publish poems through his death. In April 1919, he was promoted to president and director of the Petersburg Great Dramatic Theater. In early 1921, Blok applied for an exit visa from the Soviet Union to go to Finland for his health, but he was refused by the Politburo of the USSR. Due to interference into his personal life by the communist government, Blok by this time was financially destitute.

He died from heart disease on August 7, 1921, in Petrograd.

Outside of Russia, Blok is considered the second greatest Russian poet after Pushkin. His compositions were translated into several languages.

A book is a great thing as long as a person knows how to utilize it.

A busy person has not much extra time to squander in dreams and apathy.

A friend is a person who talks not of what is or what was, but about what can be and should be with yourself.

A poet is completely free in his creativity, and nobody has the right to demand him to prefer green meadows more than a brothel.

A weak person can be forgiven of everything except rudeness.

Art gives birth from eternal mutual activity to 2 types of music: music that is creative to the individual and music that echoes deep in the national soul.

Constant governmental worries cause a person to become less perceptive of beauty.

Death is not feared by a hero, as long as his fantasy of survival prevails.

Each day war removes culture.

Every poetic composition is a blanket that is stretched over the sharp points of a few words. These words shine like stars.

Fantasy can be abysmal. But people cannot be nourished with fantasies.

In the majority of situations people live for the present, that is, they live for no purpose, but just exist. Living only exists if there is a future.

Life is worth it only to impose immortal demands to life.

Literature must be your daily bread.

Love does not humiliate, but liberates.

Old dreams do not materialize.

Only one thing makes a person – a person. This is knowledge of social inequality.

Only truth, no matter how heavy it might be, is light.

The cruelest form of persecution is complete indifference toward him.

The direct obligation of an artist is to show, not to prove.

The discovery that something miraculous just occurred along side of us – comes too late.

The heads of busy-bodies and miscreants are harmful to the national prosperity.

The human conscience motivates a person to seek what is better and helps him in time to reject the old, comfortable and pleasant, but also mortal and dissolute, in favor of what is new, and initially uncomfortable and rude, but promising a new life.

The meaning of human life is confined in upheaval and agitation and alarm.

The more absurd it is, the more infectious it is.

The more you feel an attachment with the homeland, the more real and more willingly does it present itself to you as a living organism.

The person who grasps that the meaning of human life is confined in upheaval and agitation and alarm will cease to be a wimp.

The soul of a genuine contemporary person is the most complex, nicest and most played musical instrument.

The strength of imitation is indirectly proportional to the strength of creativity.

The work of a historian is to restore relations, cleanse the horizons of disarranged piles of useless facts that, like fallen trees, only block the view of historical perspectives.

Theater is that sphere of art of which can be said before all others, "Here art is interwoven with life, and here art and life meet face to face."

Those who are sick with irony love to laugh, but they are not to be believed.

To hate patriotism is not to know or feel national strengths.

Verses are prayers.

We have a poor ability to separate a genuine book from the trash sold at the marketplace. One and other have the same appearance of a book. But the trash is published with binding and cover that is far more elegant and expensive than genuine literature.

We should only meditate on great issues. A writer should only involve himself with great tasks. To be bold, do not be annoyed with small personal matters.

When the opportunity occurs to decide something important, it is better for your friends to keep their distance and not advise you.

When you live alone, the smallest events seem to be large.

Within a person resides a cursed, servile quality. When he becomes extremely satisfied, content, considerably materially secure, then he loses his inner turbulence, his spiritual fire. Then he becomes indifferent and psychologically torpid and content with himself. No more dignity remains in him and a crumb becomes valuable to him, when his soul – created for turbulence and joy – likewise becomes indifferent and torpid like the body.

You cannot be a human unless you love.

Valeri Yakovlevich Brusov

1873 – 1924

Poet

Valeri Brusov was born in Moscow on December 1, 1873, into a family of merchants. In 1899 he completed his education in history at the Moscow University.

Brusov's first poems were published at age 11, and which continued to the balance of his life, but he always felt he was being suppressed by the Imperial government. He considered the October Revolution as a holiday of freedom from the shackles of aristocracy, and in 1920 joined the communist party and was president of the All-Russia Union of Poets. He also organized a higher literary-artistic institute in Moscow and was its first director. Blok considered Brusov as Russia's finest contemporary poet, while others stated he was Russia's best poet since Pushkin.

Brusov died in Moscow on October 9, 1924.

A person dies but his soul is not subject to the authority of annihilation. It slithers away and lives another life. But if the deceased is an artist, if his life was comprised of sounds, paints or words, his soul is nonetheless alive and for the world and for humanity.

A poet is a artist of vocabulary. He is to words as paint is to a painter or marble to a sculptor.

All means of fighting an evil enemy is good, but only one is foolish, and that is not to use any means.

All that occurs unexpectedly changes our life, it is not accidental. This is in us and just waits for the opportune time to express these actions.

Anguish purges the soul just as fire does gold.

Any idiot has the ability to break his own neck. An intelligent person will reflect on the matter, whether it is worth expending the sweat.

Art is what in other arenas we call revelation. The creation of art is an opened door into eternity.

At the moment of fatal danger, animal characteristics return to a person.

Authors read in order to know what not to write.

Before all else a poet composes in order to explain to himself his own notions and upheavals.

Do not elicit a wife for yourself who will be beautiful. An ugly wife can flirt the husband no less than a pretty one and she will love you even more.

Do not ever fear to make a mistake. There is no need to fear distractions or disappointments.

Do not seek honor. It will be accompanied by envy and hate.

Even words will beat someone to death.

Every era believes in that deity which is compatible to it.

Every person is a distinctly defined personality who will never appear a second time.

I was able to grasp only sincere truth: that miracles are made through the effort of your own hands.

If we sin on behalf of another person, it is just half the weight against us on the scales of justice.

If you believe the one you love, this is the highest proof of love.

If you can, try to walk ahead of time. If you cannot, then walk with time, but never place yourself behind the times.

If you were not born a poet, you will never become one, regardless of how much as you may strive, or as much effort you might expend.

Inspiration lasts a moment longer than a penetrating sensation.

It is senseless to install a border where emotion ends and where genuine love begins.

Men love to exhaust women to whatever extent they can.

Only stupidity is one-sided, while truth can be turned in any direction.

Only the person who plays with loaded dice will win without fail.

Only valor lives to be immortal. The valiant are glorious forever.

Our life loses its meaning if we do not pay attention to our past.

People are differentiated based on the essence of their soul; what similarities that may exist are only superficial. The more a person becomes himself, the more profoundly he begins to understand himself, the more clear do his individual traits surface.

Science does not have the claim to penetrate into the essence of things. Science only knows the relationships of effects, it can only compare them and relate them. Science cannot investigate any thing without its relationship to another. The conclusions of science are the observations of relationships of things and effects.

The recognition of immortal deities is indispensable for the human mind in order to install order and civility in the world.

You are a woman and this is why you are right.

ANTON PAVLOVICH CHEKOV

1860 – 1904

Doctor, Dramatist (mostly humor)

Anton Chekov was born in Taganrog, in the south of Russia, January 17, 1860, into a business oriented family. He completed medical school at the Moscow University in 1884, and become a county doctor. He began writing short stories in the late 1870's and mostly humor. In 1885, Chekov devoted his time entirely to writing. His income he dedicated to assisting education and the under-privileged, and likewise as a country doctor.

Chekov contracted tuberculosis and moved to Yalta to recover, and then traveled to Germany for better medical attention. He died there on July 2, 1904.

A deed is defined by its goals. A deed is called great if its goal is great.

A dirty fly can soil the entire wall, but a small dirty trick can ruin the entire issue.

A honorable person will not lie when he does not need to.

RUSSIA'S WISDOM

A new pain will ameliorate an old pain.

A person is what he believes.

All needs to be beautiful in humanity: the person, clothing, soul and thoughts.

Among the vain and conceited people there occurs moments when the realization that they are unfortunate will provide them some pleasure, and they will every flatter themselves on their sufferings.

An idle life cannot ever be a clean one.

An indication of good schooling is not when you do not spill sauce on the tablecloth, but when you do not notice if someone else should do this.

Bachelors usually die insane. The married died also, but not succeeding in going insane.

Behind the door of a prosperous person must stand someone with a hammer, constantly beating and reminding you that misfortunes are so close, and that inevitably misfortune will enter after a short period of prosperity.

Belief is the spirit's ability. Animals do not have such a thing. Fear and doubt reside among barbarians and undeveloped people. It is accessible only to the higher organisms.

Brevity is the sister of talent.

Chew your food, father would say, and we chewed our food well, and walked 2 hours a day, and washed with cold water, and even then we ended up as unhappy and untalented people.

Critics are usually those people who would have been poets, historians, biographers, if they could have. But having made an effort with their talents in these or other spheres and incurring failure, they are now engaged as critics.

Do not get lazy! Do not let lethargy get the better of you! While you are young, strong, good, do not cease to do good! Even if you do not have happiness in your life, but have meaning and a goal, then this meaning and goal will be greater than happiness, as it is something greater. Do good!

Every person is summoned to religious activity – the constant search for truth and life's meaning.

Falling in love directs a person to what he should be.

Honor does not need to be taken from a person, he will lose it on his own at that time.

If all the residents were to become boot-makers, then who would order boots?

If I were to shoot myself, this would provide great satisfaction to 99% of my friends and devotees.

If you realize that you need to expend a lot of money to treat some illness, then accept the fact that this illness is incurable.

If you want to become an optimist and understand life, then stop believing what other people say and write, but instead observe and notice.

If you want to have little time on your hands, then just do nothing.

If you were to work just for the present, then your work will become useless. You must work, having only the future in mind.

If your wife has changed you, then rejoice that she has changed you, and not the fatherland.

In nature, a beautiful butterfly evolves from an ugly caterpillar, but among people it is the opposite: an ugly caterpillar evolves from a beautiful butterfly.

Indifference is paralysis of the soul, a premature death.

It is easier for a woman to learn a new language because she has plenty of empty space in her head.

It is never to early to say, "Is this an important matter? Or, am I wasting my time?"

It is only stupid people and charlatans who know all and understand all.

Love is goodness. Really, not in vain during all eras and almost in all cultured nations love in its wide sense and love of husband toward wife are both one and the same called love. If love often becomes cruel and destructive, then the reason is not with itself, but in the imbalance of people.

Men do not marry and women remain as spinsters, because they do not present any other interest to each other than the physical.

No matter how beautiful a woman may he, she cannot compensate her husband for her empty-headedness.

No matter how cynical some literature may be, it still cannot express life as it should be in its reality.

Science is most important, most beautiful and necessary in a person's life. It always was and will be the supreme display of education, and only with it alone will a person defeat nature and change himself.

Take care of having too dignified a speech. Your language must be plain and elegant.

That which we experience when we fall in love, perhaps is the normal state. Falling in love directs a person to the type of person he should be.

The best rest is purchased with work.

The desire to serve the general welfare must be the soul's immutable obligation, a condition of individual happiness.

The happiness of future humanity is contained solely in knowledge.

The higher a person is in his mental and moral development, the more he is free, and so the more pleasure that life will provide him.

The highest expression of happiness or unhappiness is more than often expressed unintentionally.

The meaning of life can be contained in one expression – struggle for survival.

The misfortune consists in our endeavor to resolve the simplest questions cunningly, and then we make them into the most extraordinarily complex.

The most important gear in family life is love.

The person who enjoys to share his illnesses with others has nothing else interesting in his life.

The place that serves for me as my holy of holies is my corporeal body, its health, mind, talent, inspiration, love, and absolute liberty, and this is liberty from coercion and falsity, and I will never express the latter items.

The present writer is the same as the ancient prophet: he views matters more acutely than ordinary people.

The profession of a physician is an accomplishment. It demands self-denial, purity of soul and purity of thinking.

There exists a special breed of people whose specialty is to occupy themselves with ridiculing every aspect of life. They cannot even walk by some destitute or suicidal person without making some futile statement.

There is contained within each one of us an excessive number of gears, wheels and valves, so we could judge one another based on our first impression or based on 2 or 3 external indications.

There is nothing that binds together love, friendship and respect, than a common hatred of something.

They say that in the final end truth will prevail, but this is not true.

To be idle means to unintentionally always overhear what is being said, and to watch what is being done. The person who works and is occupied, hears little and see little.

To marry will be interesting only if it is based on love. To marry some girl only because she is sympathetic toward you is no different than buying yourself something at the bazaar because it is a nice object.

To travel to Paris with your wife is just the same as being in Tule with your own samovar.[30]

---

[30] Tule, Russia, is a manufacturing center of samovars.

Unfortunate are the egoistic, bad, unjust, cruel and the stupid who are incapable of understanding each other. Such do not unite, but disperse people with their misfortune.

Vodka is clear, but it turns the nose red and your reputation black.

We busy ourselves to change our life for the better, so our posterity will be happy, but then our posterity will say in a customary manner, "Our life was better earlier; right now is it worse for us than before."

We need to raise girls in such a manner that they are able to recognize their mistakes, because, according to their opinion, they are always right.

What an immense happiness – to love and be loved.

What are called the governing classes cannot remain long without war. Without war they become bored, idleness wearies them, irritates then. They do not know why they live, eating at each other, striving to insult each other with greater provocations, as much as they can without incurring liability, and the best of them with all their strength strive not to get fed up with one another and with themselves. Then war occurs and involves all of them, encompasses them and a general misfortune binds them all.

What is primary in family life is patience. Love cannot continue very long.

When a woman destroys, as a man does, then they find this to be natural and everyone understands this. So when she wants to or attempts to create, as a man does, then they find this to be unnatural and cannot reconcile the matter.

When I married, I became an old maid.

When we love, we do not cease to ask ourselves the question: Is it honorable or dishonorable? Intellectual or stupid? And to what is this love leading? And more questions. Whether this is good or not, I cannot know, but I do know that what interferes does not satisfy me, but irritates me. This I know.

Women can shine without the company of men, but men without the company of women are unintelligible.

You need to organize your life in such a manner that work is unavoidable. Without work you cannot have a clean and joyful life.

ALEKSANDR STEPANOVICH GRIN

1880 – 1932

Writer

Aleksandr Grin was born Grinevski on August 23, 1880, in the city Slobodski, in Vyatski Province, central Russia. His family were immigrants from Poland. In 1896 Grin completed school in Vyatsk, left home and decided to become a sailor. He worked as a day laborer, deliveryman, gold digger, and also as a volunteer soldier. He deserted his military post and attached himself to the Socialist-Revolutionary Party and worked as an agitator in various cities in Russia.

In 1805, due to his agitation at the Black Sea naval shipyard, Grin was sentenced to 10 years exile in Siberia, but was able to receive an amnesty. He began a writing career in 1906, but his initial stories were discarded by order of court censurers. Beginning in 1912, his stories were regularly published in newspapers and journals. Up to 1917, Grin had composed over 350 stories, narrations, poems and satires. After 1918, his magazine was closed and he was almost executed. Grin was conscripted into the Soviet army but was immediately released when he was diagnosed with typhoid fever. After his recovery he again wrote new novels, but he was prosecuted by the Soviets for his books and he slowly declined in popularity until no Soviet press was willing to publish any of his new novels. In 1930, he moved to the village Staroi Krim, on the Crimean Peninsula, where he died of stomach cancer on July 8, 1932.

A creation of art will never produce evil. It is unable to do harm, because it possesses the ideal expression of every freedom.

A life of solitude in gloomy places develops suspicion, cruelty and bloodthirstiness.

A person's heart is defenseless. But if it is defended, then it is deprived of light, and burning coals in it are insufficient to even warm the hands.

A precious sensation that will extinguish hate almost migrates into the enemy as a divine inspiration, as a gratitude to his torture.

After 18 years, every person has a story to tell about themselves.

All that unexpectedly changes our life is not accidental. It is in ourselves and just awaits an external opportunity for expression though some action.

At the moment of the strongest shock the human spirit loses cognizance of reality, continuing in his imagination as though the incident has already concluded.

Conscience is the acknowledgement of this spiritual entity that lives in each person. And only when it is acknowledged as this particular entity does it become a reliable guide of life for people. But often people do not consider conscience as the acknowledgement of this spritual entity, but they consider it either good or bad depending on the opinion of the people that they reside with.

Every love is the first one.

Everything in life occurs accidentally, but all of it links one after another, and there is no person who in his time would not be, willingly or unwilling or unconsciously, the reason for the joy or the sorrow of others.

Having in view the inescapable natural end of all, what would be proper is to live heartily and boldly as a quality of human nature.

I understood one simple truth: that a person can perform miracles with his own hands.

Immeasurable is the immensity of life. And every person will have the opportunity and ability to love it more than a woman, yourself and brief fleeing happiness.

It is unthinkable to install a boundary where infatuation ends and genuine love begins.

Lonesomeness is a great organizer.

Much is lost for people who only seek illness and distortion in nature, instead of beauty and health.

Never fear making a mistake. There is no need to fear disillusion or disappointment. Disappointment is payment for something before its receipt, perhaps it is sometimes disproportionate to its actual value, but still be generous. Fear advertising your disappointment, and do not use it to decorate all that you have remaining. Then you will acquire strength to repel evil and will properly value its good portions.

People are foolishly trusting. All the advertisements of the world are based on 3 principles: Good, much, and cheap.

People seem to live in extreme dependence on one another, and if they were in complete cognizance of this, then without doubt, their words, statements, motions, conduct, and their attitudes would become activities that are intelligent and considerate; the activities of a thinking person.

Possess human nature with a marvelous capability to display that inner person, that sole entity that is truly compatible to its physical features. Then we would be witnesses to strange, monstrous and beautiful metamorphoses, true revelations able to shake the world.

Solitude is a cursed thing. This is what can ruin a person.

Something important needs to be said immediately, otherwise it will diminish like a wave caused by spilling oil from a ship.

Sometimes a person is satisfied with a fantasy that he has created to resolve some issue that is off to the side. So it is easier to die than to acknowledge the error.

Stupidity, if it is stated by one person, will acquire a appearance of something possibly serious if it is repeated by a hundred other stupid people.

The beauty of art is greater than the beauty of life.

The meaning of life only consists in what surrounds you. The innumerable quantity of combinations are presented to you: display, beauty, objects, people, work. Find you own combination.

The more that you do for a person, the more that he becomes similar to you.

The necessity of something unusual, is perhaps the strongest after sleep, hunger or love.

There is much beauty in the world providing joy to the eyes and rest to the heart when it beats slowly, tired from the tattered events of the day.

There is no measure of genius and no limits to it.

These items are no less miracles: a smile, joy, forgiveness, and at the proper time the right word that is stated. To possess this ability is to possess all you need in relationships.

We often become younger when we are older.

When it is uneasy to deal with people due to their excessive politeness or humility, then very quickly it will become intolerable due to their excessive demands and carping.

Women have built for themselves such an arsenal of effect on feelings that a man cannot calmly just associate with a woman. As soon as he walks up to her, he immediately falls under her spell and become stupefied.

Words can sometimes beat a person to death.

You say that stupid people surround you. If you think this way, then this is a trustworthy sign that you are one of them also.

ILYA ILYICH METCHNIKOFF

1845 – 1916

Biologist, Anthropologist, Philosopher

Ilya Metchnikoff was born May 3, 1845, in the village Ivanovka, Kharkov Province, Ukraine. He complete studies at Kharkov University in 1864. He was professor at Odessa University, and at Petersburg University. In 1882 he was forced to leave his teaching profession due to persecution from the side of the Minister of Education.

In 1886, together with N.F. Gamalei and Ya.Yu. Bardakh, Metchnikoff organized the first bacteriological laboratory in Russia. From 1888, he worked with Louis Pasteur in his laboratory in Paris as a microbiologist, and remained there through the end of his life. In 1908, Metchnikoff was awarded the Nobel Prize in medicine for the creation of the phagocytic theory.

He developed a teaching regarding orthobiosis – the concept that life and death are natural existences for any human being. Metchnikoff also provided material for further understanding in Russia on gerontology and thanatology. His religious concepts attempted to reconcile a person with death. Metchnikoff felt that it was indispensable for a person to change his physical and moral nature so he could materialize a complete physiological circle of life with a normal growth into old age, allowing him to easily adapt to his death.

Metchnikoff died in Paris on July 2, 1916.

There came to my mind this question during the course of my already long life, and not just once, "Should I be, or not be?" And so I count myself having the right to speak a word on this. I am convinced that the tragic decision that so many young persons make, those who could at their designated time produce much benefit to people, depends on the significant level of their ignorance of that basic law of psychological development, by which the meaning and purpose of life is recognized not in early adolescence, but during a later growth.

Similar to this is that young men and women do not recognize the meaning and goal of their reproductive organs until a time that is too late a period in their development. So then young people still do not attain the understanding of the true purpose of human life.

There occurs among people who attempt to deprive themselves of their life, that suddenly the instinct of life awakens within them, compelling them to somehow save their life by any means. Under such conditions it is understandable that the feeling of life can develop just as much with healthy people as with the chronically ill or severely painful. These diverse changes in viewpoint can be placed parallel with the development of psychological maturity. In light of the situation that the feeling of life is subject to development, it follows in this sense to direct education precisely in the same manner as training blind people to touch, since their vision is absent. Young people inclined toward pessimism must always be inspired to know that their psychological composition is only temporal, and that it, based on the laws of human nature, must yield its place to a brighter ideology expanding to the entire world.

Konstantine Konstantinovich Sluchevski

1837 – 1904

Classical Writer and Poet

Konstantine Sluchevski was born in St Petersburg on July 26, 1837. His career was mostly military in his early years. He attended military school as a cadet, graduating in 1855, and then became part of the infantry, and then advanced to the tsar's private battalion, and then again to officer's military training academy. But in 1861 he resigned from military service.

Sluchevski went to Europe and studied in schools in Paris, Berlin, and Heidelberg, and graduated with a doctorate in philosophy in 1865. He returned to Russia to work at the Ministry of Internal Affairs, 1867-1874, Ministry of State Property, 1874-1891. Then he became chief editor at a government published newspaper, through the end of his career.

He died in St Petersburg on September 25, 1904.

This is totally resolute, what it is that lies ahead of us in the full light of comprehension, imposing its colossal shadow of reasons and reasons. Upon all living humanity lies a certain something from the eternity of religious ideas.

Demarcations between the kingdoms of nature are imposed only by people.

If science will allocate me immortality, then why do I need belief?

It is pleasant to stride along the majestic truths of laughter.

Even digestion inside a person is mystical! The student of natural science, having a sufficiently clear understanding of how organic life develops from protoplasm, still does not understand the manner protoplasm is initially formed! The ability to act on our intellect is given to us, people, but only inside of some type of limited bright circle, beyond which exists only a great darkness that we cannot penetrate.

Regarding that there is nothing new under the sun was in the past stated by King Solomon. But in a similar sense, just as in nature, not one heart's pulse cannot be identical to another, no matter how similar they might be from the first glance, and because one pulse occurs as a predecessor to the next subsequent, and next a new iteration is accomplished. As it is with the organism, so with the balance of the world, so in the world the psychological activity of a person is its own pulsation and there is no repeating it.

Always and everywhere nature has preserved, guarded the highest of its developed forms of existence in order for it proceed further, and here upon reaching its highest form it suddenly – not from this side and not from that side – recedes from these millennia of conformance to law and kills it! One of the 2 have occurred: Either all earthly existence is something else, like insanity or irony or maybe just a soap bubble, but then why is there customary, unquestionable, immutable, mathematical laws of the universe, why all of his environment of strict logic, it is to inflate someone or for some type of important, triumphant, legitimate journey into some stupidity of emptiness? Or on the contrary, if the laws are not a joke, if life actually is logical and development in some known direction, its essence, then recognize that the annihilation of one individual personal soul, that is, the highest entity, is completely impossible, a complete denial of all remaining life, all certain laws of existence.

Any type of physical communication between the dead and living cannot be. All spiritism, all mediums, are something rather like dementia or absurdity in a person's mental faculties. Visions, undoubtedly, can have a place, as long as they are manifestations that are purely objective.

Young people beginning to live enter onto a new unfamiliar path and find on the left and right unfamiliar roads – smooth, deceiving, fun. All a person has to do is follow them and it will initially seem so much fun and good to follow them. But then you will further travel along them and when you want to return back to the original tried and tested road, you will not know how to return, and you will just continue further and further and enter into total ruin.

KONSTANTINE SERGEEVICH STANISLAVSKI

1863 – 1938

Theatrical Director, Actor, Educator

Konstantine Stanislavski was born Alekseev, in Moscow on January 5, 1863, his father was a local businessman. He attended the local Lazarevski Institute and graduated in 1881. For the next several years he worked at his father's factory, while at night he played at the Alekseevski Theatrical Circle, where many felt he had great promise as a actor in the future. In 1888, he was one of the founders of the Moscow Society of Arts and Literature, and then in 1898, he helped found the Moscow Theater of the Arts. As a director Stanislavski was original and ingenious.

He also traveled abroad acting in plays. Stanislavski died in Moscow on August 7, 1938

An actor first of all must be cultural and have the ability to extend to the genius of literature.

An actor needs to train himself to make the difficult appear customary, and what is customary – easy, and what is easy – beautiful.

Creativity is first of all a total concentration of all our spiritual and physical nature. It encompasses only sight and audibility, but all 5 senses of the human. It encompasses, other than the above, the body and mind and thought and will and feelings and memory and imagination. All our spiritual and physical nature must be directed toward creativity in order for the soul to materialize what is reflected in the world.

Each day that you do not add something more to your education, even if it be just a little, some small bit of new knowledge, consider this time fruitless and irretrievable and lost.

Geniuses are born ages apart, those of great talent – decades apart, those of moderate talent – years apart, those of little talent – days apart, and mediocre people – hours apart.

If the meaning of theater was only scenes of entertainment, perhaps it would not even be worth to exhaust much effort into it. But the theater is an art to imitate and reflect.

Inspiration seems to appear only during holidays. For this reason the actor needs to possess some type of more accessible and previously traveled road, and not a road that will dominate the actor, as following personal feelings will do. But the easiest road of all for the actor to travel and upon which he can fix his sights is the line of physical motions. When these physical motions are clearly defined, the actor becomes nothing more than a robot with his motions.

Let old wisdom direct young motivation and strength. Let young motivation and strength support old wisdom.

Nice decorations for its admirers is the salvation of mediocre theater. How many errors in acting are covered by scenery, and which so easily provides an artificial façade for the entire spectacle. It is worth while to note how many mediocre actors and actresses exert effort to hide behind the scenery, decorations, costumes, colors, hardware, styles, special effects, and other objects, as a means of deceiving the inexperienced and naive spectator.

Theater is the strongest weapon, but just as with the use of all weapons, it has 2 means. One can provide great benefit to people and perhaps be the greatest means of inflicting wrong.

There exists no art that does not require a virtuoso.

To perform in a full and inspiring auditorium is not much difference than singing in a house with good acoustics.

Aleksei Konstantinovich Tolstoy

1817 – 1875

Poet, Writer, Historian

Aleksei Tolstoy was born in St Petersburg on August 24, 1817. He was a second-cousin to Leo Tolstoy, and they led parallel lives, although never crossing. The family was wealthy and his early childhood was spent in Ukraine at the estate of an uncle. At the age of 10, he traveled Europe with his parents, and was in the same circle as the children of the royal Romanoff family, including the future Tsar Alexandr II.

For his education, it was not in upper educational institutions, but working at government offices. From 1834, working at the Ministry of Internal Affairs, then from 1837, at the Russian Embassy in Italy, from 1840, in the royal court of Tsar Nicholas I, where he continued until his retirement in 1861. Tolstoy – like his namesake Leo – was also in the military during the Crimean War. In Odessa he contracted typhoid and was nursed back to health, and then in 1856, returned to St Petersburg. Tolstoy rejected Christianity as an institution but believed in a higher power and that this entity provided humans all they needed for a life and future.

After his retirement, Tolstoy lived in the village Pustinka on the shore of the Tosna River near St Petersburg, or else at the family estate in Chernigov Province, Ukraine. During the 1860's

RUSSIA'S WISDOM

and 70's, Tolstoy traveled Europe, and lived a life of high style and squandered all the family inheritance, including all his income from his books. He distributed his wealth also to the serfs of his estate after the Emancipation of 1861. Isolated from Russian culture at his family estates, this had a bad effect on his mental faculties and his disillusion of Russian government affairs set in. Subsequent illnesses led to his decline in health and pain, and as a result Tolstoy began to take morphine.

Tolstoy died of an accidentally morphine overdose taken to relieve his migraine head pain, at his home in Pustinka on September 28, 1875.

Most of his books were historical fiction of characters in Russian history, such as Ivan the Terrible, Kagliostro and Boris Godunov, as well as writing many parodies of life in imperial Russia.

"Why," says the egoist, "should I work for my posterity, when it plainly will do nothing for me at all?" How unjust you are, stupid! Posterity will do for you what you, connecting the past with the present and the future, can do by considering yourself as a child, adolescent and adult.

A magnet points to the north and to the south. It depends on a person to select a good or a stupid path of life.

A married playboy is like a sparrow. Life is an album. A person is a pencil. Deeds are a landscape. Time is a gymnast, continually in motion.

A person's memory is like a page of white paper. Sometimes good is inscribed on it, and sometimes the bad.

All say that health is most valuable of all, but very few observe this.

Digging a hole for someone else, do not fall in it yourself.

Do not irritate the wounds of your close associate, carefully propose to him some ointment.

Do you need to remember that this duck hunting boat being sold at the marketplace in the recent past is nothing but the person selling himself?

Genius is like a hill that rises above the plain.

Happiness is like a balloon that moves about: today it is over one person, tomorrow over another, the day after over another, and then over the next and the next, and according to the number of happy people that it finds, each having his turn.

Have the same attitude toward yourself as you would that others will have toward you. This is a very trusted means of getting people to like you.

I do not completely know why many call destiny – Indian,[31] and not something else that is closer to destiny like a bird?[32]

I will boldly compare the pen that writes for money with the street-organ in the hands of some wandering foreigner.

If you have a fountain, plug it on occasion to allow it to also rest.

If you try to chase love out the door, it will fly back in through the window.

If you want to be happy, then be happy.

---

[31] meaning Hindu, referring to the concept of Karma.
[32] The Russian word for Indian (In-dei-tz) is similar to the word for Turkey (In-dei-ka).

If you want to be tranquil, do not accept sorrow and troubles on your own account, but always take them to the bank.

Intellect displays to a person not only the external appearance, beauty and goodness of each subject, but furnishes it for some actual utilization.

Live forever – learn forever! And in the end you will attain what you have the right to say, like a sage, that you in reality know nothing compared to what can be known.

Measure goodness proportionally, because how do you know where it will penetrate? The rays of the spring sun, predestined only to warm the surface of the earth, unexpectedly penetrate deep underneath where jewels are located.

Never lead something to the very extreme. A person who desires to dine very late at night risks eating early the morning of the next day.

Never lose from sight that it is considerably easier to enjoy the many, than to satisfy the many.

New boots are always tight.

Nothing in the world falls to the wayside. Every work and every word and every thought grows as a tree.

Often words written in a cursive form are more unjust than those printed using straight lettered type.

Only people who are capable of strong love can tolerate strong resentment. But this requirement to love serves for them as a reaction to their sorrow and heals them. As a result the moral nature of a person is even more tenacious than the physical nature. Sorrow will never defeat them.

RUSSIA'S WISDOM

Our life can comfortably be compared with a meandering river: on its surface canoes float, on occasion a small wave will agitate the water, often it will be restrained by the motion of a watermill, and then be beaten as it flows over underwater rocks.

People see poetry in whatever they do not lie about.

Prosperity, misfortune, poverty, wealth, joy, sorrow, destitution, contentment, are all diverse displays of one historical drama, where persons repeat their roles for the edification of our world.

Take the opportunity to speak on 2 occasions: either when you have thought clearly through on the subject of your talk, or when something needs to be indispensably stated. Because only in these 2 circumstances is talk better than silence, and so in the balance of situations it is better to be silent, than to speak.

The income of some dissolute person is the same as having a blanket a little short: if you pull it to your nose, you will expose your feet to the cold.

The present is the result of the past, and so continually turn your attention to your rear, so you will not repeat the same mistakes of the past.

The utilization of talents is measured by the successes of civilization, and they are presented like milestones of history, serving as telegrams from the ancestors to us the contemporaries, and then to posterity.

The wind is the respiration of nature.

They say that work kills time. But time is something that cannot be reduced, and continues to serve humanity and all the world continually in the same fullness and without interruption.

Time is like a gifted director, continually introducing new talents to replace those disappearing.

Under sweet expressions lie hidden malicious thoughts. So the tobacco smoker often uses perfume to cover his stink.

Very important consequences can result from small reasons. So, chewing his fingernails was the cause of my friend's infection.

Virtue serves as its own reward. A person transcends virtue when he serves and does not receive a reward.

Watching the sun, blink your eyes and you will see sunspots.

When speaking with a sly person, always weigh your answers.

When you watch people in high rank having high objectives, keep your wallet in your eyesight.

Evgeni Nikolayevich Trubetzkoi

1863 – 1920

Attorney, Soldier

Evgeni Trubetzkoi was born September 23, 1863, in the village Akhtirka, in Moscow province, central Russia. He evolved from an aristocratic family of many princes in Russian history. He received an excellent schooling at home, and in 1881, entered Moscow University to study law. Finishing in 1885, he taught jurisprudence at the Demikovski Law School in Yaroslav, and then later at Kiev University.

As far as his political views were concerned, he first was inclined toward the state views, but then later toward peace implementation. Trubetzkoi was one of the organizers of the Party for Peaceful Restoration, in 1912, and which was transformed into the Party of Progressives. At the same time he was editor of several journals and literary publications, including the publication of his own compositions dealing with religious philosophy.

With the Russian Revolution, Trubetzkoi joined the White Army under Denikin against the Soviet authority. He died in battle in Novo-Rossiysk, Ukraine, on January 23, 1920.

A person sacrifices himself only when he believes that this is something great, something immortal, something that will outlive his death.

The entire pathos of freedom has not even the smallest meaning if a person possesses nothing sacred that we must venerate.

In every heroic feat, in every act of self-sacrifice, there exists this conscious or unconscious belief in some meaning of life beyond the grave, and which will lead us beyond the boundaries of our present existence. With such a feat we declare that it is not worth living for just our personal convenience, happiness, egoism; but that the meaning of the life of each of us prevails in some type of permanent global goals.

Our entire life consists in striving toward a goal. From the beginning and to its end it is presented to us in a vision of a hierarchy of goals, where one is subject to another depending on the quality of means to accomplish each. There are goals that are desirable, not just on their own sake, but for the sake of something else, for example, we need to work in order to sustain ourselves. But a goal does exist that is desirable on its own. Each of us possesses something eternally valuable, for which sake we live. Every person, consciously or unconsciously, supposes that it is worth living for the sake of this goal or valuable and unconditionally. This goal, or its equivalent meaning of life, is a proposition that is fearless and inescapably tied with life in this manner. And this is why no failure of any type can stop humanity in the search of this meaning.

Only what is perishable can be consumed by fire. It is only what eternally endures, having a solid religious basis, that can withstand the general destruction and fire.

It is characteristic of the Russian liberation movement that it values equality more than it values freedom itself. It is ready to prefer slavery to private freedom. Between general equality of slavery and general equality of freedom it does not permit a middle ground. It cannot think otherwise except in the form of a generality.

There are 2 types of democracy, 2 contradictive understandings of democracy. Of them one confirms the authority of the people for the right of power. Such an understanding is incompatible with freedom: from the point of view of power there cannot be talk of any kind whatsoever of inalienable and solid rights of the individual. The other understanding of democracy places as its foundation of the authority of the people – moral principles, and first of all, the recognition of human dignity, the unconditional value of human individualism as such. Only with such an understanding of democracy will the issue of freedom stand on a firm foundation.

The cemetery is a classic expression of communalism, equality and the secret of death, the direct destiny that stands before each of us.

The most dangerous characteristic of the contemporary era consists in that the conduct of civil war, to which the Bolsheviks have accustomed us, has become regular. Not only have the adults adopted it, but also children. The instability of all moral principles, the intensive arbitrary conduct, habit of pillage and cruelty, such a poisonous legacy of a turbulent epoch, has impressed it traces in the national soul for many years. Traces of the Bolshevik character will continue to be preserved in Russian administrations, wars and community activism, even when we have long forgotten and no longer think about the Bolsheviks.

The essential character of national messianism includes the national exclusion of religious comprehension. One way or another Russian messianism is always expressed in the confirmation of a

Russian Christ, and more or less is a subtle Russification of the Gospel.

To not be able to well express your thoughts is a shortcoming. Not to have independent original thought is even a greater shortcoming. Independent original thoughts flow only from independently acquired knowledge.

Under the influence of anger we often bring such accusations against the person who causes us to become angered, and accusations that would otherwise be humorous if under carefree circumstances.

Each person knows what he should not do in order not to isolate him from other people, and a person knows what to do in order to unite him with people, not because it was ordered him by somebody, but because the more he unites with people, the better life will be for him, and also the contrary, the worse he lives the more he is separated.

The life of each person consists only in becoming better and better every year, month and day. And as people become better, the closer they draw to one another. And the closer people draw to one another in unity so the better their life.

One the most sorrowful results of the reforms of Tsar Peter I the Great is the institution of the official government ranks. He created a class of artificial, uneducated, hungry, busybody people who are unable to do anything at all, and who know nothing except chancellery bureaucracy. He installed some type of civic priesthood performing their sacred rites in courts and police stations, and using their thousands of starved and unclean mouths to suck the blood from the balance of the population.

Konstantine Dmitrievich Yushinski

1824 – 1870

Educator

Konstantine Yushinski was born in Novgorod-Seversk, Ukraine, on February 19, 1824. He studied at Moscow University, graduating in 1844, concentrating on science and education. He began writing articles on education in 1857. By 1859 he was hired as director of the Smolny Institute in St Petersburg, as well as working with the Ministry of National Education. His efforts had a large positive effect on the modernization of education for young people in Russia, including writing textbooks for elementary students.

He died in Odessa, Ukraine, on December 22, 1870.

A conviction only then becomes an element of character when it changes into a habit. In particular a habit is that process by means of which a conviction becomes an inclination and a thought is transformed into an act.

A person not only likes to be surprised, he also likes to surprise others.

A person is born to work. His earthly happiness consists in work, and work is the best preserver of social morality, and work must be the best education of a person.

A person needs freedom to work as an inherent part of his individualism, for development and support of feelings of personal dignity.

A person's body, heart and mind require work, and this work is so urgent, that if a person does not display his personal work in his life, then he will lose the genuine road, and in front of him will appear 2 others, both identically destructive: the road of insatiable dissatisfaction with life or the road of voluntary unnoticeable self-destruction.

A strong character, as with a strong stream, incurs obstacles, which only cause it to become more stimulating and forceful. But should such obstacles be removed, it has the ability to place a deep rudder in the water.

Attention is the one door entering our soul through which all comprehension indisputable enters.

Fear of corporeal punishment will not make an evil heart – good. And mixing fear with malice is the most repulsive display in a person.

Humanity's lives would have long died at some point if it were not for young people dreaming, and the seed of many great ideas did not ripen unnoticed from the rose-colored shell of young utopias.

If education wants to provide happiness to some person, it must educate him not for happiness, but to prepare him for hard work.

If you successfully select a vocation for yourself and dedicate yourself to it with all your soul, then happiness will seek you and find you.

In order for an education to be able to create a second nature for a person, it is indispensable that the ideas of such an education migrate as convictions of the student, and such convictions evolve into habits. When such convictions are inculcated into a person, and his attitude develops to the point that he obeys them before even thinking about the fact that he needs to obey them, only then have they been made an element of his nature.

In order to overcome feelings of embarrassment, what is needed often is nothing less than heroism, just as you would need to overcome feelings of fear.

In particular it is labor – even though labor is not always interesting, although always thought-provoking and useful – that is the supreme mover of mental and moral development of humans and humanity.

Is not mental work the most difficult work for a person? It is easy and pleasant to dream, but difficult to think.

It is not within the mental faculties of a woman, but in the character of her nature that is hidden the rich means of her ability to nurture children. The concentration of attention, precision, patience, persistence, love of protocol, kindness, manners, taste and, finally, inherent love of children – all of these are such qualities that reside in a woman a lot sooner than in a man.

Never promise a youngster what you cannot fulfill, and never deceive him.

Only the inner, spiritual, life-providing strength of work serves as a source of human dignity, and along with it is morality and happiness.

Our will, just as with our muscles, strengthen after constant increasing activity. But by not allowing them exercise, you definitely will acquire weak muscles and a weak will.

Pedagogics is not a science, but an art. It is the most expansive, complex and highest and most indispensable of all the arts. However, the art of education depends on science. As art is complex and expansive, it depends on a multitude of expanded and complex sciences. Knowledge requires ability and inclination, and it strives toward the ideal of a complete person.

Satisfy all the desires of a person, but then remove from him his goal in life and you will see how unhappy and miserable an entity he will become.

The art of education has this feature, that it seems to almost everybody to be an activity that is familiar and understood, and likewise an activity rather easy. But the easier and fluently this is said, the less that person actually knows about it, both the theoretical and practical aspects.

The courageous person is not the one who crawls about seeking danger, while not sensing fear, but the one who can suppress his greatest fears and think about danger, while not submitting to fear.

The head filled with fragments and disconnected pieces of information is similar to a warehouse where everything is totally disorganized and where the boss cannot seem to find anything. And then you have the head that is totally organized but without any knowledge, and this is similar to a grocery store, where all the shelves are clearly labeled, except the shelves are empty.

The independence of a student's head is the sole durable basis of all productive teaching.

The most important part of education is the formation of your character.

The right to happiness comprises one of the inalienable rights of a person.

The state of unjustifiable, unrestrained anger is just as destructive as the state of unjustifiable or unneeded goodness.

There is nothing – not words, not thoughts, not even our actions – that can express so clearly and reliable ourselves and our attitude toward the world as our feelings. Our character can be heard in them, not as separate thoughts or separate resolutions, but as the entire content of our soul and all of its traits.

To ameliorate the mass amount of human suffering and increase a mass amount of human enjoyment is a goal that people incline towards – consciously or unconsciously, directly or indirectly, using all the strengths of intelligent and honorable people.

The expansion of your knowledge can only occur when you look directly into the eyes of your ignorance.

What is supremely valuable in an individual's education is conviction, and only one person's convictions can effectively impact another person's convictions. Every educational program, every method of instruction, no matter how good it might be, if it does not migrate as a conviction into the student, remains a dead letter, not having any strength or effectiveness.

Do not believe that equality is impossible or that it will only materialize sometime in the distant future. Learn from children. This can apply to every person and laws are not needed with this type of education. You in your own life can institute equality with all people, all those with whom you associate. Only do not display especial importance to those who count themselves great and high. But primarily, display yourself as having respect toward those who count themselves contrite and humble.

If you are stronger, wealthier, more educated than others, then strive to serve people with what you have that they do not. If you are stronger, help the weak. If you are more educated, help the uneducated. If you are wealthy, help the destitute. But proud people do not think in these terms. They think that if they have something that others do not, then they not should not share it with people, but only use it to magnify themselves.

It is foolish for people to boast of their appearance, their body, and it is even more foolish when people boast of their parents, ancestors, their friends, their genealogy, their nation. The greater portion of evil in the world is due to this foolish pride. This causes arguments between people and families and causes wars between nations.

The Soviet Era

Anna Andreevna Akhmatova

1906 – 1966

Poet

Anna Akhmatova was born Gorenko on November 23, 1906, in Odessa, Ukraine, into a family of naval and mechanical engineers. She was educated at Mariyenski Woman's Academy, and then after graduation she migrated to St Petersburg, where together with her husband and poet N. Gumilev in 1922, she became part of a growing number of poets dedicated to the new socialist system. Anna Akhmatova received numerable awards in Europe likewise for her poetry. She died near Moscow on May 3, 1966, and is buried near St Petersburg.

Anna Akhmatova wrote under the family name of her maternal grandmother.

A poet is a person from whom no one can steal anything, but at the same to whom no one can give anything.

All of us spend some of our time as guests. Life – this is only a routine.

All those you truly love will always remain alive for you.

An honorably educated person will not arbitrarily insult another. He will do it deliberately.

Do not give me anything to remember, because my memory is short.

Genuine gentleness you can never entangle in any manner, since it is very subtle.

I possessed great credit. I also tolerated immense discredit. And I became convinced that essentially both are one and the same.

In essence, no one knows in what epoch he lives. So we did not know at the beginning of this decade that we were living on the eve of the European War and the October Revolution.

It is possible to be a famous poet, but still write bad poetry.

It is possible to forgive treachery, but an insult never.

It is terrifying to admit that people see only what they want to see, and hear only what they want to hear. It is due to these specific qualities of human nature that 90% of all fantastic rumors, false gossip, and holy-woven scandals are preserved. I only ask those who disagree with me to remember what they had heard about themselves to ascertain whether this is true or not.

Strongest of all in the world are the rays of a calm eye.

The future, as we know, throws its shadow long before we enter it.

The properly educated person does not accidentally insult another. He insults only deliberately.

When someone in the street calls out loud, "Hey stupid," you do not have to turn around.

DANIEL LEONIDOVICH ANDREEV

Poet, Mystic and Visionary, Political Activist

1906 – 1959

Andreev was born November 2, 1906, in Berlin, Germany, but spent his entire life in Russia. He was the son of the poet of the Silver Age, Leonid Nikolaevich, and was raised in a household that remained deeply religious, Andreev began writing poetry and prose in early childhood.

He graduated from high school having concentrated on literature but was not allowed to attend university. He supported himself as a graphic artist and wrote poetry in his spare time. Prior to Second World War he wrote considerable poetry and produced 2 volumes: *Russian Gods* and *Iron Mystery*, but they were not published until long after Andreev died. He married but the marriage was short-lived. In 1937, he met his future second wife, Alla Aleksandrovna, but they did not marry until after the war.

Andreev was conscripted into the Red Army in 1942, serving in World War 2. Due to medical problems and unable to serve at the front, he served as a noncombatant, and helped to transport supplies. The impact of the war had a psychological effect on Andreev that turned him toward religion in a serious manner and he began to have visions and became mystical. Oppression, war and dictatorship become totally repulsive to Andreev. After the war he returned to civilian life and worked in Moscow in the literary field, but he was arrested by Soviet authorities April 21, 1947, and sentenced to 25 years of imprisonment, being charged of anti-Soviet propaganda. Alla was also arrested and exiled to a prison in Moldova, but her incarceration was short.

Andreev suffered a heart attack in prison in 1954, the first that would eventually cause his death. In the same year his sentence was reduced to 10 years, and he was released on April 22, 1957, already seriously ill. While in prison Andreev had mystic visions and started writing *Roza Mira (Rose of the World)*, finishing it after he was released. The book was known in the Soviet Union via underground publishing, but was only officially published in 1991.

Both the war and subsequent imprisonment took a serious toll on Andreev's health and he died in Moscow on March 30, 1959, at age 52, only 2 years after his release from prison.

Andreev was an adherent of religious spiritualism. A central viewpoint of Andreev's thought is that the life of the created universe is filled with the struggle between the powers of light and the powers of evil. Andreev divided time in eons of life to designate world periods. The mystery of the first eon is consummated by the annihilation of the antichrist and the salvation of a few. During the second eon the salvation of all without exception will be consummated and the emanation of evil will be terminated. During the 3rd eon the redemption of the very devil will occur.

One trait characteristic of the 20th century is the aspiration to be worldwide. The external pathos of various movements of our age has been directed toward the constructive programs of their national development. But the inner pathos of the most recent history has been directed toward becoming worldwide.

Until we are finally liberated from our national-cultural arrogance, until we finally cease to feel that Russia is surely to be the best country in the world, until that time none of our immense massiveness will gain anything, except despotic threats for humanity.

For the meta-historian, doubt never arrives for the hero who has passed through his fatal moment, that by this very means, new and newer paths of creative abilities are opened to him on the historical level, from top to bottom. That state of being without a glimmer of light is alien to the meta-historical view of world progression. For the meta-historian, the doubt never arrives that great national love and activity, its summons, is not subject to the law of annihilation, if its activities were bright and its love was justified.

The Lord is an immutable and inexpressible and initially-supreme aspiration. He is a spirit-creating authority acting in all souls, not silenced even in the depths of demonic monads and governing worlds and more worlds, from microcosms to super-galaxies, and He holds greater perfection than any goodness, and more supremacy than any grace or virtue.

God possesses all-encompassing love and inexhaustible creativity molded into one entity. All that lives, and people included in this number, draw close to God through 3 divine qualities that are inherent to Him: freedom, love and divine-creativity. Divine-creativity is the goal; love is the path; freedom is the condition.

The experience of history leads humanity close to understanding this obvious fact, that dangers will be circumvented and social harmony attained not by the development of science and technology on their own, not by the redevelopment of government principles, not by the dictatorship of a strong person, not by the approach to the authority of pacifist organizations of the social-democratic type that are rocked by historical winds to right and to the left as a result of the powerless scatterbrain idealism, and all the way to revolutionary maximalism — but by the acknowledgement of the essential indispensability of one-sole path: the installation of some type of untarnished, highly authoritative institution over a worldwide federation of states, and one that is immune to bribery, one that is a ethical institution, outside of the state and over the state, and this is because the state is secular due to its fundamental essence.

It will not be a hierocracy, monarchy, oligarchy, or republic, but it will be something new, qualitatively distinct from all else that has existed up to this time. This will be a world-wide national arrangement striving toward sanctification and enlightenment of the entire world's life. I cannot describe in exact detail using any of the words in my vocabulary the new religion, internal religion and church. The list of its fundamental distinctions from old religions and churches over time compels me to develop new words to apply to describe it.

This is not an isolated confession, that can be determined to be true or false. It is not an inter-national religious society similar to the theosophical, anthroposophic, or Masonic, which are instituted like a bouquet, each flower representing some religious truth eclectically selected by them from every possible religious meadow. This is internal religion or pan-religion in the sense that it needs to be understood as a universal teaching indicating this angle of view of the religion that appeared earlier. They all seem to be reflections of various layers of spiritual reality, different rows of informational facts of different segments of the planetary cosmos. This direction of view is accepted by Earth as a complete as well as a part of the divine cosmos of the universe.

Each soul is the playing field of the struggle between light and demonic principles. The soul is like the traveler attempting to cross a shaky bridge. Hands of assistance stretch to him from each shore, but to accept this help, the traveler must stretch his own hands. Such a hand on the shore of light is every good choice, every good action and every bright movement of the soul and every prayer.

Even the millions of such people who earlier were distant from questions of religion, who were immersed in the worries of their puny little world on in artistic creativity and scientific research, will feel that in front of them stands a certain selection, and it is the only one, and it is so scary that even tortures and executions are trivial next to it.

But to whom more is given, from him more will be required. Just as for the individual, so and for the nation that is supremely gifted. Endowments and weight are an obligation for the greater, but this does not give them the rights, that the balance of mortals do not have.

This struggle appears just as much in the life of individual persons in the form of confrontation between the bad and good sides of a person's soul, as much as in the development of humanity as a whole – in history. However history is only the visible part of the iceberg that is passing. The fundamental struggle cultivates in a reality consisting of another form of matter. The term metahistory in the *Rose of the World* is introduced as the revelation of the entire fullness of this struggle. Metahistory encompasses not only the historical processes, but also what is apparently the reasons behind it all, that is, the struggle between anti-religious propaganda and the divine providential powers.

O, there was no reason for Christ to die, not a violent death, not even a natural. After many years living in the Enroth[33] and involved in the resolution of such problems, for whose sake He accepted this life, a transformation awaited Him, and not a death. A transformation of His entire substance and His transfer to the Olirna[34] for all the eyes of the world to see. Once culminated, the mission of Christ would have summoned the following: that on earth within 2 or 3 centuries, in place of governments with their armies and bloody Bacchanalians there will be established an

---

[33] This universe
[34] The first of the levels, where the dead reside

ideal Church-Brotherhood. The number of sacrifices, the sum of sufferings and times of recovery from disaster would immeasurable terminate.

How should we understand, for example, the phase *materialization as a human*, in its application to Jesus Christ? Should we now imagine that the Logos of the universe was clothed by the same substance as given to human flesh? Is not such a disproportion of scales intolerable for us: the close proximity of the category of the cosmic in the same limited sense as the category of the local-planetary, narrow-human? So would it not be more precise to speak not of the materialization of the Logos into a human, into the substance of Jesus Christ, but as this being his expression by means of the great monad that was born of God? God is not incarnated, but expresses Himself in Christ. And if it is so, then one more obstacle to the agreement of Christianity with certain other religious trends falls aside.

Before attaining materialization as a human, which would fully reflect its substance, the great Spirit accomplished the preparatory descent, incarnating itself some 7,000 years ago in Gondwana.[35] There It was the great teacher. However humanity still was not ready to accept spirituality, descending like rain through the incarnated Logos. Yet there was established a profound and immaculate esoteric teaching, the first kernels were spread, carried by the winds of history upon the fertile fields of other countries and cultures: into India, Egypt, China, Iran, Babylon. The incarnation of the Logos in Gondwana still did not possess the character of such fullness, as it later displayed in Jesus Christ. It was in essence still preparatory.

We name Christ – the Word. But the speaker becomes its incarnation, and in particular expresses itself in word. God does not incarnate Himself, but expresses Himself in Christ. Particularly in this sense Christ is truly God's word.

---

[35] A primal super-continent, before the separation of the continents into what they are at present.

Because every nationalism – and to understand this word as meaning the preference of your nations over the balance and the advancement of its interests at the expense of the balance of nations – is nothing else other than patriotism raised as a principle and confessed as a world ideology.

But it is time to explain to yourself, that these historical events, whose scale blinds us and compels us to romanticize them, nevertheless stand in particular as the struggle between meta-historical monsters. In particular, this is why such historical epopees were so bloody, and why their concrete and positive results were so doubtful.

Creativity, as with love, are not exceptional gifts, known only to selected individuals. What is known to such select individuals is virtue, holiness, heroism and wisdom, ingenuity and talent. But all of this is unveiled potential residing in each heart. The depth of love, an inexhaustible fountain of creativity, boils beyond the threshold of each of us.

Freedom is freedom when it consists of the possibility of a selection of the individual's desire.

I will repeat what I wrote earlier, that in particular this world must become the Kingdom. The Old Testament Hebrews were right, thinking of the Messiah as a good earthly sovereign. The New Testament transferred the time and place from here to the heavens.

It is a firm axiom that a person living only for himself is not even a zero, but a negative value in society.

Love is a feeling of mutual joy and desire, the belief in another person's enlightenment.

The fallibility of religious dogmas consists, for the most part, not in their content, but in the pretensions that these established dogmas claim to have, being as if laws of a cumulative, universal or cosmic significance, that these confirmed dogmas as a fact must be confessed by all humanity, and that as though without it there is no salvation.

The most terrifying dangers that threaten humanity at the present and will threaten us for well over another century, this is great suicidal war and absolute worldwide tyranny.

The substance of governments is soulless automation. It guides material interests of the greater or lesser of humanity's masses, considering them as a single entity. But it does not participate in the interests of the individual as a single entity.

You must not nurture in your soul any love toward dark powers. This signifies subjecting your undefended soul to the temptations that it will meet on the road ahead.

You need to be able to disdain alien opinions, if you feel yours is correct.

ALEKSANDR MIKHAILOVICH DOBROLUBOV

1876 · 1943

Sectarian Mystic, Poet, Pilgrim

Dobrolubov was born 1876, in Warsaw, Poland, where his father worked for the Russian government as a civil servant. Otherwise there is no information available regarding his early life. After his father's death in 1892, Dobrolubov moved to St Petersburg with his mother.

He began writing poetry while in school as an adolescent. Once in Russia he dedicated himself to writing and followed the style of western European symbolists and decadence. He attended Petersburg University and studied history and philosophy. With his circle of associates, he smoked hashish and opium, and preached fatalism and suicide. As a result of his moral corruption and bad influence, he was expelled from the university.

In early 1898, Dobrolubov experienced a religious transformation and overnight he became an entirely new and different person, now with a search for God and spiritual experience. First he went to John of Kronshtadt for counsel, and then on a pilgrimage to Troitzki-Sergeev Monastery, and then at the end of 1898 he departed to Solovetski Monastery with the intention of becoming a Russian Orthodox monk. After a year at Solovetski, he left, not able to adapt to the regimen, and he began his life-long pilgrimage and nomadic travel throughout Russia, while preaching his version of Christian mysticism. One durable conviction of his was that the Orthodox Church with its theology and rites only suppressed the advancement of Christian mysticism, and he rejected the Orthodox religion as an institution. His attitude likewise reached to opposition to the state, and he declared himself a pacifist. As a result, he was arrested for refusing induction into the military in 1901, but was released by the intervention of family who claimed he was mentally ill.

In some respects, Dobrolubov was a parallel of Leo Tolstoy, except his revelation was 20 years later, and he began his nomadic life earlier. They visited together in 1903 and again in 1907 at Yasnaya Polyana, near Tule, and Tolstoy in his diary complements Dobrolubov for his convictions, the 2 of them having many similarities. This also strengthened Tolstoy's convictions.

His wanderings were from Nizhni-Novgorod to Orenburg, along the Volga River valley, and occasionally back to Petersburg to visit his mother. The adherents he gathered called themselves Dobrolubovtzi, and they were few and scattered, separating from Orthodoxy, and denying the validity of the state, and living in isolated communities. Most of them were in Samara Province. His convictions were recorded in his book, *From the Invisible Book*, published 1905.

Dobrolubov's activity almost disappears after the Russian Revolution when he moves to Omsk, Siberia, in 1921, since now he was always one step ahead of Soviet police. In 1923-1925, he is again near Samara; 1925-1927, now in Bukhara and Dushanbe, central Asia; and then his history is lost until near his death in 1942/1943 in Azerbaijan, in the Caucasus.

I am a person raised in what is called an educated society, but God placed me on a different road. I expended several years in isolation and in a religious wilderness, in search and in labor and in silence among the silent working people. With a child's steps – and this may seem funny to many – I entered the path of belief and conduct, this sincere path of mine.

Songs were born in my heart since childhood. When I entered the path of repentance, I held my tongue for several years. Once they opened, I could not forbid them and I sang in winter among the trees on an empty road. Now I realize that this was not a road with signs, but only a trail. And it was one of the straightest and most comfortable of trails, and maybe it just might exit to a main highway. Even then you will never exit some distant corner without a trail to follow.

All of these songs were born already fully prepared in my heart, they were sealed upon my heart so I would remember them. For several years I lived with one book of life, the life of belief and conduct, and I sang all that I sang, but only for the closest of my brethren and for God.

Accept this statement, brethren, as a creed. Forgive me, you the bad and good, high and low, familiar and unfamiliar, men and women, children and aged, and all whom my infection affected, and those whom it is not affect, friends and enemies, those who remember me and have forgotten me, those who hate me and love me and laugh at me. Forgive me, those who walk the path of purity, and the corrupt and murderers, those incarcerated in distant prisons and concentration camps. Forgive me, every creation and animal and cattle, every free bird, and the mountains and eternal hills of the world, and the heavens that calmly shine. All of you forgive me, my sisters, and the grass upon which I laid on those June days outside the church, for offending all of you. The steppes respire with heavy fragrances, while my hand – so accustomed to doing wrong and for no apparent reason – plucks your silent leaves. Forgive me, you Angels, as well as all the unsubmissive spirits who have risen against God, all the daemons. Why was I your helper for such a long while, helping you to blind others?

All of us are one body. One secret sin, one most secret evil act, one most secret evil word, adds to the difficulty of all and loads the yoke held over all the offspring of Adam, and makes it more difficult for all in the world. And one most secret benevolent act, one most secret immaculate statement, adds to the joy of all and makes it easier for all to proceed forward.

All of us will stand on the porch with the Master, friends, and friends and enemies, animals and Angels and flowers and rocks and rivers and children of the heavens. Green leaves cover the patio from the heat, the grapevines pour its wine.

Then he will say, "Friends, I provide to you My kingdom, I decline My crown. I am the slave of all of you, I want to be a slave unto all of you." He holds a towel, He will wash the lowest reaches of our bodies, that closest to the dirt. "I want to wash your feet, and want to always conduct Myself as only your slave. I am your Lord."

I have provided you corporeal food and life and respiration, and I have provided you the ability of movement. I have constantly walked behind you, brought everything to you, served you. I am your Lord.

In His infinite love, just as a boyfriend with his bride, or like a son with his father, or like a friend among other friends, He will fall to my feet just like the woman who wiped His feet with her hair and covered Him with her holy kisses, so shall He display his infinite love. And this will be awesome for the previous eternal mistakes of His friends. Because He was tempted in all manner just as we are, only He remained immaculate. Often, often did His sorrowful gaze stare into the abyss of sin, and death was almost able to defeat Him. But just one time for the sake of His friends did He descend into the valley of this world.

So many accomplishments of Yours, my God. I see the kingdom of Your labors. I see that thousands of Your assigned duties await Your laborers. Work under the supervision of the Master. But in your spare time, work on your own behalf, you have little time to squander.

When He sends you a holiday, utilize it as you would your free days: attend church, pray, breath the pure air of the spring morning. Meditate at night, the best manner to attend to your work, waiting for it to be assigned to you. Ask of elders, friends, and see how they respond to you.

And the Angel cries, "There is no end, no end to His work, no end to His progress." He does not reject even the most menial of tasks that need to be accomplished, and on occasion will assign major ones, but He asks not to ignore the simple tasks.

He arrived in my valley in the springtime, when birds were mating among the braches of the cherry trees. Upon my hills His stopped His feet, and I followed after Him and sought Him. Wherever he placed his feet, the grass flourished like silver strands.

On Sunday He was walking through the village, and when peace was already settled in my cities, when the sound of the bells greeted those who were still in their beds, who had worked the entire week, when the clear and damp morning began that spring day, when children laughed while on their cots near the stove and biscuits were ready to be baked.

Girls, walking for water at the well, saw Him, how quietly and majestically, yet non-stop, the almost unnoticeable Pilgrim walked through the village along its main road. For a long while they watched, pouring the water from the well into their buckets, and spilling some on the green grass. The city had been cleaned some time back and Angels stood at the corners of all the main streets.

Living among contemptible people of all sorts, I heard their simple yet profound language and saw that they can explain everything and just as good if not better than the emaciated words of the scholarly.

Who assigned me this law of death? I want to live, and so I will live.

You say a law of death exists? I searched within myself for it everywhere and did not find it. Only immortality, and this is will. For a long while my will weakened. For a long while it could not find life without death. But through death it aspired indefatigably. Even in your present mortal life – immortality exists.

The mortal imitates the immortal; it aspires to be eternal and mortal. The thousands of incarnations, these tens of thousands of rebirths, these are the beginning of immortality.

And an Angel walked to me and showed me a book and ordered me to write, although I read nothing in it. And then he said to me, "This book is plain, a book of simplicity. Without simplicity I will not show you its secret. Abandon, abandon, your will. Did I not teach you this all these years? Did not your friends sing this with you among the green field before we bid farewell? Do you remember?"

And I said, "Lord, how can I recognize your paths? They demand peace from everybody, while those demand only battle. Did you not lead me earlier? If I erred, I am ready to reject it. But I saw just the weak side, but it was Your true church. I saw it in the morning fog and I rejoiced."

Myself plain and in plain destitute clothes, I come to You, the ancient Plain Person.

I abandon, I abandon my will! In this, in this is my will, Lord! I abandon worry, but not about food, not about tomorrow's day, because I abandoned this long ago. I abandon sorrowful worries about my rectitude, deeds, words, fasts, my prayers. I do not want, I do not want to do anything; it is best for You to command me. For a long while I was perishing due to these worries, but now I will not worry even about my friends. Send to me and tell me, O, Omniscient One, all the actions, all the words and all the feelings residing in Your radiance. You love me with a love that is uncontrollable for me. Your enemies You have long forgiven. Will You now lead me to my friends, Lord?

PAVEL ALEKSANDROVICH FLORENSKI

1882 – 1937

Russian Orthodox Theologian, Martyr

Pavel Florenski was born in the city Evlakh, Elizavetski Province (today known as Azerbaijan) on January 9, 1882. His father was Russian but his mother was Armenian. His local education was in Tiblisi, Georgia, and then he entered the physics-mathematics program at Moscow University, and later attended Moscow Religious Academy. In 1911, he was ordained as a priest in the Russian Orthodox Church. From 1912-1917 he was editor of the magazine *Bogoslovksi Vestnik* (Theological News).

With the Russian Revolution, Florenski continue to incline toward a theocratic monarchy in his philosophic and political views. As a result of this, he was continually under surveillance by Soviet police. Nonetheless, from 1916 to 1925, Florenski continued to write religious articles and publish them. In between he would work utilizing his education in physics and mathematics working for the Soviet government. At the same time Florenski worked to preserve churches and monasteries as works of artistic value, for them not to be destroyed, and especially the Troitzki-Sergeev Monastery, and preserving other ancient works of Russia art.

In 1928, Florenski was exiled to Nizhni-Novgorod, and his surveillance intensified. He was formally arrested on February 26, 1933 and on July 26, he was sentenced to 10 years imprisonment. His exile was an eastern-Siberian concentration camp, where he arrived December 1, 1933. He continue to write while in prison, now on political views against the Stalinist suppression of religion. In August 1934, he was placed in solitary confinement, and then in September 1934, he was sent to Solovetski Island concentration camp, arriving there in November.

On November 25, 1937, Florenski was sentenced to death by the Communist party and executed by shooting. On December 8, his body was brought to Leningrad and buried at a local cemetery for executed criminals.

The pillar of truth is the Church, this is assurance, this is the spiritual law of identity, this is accomplishment, this is the Tri-hypostasis Unity, this is the light of Tabor, this is the Holy Spirit, this is prudence, this is wisdom, this is the Immaculate Virgin, this is friendship, this again is the Church.

Let us remember in its true sense, what is the entirety of the Christian concept of life? It is comparable to the development of a musical score that is a system of dogmas and dogmatics. And what is dogmatics? It is the Creed of Faith in its individual parts. And what is the Creed of Faith? It is nothing else than the maturely developed baptismal statement – In the name of the Father and Son and Holy Spirit.

This way or otherwise, but between the Three-in-One Christian God and dying in insanity, there is no 3rd alternative. Do turn your attention to this. I do not exaggerate when I write this, but precisely the situation. I even do not suffice in words to express this more sharply. Between eternal life in the womb of the Trinity and eternal second death there is no interval, even to the extent of a hair. It is one or the other.

My dear friends, the sin which is especially difficult for me to see in you is envy. Do not be envious, my precious friends, of anybody. Do not be envious, this crushes the spirit and reduces its effectiveness. If there is something that you want, then humble yourself and ask it of God, so you will receive what you need. But do not envy. Shallow thinking, narrow-mindedness, triviality, weaving webs, malice, intrigue – all of this evolves from envy. Comfort me by not having envy.

Only by depending on direct experience can you acknowledge and value the spiritual treasures of the Church. Only being led through the ancient lines of moisture-filled bays can you wash them with living water and decipher the letters of ecclesiastical literature. The ecclesiastical champions are alive for the living and dead for the dead.

The religious activity that provides us the knowledge of the pillar of truth is love. But this love is gracious, displayed only in a cleanse stream of knowledge. We need to attain it by long-term effort. In order to aspire to it, and which only pertains to humanity, we must receive an initial push and must have support in further movement forward. Such a push is a revelation and a meditation directed at the individual. To accept such a revelation, love of God must already be inherent.

All rotates, all slides into the abyss of death. Only One resides, only in Him is there immutability, life and rest.

I learned kindness when I firmly learned that life and each one of us, and nations and humanity, is led by the Good Will, so there is no reason to be anxious over anything, other than the problems of the present day.

In agreement with our daily-mundane understanding, jealousy is harmful for love and is its ugly tumor. The reasons for jealousy are alien to the essence of love, and so jealousy unusually is recognized as estranged from love.

It is necessary to live and utilize life, depending on whatever is available at that present moment. Once time is squandered on discontentment, nobody and nothing can return it.

Love is infinite. It is not limited by space or time. It is ecumenical.

Our philosophers aspire to be not so much intelligent, as much as wise; not so much thinkers, as much as sages. I cannot decide whether the Russian character has been molded by historical conditions. But undoubtedly, philosophy has not been an important issue among us.

Sin will paralyze holiness and will continue to do so, since holiness is still not completely distanced from it, just as the wheat and weeds grow together until the designated time.

The heart wounded by a friend is not capable of being healed, except by time or by death. But time will wash its wounds, removing the greater part of the heart, while a part will die. But death reduces the entire person.

Culture is the rope that you can throw to a drowning person, and which you can also use to strangle your neighbor. The development of culture progresses in the direction of a use for benevolence as much as it does a use for evil. Contriteness grows, and so does cruelty; altruism grows, and so does egoism. The matter does not occur such that with the increase of goodness – evil will decrease. It is faster than an electrical current. Every appearance of a positive electrical current is parallel with the appearance of a negative. For this reason the struggle between good and evil is not extinguished, but intensifies. It cannot end and apparently it cannot not end.

MAXIM GORKI

1868 – 1936

Soviet Writer and Dramatist

Maxim Gorki was born Aleksei Maksimovich Peshkov in Nizhni-Novgorod on March 16, 1868. He was orphaned early in his life and began work at the age of 11 to support himself. Diligently working, he was able to enter Kazan University in 1884. He became familiar with Marxist literature and worked to propagandize it. Gorki joined the group headed by Nikolai Fedoseev, a Marxist promoter, and was arrested. After his release, he continued under police surveillance.

His literary career began in 1892 with the publication of his first short stories. His plays were first published in 1901, and all met with success.

Gorki became friends with Vladimir Lenin in 1905 and became a member of the Russian Social-Democratic Workers Party. The following year he went abroad and wrote satires on the failure of the cultures of France and America. He lived in France, America, Finland, Germany, Czechoslovakia, and Italy. From 1906-1913 he lived on the island of Capri off the coast of Italy, for both health reasons and to isolate himself from the upheavals occurring in Russia.

He returned to Russia and supported the Bolsheviks in the new government. However he became disenchanted with the results of the revolution and left Russia for Italy in 1921, and for health reasons, he had tuberculosis. There he stayed until 1928.

Eventually, Gorki's finances declined and also any popularity, and he traveled back and forth to USSR a few times up to 1932. Then Joseph Stalin asked Gorki to remain permanently in the USSR and so he did.

Gorki organized the first union of Soviet writers, started several newspapers and journals, and continued writing. Matters though did not go as well as he expected: he was placed under house arrest for a while in 1934. His son likewise died suddenly that year.

Gorki died in Moscow on June 18, 1936. He was cremated and his remains are in an urn in the wall of the Moscow Kremlin. Some scholars suspect foul play in Gorki's death at the age of 68, that he was a puppet of Stalin, who awarded him heartily after his return from Italy.

A good joke is a reliable sign of psychological health.

A person must always live loving something that is inaccessible to him.

A person will become taller as a result of extending upwards.

A stupid person introduces questions more often than an inquisitive person.

A writer who does not possess a fluency in folklore is a poor writer. A limitless wealth is hidden in the national compositions, and the prudent writer must possess it. It is only here in Russia that a person can properly learn our native language, and it is very rich and glorious.

All men make themselves interesting in the presence of women.

All my life I saw genuine heroes as only those people who love and can work.

All want order, except their minds are insufficiently in order.

All women are artists, and this is the whole matter! Russian women for the most part are dramatic actresses, they all want to play the role of the heroine.

All work is difficult for a while, until you start to love it, and then it will motivate you and it will become easier.

Anger is temporal. Love is eternal.

Any person and each of us is the exit of previous dispatches and is the non-circumventable dispatch to the future. And I do not know of any name that can be spoken with greater pride and live than the name of some person.

Belief is always good for the soul's comfort, its tranquility. It will sometimes blind a person, permitting him not to notice the torturous contradictions of life.

Children are living flowers of the soil.

Children are our destiny of tomorrow. They are the critics of our viewpoints and actions. They are people who enter the world for a great work in building new attitudes of life.

Cultural superiority is defined by a nation's attitude toward women.

Do not be indifferent, because indifference is fatal to a person's soul.

Even if you have a high intellect, you cannot live without a conscience.

Every government – and whatever it wants to call itself – strives not only to govern by the will of the national masses, but also to educate this will to be conforming to its principles and goals. For the most part the demagogic and cleaver governments customarily embellish their aspirations to govern the national will and educated it by using the epithet: We express the will of the nation.

Falsity is the religion of slaves and masters. Truth is the god of the free person.

For an elderly woman to marry as a virgin is her jumping into an ice hole in winter.

Great and beautiful is the person striving to become something better.

Happiness with women is possible only if under the conditions of complete sincerity.

If a person will tell himself over and over that he is a pig, eventually he will start to snort.

If life was already interesting, no one would play cards.

If we were to value a person based on his work ethic, a horse would be better than any person.

If you are a counterfeiter, do not imagine that you are an original.

If you are not able to hold an axe properly in your hand, you will never hew a tree. Not knowing the language well – to eloquently and comprehensively speak – you will not be able to write.

Imagination is one of the most essential traits of literary technique, the ability to create entities.

It is impossible for a person to live without love. This is why he has a soul, so that he can love.

It is not true that life is gloomy; it is not true that it is filled with only plagues, groans, sorrows and tears! All situations occur in life, and whatever a person wants to find. And he has the strength to create what he feels is lacking in his life.

It is our mother who saturates us with love toward life.

It seems that a wife is connected to you by a chain your entire life. And both you and she are similar to convicts chained together. So strive to walk carefully and closely to one another, otherwise if you attempt to stray you will feel the chain.

Life is ludicrously short. So how should we live? Some stubbornly decline from life, others dedicate their entire selves to it. In the twilight of their years the former will be melancholy and retain few good memories, the latter will be rich in mood and memories.

Life moves forward, and if a person does not keep up with it, he will find himself alone.

Life will always be lacking in some area so that the desire for improvement will not be extinguished in a person.

Life without love is not life, but just existence. It is impossible to live without love, and this is why a soul is granted to a person, so he can love.

Life's realism is not much different from a good fairy tale or fantasy story, if you look at it from the inside, from the side of desires and motives, by which a person is guided in his activities.

Love a book. It will ameliorate your life, help in a friendly manner to untangle the webs of your thoughts, feeling, and accidents, erase the blemishes. It will teach you to respect humans and yourself. It will open your mind and heart with a feeling of love for the world, for humanity.

Moralists strive to hammer their moral principles inside of people, while they always carry them on the outside, like a tie or gloves.

Movement forward is life's goal. Let your entire life be a movement forward and beautiful time will be spent in moving upwards.

Never approach a person thinking that he is filled more with stupidity than with intellect.

Not knowing the past, it is impossible to understand the genuine meaning of the present or the goal of the future.

One misfortune of the majority of people is that they consider themselves capable of doing more than they actually can.

Only 2 forms of life exist: decay and fervency. The cowardly and greedy will select the former; the courageous and generous – the latter.

Only the person who is saturated with belief in himself materializes his will, directly implanting it into life.

Particularly in effort and only in effort is a person's greatness, and the more fervent his love for effort, the more majestic he is, the more productive, the more beautiful his work.

Pessimism is the philosophy of the failures.

Pity is a cheap imitation of love.

Politics is inescapable, like bad weather, but cultural involvement is needed in order to make politics a noble profession, and long has been the time to bring emotions of goodness and benevolence into the sphere of evil political emotions.

A smart poor person will look nice to deceive others; a smart wealthy person will not look as nice to deceive others.

Science is the supreme intellect of humanity. This is the sun that the human created from his flesh and blood, created and lit in his own presence in order to illuminate the darkness of his difficult life, in order to find an exit to freedom, justice and beauty.

Short speeches are always more retained and have a better ability to leave a strong impression.

Sometimes a woman can fall in love with her husband.

Talent is belief in yourself, in your abilities.

The atheists of our era, laughing at Biblical legends, count God as a pseudonym of humanity's stupidity.

The best consolation, the highest joy in life, is to feel yourself needed and close to people.

The future belongs to people of honorable effort.

The hero is the one who creates life as opposed to death. He is the one who defeats death.

The life of humanity consists in creativity, aspiration toward victory over the opposition of dead matter, the desire to possess all of its secrets, and to compel its strengths to serve the people's will for their happiness.

The meaning of life consists in a person's aspiration toward self-perfection.

The most intelligent ability a person can acquire is to love a woman, to respect her beauty. All that is beautiful in the earth results from love for a woman

The person who does not know what he will do tomorrow is an unfortunate person.

The responsibility of art is to provide aesthetic and moral value to all substantial aspects of life, among them also the negative, in order to help a person understand himself, increase belief in himself, develop aspiration toward truth, struggle against trivialities, find the best in other people, to excite embarrassment, anger and courage in them, to do all expected for people to be honorable, strong, and to inspire their life with a holy spirit to be beautiful.

The result of life is always one and the same – a new person! I speak not about a child, but of people who love, since this sensation renews the soul, makes people something else than they are – better and more beautiful.

The tongue is the weapon of literature, just as a gun is for the soldier. The better the weapon, the stronger the soldier.

The wise strength of a builder is hidden within every person. It is necessary to provide it the will to develop and flourish, so it will enrich the world with greater miracles.

There is no force that is more potent than knowledge. A person armed with knowledge is invincible.

There is no strength that makes a person great and wise, as much as does the strength of effort: a collective, friendly, voluntary effort.

To prove to a person the absolute necessity of knowledge is the same as trying to convince him of the usefulness of eyesight.

RUSSIA'S WISDOM

To remember does not always mean something, but the more you understand what you remember, the more this will be a benefit to you.

Until the time that we learn to admire the individual human as the most beautiful and marvelous manifestation on our planet, we will not be liberated from the depravity and falsity of our life.

Up to this time I still like people, as long as they want something, are going somewhere, seeking something, are motivated. But once they have reached their goad and stopped, then they have become uninteresting.

What is good always ignites the best desires in another.

When a person loves accomplishments, he will always have the ability to do so and will look for ways to do them. There are always room for accomplishments in life, and those who do not find this for themselves are simply lazy or cowardly, or else do not understand life, because if a person was to understand life, each would leave behind their shallow self after they pass away.

When a person speaks less, he appears more intelligent.

When labor is pleasant, then life is good. When labor is a duty, this is slavery.

Who works has no time to be lonesome.

Women will always love the man who will flatter her excessively, even though he might be gray, his face covered with wrinkles, his skin emaciated and cheeks worn red.

Your entire soul is invested in the one you love.

Ilya Arnoldovich Ilf

1897 - 1937

Evgeni Petrovich Petrov

1903 – 1942

Writers of Humor and Satire

Ilya Ilf was born Fainzilberg on October 4, 1897, and Evgeni Petrov was born Katayev on November 30, 1903, both in Odessa, Ukraine. They changed their names after the Soviets instituted a new government in order to disassociate themselves from their Jewish roots.

Beginning in 1927, they teamed together to write a series of humorous and satirical books on Soviet life, including some parodies of American life, used as propaganda.

Ilya Ilf died April 13, 1937, and Evgeni Petrov died July 2, 1942, both in Moscow. Neither of them lived to 40 years of age.

A balloon is always a balloon, whether empty, whether inflated.

A dog is so devoted that you cannot believe why a person should merit such love.

RUSSIA'S WISDOM

Actresses do not enjoy being killed during the 2nd act of a 4-act play.

Before the revolution he was the general's buttocks. The revolution liberated him and he began an independent existence.

Do not fight for cleanliness, just sweep instead.

Financial abyss is the deepest of all abysses, since a person can fall into it all his life.

God sees what is right, but does not quickly say so, because of the red tape.

He is not a chess player who, losing a game, does not announce that he had a winning move.

I am unable to start my millionth project since I have just felt in my pocket an insufficient amount of banknotes.

I know that many who have attempted to acquire glory from being stingy only had their nose broken.

If a competition of liars was to be organized, then the victor could only be the one who would tell the truth.

If there is no love, it is not a nice place to talk about money.

In the final end, what is love? Love is a miraculous moment.

It is not so bad to be destitute, especially with a moderate education and a weak-sounding voice.

Life, the foreman of the jury, is a complex joke, but for the foreman of the jury, this joke easily opens like a box. It is only necessary to be able to open it. Who cannot open it fails in life.

Money must be able to easily depart from you, without moans.

People read in a railway train because it is lonesome. People read in street car because it is interesting.

The road to true credit is always very difficult, but in our age it is easier due to the many roads available to reach it, even to the point that we no longer need virtue to acquire such credit in our life.

The time that we have is money, which we do not have.

There is still one pedestrian that an automobile driver has not yet run over, nonetheless, the automobile drivers are still dissatisfied.

What was prominent in early science fiction novels was the radio. Then they waited for humanity's happiness. Now we have the radio, but no happiness.

When I see this new life, these alterations, I do not want to smile, I want to pray.

When a woman ages, her body incurs many unpleasant affects. Her teeth fall out, her hair turns gray and thins, she develops asthma, she may gain a few pounds, or lose a few pounds. Yet, her voice does not change. It remains the same as it was when she was in high school, or as a bride, or as the lover of some young playboy.

ANATOLI VASILYEVICH LUNACHARSKI

1875 – 1933

Soviet Writer, Government Activist

Anatoli Lunacharski was born in Poltava, Ukraine, on November 11, 1875. He was educated 1895-1896 at Zurich University, and joined the Bolsheviks in 1904 while in Europe. He participated in the October Revolution in St Petersburg, and in 1917 was a member of the National Ministry of Education. From 1929, the president of the Scholar Committee of the USSR.

In 1933 he was assigned to be ambassador to Spain. Lunacharski died on December 26, 1933 in Menton, France, on the journey to Madrid, Spain.

What does it mean to have religion? This means to have the ability to think and sense the world in a manner that would allow the contradictions of life's laws and nature's laws to be resolved for us. Scientific socialism resolves these contradictions, promoting the concepts of the victory of life, subjecting the elements of the mind through a path of knowledge and labor, science and technology.

And so we confirm that religion is alive and will live, but that it has completely changed it forms. In essence, earlier religions expressed a thirst for happiness, and the people earlier ran to it seeking knowledge and purpose. But now this knowledge, finally, has been purged, and purpose has been purged. This cleansing of the great instruments of humanity from slag, stupid hypotheses and false presumptions was now able to raise religion to a new height, but not at all to eradicate it.

A pedagogue is the person who must transmit all the valuable accumulations of the ages to a new generation, and not transmit their prejudices, vices and illnesses.

A poor instructor only knows what needs to be done. A good one will show how to do it.

All of Smolni[36] was brightly illuminated. The excited crowds of people streamed through all of its corridors. You remember how some special music, how some special psychological fragrance, this atmosphere of the explosive past. These were the hours where all seems to be gigantic and where all hung on a hair, the hours and every minute that brought with it enormous news. Who was able to live though this will never forget this, the event that causes Smolny to remain the center of his life. All were huddled around a poorly illuminated table. They selected the leaders for the new Russia.[37]

And every one of use who supposes that he is able to guide others must first continually and intensely study.

Authority needs to be won only though parliamentary procedures.

---

[36] The Smolni Institute, a girls school in Petersburg for the wealthy families.

[37] When Vladimir Lenin returned from Germany, he selected the Smolni Institute in 1917 to be the headquarters of the Bolshevik party.

Great music was always recognized at its opportune time. Very potently does it huddle in our hearts. I do not know if there exists even one great musician of whom it would be proper to say that he has become old. Even the simplest song proceeding from the depths of thousands is invigorating.

If you are old, you know this. If you are young, you will know this. If you are old and do not know this, then I am sorry for you.

Is this the reason a person lives, to every day put on his pants, eat a piece of meat at lunchtime, and then at night lie back on his bed? No. All of this is just a means to attain a happy life. A person does not live for the sake of the means. He needs to dress, eat, rest and work in order to unfurl his comprehensions, develop feelings and sensations, in order to recognize happiness, to be happy and transmit this happiness to others.

Laughter is not just an illusion of strength, it is strength.

Sports installs a culture of optimism, a culture of vigor.

The atmosphere of a family's home will define the selection of life's path.

The corporeal education of a child is the basis of all else that remains. Without a correct application of hygiene in the development of a child, without a correct implemented physical culture and sports, we will never receive a healthy generation.

VALERIAN NIKOLAEVICH MURAVYOV

1885 – 1930 or 1932.

Civil Servant, Historian, Political Activist

Valeria Muravyov was born in Moscow on February 28, 1885. He attended private school at the Aleksandrovski Lyceum near St Petersburg, graduating in 1905. He then attend the School of Science and Politics in Paris, France. He then entered state diplomatic service working at Russian embassies in western Europe: secretary at the Russian Consulate in Paris, Hague and Belgrade, and then returned to Moscow, and went to work at the Ministry of Internal Affairs. At the onset of World War I he was back in the embassy.

However, after the Russian Revolution, he became involved in contra-revolutionary activities. He was arrested in 1920 and sentence to execution, but it was reduced to prison incarceration, but soon after he was able to gain amnesty. Muravyov again went to work in the embassy with the National Commissariat of Foreign Affairs. In 1920-1922, he participated in the work of the Free Academy of Religious Culture, and 1926-1928, worked at the Central Institute of Labor.

When the purges began in 1929, he was forced to resign from his position with the state department. Muravyov was arrested in October 1929 and sentenced to 3 years at a concentration camp for anti-Soviet agitation. There is no information regarding the date or place of his death, but what little is available indicates that he died of typhoid fever a few months after he entered the concentration camp.

A fundamental problem is the problem with eternity. There is no meaning in anything if there is no eternal fundamental nature in the world.

We do not overwhelm ourselves deliberating on the strange character of the feeling of love, that it as though does not coincide with any other item in our reality and, on the contrary, contradicts much, exciting us to paradoxical and illogical actions. Love does not recognize our corporeal limits and prohibitions. It is unable to be measured by our scales, it displays an extraordinary power in comparison to our small criteria. If we were to meditate on all this, then it will become clear to us that love is – in our dark, alienated and unenlightened world – a part of the transformed world, penetrated with rays still unknown to us, born and perfected in eternity.

Perhaps this is an opportunity to implement the tie between the 3 moments of time: past, present, and future, with the 3 views of psychological experience – knowledge, sensation, will. The past is only knowledge, and knowledge is only comprehension of the past. The present is only sensation, and sensation lives only in the present. The future is only will, and maintaining the will is only the future.

One of the inculcated preconceptions is the conviction in the irreversibility of time. Indeed time is not only reversible in principle, but we ourselves continually reverse it, completing these or some other expedient transformations of what surrounds us and repeating its former situation according to our will. Every intelligent act is an example of such an act, because it can be repeated if desired.

Deliberations about the nature of time, about its manufacture, its eternity, seems to be metaphysical and deprived of practical meaning. Right now with speed that makes your head whirl a person is attempting to win the war of space and subsequently time. We stand on the eve of such advancements in space that will create our ability to be close to the omnipresent. Time does not exist for the omnipresent.

In the final end, all seems to lead toward the task of creating the Sole Supreme Entity from disconnected individuals. The Supreme Entity is continually resurrecting himself, separating into a multitude of distinct primal individuals, and then again regathering and reuniting them. Eternity is included in the incessant birth of unfathomable wealth. God resurrects by means of the growth of our intellect, expanding and deepening our love and combining our activities in a collective matter.

From God's point of view, the path we traverse is the path of His personal creativity and increase. God eternally increases and restores all out of Himself. All of this occurs for us in time, because time is nothing else other than the accomplishment of each of these individual processes. For God time is eternal. It is distinct from being torn into past – present – future time in human terms, to the extent that He is omnipotent, while we are limited in our possibilities.

BORIS LEONIDOVICH PASTERNAK

1890 – 1960

Contemporary Poet and Novelist, Nobel Prize Winner

Boris Pasternak was born in the city Peredelkino, Moscow province, on January 29, 1890. He entered Moscow University to study law in 1908, but changed the following year to history and philosophy. After graduating in 1912, he continued his studies in philosophy at the Marburg University in Germany. Returning to Russia he joined a circle of Moscow writers, and himself began writing poetry with the first collection published in 1913, and his talent was immediately recognized by the public and so he made his decision to be a professional writer.

Pasternak spent 1916 in the Urals to help in a business and finance office. His experiences in the area and the city Perm provided him background information for his future novel *Doctor Zhivago*. In 1921, Pasternak's parents and sisters left the Soviet Union to relocate to Berlin, Germany. He visited them in 1922-1923 and there married his first wife, Evgenia Lura, and they had a son the following year. They returned to Russia and Pasternak continued to write poetry and subsequently novels. In 1934, Pasternak was a participant in the Union of Writers of the USSR, and he received honorable mention for his poetry.

With his 2nd wife Zinaida Eremeeva he traveled to Georgia in 1931. In 1935 he traveled to Paris as part of an International Congress of Writers for the Defense of Peace, and where he suffered a nervous breakdown. This was his final journey abroad.

Even though Pasternak praised Joseph Stalin in a couple of his poems, in 1936 the Soviet state changed its attitude toward him, and Pasternak was denied official publications of his writings. He retired that year to his family estate at Peredelkino, where he spent the balance of his life. He translated Shakespeare into Russian, and also Goethe and Sheller. Fortunately Pasternak was never arrested by the Soviet police, since they felt he was too popular a person to prosecute. He was able to visit soldiers at the front to encourage them in 1943 during World War 2.

His most famous novel, *Doctor Zhivago*, was completed in 1956, but was censured by the Soviet state. It was first published in Italy the following year and then in English in 1958. Pasternak was declared the winner of the Nobel Prize in literature for 1958, however due to fear of the Soviet government, he declined to accept the prize. At the same time a massive anti-Pasternak campaign was underway in the Soviet press and the Soviet government created artificial demonstrations demanding the exile of Pasternak from the Soviet Union.

Pasternak died of lung cancer at his family estate of Peredelkino on May 30, 1960.

All of us become people at least to this extent, among those who loved us and those we had the opportunity to love.

All people that we encounter in life are a reflection of ourselves. And they are sent in order for us, watching these people, would rectify our own mistakes, and when we rectify them, these people will also change, or else just fade away out of our life.

And carefully, petal after petal, your natural perfection would have been revealed, but having been revealed, saturated like a rose, you inevitably would belong to another.

From childhood I have been amazed at the passion of the majority to have this attitude to be typical or just like everybody else, the necessity to be part of some type of series or category, but not to be yourself. Why is this? Why is there such a strong impulse in our generation to just be typical? However you look at it, being typical deprives a person of their soul and individualism, it is a destruction of your destiny and name!

Her kiss was like the summer. It was slow and slower, until the storms came.

I am a repulsive person. I find only stupidity to my benefit, while the good is to my harm. Truly, I am just like a lobster that becomes best after boiling in water.

I knew 2 people who were in love, who lived in Petrograd during the days of the revolution, and I did not notice they were in love.

I love you so much, that I am even neglectful and indifferent toward other items. You are so much mine, just as though you have always been my sister, and my first love, and wife and mother, and all of what a woman is to me. Yes, you are this woman.

Peace is music which is seeking for words.

Silence is the best of anything I have ever heard.

The first place in the series of feelings of love is occupied by pseudo-humble cosmic elements. Love is so simple and unconditional like comprehension and death, nitrogen and uranium. This is not the composition of the soul, but the immemorial foundation of the world.

The future is the worst of all that is abstract. The future never arrives in the manner that we await it. Would it not be more true to say that it in general never actually arrives? If you await A, but B arrives, can you say that what you awaited did arrive? All that exists in reality, only exists in the frame of the present.

The inability to find and speak the truth is a fault that no ability to speak lies can ever cover.

The years will pass and you will get married. You will forget your earlier disorder.

There is no first page to any true book. Like noise in a forest, it occurs wherever God decides, and increases and echoes, beating against ancient trees, and suddenly in the darkest, stunning and panic moment, all the noises are beyond your ability to decipher and the echoes diminish.

To lose in life is more inevitable than to acquire. A seed will not sprout unless it dies.

You need to put a problem in front of you that is beyond your abilities. First, because there are so many you do not know. Secondly, because your strengths will develop to the measure of fulfilling the unattainable resolution to the problem.

Faina Georgievna Ranevskaya

1896 – 1984

Actress – Movie and Theater

Faina Ranevskaya was born Fanni Girshevna Feldman on August 15, 1896, in Taganrog, southern Russia. She was a Soviet actress in the theater and movies. She was considered one of the greatest Soviet actresses of the 20th century. She also contributed a large amount of aphorisms during her career.

Faina died July 19, 1984, in Moscow.

In order for us to know how much we overeat, our stomach is located on the same side of the body as our eyes.

I am comforted, having noticed in your recent letter, that you are not as smart as you were before.

When I was in the theater, talented people liked me. The mediocre people hated me. The vulgar audience bit at me and shredded me into pieces.

Memories are the riches of old age.

"And whom do you consider more intelligent? A man or a woman?" they asked Ranevskaya.
"A woman, of course, is more intelligent. Have you ever heard of a woman who would lose her head over some man's beautiful legs?"

"Why do women dedicate so much time and means to their external appearance, and not the same toward developing their intellect?"
Ranevskaya answers, "Because there are considerably less blind men than there are stupid."

One person asked Ranevskaya, "Why did God create some women beautiful and other women stupid?"
She responded, "Beautiful, so men would love them. Stupid, so they would be able to love men."

For a woman to succeed in life, she needs to possess 2 qualities. First, she must be sufficiently smart to be liked by a stupid husband. And second, to be sufficiently stupid to be liked by an intelligent husband.

"What was your mother before she was married?" one interviewer asked Ranevskaya.
"I did not have a mother before she was married."

"Today, I killed 5 flies: 2 males and 3 females," Ranevskaya once said.
"How did you know the difference?" the interviewer asked.
"Two sat on a beer bottle, and 3 sat on a mirror."

Optimism occurs due to a lack of information.

Old age is for the pigs. I consider it to be God's ignorance for Him to permit people to live to old age.

Life takes away so much of my time from me that I have no time to write about it at all.

Life is an extended jump from the (*unfit-for-print*) and into the grave.

Life is a short walk through an endless dream.

"Look, Faina Georgievna! There is a fly swimming in your beer."
"There is just one, dear. And how much can it really drink?"

Life is too extremely short to just squander it on diets, greedy men, and a bad disposition.

There are people in whom God lives. There are people in whom the devil lives. And there are people in whom only parasites live.

How I envy brainless people.

I am Stanislavski's abortion.[38]

Old age is not when bad dreams bother you, but bad reality.

I have enough intellect to live my life stupidly.

I do not recognize the word – play. Cards, checkers, jump rope, is what you play. On the stage it is what you live.

---

[38] Referring to Konstantine Stanislavski, Soviet movie and theatrical director, also in this volume. He was her mentor.

Ranevskaya and a friend were walking along Tverski Blvd, and the friend gave charity to a blind person. Ranevskaya tells her, "That blind person you gave a coin to is not pretending. He definitely is blind."

"How do you know this?"

"Because he said, 'Thank you, beautiful.'"

"Ranevskaya, how can a person be comforted when he suffers some misfortune?"

"The intelligent person is comforted when he realizes how small his misfortune compared to all else existing. The stupid person is comforted because he notices that others have the same misfortune."

It has been a long while since someone called me a (*unfit-for-print*). I must be losing my popularity.

Think and talk about me all you want. Have you ever seen a cat that was interested in what mice said about it?

If a woman is walking with her head down, she has a lover. If a woman is walking with her head proudly up, she has a lover. If a woman is holding her head straight, she has a lover. In general, if a woman has a head, then she has a lover.

ALEKSANDR ISAIYEVICH SOLZHENITZIN

1918 – 2008

Historian, Poet, Political Activist, Nobel Prize Winner

Aleksandr Solzhenitzin was born in Kislovodsk, near Stavropol, southern Russia. He completed studies in physics and mathematics at the Rostov University, and in 1942 was conscripted into the Soviet army during World War 2. He was wounded in battle and received a military honor.

In 1945, Solzhenitzin was arrested for critical statements he made about Joseph Stalin in a private letter he sent to a friend, and he was sentenced to 8 years in a concentration camp. At the conclusion of his incarceration, the sentence was increased another 3 years, and he was released in 1956. His book published in 1962, *One Day in the Life of Ivan Denisovich*, was a narrative of concentration camp life based on his experiences. But after 1966, not one of any of Solzhenitzin's literary works was allowed to be published in the Soviet Union, but his manuscripts were smuggled out of the Soviet Union and published abroad, such as *First Circle* and *Cancer Ward*, and his masterpiece on the Soviet concentration camp system, *Gulag Archipelago*.

In 1970, Solzhenitzin was awarded the Nobel Prize in literature, but fearing retribution from the Soviet government, he did not go to Sweden to receive the prize. In 1974, Solzhenitzin was exiled from the Soviet Union, and then went to Sweden to receive the prize. He lived in Germany and Switzerland, and then migrated to the USA in 1976, where he lived for the next 17 years, continuing to write against the evils of communism and living off the income from his books. Solzhenitzin was also a fervent critic of western culture, that it was decadent. Some Americans resented his residency here as a result, and especially with his promotion of Russian nationalism as well as Russian Orthodox Christianity.

In 1994, after the collapse of the Soviet Union, Solzhenitzin returned to Russia. He died in Moscow of heart failure at the age of 89, on August 3, 2008.

Being completely fed does not depend on how much we eat, as so much on how we eat! So with happiness, so with happiness, it is not at all dependant on the volume of external prosperity that we acquire in life. It depends on our attitude toward it. The person who attains contentment will also be content.

Now beaten by life, he knew that objects and events have their own relentless logic. In conducting their daily activities people have no time to deliberate on the results that will occur due to their conduct, the consequences of their actions. So we have [Alexandr] Popov who create the radio. Did he ever think that he was preparing a loudspeaker for the verbosity of thinking people during the night? Or the Germans who permitted Lenin to escape to Russia to convert it into ruins, even though 30 years later it was Germany that was turned into rubble? Or Alaska? It seems to have been such an oversight to sell it at such a bargain., since now Soviet tanks do not have an overland passage to America! Some incidental fact decides the fate of our planet.

Even prosperity that is not entirely equal will provide happiness to people, and the attitude of our hearts and our point of view will also affect our life. One and the other is entirely in our authority, meaning, a person is always happy if he wants to be, and nothing can interfere with it.

It is good to have a strong head. You always possess an exit even at the last minute. All paths of events are subject to you.

Literature is life's instructor.

Often thoughts that are so fixed at night when we are half-asleep become so vague at the light of the dawn.

The line that divides good from bad cuts across the heart of each person. And who will destroy a piece of his heart? In the course of the life of one heart, this line moves place to place, at one time it will restrict happiness due to malevolence that occurs, at another time it will enlarge to allow expanse for benevolence to flourish.

The more fragile a person, the more dozens, even hundreds of accidental circumstances are needed in order for him to attract someone like himself. Every new coincidence just increases the chances of intimacy a little. And even then, just one sole separation can quickly ruin all of it.

The Russian spirit and Russian culture has existed for ages, and every soul that is attracted to acquiring this legacy through knowledge and intimate pain, these are genuinely Russian.

The universe has as many centers as its does living creatures.

They say, "You cannot suppress an entire nation without end." What a lie! Yes, you can! Do we not see how our nation has become desolate, barbaric, and indifference has descended on it not only as the fate of our country, not only as the fate of neighbors, but even our individual fate and the fate of our children. Indifference is the last reaction for the deliverance of an organism, and it has become our defining characteristic. As a result the popularity of vodka has reached a scale unseen in all of

Russia's history. This horrible indifference, when a person sees his life not as being split in half, not with corners broken off, but as hopelessly hewn to bits, sanded down back and forth, but for the oblivion caused by alcohol, it is still worth living. But if they were to prohibit vodka, immediately a revolution would flare.

Two dilemmas in our life: how we were born, we do not remember; how we will die, we do not know.

We should not be so excessively practical so to judge by the results, humanity is judged by its intentions.

You suffered the misfortune of seeking a counselor in me! And I in general do not believe that on earth it is possible to build something good and stable. How will I be able to handle the responsibility of providing advice, if I cannot pull my own foot out of doubt?

MARINA IVANOVNA TSVETAEVA

1892 – 1941

Contemporary Poet

Marina Tsvetaeva was born in Moscow on September 26, 1892. Her first complete book of poetry was published in 1910 and reflected her childhood memories, home, and the loss of her mother. The critics were impressed with her early poetry and she began to circulate with them.

Marina and her husband Sergei Efron alienated themselves from the October Revolution, and Efron journeyed south to the Ukraine and joined the anti-Bolshevik White Army. Tsvetaeva remained in Moscow. After the defeat of the White Army, Efron left Russia for Prague, and then in 1922, Tsvetaeva likewise left Russia with their daughter, first to Berlin for a short while, and then to Prague to her husband. In 1925, the family moved to Paris, and during those years to 1939, she wrote immensely, but they were living in destitution.

The family decided to return to the Soviet Union. First Efron in 1937, and then Tsvetaeva in 1939. But matters turned out opposite than what they thought. Efron was arrested in 1939, and then in 1941 he was executed at the Lubyanka Prison. Their daughter Ariadna, age 30, was arrested about the same time and sentenced to 15 years in a concentration camp (she was released in 1956). Tsvetaeva was alone with her son, and she made money by translating.

With the German approach to Moscow, Tsvetaeva and her son were evacuated from Moscow to the city Yelabuga, in Tatarstan Republic, in the eastern part of European Russia. On August 31, 1941, Marina Tsvetaeva committed suicide by hanging.

Men are too honest: I love it when they talk about the person they love, and then they marry.

Relationships based on blood are coarse but stable, while relationships that are selective are subtle, and if they are subtle they can easily break.

Have you thought at any time, that at this very moment, at this very minute, at this very second, somewhere in some port city, perhaps on some island or another, a person is boarding a ship, the one that you could love? But perhaps he is disembarking the ship, the one that is mine and always a sailor, in general a seaman, officer or sailor, all the same he is disembarking the ship and wandering through the city seeking you, who are here, at the Borisoglebski crossing. And perhaps he is just rambling toward the Tretia Meschanskaya (and have you noticed that right now here in Moscow they are many sailors? After 5 minutes you need to wipe them out of your eyes). But Tretia Meschanskaya is so far a distance from Borisoglebski crossing, as far away as Singapore. And what is most terrible, Marina, is that there are so many cities and islands, the world is full of them! And at every point on this earth! But looking at an atlas the world seems small in our view, yet there is no doubt a thousand, or many thousands of those whom I could love.

Her eyes were exceptionally fiery, and even should some tears be allowed to flow, they would dry immediately. And so these beautiful eyes, always ready to weep, were not moist, on the contrary, the tears glistened and radiated the heat, displayed her image, rays of warmth, but not moisture, and no matter how hard she tried, she could not shed one small teardrop.

How I love to love.
    And do you sometimes forget that you are loving when you love? I – never. This is like a toothache, only opposite – an opposite toothache. That digs into my jaw, but the other I cannot express.
    They are such barbaric stupid persons. Those who do not love, love not themselves, it is as though they only want others to love them. Of course, talking to such people is like talking to a block wall. But you know that there is no wall that I cannot break.
    But you notice how all of them, even those who are kissing, even those who seem to be in love, are so afraid to say this word? So why do they never utilize it? One explained it this way, "Why use a word when you can express it in some action, like in kissing, and other motions." And I respond, "No, an act does not entirely prove it, but the word will testify to all."
    This is all I need from a person, Say, "I love you," and nothing more. If you do not want to love me, it is up to you, but with your motions I will not believe you. This is why the word was created. It is only this word that sustains me. Otherwise all is unproductive.
    But they are so meager, calculating, cautious. I always want to say, "Just say this to me. I will not ascertain your truthfulness." But they are not saying it, because they think you want them to marry you, to bind you and never untie you. "If I first say it, then I will never be able to be the first to walk away." But they will not even be the second to say it, not at all. It is as though I do not need to be the first to leave. In my entire life I have never been the first to leave. And as much life that God still permits me, I will not be the first to leave. I plainly cannot do that. It will always be the other who will leave, because it is easier for me to cross over my own dead body than to be the first to leave.
    What an awesome word. Completely dead. I understand. The one who is dead is the one whom no one has ever loved. But you know that such a dead person does not exist for me. Even within

myself, I have never been the first to leave. I have never been the first to stop loving. Always to the final possible moment. To the final and last drop. Like when you drank from a glass as a child, and the glass was hot and empty, but you turned it upside down and shook it, and all that came out was your exhale.

You will laugh, but I will tell you one short history, and this is my turn. It is not important who, but he was very young and I was insanely in love with him. Every evening he would sit in the first row, and he was poorly dressed, and he did not sit their because he had a front row ticket, but because he wanted to see. On the 3rd evening he watched me so intently, that I thought his eyes were going to jump right on stage. I am speaking and moving, but trembling inside, "What is going on? He is still sitting there." But only this needs to be understood, he was not an ordinary man in love, devouring me with his eyes. He was almost a child. This was a drinking gaze. He watched as though he was mesmerized. Precisely with every word I was able to attract him, as with a string, a string, a string. Fairies can understand this feeling. And likewise the violinists or those playing the other stringed instruments, and the rivers and the fires. And this is what was dragging me into the bonfire. I just do not know how I was able to complete the scene. All this time I had such a feeling, and I was able to feel it just in his eyes. And behind the scenes I was with him, and behind these unfortunate scenes we kissed, and I knew this was vulgar, but I had not other feeling, except this one, "I was delivered." This lasted terribly short and we had little to say to one another. Initially I was the one who spoke, who spoke, who spoke, and then I was silent, because I was waiting for a response to my words, other than just eyes and kisses.

And so in the morning I lie, until morning. I still sleep, but yet not sleeping. And all this time I repeat something to myself. With my lips, words. Listening to myself, and do know what was said? "You will enjoy it more. Just a moment, in a minute you will enjoy it more." But you do not think that I was not his, sleeping, asking. We living in separate quarters and I needed some air. But perhaps I was petitioning God. Reach out a little more. I reached. He could not, but I could. And he never knew it. And his strict father, a general in Moscow, who did not know that I was an actress. Then he became just a friend, otherwise we would have gone off together.

And I will never forget, and this is no lie. Because love is loving, and virtue is virtuous. He is not to blame that he liked me no more. This is not a blame, but a misfortune. He is not to blame, but it is my misfortune. All the same, if it was strong as iron, it would not have broken.

I understood one matter. In the presence of others, I had a favorite letter, *R*, which I preferred of all the letters of the alphabet. It seems to me the most courageous: frozen, mountain, hero, Sparta, beast, all that in me was straight, stern and severe.[39]

In your presence, the letter was *Sh*: flattery, whisper, silk, silence, and especially, cherry.[40]

But this seems to occur to me so rarely, almost never. All the time I fear that I dream and will right now awaken, and then again mountain, hero.

---

[39] All these words in the Russian have the letter R.
[40] All these words in the Russian have the letter Sh

VIKENTI VIKENKYEVICH VERESAYEV

1867 – 1945

Doctor, Writer

Vikenti Veresayev was born Smidovich on January 4, 1867, in Tule, central Russia; his father was a doctor. He attended school in Tule, and then progressed to St Petersburg University, completing his education in history in 1888, but then he continued to complete medical school in Dorpat (Tartu), Estonia. He went to work at Russian hospitals as a doctor.

As a poet, his first published work was in 1885. But in April 1901, a story about the lack of proper medical care and attention in Russia forced the hospital to terminate his employment. Such political views were unacceptable and the government told Veresayev not to live in either Moscow and St Petersburg, and this continued for 2 years. With the start of the Russo-Japanese War in 1905, he joined the army as a doctor and was transferred to the Far East. His book dealing with the heroism of the soldiers as well as the corruption of Imperial Russia was to his benefit and he was reinstated with his return.

Veresayev welcomed the Russian Revolution and he continued to write. His special achievements were the translation of Greek and Roman classics into Russian, including Homer. As a result of his literary achievements, Veresayev was awarded the USSR State Prize and the Order of the Red Banner of Labor in 1943.

He died in Moscow on March 3, 1945.

Marriage based on love! O, this is of course a very good thing! But it is a pity that such weddings are very rare. More than often, such are actually understood as marriages due to infatuation. But know that such marriages are the most horrible of all! They are more horrible than cold marriages that are arranged based on mutual agreement, although at least they can see what they are getting into.

A human is not the image of God, but the descendant of a wild, predatory beast. But we must not be surprised at the amount of ferocity and voracity in humanity, but at the amount nonetheless of self-sacrifice, heroism and philanthropy.

A woman attributes little toward minor issues but much toward major items. But a man never conducts himself contritely in petty items and is never forgetful in accomplishments.

As children we see life with personal impartial eyes and are amazed that adults completely do not see the same that we do.

Great artists in prophetic inspiration rise high above interfering people who just get tangled in their feet, and then they direct them to impossible ideals that inevitably and brilliantly materialize in the future.

If you want to recognize the containment of a person's soul, watch his lips. The eyes may be impressive and bright, but the lips are conniving. With a young girl her eyes are innocent but her lips are rotten. A friend may have happy eyes but as an official he possesses a fiery mouth and unconscionably expels hot coals from deep inside him. Beware of the eyes! It is because of a person's eyes that people are so easily fooled. But the lips do not fool.

If you want to value a person, then as soon as possible you must unclothe his ambition and vanity. But then what is left will probably not be your hero or champion or sage.

It touches me when people are grateful to me for some charitable effort I have done. I an grateful when people do something good for me. But what deeply agitates me is when people expect gratitude for the good done on my behalf. Then all of the goodness that person has done becomes valueless, and I feel like paying him with interest for what he did and reject the entire event.

Life is not a burden, but is wings of creativity and joy. But whoever converts life into a burden, this is his own fault.

Sincerity is a difficult and very subtle matter. It requires wisdom and great psychological tact. Even a minor inclination toward one side and you will be exposed, or toward another side and you will face cynicism. The ability to display genuine sincerity is to have integrity and prudence, and this is a great and very rare gift.

The eyes as the mirror of the soul? What nonsense! The eyes are a deceiving mask, the eyes are a screen that hides the soul. The mirror of the soul is the mouth.

The public is completely deprived of individual thoughts. With identical and mundane enthusiasm it claps its hands for completely opposite opinions.

There is nothing so repulsive and nothing so beautiful as elderly faces. And not one excels another. With a young elastic face without wrinkles, its character disappears, that which penetrates the skin, those meditations and moods of a person. The soul's life is engraved on an elderly face and apparent to all, an impression that cannot be simply washed off.

We should enter life not as a joyful stroll in a pleasant garden, but with reverent trepidation as in a sacred forest filled with secrets.

Vladimir Ivanovich Vernadski

1863 – 1945

Scientific Researcher and Educator

Vladimir Vernadski was born in St Petersburg on February 28, 1863. His higher education was in physics and mathematics at the Petersburg University. In 1912, he became a member of the Russian Academy of Sciences, having published over 700 scientific dissertations. He was a founder of the concepts in Russian schools of geochemistry, mineralogy, radiogeology, and teachings of the biosphere. He also organized scientific organizations, such as the Ukrainian Academy of Sciences. Vernadski was important in the early development of atomic energy and the atomic bomb in the USSR, and he conducted experiments at his Radium Institute, but he died before being able to complete his work.

In his philosophic compositions, Vernadski promoted the concept of the noosphere, the sphere of human thought, and continued the ideas of Russian cosmism, even though he was an atheist. The activities of Vernadski had an immense influence on the development of science in the USSR.

Vernadski died January 6, 1945.

The entire history of science at every step indicates that individual personalities were more right in their affirmations than entire corporations of scholars, or hundreds or thousands of researchers who were adhering to state view. Truth is often to a great extent revealed to these scientific heretics rather than to orthodox representatives of scientific thought. Of course, not all groups and persons standing off to the side of scientific ideology possess this great vision of future human thought, but just hardly a few, a handful. But such present day people possessing the maximum true scientific ideology available for the present era are always found among them, among these groups and persons who stand to the side, among the scientific heretics, and not among the representatives of state scientific ideology. To distinguish them from those standing off to the side is not for their contemporaries to decide.

Difficult, stubborn and undependable, thanks to the possibility of errors, is the struggle of scientific ideology and the concepts of philosophy and religion that are alien to it, and even with their obvious contradictions with the government instituted scientific theorems. Philosophy and religion are tightly interwoven with something more profound than logic by the strength of people's souls. Their influence has a powerful affect on the acceptance of logical conclusions or their understanding.

Educated visionaries and artists do not do whatever they want with their ideas. They can work hard, work long on what their thoughts pertain, to what their senses draw them. But their ideas change. Often they appear impossible, often insane. They swarm together, circle, mix and separate, and they live among such ideas and work on their behalf.

I entirely comprehend that I can be attracted by something false and deceptive, follow its path and it will lead me into some dark forest. But there is no way for me not to follow it. I hate every shackle and fetter of my mind. I cannot and do not want to force it to walk by the road that is practical and important, but this mind of mine does not allow me – and even a little bit – to understand these questions that torment me. And this search, this aspiration, is the basis of every scientific research.

All of whatever it is we know, we know as a result of the dreams of dreamers, fantasists, and scholars and poets.

Democracy is freedom of thought and freedom of religion.

I heard said that the natural sciences raised people's faculties, gave them some type of unknown potency. They quickly brought nature to the level of humanity, gave them the possibility of predicting its delicateness, predict after needed research that it will fall into a certain order, just as the nature of a person.

In every philosophical system a soul's mood is unconditionally reflected and its creator.

In the history of humanity's development the significance of the mystic mood – inspiration – can be too highly valued. In one or another form it penetrates the entire psychological life of a person and appears as a foundational element of life.

It is time to deliver ourselves from the narrow Christian division of spirit and body. The genuine intrinsic or psychological life, the present ideological facet of life consists particularly in the utilization of the best facets of body and spirit.

Just as Christianity did not defeat science in its sphere, but in this struggle it has defined its essence deeper, so science in an alien sphere is not able to break Christianity or any religion, but defines and explains the forms of its knowledge more precisely.

Minor, unnoticeable discoveries, processes, that occur at every step and which we do not sense due to their insignificance, accumulate in time and accomplish the most grandiose upheavals and changes.

Scientific hypothesis always evolves from the accumulation of facts that serve as the basis of its formation.

Socialism is based always on the subjection of the individual to the best interests and prosperity of the majority.

The acknowledgement of full freedom of the individual, the personal spirit, is indispensable for scientific development, because it is only under such conditions that one scientific ideology can be exchanged for another, and one created freely, the independent effort of the individual.

The present is the display of the past, so it will not become so distant from us.

The roots of all discoveries lie distant in the depths and, like waves beating on the shore turn after turn, the individual mind lashes many times at the nearly prepared discovery, until the highest wave comes along.

The victory of some type of scientific view and its inclusion in ideology does not still prove its validity. Often we discover the opposite. Scientific truth is developed in a complex and convoluted path, and its expression is far from every scientific ideology.

What one individual might accept as truth, really never appears as absolute truth to another individual.

THE IMMIGRANT THINKERS

RUSSIA'S WISDOM

ALEKSANDR VALENTINOVICH AMFITEATROV

1862 – 1938

Journalist, Historian

Aleksandr Amfiteatrov was born December 26, 1862, in Kaluga, central Russia, and attended Moscow University, where he completed law in 1885. His entire career was concentrated on being an editor and journalist for many newspapers in Russia and subsequently the Soviet Union.

On August 23, 1921, Amfiteatrov and his family escaped from Petrograd to Finland. From there he moved to Prague, Czech Republic, and then in his later years to Italy. He worked again as a journalist for several Russian newspapers that were published in Europe for immigrants, and especially since he was also fluent in several European languages.

Amfiteatrov died February 26, 1938, in Levanto, Italy.

At one time we had inquisitors who, due to imposing tortures during investigations and inquiries, were themselves unable to endure the repeated bestial insanity and agitation systematically inflicted, and so their nerves began to affect them. As a result they were unable to remain stable and so committed suicide.

I am a genuine Russian by nature. In what ever social circle I will enter, I will immediately enter their mood, and then I absorb their views, tastes, manners. One scholar proved to me that a great quality of Russians is that they become the best of colonizers. Lermontov praised his Maxim Maxsimovich[41] for having this character, while Gorcharov did the same for Russian sailors from Japan. Perhaps they are right, I cannot judge. Only this quality, as it seems to me, possesses inclinations of great resignation, the absence of independent thought and independent conviction.

If a woman lets her beauty go into disrepair when she appears in public, her soul will likewise be in disrepair.

My husband does not at all look at me as at a woman, as a member of the female gender, as a pleasant object, because I am pretty, submissive, and that I provide him many comforts, income as a hard worker and fulfill domestic responsibilities, but as an object that does not possess an independently self-maintained will or opinion, that has to live in the manner that the husband dictates, and is not to speak unless first requested, and only when someone kindly asks for my advice, and nothing more am I. Never has he asked me for my advice. He does everything first and then shows me what he has done.

Our age is a clandestine and colorful masquerade, that you will not find in any song or fable. Here the mind for a long time now has been wearing the clothing of a idiot, while stupidity looking importance strides wearing a mask of intelligence.

Remember that people are young only once in their life. Take hold of happiness however it may find you.

---

[41] A character in *Hero of our Time*.

NIKOLAI SERGEEVICH ARSENYEV

1888 – 1977

Professor of History and Religion

Nikolai Arsenyev was born May 16, 1888 in Stockholm, Sweden. He completed studies in history at Moscow University in 1910, and continued his studies in Berlin, Germany. Returning to Russia in 1912, he taught Western European Literature at the Moscow University, and in 1914 became professor. During the First World War he was in the military and received the Red Cross for his bravery, and subsequently continuing teaching Western European literature at the Saratov University, 1918-1920.

Arsenyev was twice arrested in 1919, and fearing further persecution he illegally crossed into Poland in March of 1920. After his emigration from Russia he taught in Warsaw, Berlin, and then in Konnigsburg until 1944, teaching religion and philosophy. From 1945 to 1948, he taught in Paris, France. Arsenyev then migrated to the USA in 1948 and became a professor at Vladimir Seminary, New York, and also teaching at Columbia University. Arsenyev's research dealt with antiquity, the Middle Ages, the Renaissance and contemporary history.

Arsenyev died December 18, 1977.

The basis of belief in God is meeting God. Speaking in theological terms, this is God revealing Himself. God Himself speaks to the soul. He discloses Himself to it, approaching and touching it. This is the mystical experience that is the root of religion, the direct and immediate meeting with God in the soul's depths. But sometimes this meeting attains a special intensity and brilliance. All remaining, all terrestrial, all created, then withdraws to a back stage, and only God alone is in the soul's presence. Such decisive meetings occur among certain saints and righteous and especially people that are gifted with mysticism. These meetings are often just a moment of spiritual cataclysm, a crisis of a person's entire internal life. Their characteristic trait appears as an overwhelming reality, another and higher, all-submitting reality rushing with victory, an undefeatable power entering the regular phase of a person's psychic life. It is not any longer *I,* but now *He.* Not my life's experiences, whether good or bad or even affectionate, but He who is above all of my life's experiences. He is before me, His subject: grasped, small and reduced to nothing. He is in my presence in His majesty and potency, and there only remains for me to condescend to Him, fall before Him.

God's immeasurable love was spilt at the cross of Christ. There is no parallel to the cross of Christ. There is nothing in religious history comparable to it. In physical reality he was surrounded by 2 other crosses – 2 criminals also being crucified at the same time. But on the spiritual plane he hangs above them, not at their same level. He alone is the path of reconciliation between God and the world. This is the event completely exceptional, paradoxical, striking us, perplexing and joyous, and nothing is comparable to it. This matter definitely being extraordinary and unrepeatable.

We stand in front of a question motioning within us, and on all sides is motioning around us, it is crushing and departing into nonexistence, and at the same time continuing to exist in the world that is full of death, destruction and struggle. And along with this we can touch and realize it – although at a very incomplete level – something sturdy, complex, that is disclosed to us in all new and newer horizons that we grasp: it is the structure of the world. There exists in this structure of the world an immense potency. In these circulating orbits of electrons, in this immense effort and drive of power, from whose mutual activity is born what we call matter, here is not only a summons from the depths that transcend infinity that envelops us, but also beauty and systemization that is striking to us. We begin to understand words about wisdom that lie at the foundation of the universe, similar to the wisdom that inspired the authors of the books of Job and Psalms, when they were raptured due to the majesty of God who disclosed Himself in the sun's brilliance, in shining stars and in the barricade placed for the wild waves of the ocean's elements, and in the joy of fields and hills and pastures, and in the strength of Lebanon's cedars. The words of God's wisdom, of God's plan in creation, is involuntarily wound in the person who is a believer in God.

The school of love! The stronger that I learn in God to love my surroundings, my nation,[42] that life-providing field upon which I have been assigned to work, to love in particular this nation with its sufferings and weaknesses, demanding compassion and healing, but to love is particularly in God. The more I learn in God to love the separate peoples and groups of peoples that I have greeted on life's path, not excluding my own people,[43] suffering and so needful to me, the more my strength of love in God grows. There is no contradiction between the tie of the blood and the religious since both are tied together in empathy and love with my people and spiritual valuables and gifts that were entrusted to it and which He has placed as the foundation of the higher valuable of its culture, and the virtues of God.

God's virtue then sanctifies this life and my cultural effort. Because the understanding of religious valuables of culture is already a participation, although a humble one, in the living stream of cultural tradition, cultural creativity: the dynamic

---

[42] The USA in this case, where he was residing at the time.
[43] The Russians

tradition that grows from the better, by which our past lived and was inspired, and it aspires ahead uniting the past, present and future. And the warm breath of love, in an unconscious instinctive aspiration drives toward the revelation of the love that existed before the beginning of time, and disregarding our weakness and sinfulness.

To be a person in society is not at all a difficult obligation, but a simple development of an inner need. No one tells a bee that it has a sacred debt to make honey. It make honey because it is a bee. A person who reaches the cognizance of his dignity conducts himself in a dignified manner because it is natural, easy, pleasant, reasonable and inherent for him to conduct himself this way. I am not praising him for this; he conducts himself this way because he cannot conduct himself otherwise. A rose cannot have any other fragrance.

KONSTANTINE DMITRIEVICH BALMONT

1867 – 1942

Poet

Constantine Balmont was born March 6, 1867 in the village Gumishi, Vladimir province, central Russia, to a wealthy family. In 1885, he first published his poems. The following year however he entered law school at the Moscow University, but left, never finishing the curriculum. The subsequent years he translated French and German poetry into Russian, and anthologies of his own poetry, and also published histories of European literature in Russian. Balmont did not accept the Revolution of 1917, and in 1920 left Russia for Paris, France. There he continued his own poetry and translated into Russia the poetry of other nations.

He died December 23, 1942 in Paris, France.

A revolution is good when it discards the whip. But the world should live by evolution, not by revolution.

All that resides in heaven also resides in the heart, and much more.

Every soul possesses many faces; within every person is hidden a number of people, and many of these faces that form one person must be ruthlessly discarded into fire. A person needs to be merciless to himself. Only then can you attain something.

It is an amazing intensive state of the mind when a person is actually stronger, more intellectual and more beautiful than himself. Such states of existence that draw us to out-of-bounds' worlds occur with each person as if an affirmation of the great principle of the fatal parity of all souls. Such states of self-consciousness are greeted by some just once in their life, and for others it is stronger or weaker and they extend almost an uninterruptible influence. And there are some select people to whom are given foresight almost every night, and with every new dawn they hear the bellows of new lives.

The heart's holiday is the joy of loving someone. The heart's holiday is to find some unexpected treasure. And the heart's holiday is to find yourself in another, to see what is better than your own heart in the mirror of another's heart. And to shatter the wall of disassociation with the heart that is sharp as a diamond is joy This occurring is the heart's true holiday.

There is no joy without some sorrow. Among flowers a snake is always slithering.

Upon all of us lies the obligation to better this world, the one in which we live. To worry about the welfare of the oppressed and suffering, to worry about ameliorating the difficulties that they endure.

Nikolai Aleksandrovich Berdayev

1874 – 1948

Religious and Political Philosopher

Nikolai Berdayev was born March 6, 1874 in Kiev, Ukraine. He was educated at the Kiev University in natural science, but was expelled for participation in a revolutionary student demonstration and was exiled to Vologda province in the Russian far north. After his release in 1904, Berdayev led an active involvement in various religious and philosophic societies in Petersburg. Several of his compositions were very critical of western philosophy. In 1918 he formed the Free Academy of Religious Culture, and in 1920 was selected as a professor at Moscow University.

In 1922 Berdayev was exiled from the USSR. In 1924 he settled in Paris where he began his philosophical career with over 500 books and articles. Berdayev's views were formed from his influence by various religious innovators, such as Origin, Gregori of Nyssa, Jacob Boehm, Dostoyevski and Tolstoy. Berdayev's basic concept consisted in that freedom is not determined by existence, not defined even by God, but has a primacy over them and discloses the possibility for the creation of what is new and not yet materializing in the world.

Berdayev died March 23, 1948, in a small city near Paris, France.

What is the cause of illness and deathly sorrow in our age? It is in our inability to live to fullness and joy in the present in order to attain eternity, and the impossibility at the moment of the present – even though it may be filled with value and joy – to free oneself from the poisons of the past and future, from past sorrow and from fear of the future. A moment's joy cannot be lived as the fullness of eternity, because it possesses a poison rushing through time. A moment – as a part of departing time – carries with it all disruption, all the torment of time, an eternal division into the past and future. And it is just the moment, as an attachment to eternity, that has another quality. There exists a profound melancholy in the thought that all is not stable, but departing.

The *I* can realize personality, become an individual. The realization of individuality always supposes beforehand self-limitation, so what is needed is free subjection to what is beyond yourself, creating valuables that are beyond yourself and evolving out of you and toward another. The *I* can be ego-centric, self-affirming, inflating, and incapable of leaving itself for another. Ego-centrism destroys personality, it is the greatest obstacle on the path of realization of the individual. Not to be devoured by yourself, but to turn to *you* and to *us* is the foundational condition for the existence of good personality.

The creative life is eternal life, and not mundane. And how weak and pitiful are moralizations in comparison to great creations. What is born of a creative act of beauty is already a migration from this world into the cosmos, into another existence, where darkness cannot exist, which was already residing in the sinful nature of the creator. The original picture or poem do not belong to the physical plan of existence, they not having a material burden directly enter the free cosmos. And the creative act is self-revelation and self-evaluation, not acknowledging any external criticism of itself.

Ingenuity is another world within a person, a supermundane nature of a person. Genius overwhelms a person like a demonic possession. Ingenuity also is the revelation of a person's creative nature, his creative assignment. The destiny of ingenuity in prehistoric world periods was always sacrificial and tragic. Creativity disclosed in ingenuity is destined to ruin in this world. Destined ingenuity has not the strength to preserve itself in this world, it does not possess the strength of adaptability to the demands of this world. For this reason the ingenious life is a sacrificial feat. The ingenious life knows the minutes of ecstatic bliss, but does not know rest or happiness that is always found in tragic discord with the surrounding world.

Clearly because a person is defined as either male or female, gender is an element that is dissipated throughout the entire substance of a person, but not a differentiation of function. If gender is a handicap, then it is a limited handicap, and not a functional handicap of the entire person, entire physique and entire metaphysic. Gender is not only a point of severance of the 2 worlds in the human creation, but a person's point of severance with the cosmos: the microcosm with the macrocosm. A person is interwoven with the cosmos first of all through gender. The source and true unity of a person with the cosmos and his servile dependence is found in gender. The categories of gender – male and female – are cosmic categories, and not just anthropological.

Christian symbolism of Logos and the world's soul, Christ and his church, speak of the cosmic mysticism of male and female, of the cosmic mystery of marriage. But only in a person – but not in the cosmos – does the sexual separation of male and female and their sexual union exist. The world's soul is the earth, which is female in relationship to the Logos, the light-bearing husband and it hungers for unity with the Logos, to accept it within itself. The earth-bride awaits its groom – Christ. Nature awaits its king – the human. Within the world order the male for the most part has the anthropological human principle, while the female principle is the natural or cosmic. The male-human is tied with nature and the cosmos through the female. Outside the female he is severed from the world's soul, from the mother-earth. The female would not be a complete person outside the tie with a male, because there exists an especially powerful and clandestine natural element in her, one that is impersonal and unconscious. There is no individualism in the female element if it is severed from the male. The male recognizes the active problem of the anthropos in its relationship to the cosmos and the unavoidable victory over time and the clock. The female is part of the cosmos but is not a microcosm. She does not recognize the cosmos because by way of the cosmos she considers her temporal state, for example, her undivided love.

The differentiation into male and female is the result of the cosmic fall of Adam. The created person in the image and likeness of God falls, separates himself from the natural-maternal elements and alienates himself from the cosmos.

SERGEI NIKOLAYEVICH BULGAKOV

Theologian, Economist

1871 – 1944

Sergei Bulgakov was born in Livna, Orlov Province, central Russia, on June 16, 1871. He finished Moscow University Law School in 1896. He was professor of political economy in Kiev, 1901-1906, and in Moscow, 1906-1916, and was a stern critic of the legitimacy of Marx's economic doctrines.

Bulgakov was ordained as a Russian Orthodox priest in 1918, and immigrated to France in 1923. From 1925 to his death in 1944, he was a professor of dogmatics at the Russian Theological Institute, Paris, France. He wrote intensively on the Gnostic concept of Sophia, the wisdom of God, and was considered by many as a heretic to Russian Orthodoxy.

He died in Paris, France, on July 13, 1944

Religious truth is universal, that is, catholic, conforming with the whole and not with its parts. According to its inner drive, all is collected in the truth as one, or the one is in all. If we love one another, we confess a unity of thinking. The council's announcement of the truths of belief[44] flows from a unity in the fully-developed and fully-immaculate truth. It is not the majority of voices that decided this, but a certain life-possessing unity in truth, its inspiration, communion with it.

We can define 3 distinct paths of religious comprehension: geometric or analytic; natural or mystic; historical or empirical. Otherwise stated, these divine comprehensions are an abstract deliberation, a mystical self-commitment, and a religious revelation. The initial 2 paths receive their relative meanings only when tied with the 3rd, but are incomplete if the attempt is to confirm each as individual aspects.

Alongside the supra-existent entity of the Absolute there surfaces existence where the Absolute reveals itself as Creator, appears in the creation, materializes itself in the creation, associates with it, and in this sense, the world is the installation of God. We must not talk of Him in an unconditional sense: God is only in the world and for the world. Having created the world, God installs Himself into His creation, and as if makes Himself part of His creation.

The word is the world, because this is what He thinks and speaks about Himself. However the world is not the word, precisely it is not only the word, because this also has an existence that is metalogical and silent. The word cosmically exists in its own essence, since it belongs not only to creation, where it flares, but existence and the human are the world arena, the microcosm, because in it and through it the world echoes. The word is anthropo-cosmic, or should we say this more precisely, anthropological.

This common evolution – the emanation of the individual – is provided by religion and is in this sense the religious truth of absolute character. But for its gradual historical materialization, it requires relative historical means, which direct circumstances

---

[44] referring to the Nicene Creed.

and change together with them. These means must be found by reason, in agreement with an indication of scholarly experience and this discovery composes the research of general science.

The worldwide-historical departure of the prodigal son from his father's house, the epoch of humanism, during which course humanity tests its strengths and makes a desperate attempt to build and live without God, has its meaning and its indispensability. Building the Kingdom of God, which is the process of making humanity divine, is based on humanity's personal-independent adoption of the divine content of life, what is indispensable is the free development of purely human elements. For this reason the humanistic, extra-religious and even anti-religious, period of historical creativity is absolutely needed for the event of making humanity divine.

The voice of passion can be louder than the voice of conscience, but the voice of passion is completely different than that calm and tenacious voice which is how conscience speaks. And no matter how loud passion cries it nonetheless retreats in the presence of the quiet, calm and tenacious voice of conscience. It speaks with such a voice within a person regarding matters that are eternal, divine and living.

You never know in secular matters for sure if you really need to do something that you feel needs to be done, and whether the result will succeed in the manner you want. But it is not this way when you live for the soul. Living for the soul you will surely know that what needs to be done is that which is namely what the soul requires. Surely you will also know that the result of what you do will be good.

Ivan Alekseevich Bunin

1879 – 1953

Writer, Nobel Prize in Literature

Ivan Bunin was born October 10, 1879, in Voronezh, central Russia, in a simple village family and he did not get any formal education until he was 11 years of age, and only at a district school. At age 15 he returned home to be home taught by his older brother. At 17 he began to write poetry and at age 20 moved to Oryol to work at a local newspaper, continuing to write in his spare time. He then moved to Moscow to continue as a newspaper journalist. In 1918 he escaped the turbulence of Moscow and traveled to Odessa and joined the White Army of General Denikin. With the approach of the Red Army, Bunin left Russia and migrated to Paris, France, and which became his home for the balance of his life.

He continued writing and especially against the Communists and their regime. In 1933, Bunin was awarded the Nobel Prize in literature, the first native Russian to receive this award. Bunin's books were not published at all in the Soviet Union in the years 1929-1954, and only began in 1955 after his death, with a few of his popular volumes that were not threatening to the Soviet regime.

Bunin died in Paris on November 8, 1953.

A beautiful woman must rise to the next step. The first step belongs to women of kindness.

A human's happiness consists in not wanting anything for yourself. The soul rests and begins to find goodness where it completely never expected to find it.

Ambition selects, true love does not.

And on this occasion let us drink to a broken soul! Drink for everybody, for those who love us, for all whom we, idiots, do not value, for those with whom we were happy, blessed, and then separated, for whom we dissipated our lives forever and without end, and even then forever we are tied by the most horrible bond in the world.

Be generous like a palm. And if you cannot, then be a cypress tree trunk, straight and plain and noble.

Essentially, a long time ago we should have rejoiced. But we were beaten, treated as intruders, deprived of all rights and laws, living in such a vile slavery, among incessant slapping and ridicule.

If a person has not lost his ability to expect happiness, he is happy. This is definitely happiness.

Is this really unknown, that there exists a quality that is overwhelmingly strong and in general not a totally regular type of love that would allow you to circumvent marriage?

Life is like the steppes, empty and vast.

My older bother at one time decided to portray my future. "This will be it," he says, laughing, "you will go to school someplace.

When you grow up you will complete your military service, get married, have children, accumulate a little, buy a small house." I then suddenly felt and I felt this so stimulatingly, the entire horror and entire humiliation of such a future, that I wept.

Remembering all that I lived through from that time, and I always ask myself, "Yes, and so what is it that occurred in my life?" And I answer myself, "Only this cold autumn night." Did this really occur at some time? All the same it did. And this is all that had occurred in my life, the balance is just an unnecessary dream. And I believe, fervently believe, that somewhere he is waiting for me, with that love and youth, just as it was that night. "You, live a bit longer. Enjoy the world, then come to me." I lived a bit longer, enjoyed what was available, now soon I will arrive.

She was enigmatic, to me not understandable, strange were the attitudes between her and I, yet we were not yet so close to one another. And all of this without end held me in an indestructible restraint, in a torturous expectation, and along with this I was inexpressibly happy every hour.

So I was able to survive it, death. Then I hastily said the following at some time, that I will not survive it again.

The person who risks nothing is the one who risks all.

The person who is astonished at his personal existence is the one who thinks about it. This is his chief distinction from other entities, who are still in paradise, not in deep meditation over themselves. And this is exactly how people are different from one another, by the stages or levels of this astonishment.

There are female souls that eternally anguish over some type of sorrowful and hungered love and who as a result do not love anyone and never.

There is not one soul capable of not lying, and who cannot add to his lie if he has to, or to add some distortion to some rumor he heard that he knows is a lie. This all evolves from an intolerable thirst, so matters will be as intolerable for him as possible.

We in general should all be very guilty, each in the presence of another. But only during a separation do you feel this. Even then – how many years of our life would we have left together? If we have a few years left, what is the difference since there will be fewer and fewer. And the future? Each of us will go to our assigned grave! It is so painful, our feelings are aggravated, all our thoughts and memories are so severe! And how insensitive we were! How tranquil! And is this pain really needed, for us to value life?

What is this old Russian illness, this anguish, this lonesomeness, this imbalance. Our eternal hope is that some frog will come along with a magic ring and will solve all your problems for you. All that's left is getting on some leaf and tossing a ring from one hand to the other.

When you love someone, no forces of any type can compel you to believe that you cannot love the one who loves you.

Women are never so strong as when they arm themselves with weakness.

We have here the sun, flowers, grass. We can play, run, while they always lie there in the darkness, as at night, in large and cold iron boxes. Grandmothers and grandfathers all old, while uncle is still young.

Aleksandr Ivanovich Herzen

1812 – 1870

Political Philosopher and Activist

Aleksandr Herzen was born March 25, 1812 in Moscow, although his father's family name was Yakovlev. His family were wealthy businesspeople. He received an excellent education at home, including the study of foreign languages. Herzen's repulsion toward the government of Imperial Russia began at the age of 13, when he heard of the Decembrist Revolt and its consequences. In 1833, Herzen completed Moscow University in physics and mathematics. While there he further developed his thoughts on a renovation of the existing government.

In 1834, all the members of Herzen's circle of progressive thinkers were arrested. Herzen was exiled to Perm, and then to Vyatka, where he was assigned to work in the government office. He then was relocated to Vladimir, where he married, and spent the happiest years of his life. It was now 1840 and Herzen was moved again, now back to Moscow, and then to Novgorod, and back to Moscow in 1842. Here he faced conflicts with Stankevich and Belinski, who were dedicated Slavophiles. Herzen was labeled a Westerner, because of his views that Russia would advance further if it would more associate with Europe, and in about 1844 a new circle was formed.

In 1847, after the death of his father, Herzen migrated from Russia, never to return again, he was 35 years old. He settled in Paris and joined a newspaper as a journalist and wrote on political issues that affected Russia, advocating its transformation. Due to opposition from French state authorities, he was forced to leave France and went to Switzerland, and there became a naturalized citizen. He then went to Nice, France, and surrounded himself with a circle of radical European immigrants, and he further developed ideas of implementing socialism in Europe and Russia. While in Europe in 1849, Tsar Nicholas I confiscated all of Herzen's remaining wealth and property in Russia.

After the death of his wife in 1852, Herzen moved to London, England, where he lived the next 10 years of his life. There he opened a publishing house for books that would otherwise not be printed due to their political convictions. One of his prime concerns was the liberation of the serfs and abolition of the feudal system in Russia. Then pressure from Russian authorities in 1865 forced Herzen to close his publishing house, and so he returned to Switzerland, to there live the balance of his life. He again opened a publishing house there, but it was short lived.

Herzen died of pneumonia on January 9, 1870, in Paris, France.

"Sooner or later truth will always prevail." But we think that it will be very late and very rare. Intellect from time immemorial has always been inaccessible or repulsive to the majority. To have an effect on somebody, you need to instill dreams in them that are more clear than the dreams they see themselves, instead of attempting to prove your convictions to them in the manner that some geometric theory is proven.

A nebulous premonition states that philosophy must resolve all, reconcile and calm. The validity of this is based on its ability to prove its own convictions, every hypothesis, and find comfort in failures, and only God knows what else is needed. The impersonal nature of science, its distance from pathos and its definitive nature, overwhelms them. Notice that every person considers himself a independent judge, because every person is convinced in his own mind and in his personal supremacy over science, even though he hardly reads past the introduction.

As long as a person walks with quick steps forward, not stopping, not thinking about where he is going until he arrives at a cliff or almost breaks his neck, all the way he supposes that his life is forward, haughtily reviewing the past and without the ability to value the present. But when experience tramples spring flowers and fades the bright summer colors, when he finally and personally guesses that life has passed, and all that remains is to somehow extend it, but all he can do is return to the bright, warm, beautiful recollections of his initial youth.

As many times that I had started to read philosophic compositions, all of it is nonsense. All of them are always reminding me of the philosophic stone – the worst of all rocks because it is something that does not exist, but people still search for it. Whether this be science or some conference, if a person wants to talk some stupidity, some general opinions, improbable hypotheses, he immediately stipulates that this is only philosophic, that is, not a legitimate viewpoint.

Fortunate is the person who continues what he starts, to whom work is successively assigned. Early in his life does he learn to do it. He does not squander half his life selecting something, he concentrates and limits himself in order not to expend himself, and accomplishes what he starts. More than often we begin again. We have inherited from our father only personal property and real estate, and yet we preserve this poorly. As a result for the most part we do not want to do anything, and if we do want to do something, then we exit to an immeasurable vast steppe: go where you want in any direction, wherever your will is willing, but you will not arrive in any place. This is our diversified inactivity, our motivational lethargy.

In our age, proud due to its excessive success, the majority of humanity that is proclaiming itself Christian and achiever of overwhelming good has surged to the consummation of the truth of our fallen nature, rejecting with contempt the virtue of the Gospel. The achiever of human virtue is saturated with doubt, egoism, self-deception. He preaches, trumpets about himself and his activities, not turning any attention to the Lord's prohibitions. He repays using hate and vendetta those who were bold enough to open their lips to expose the basic and well-intended contradictions of his virtue that he claimed. He recognizes himself as worthy and even more worthy of the rewards of earth and heaven.

Is it not simpler to comprehend that a person lives not to accomplish some destiny, not for the incarnation of his ideas, not for progress, but solely because he was born and was born for the present, and this is not difficult to grasp, and that it should not bother him not to receive a legacy from the past or leave some inheritance for someone else? Our entire great significance consists only in our own nothingness, a moment's captured sparkle of personal life. This is of what it consists while we live, as long as we have not yet dissolved into the elements of the bundle that ties us together. We are nevertheless ourselves and not dolls destined to suffer progress or to materialize some type of abysmal idea. We should boast that we are not strings and not needles in the hands of some fate using us to sew their particular fabric of history. We know that this fabric cannot be sewn without us, but this is not just our goal, not just our purpose, not just the lesson assigned us to complete, but the result of this complex sewing circle is because of us, tying all that exists, the ends and beginnings, reasons and activities, together.

It seems to me that in the Russian life there is something that is much more higher than community and stronger than authority. This something is difficult to express in words and is even more difficult to point at with a finger. I speak of that inner and not fully comprehendible strength which so miraculously has maintain the Russian nation while under the yoke of the Mongol hordes and German bureaucracy. I speak of that belief in yourself which storms our breast. This strength, independent from external events and contrary to them, has preserved the Russian nation and supported its undefeatable belief in itself.

Moralists often speak nicely of the destructive flaw of ambition, which we know, as with all other passions, when brought to an extreme, can be humorous, sorrowful, harmful, depending on the circle of effects. But ambition on its own evolves from a good source, from the cognizance of your individual dignity. Based on this, a person is so courageous, so boldly proceeding everywhere in a struggle against nature. It is a completely different matter when the moralists reduce respect of authority and subjection based on self-contempt, on the annihilation of your dignity. It is so common that it is like an epidemic that plagues entire generations and entire nations, but yet they are silent about it, although it is so important to mention. To consider yourself stupid, incapable of understanding truth, weak, disdained, and finally, defining your significance on something else external, is not virtuous.

The moralists indispensably want to compel a person toward goodness, to force him to act ethically, in the same manner as a physician would force someone to drink some repulsive tasting medicine. They feel some dignity in conducting themselves in this manner, so a person would even unwillingly fulfill their obligations. It does not enter their head that if these obligations were true and ethical, then what person would actually be against their observance? The need to reconcile heart and mind does not enter a person's head when he feels that the fulfillment is a demanding debt or a difficult burden, but if he finds in it a consolation and comfort, one that is natural to him and conducive to his intellect.

Their fatal mistake is that they, enveloped with a noble love to close associate, to freedom, are carried away with intolerance and contempt, yet they have thrown themselves to liberate other people before liberating themselves. They have discovered within themselves the strength to break the iron, course chains, not noticing that the walls of the prison still remain. Not exchanging the walls, they want to give them a new designation, as if the prison's plans are also worth using for a liberated life.

We cannot be but impressed with the influence of a person with whom we associate that has a strong personality and imposing character, and we cannot but absorb the rays emanating from him and grow in them. Such a mental attraction – and which we highly value – provides us inspiration and new strength, confirming what is precious to our heart. But this natural reaction is still far from imitation.

No one can commit more of a mistake than to discard the past, since it serves as a means of attaining the present. It is like a development that is an external stage deprived of any internal scenes. Then history would be insulting, an eternal sacrifice of the living for the benefit of the future. The present human spirit envelopes and preserves all the past. It has not vanished for the present, but developed for its purpose. Past events have not been squandered in the present and not exchanged for them, but fulfilled in them. What vanishes is the false, transparent, non-existence, since this personally has never had a genuine existence. It was a still-born. But for truth there is no death.

"The time for words has passed. The time for action has arrived," they say. As if the spoken word is not an action? As if the time for words can actually pass? Our enemies never separated words and actions and executed for words spoken just as they did for actions done, and likewise in the same brutal manner.

A good environment requires good people. Every person should produce a harvest as much as a vineyard.

A person boasted that he survived about 20 duels, Suppose that there were actually only 10 and even then it is apparent that he does not consider his life very seriously and neither should we.

A person considering himself alienated from contemporary events is unpractical, and for the most part is not of a high nature, but an empty person, a dreamer, romanticist, a sacrifice to artificial civilization.

A person is unavoidably subject to external irritations. He needs a newspaper so that every day he can be in touch with the entire world. He needs a magazine to provide him with every progress of contemporary thought. He needs conversation, he needs theater. Certainly it is possible to get out of the habit of all of this if it seems that as if all this is not necessary, and then in reality it will become completely unnecessary, that is, at the time when this person himself has become completely unnecessary.

A person may read a book, but he understands what is in his head.

A person will sooner or later reach their horizon, reach their pit, across which they cannot jump.

A science that does not have some kind of goal other than genuine knowledge is not a science.

Actual truth must reside under the influence of events that reflect it, leaving something behind to prove its accuracy, otherwise it would not be living truth, eternal truth, resting from the upheavals of the world, in the dead silence of a holy stagnation.

An abundant earthly success and immense earthly accomplishments that are obvious to everybody are presented by

God's word as a portent of the final era and ripening of humanity's sinfulness.

An exceptional feeling of patriotism will never lead to any good.

An old heart is terribly hardened due to the egoism of self-preservation.

And if there are no goals, then anything can be a goal.

And so in order to understand the contemporary condition of thought, the more trusting path is to recollect how humanity has been able to reach this far.

Conversation is so joyous when your listeners have a good ability to deeply understand and sympathize.

Delusions develop on their own, while at their base always lies something true, overgrown with layers of mistaken interpretations. But falsity copied over and over through the ages, now gray from time, depends on memories as it passes from generation to generation.

Disappointment is a word that is beaten, trite and vague, under which the heart's lethargy and egoism hide. It passes itself off as a form of love toward the object, but it is a noisy and empty self-interest with a tie to everything, yet with no strength.

Emigration is the first sign of the approach of upheavals.

Every reduction of authority is a revolutionary act. The person, having been able to liberate himself from the oppression of powerful masters and scholastic despots, cannot be in his full capacity either a slave in religion or a slave in society.

Explain to me please, why it is a joke to believe in God, while believing in humanity is not funny? To believe in the Kingdom of Heaven is foolish, but to believe in an earthly utopia is intelligent?

Flattery damages the natural character of a person with a lie. All of us reside somehow in flattery. Knowing this is the greatest protection from flattery. The greatest flattery is to recognize yourself as being free from the effects of flattery. All of us are deceived, all are manipulated, all reside in a fallacious state and we need a liberation by the truth.

Freedom of an individual is a supreme matter. Upon this, and only upon this can the actual will of the people genuinely grow. A person must first respect his own personal freedom and honor it no less than he would in an associate or in the entire nation.

He was not entirely stupid, but belonged to the number of those bright practical minds, minds that reside beneath the surface of the skin, those that do not travel and cannot travel beyond rational categories and generally accepted opinion.

History in general is not a subject that is an obligation to study: what each person did and what was done everywhere. So it is with whatever settles out of the common riverbed or does not flow into it, or dies in it due to stagnation, or becomes exhausted and falls by the wayside, or an accident, or a private matter. What remains in the stream only has the right to historical significance, all that is traceable. From the opposite side history forgets and this is also a great merit.

History is nothing else but the interwoven narrative of the insanity of successive generations in chronological form and its slow treatment. I relate this aphorism because on its surface it gives us the complete right to hope that after the course of a thousand years, there will be 2 or 3 less stupid than at present.

I do not know why some type of monopoly is given to recollections of first love over recollections of young friendship. First love is so fragrant that it forgets the distinction of genders, that it is actually passionate friendship. From my own side, friendship between young people possesses all the fervency of love and all its character.

If a person makes his goal some passions that captivate him, he gives these passions strength and supremacy which they do not have on their own. He places them as opponents to reason.

Illnesses resulting from over-eating do not heal quickly.

Is the genius to blame if he resides above the crowds? Is the crowd to blame if is does not understand him?

It is as if someone (except for ourselves) promised that all in the world will be elegant, proper and flowing smooth as oil. We have sufficiently been amazed by the distracted wisdom of nature and its historical development. It is time to guess that in nature and history there is much accidental, chanced, unsuccessful and complex. In general more than often we know success and advancement in nature and history. We have at present only started to feel that not all is so well and arbitrary as it seems.

It is doubtful that external measures have restored somebody, but they retain the person in fear and so indirectly they achieve their goal. Criminal laws are legislated for the benefit of society and not for the benefit of the criminal.

It is easy to say that he is guilty and so this is his fate. But how are we to evaluate and weight the destiny that befalls a person or the one that falls in the middle?

It is incomparably more difficult to speak about what others are silent, than to speak about what has never entered into the mind of others.

It is not necessary to overly trust in the future, not in history, not in nature. Not every conception attains maturity, not all that resides in the soul will materialize, although in other circumstances all could develop.

It is so necessary to create the new with the sweat of your face, while the old will continue on its own and will be firmly supported on the crutches of custom and tradition.

It is terribly difficult for an old person to open his wallet.

It is very natural that the devil will utilize all efforts to retain a person in his previous attitude toward him, or even lead him to a greater enslavement. In order to do this he utilizes his former and his ever-present weapon – the lie.

It seems that ordinary persons' lives are as though uniform, but it only seems this way. There is nothing in this world that is more original or diverse than the biography of unknown persons, especially where no 2 persons are bound with the same common idea, where each young person develops into his own individual self, without looking back.

Laziness and habit are 2 indestructible pillars upon which authority sets. Authority personally presents a guardianship over immaturity. Laziness among people is so great that they willingly comprehend themselves as under legal age or insane as long as they will be taken under guardianship and be given leisure time to eat or die from hunger. But chief is not to think and be occupied with nonsense.

Letters are worth more than recollections, upon them the blood of events has dried as the ink. This is how the past is remembered, retained and immortalized.

Life only progresses agilely and well when you do not feel the blood flowing in your veins, and you do not think about your lungs respiring.

Napoleon once stated that fate is a word that has no meaning.

Nonetheless, experience is still the worst means of comprehending something.

Not intellect, not logic, leads nations, but belief, love and hate.

Nothing so much suppresses an army's spirit as the malicious thought that behind your back treachery is being prepared.

Now, 30 years from his birth he, like a 16 year old adolescent, is preparing to begin his life, not noticing that the door more and more opening is not the one through which enter gladiators, but the one through which exit their dead bodies.

On the one side inheritance contains a deep unethical problem. It distorts legitimate sorrow over the loss of a close associate introduced by the future acquisition of his property.

One activity can fully satisfy a person. This activity is his personality. In his intellectually unrestrained and moral and passionate energetic activity a person attains the ultimate reality of his individualism and immortalizes himself in the world of events. In such activity a person is eternal within the temporal realm, he is infinite in the finite world, he is the representative of his generation and himself, a living and cognizance organism of his epoch.

One extreme seems to always summon the same type of extreme from the opposite side.

Only in solitude can a person work at the full strength of his potency. The will to arrange time and the absence of unavoidable interruptions is a great matter. But when a person becomes bored and exhausted, he takes his hat and seeks people and then rests with them.

Only under autocratic governments is speaking of harvest failures, plagues and the number dead in war, forbidden.

Patriotism like a banner, like a war cry, is only surrounded by a revolutionary aura of awe when the nation fights for independence, when it overthrows a foreign yoke.

People are so superficial and inattentive that they observe words more than actions, and they give incidental mistakes more weight than the completeness of a person's character.

People think that it is sufficient to prove truth as you would a mathematical theorem to make it easier to accept; that to believe it yourself is sufficient enough for others to believe it. But the reality is otherwise. Some say one thing, others listen to them and understand something else, and this is because their development is different.

People, due to their immaturity, only consider the following misfortunes to be great: where chains cause noise; where blood flows; or black and blue bruises are noticed; or illnesses requiring surgery. Psychological illnesses are discounted.

Personality is created by environment and incidences, but incidences materialize due to personalities and possess their impression. Here is mutual effect.

Prejudices are a large chain that restrain a person in an undefined, limited circle of ossified interpretations. The ear becomes accustomed to it, the eye has seen what it needs, and the ugliness slithering using ancient conclusions, becomes the generally accepted truth.

Publicity and disclosure are the great enemies of unethical conduct. Vice covers itself in the gloom, immorality fears the light. For its darkness is indispensable not only for clandestineness, but to increase impure excitement for those hungry for the forbidden fruit.

Reconciliation in general is then only possible when it is not needed, that is, when personal malice has long passed or opinions have now coincided and the people themselves see that there is no longer any reason to argue. Otherwise every reconciliation will be a mutual weakening, both sides will molt, that is, both will allow their sharp colors to fade.

Religions have always been instituted and retained due to a fervency of heart and a strong fist.

Repentance causes all the soul's blemishes to surface.

Science is an available table for all and each, as long as they are hungry, as long as the demand for heavenly manna has developed. The aspiration for truth, for knowledge, does not exclude in any form the private utilization of life. So it is possible to equally be any of a chemist, physician, artist, businessman. In no manner should a person think that some specially educated has a greater right to truth; he would only have a great attraction to it within his own field.

Small cities, tight circles, horribly ruin our perspective and vision. If we are daily repeating the same thing over and over we will naturally come to the conviction that everywhere everyone says the one and the same.

Social inequality nowhere appears with such a humiliating and sorrowful character than in the relationship between master and servant. Rothschild on the street is much more equal with a destitute person standing with a broom and sweeping the dirt in front of him than with his chamberlain in silk stocking and white gloves.

The beginning of knowledge is the personal recognition of a contradiction and the drive to remove this contradiction by thinking it through.

The ideal for every epoch is the epoch itself once purged of incidentals, a transformed contemplation of the present. It seems the more all-encompassing and more complete the present, the more all-peaceful and true its ideal.

The more a person knows, the more his contempt toward the ordinary, to what surrounds him.

The matter can be concluded in discarding something of value if we are convince that it is not truth.

The military uniform and regimentation is a passion of despotism.

The mind possesses its justification not in a majority of voices, but in its logical ability to define its own laws.

The most virtuous person in the world who cannot find in his soul the cruelty to even kill a gnat will not hesitate with great satisfaction to lacerate his close associate's good name on the basis of morals that he himself does not observe.

The past is an uncorrectable page, a guillotine blade that after its fall does not allow restoration or reattachment. It is metal poured into a cast that is unchangeable. People in general forget only what is not worth remembering or what they do not understand.

The possibility to remember, feel, love, bind, indispensably draws after itself the opposite possibilities of unhappiness, suffering, deprivation, insult, bitterness. The more lovingly the inner life develops, the more cruel and destructive are the caprices and accidents occurring, and they seem to have no accountability for any of their impacts.

Theory inspires convictions, example defies the means of its effectiveness.

There are truths that, like political rights, are not summoned any earlier than the appropriate time.

There exists no stupidity that is as bad as to force some empty dialectics into a form attributing to it some profound metaphysical appearance.

There is no good feeling residing in a person's soul that will not get worn out.

There is no more ungrateful a vocation in the world then to war on behalf of a dead person. They win the throne, forgetting that no one remains to sit on it since the king is dead.

There is nothing more stubborn in the world than a corpse. You can beat it, sever it into pieces, but convince it you cannot.

This came into my head today that the supreme form of egoism is a person's most self-denying love, this is also the highest humility and contriteness. But hiding cruelty is a terrible pride.

This is obvious on its own merit that wherever people are to be found, there they will lie and pretend. But they will not consider vices a matter of disclosure, they will not mix some boldly stated conviction of a thinker with his impropriety with a dissolute woman and boasting of his fall. Never is hypocrisy raised to the level of a social and acceptable virtue.

To have respect for a thing is in general senseless, but to respect money is twice as senseless. Occasionally I will respect a thing for its beauty, memory, effect on my life. But money is like a mathematical formula representing the value of a thing, but it is not a thing.

To subject yourself to something that is against your convictions, when the possibility exists not to do so, is immoral.

We become angry at science during our mature years in the same manner as we become angry at grammar when we are 8 years of age. In general it is somewhat inappropriate, lazy and not meriting reflection to eternally blame this on its difficulty.

Will the next generation of people understand, and value, all the terror, the entire tragic side of our existence? And meanwhile our sufferings are buds out of which their happiness will blossom.

Without natural sciences there is no salvation for the contemporary person. Without this healthy food, without this strict education of the mind with facts, without this closeness to life that surrounds us, without this independent humility – somewhere in the soul there remains a monastic cell and there a mystical seed that can distribute dark water throughout all comprehension.

Worry-free is a quality of all young people who are not deprived of their strengths, and assurance of life and themselves is expressed in it. The feeling of a total possession of your destiny numbs us, while dark power and dark persons draw us, not speaking a work, to the edge of the abyss.

You think that there is no salvation for the world if circumventing your revealed paths? You want the world to dance at your flute because of your devotion? And as soon as you note that the world has its own steps and its own tact, you become angry and despairing. You even do not have the curiosity to examine its own individual dance.

IVAN ALEKSANDROVICH ILYIN

1883 · 1954

Philosopher, Political Activist

Ivan Ilyin was born March 28, 1883, in Moscow, and completed his elementary education in Moscow, and continue with studies in Latin, Greek, French, German, and Slavonic languages, finishing in 1901. He then entered law school at the Moscow University, graduating in 1906, and remained to teach there. In 1910 he traveled to Germany and France to study the latest trends in European philosophy, and returned in 1918 to be professor of law at Moscow University.

In 1922, Ilyin was exiled from Russia for being a supporter of the While Guard, which later became the White Army against the communist Red Army, and for his anticommunist views. He was put on a ship with 160 other philosophers, historians and economists, and the ship landed in Germany. Ilyin was also inclined toward the philosophy of the Slavophiles, to isolate Russia from European influence. The years 1923-1934, Ilyin worked as a professor in the Russian Scientific Institute in Berlin, Germany. Within this period, 1927-1930, he was an editor of a Russian anti-Soviet journal. However, in 1934 he was forced from his position and was under surveillance by the German Gestapo for his political views that now Germany felt dangerous for its population.

In 1938, Ilyin left Germany to live in Zurich, Switzerland, where he worked in one of their scientific institutions for the balance of his life. Ilyin died in Zollikon, Switzerland, near Zurich, on December 21, 1954.

Ilyin researched and interpreted Hegel, and as a result created an original concept, where he proved the validity of *the believing mind*, and the fruitless *thinking without a heart*. He was also very critical of Leo Tolstoy's non-resistance to violence.

A person does not create out of a void. He creates out of what is already created, from what is existing, creating something new within the limits of the substance that is provided him – the external material and the internal psychological. The creative person must heed the worldwide depth and sing along with it. He needs to learn to contemplate with his heart, to see with love, to leave his small personal cocoon and enter the bright expanse of God. To find in it the great, the related, the belonging; to identify with its feeling and create the new from the ancient and the invisible from the primeval. This is the achievement of all the chief spheres of humanity's creativity: in all arts and sciences, in prayer and in rectitude of life, in association with people and in all culture. Culture without love is a dead, fated and hopeless effort. And all that is great and genuine, what was created by humans, was created from a contemplated and singing heart.

My spiritual *I* was revealed to me when I became convinced that I am a creative energy, such an energy that itself is not material, but has the summons to control its body as a symbol, an instrument, or a shell or clothing. This spiritual energy possesses the strength not to serve its corporeal body, but dominate it. It possesses authority to strip itself from [the body] and overpower it. It does not recognize [the body] as the measure of all things. This creative energy lives for the sake of other values and serves other goals. Other criteria and methods of measurement pertain to it. It possesses completely other forms, other laws of life, other paths and states, than the body or material in general. These forms are spiritual independence and freedom of the self; these laws are spiritual integrities and obligations; these paths are spiritual cleansing and self-perfection, this state is immortality and the adoption as an offspring. This energy, in this condition, is the primal and essential spark of God, and the human is summoned to it to accept and confirm in himself this spark of God as his personal and genuine essence. A person must devote himself to this high spark, lose himself in it and so find himself again. Then he will arise as God's spark and be able to ignite it so it becomes a large flame, while himself he will transform into an inconsumable burning bush of spirit.

There exists a great artist who created the external world using all of His majestic and beautiful laws and austere vastness, and who to this time continues to create the world of human spirits. We are His sparks, or His artistic creation, or His children. And in particular, in this power we are immortal. And our corporeal death is nothing other than our supra-terrestrial birth. True, a person seldom succeeds to abandon his freedom in its entirely to God's flame. So seldom does a person arise in all of his freedom as a perfected artistic creation of Spirit. But every person has a defined level of perfection he can attain. His entire life he ripens and matures, ascending to this level. His entire life he foresees death. And his corporeal life arrives when he can no longer ascend any higher, when he has nothing more he can attain, when he has ripened to this exit by demise.

There exists only one sole power in the world that is capable of prevailing over a person's solitude – this power is love. There exists in the world only one possible manner to exit from life's dust pile and not allow a whirlwind to dissipate it – this is the religious life. And so true friendship is spiritual love that unites people. While spiritual love is the substance of God's flame. Who does not know God's flame and has never experienced it, will not comprehend true friendship and will not be able to materialize it.

And he will likewise not be able to understand fidelity or true sacrifice. This is why only people of spirit are capable of true friendship.

There is no true friendship without love, in particular because love binds people. And true friendship is a voluntary tie: within it a person is both free and connected. And this connection does not violate or decrease freedom, because the freedom performs the tie. And this freedom, materializing in this connection, ties the corporeal person with the spirit-person. The tightest connection on earth is a free connection, if it is arranged in God, who unites people through God and this connection is strengthened in the presence of God. This is why unrestrained spiritual friendship lies at the foundation of every legitimate marriage and every healthy family. True friendship, as with the true marriage, is confirmed in the heavens and does not dissolve on earth.

All the meaningless trivia of our existence, all these misfortunes, unessential and empty circumstances of life, which want to have weight and significance, but indeed are deprived of every higher substance; all of these idle, outcast contents of life that are imposed on us like bursting rivers; all of the mundane that buries us, that consumes our time and our attention, that vexes and annoys us, that excites and mesmerizes us, that amuses us, exhausts us and depletes us, all of this is dust, the dust of life that interferes with it and diminishes it. And if we are not able to deliver ourselves from it, if we do not train ourselves to having a better taste, and not withstand it by using our greater strength and the honorable depth of our spirit, but rather live according to it, then the ordinary and mundane will swallow us. Our lifelong activities now will desolate the higher meaning, become meaningless and unaccountable. Our lifelong level will become a flat plane. Our love will be capricious, defiled and sterile. Our activities will become incidental, unreliable and treacherous, and our spirit will suffocate in the dust of existence.

Toleration is not at all passive weakness or blind submission, as some people think, On the contrary it is a restrained action of the spirit. The more that it is strengthened with the meaning of defeated suffering, the stronger becomes its creative action, the more reliably he attains his victory. Toleration is not only the art of waiting and suffering. It is, other than this, belief in victory and the path to victory. More than this it is the victory itself, prevailing over weakness, deprivation and suffering; the victory over reaction, over time, over determination; the person's victory over his corporeality and over every one of life's circumstances. Toleration is truly the staircase to perfection.

In order to be sincere, a person must become inwardly unified. While his spirit lives in division or torn apart, he does not sincerely love, think, speak or act, because within him proceeds this civil war against himself. He pursues at the one and same time various goals and serves at one and the same time various values – gods. Within him reside several life-centers competing against each other, while he is regularly betraying one to another. All within him is ambiguous and questionable. His love is not strong and worth little. His thinking is conditional and relative. He goes astray, doubts and does nothing creative, and his words are malicious. He always places his concerns first in decisions he makes. He no longer has a concept of trust in what he does and is unreliable. He deteriorates into a weak character and is not longer dependable.

The first and fundamental law of individualism is the law of inner indivisibility. This law he does not observe and does not live by it. This is why he is always insincere, and even when alone with just himself and when he meditates about himself, and so he accepts identical decisions that coincide with his insincerity. He possesses no internal unity, and without this there is not sincerity.

A person becomes sincere only when a certain sacred concentration resides in his soul, with which he deals in a serious and wholesome reverent manner, and when he in his lifelong choices and activities otherwise cannot but want. Then he stands firm. Then he possesses a sturdy anchor, or a living and potent root. Then he would not have it otherwise. And then what he still needs is courage, in order to preserve the fidelity of his sacredness and to make all of his lifelong choices based on sincerity.

The patriarchal unification of people rests on certain characteristics of theirs, the ones that are indispensable, natural and sacred. Spiritual time and purpose and a spiritual means of life now become for that person indispensable, natural and sacred. People bind themselves into one nation and create one homeland in particular due to the similarity of their spiritual structure. And this spiritual structure develops gradually. From a historical perspective it is based on experience: the internal hidden within the person himself: race, genealogy, character, psychological stability and mental faculties; and the external: climate, environment, neighbors. The entire internal and external experience is received from God and from history, and must be developed by spirit, and so from these facets there is formulated the spirit of the nation, sometimes ameliorating its paths, or sometimes making them difficult or even installing barricades. The result is the appearance of one national-religious structure that ties the people into a patriarchal unity.

The defeated and old do not immediately descend into the grave. Longevity and stubbornness of the person departing is based on the inner protecting strength of all that exists. This is what to an extreme extent protects all who are summoned to life and all at the same time. The worldwide economy does not permit any real person to descend into the grave until all strengths are exhausted from him.

The history of thought is the continuation of the history of nature. Not humanity and not nature is possible to be understood if bypassing historical development. The difference of these histories consists in the fact that nature remembers nothing. For it there is no past, but a human possesses all of his past deep in himself. As a result a human presents himself not only as a part of something, but also as patrimonial.

NIKOLAI ONUFRIYEVICH LOSSKI

1870 – 1965

Historian, Religious Philosopher

Nikolai Losski was born in Kerslavka, Vitebsk Province, Russia (today known as Kraslava, Latvia), on November 24, 1870. His father was Russian, but his mother was Polish. His education began in 1881 in a private school in Vitebsk, but in 1887, he was expelled for distributing atheistic and socialist information. He then went to Bern, Germany to study philosophy. Returning to Russia he attending Petersburg University studying history and philology. It was about this time that Losski experienced a religious transformation and dedicated his life to God.

In 1916, Losski became history professor at Petersburg University. After the Russian Revolution he was expelled from his position due to his Christian ideology and in 1922 he was exiled from the Soviet Union. He first lived in Berlin, and then he lived in Prague to 1942, and was a professor at the Russian University, teaching theology and philosophy. The years 1942-1945, he was professor of philology in Bratislava, Czechoslovakia. Losski likewise lectured at the Holy Sergeev Theological Institute in Paris.

He migrated to the USA and in 1947 became a teacher at the religious academy at St Vladimir Seminary, New York, and taught there until 1953. He then returned to France.

Losski died in Paris on January 24, 1965.

Love of freedom and its higher expression – the freedom of the spirit – belongs to the number of primary essential qualities of the Russian people, together with their religious devotion, the search for absolute goodness and strength of the will. This quality is tightly bound with the search for absolute goodness. Indeed, perfected goodness exists only in God's Kingdom. It is supra-terrestrial. Subsequently, in our kingdom of egoistic entities, only what is half-good materializes, the unification of positive values with some type or others of imperfect ones, that is, goodness in a union with some type or other aspects of bad.

When a person decides which of the possible paths of conduct to choose, he does not have a mathematically proven knowledge of the best method of practice. And so the person, the one who possesses freedom of the spirit, is inclined to subject every valuable item to a test, not only mental, but also in experience.

The search for absolute goodness, an inherent quality of the Russian people, leads to acknowledgement of the highest value of every individual. For this reason the Russian intelligence always displays an ascended interest toward social justice and a concern about improving the conditions of the serfs, who have existed as a deprived class.

Goodness that is profound and supported by the search for absolute goodness and religious devotion belongs to the number of the primary essential qualities of the Russian people. However, tormented by malevolence and destitution, the Russian person can display greater cruelty. Tied with the experience of the search for absolute goodness, among the Russian people there has developed a high and diverse talent, a theoretical and practical mind, an artistic creativity in various spheres of artistry. Sensitivity to goodness in the Russian people is united with a satirical direction of the mind, with the inclination to critique everything and never to be satisfied.

If the final judgment consists in one person becoming worthy of eternal bliss in the Kingdom of God, while others will be sent for some long interval to hell, then it comes to mind, deducting from observations of our imperfections at the end of life, that very few will be saved, the infinite multitudes of the people remaining are doomed to eternal infernal torment. In such a case it would be unavoidable for us to accept that the creation of the world was unsuccessful for God, and theodicy would be impossible. We then extract that God is not a perfect entity, that He is not omnipotent, not omniscient and not all-benevolent. But religious experience convincingly witnesses that God absolutely is perfect and that He is love. Base on this it is without doubt the world He created is capable of materializing the most supreme levels of benevolence.

The deification of creatures cannot be identified with God. The border between the created world and divinity cannot be trespassed. But if isolated from God, the created and limited entity, based on only individual strengths, cannot attain absolute fullness of existence that we mentally conclude in the understanding of deification. It is the 3rd path that causes it to remain mental. Remaining to the end distinct from deity, the created entity can become worthy of a tight union with deity, grateful that all its activities will materialize in an intimate tie with the divine life, and in this manner, it will actively participate in the absolute fullness of existence. The ecclesiastical fathers named such an ascension to the height of the divine life, consummated with the help of God, as deification by grace.

The members of God's Kingdom will possess a type of body that cannot be destroyed by any type of power, not external, not internal. Indeed, they cannot produce any exertion, and so are not subject to any attack from the outside, subsequently, their transformed body is invulnerable to, and indestructible by, mechanical means. What pertains to the inner relationships among the members of God's Kingdom, consummate love lies at their base, excluding the possibility of dissolution. In this manner, death is impossible in God's Kingdom.

The fear of death is only useful at the beginning of the path, but later it must be defeated, so that when we stand before God we will be free from all conceited and selfish motivations and attitudes. Christian heroism assumes that purity of heart already exists, where fearlessness unites with humility. In the opposite situation, if courage develops on the basis of an arrogant and high opinion of oneself, the liberation from fear of death is attained easier, but no inherent goodness prevails, but only evil, and as a result this will provide demonic asceticism on your path.

The answer to the question on absolute goodness as provided by religion has a character of truth expressed in concrete form, that is, in a form of full-blooded life. Such an answer stands higher than philosophy that provides knowledge in an abstract form. A concrete answer has a character that embodies stability. Grateful for its concreteness, religion skillfully and more correctly expresses truth than philosophy.

The general consensus is that what we call ourselves is only the body. It seems that what my intellect and my soul and my love are evolves from the body. And it seems that what we call our body is actually what our body is fed. True that my body is only food that have been reconstituted by the body, and that without food there would not be a body. But my body is not food. Food is what is needed for the life of the body, but it is not the body.

The same with the soul. True that without my body there would not exist what I call the soul, but nonetheless my soul is not body. The body is needed in order to preserve the soul, but the body is not the soul. If there was no soul then I would not know about my body. The beginning of life is not in the body, but in the soul.

DMITRI SERGEEVICH MEREZHKOVSKI

1865 – 1941

Poet, Historian, Religious Philosopher

Dmitri Merezhkovski was born in St Petersburg on August 2, 1865. In 1888, he completed his education in history at the Petersburg University. Merezhkovski was one of the most prolific writers of the Silver Age in regard to the implications of religion on politics and contemporary history. He was one of the organizers of the Religious-Philosophic Society in Petersburg. He is one of the founders of Russian symbolism and his novels introduced into Russian literature the new genre of fictional historico-philosophy, where historical fiction is impregnated with religious and philosophic concepts.

Merezhkovsky was 9 times nominated for the Nobel Prize in literature, which he came closest to winning in 1933. His religious-philophical masterpiece was his trilogy tragedy *Christ and Antichrist*, on which he worked for 12 years, 1893-1905. He lived in Paris, 1906-1908, which was his first exile. In 1918, his 2nd exile, he migrated from the Soviet Union to Paris, France, where he lived until his death. During those years he was a fervent anticommunist and wrote considerable essays criticizing and exposing its faults.

He died in Paris, France, on December 9, 1941.

God is endless, the creator of all beginnings and ends. The devil is the state of a denial of God, and subsequently the denial of He who is endless, the denial of all ends and beginnings. The devil has a beginning but has not yet reached his end, although he attempts to display himself as beginningless and endless. The devil is a nominal and mediocre entity, his essence denies all depths and heights. However he is eternally linear, eternally mundane.

We understand that the more dangerous enemy of every positive religion is not atheism, not an honest denial of God, but individualism, a malicious attitude toward religious values. Triumphant atheism is a philosophical naivety or semi-illiteracy. "I do not know if God exists," is all the follower of positivism or agnosticism can say. Belief in the non-existence of God is the same type of belief as though in His existence. Both confirmations are identically not provable. The choice between them is made not only with the intellect, but with the senses, the will, with the entire consummate psychological strengths of a person. No one will now debate over the inner possibility of religious experience. Philosophical foundations of atheism inevitably surrender.

As a natural human weakness – "I believe; help my unbelief," – atheism is the point of departure of every religion. Belief is nourished by unbelief, as fire is by dry wood: the dryer the wood the hotter the fire. In this sense unextinguished, seeking and suffering atheism is closer to belief than individual self-sufficient dogma.

But when the role of dogmatic atheism is fulfilled by religious individualism, the matter proceeds not by considering if you can believe in something, but whether you can believe with someone. "Religion is a private matter." Believe and be silent; hide your faith. Personal observance is incompatible with social protocol, and every attempt of combining them is fatal to the both of them.

People with isolated beliefs are saved, but together they will perish, but common ruin does not interfere with personal salvation.

Godless association is a valley of sorrow that needs to be traversed in order to attain the heavenly kingdom. Such are the confirmations of religious individualism. Especially difficult is to fight with it, because he, the evil enemy, is hidden.

The roots of religious individualism descend into the depths of Christian dogma, where a new religious experience is perfected. All of us are religious individualists. But this is not our old clothes that are easy to remove, but an old shell, out of which to exit is painful and scary.

The Christian idea of personality is so distorted and clouded in individualism, that it is almost impossible to return to its original source. The personality of Christ has been sealed on the Christian, and it is indelible, and more than can any other religion. In essence, the sole source of the Christian dogma is that defined, historically-visible, touchable person – "Jesus, crucified during the reign of Pontius Pilate," – who is the 2nd hypostasis of the Trinity. The person historically-visible, touchable and likewise extraordinary and unique, incomparable to any other, and not similar to any other, 2,000 years ago was nonetheless new, known and unknown, identifiable and unidentifiable, close and far. The more that we gaze at Him, the more we as astonished. Who is this? What is he?

Healthy lungs do not sense the air that they breathe, just as we do not sense the dogmas by which we live. But it is worth comparing our world with other worlds, in time and space, with the non-Christian East or the pre-Christian antiquity, in order to touch the oxygen of our air. The impersonal Buddhist deity, the Jewish God in their history, the Roman-Greek mythology, all of these worlds are uninhabitable for us.

At the furthermost limits of anti-Christianity, we return to this Christian dogma: If it was not Christ, the God-person of the past, then it will be the antichrist, the deified person, the superhuman, of the future. Whether it is Christ or antichrist, we have no place to hide from the Absolute individual. Whether we go above or below, the pyramids of humanity still conclude at a sharp corner.

The Person of Christ is one half of the Christian dogma, the other half is community.

If Christ was, then we can say, "I am," meaning, to say, "I am in Christ, in the Absolute person." Then the entirety of humanity's persons are splinters of the single Christ.

In every living organism exists a center that will be at some time the center of consciousness, the one cell, the monad. With the union and weaving and subjection of this monad of all the lower cells, the *I* is isolated from the *non-I*, the living from the dead. Such a monad is humanity – Christ; not only every person as an individual entity, but all humanity speaks in Christ, "I am." As there are individual cells in an organism, so in the Church the individual persons unite, are woven together with great strength, with the only one that exists in the world to do this, being the strength of love as the absolute unity in God. "Let us all be in one, as You Father are in me and I in You, so they can be One in Us."

This single absolute community is the Church.

I thirsted for God, and did not know it. Even before I believed, I had love. When I rejected intellect, I felt You in my heart. You revealed Yourself to me: You are peace. You all everything. You are the sky and rain. You are the voice of the storm. You are the ethereal. You are the mind of the poet. You are the stars. So long as I live I will pray to You. It is You whom I love, and You are my respiration. When I die I will assimilate into You, like the star at the morning twilight. You are the midnight and the dawn. I thank You at my birth and at my death.

The primary tenet in Christ's teaching is that he considered all people as brethren. He recognized a brother in a person and so loved every one whoever and whatever he was. He viewed not the external person, but the internal. He did not look at the body, but through the elegant clothing of the wealthy and the rags of the destitute he saw an immortal soul. In the most depraved and fallen person he saw the possibility of his transformation into the greatest and holiest person, into becoming just as great and holy as he was himself.

A person will find his own providence only when in service to associates. And he finds providence in service to associates because in serving associates he is uniting with the spirit of God that is within them.

It seems to people that they are distanced one from another. Meanwhile if each person does precisely live only for a life that is distanced from all others then the live of the people cannot continue. The life of humanity is only possible when all are aware that the one and same spirit of God live in all people.

Other that what is tangible with ourselves and in all the world, we know that there is something intangible that provides life to our body and is attached to it. This something intangible, attached to our body, we call the soul. What is intangible and is not attached to anything but provides life to everything is what we call God.

In the house of Romanoff a secret curse migrates from generation to generation. Murder, treachery, blood and mud. Peter 1 killed his son; Alexander I killed his father; Catherine II killed her husband. And besides all these great and known sacrifices, there exists pathetic, unknown and unfortunate abortions of the autocracy that were suffocated, like mice in some dark corner, in the cells of the Schlesselburg fortress. The executioner's block, the whip and poison are actually the true symbols of the Russian autocracy. The anointment placed on the forehead of the kings at their coronation truly has become the mark of Cain.

LEV ESAIAKOVICH SHESTOV

1866 – 1938

Existentialist Philosopher

Lev Shestov was born Yehuda Leyb Schwarzmann in Kiev, Ukraine, on January 31, 1866. He changed his name to cover his Jewish roots. His family were wealthy factory owners. Shestov first attended Moscow University to study physics and mathematics, but due to ideological differences, he was expelled. He returned to Kiev and completed law school at the Kiev University in 1889. He began writing on topics of philosophy and literature in 1895, but the first 2 were censured and not published and the 3rd was completely rewritten by the censurers.

Further suppression of his work led to his decline in health and he spent 1896-1897, in Switzerland recovering, and then continued to live there until 1914, but also in Germany in 1906-1908. During his years in Switzerland, he continued to write on philosophy.

Shestov returned to Moscow in 1915, and taught philosophy, but after the revolution in 1918, he could not deny his religious convictions and capitulate to the Marists. He was unable to accept the new communist government and so voluntarily left his position and moved to live in Kiev for 2 years, there to teach Greek philosophy at Kiev University. Shestov's repulsion of the Soviet system caused him to again leave and he immigrated to Europe in 1920, to live in Berlin, and then in Paris. He continued to write and lecture in Europe, the majority of his books composed between 1921 and 1938. He called his concept – the philosophy of tragedy or despair.

Shestov died in Paris on November 19, 1938.

A person is so much a conservative creature, that every change, and even a change for the better, scares him.

Educated people, those who read a lot, must constantly keep in view that literature is one matter, while life is another.

Europe has forgotten about miracles a long, long time ago, and it has not traversed further than ideals. We in Russian continue to this time to mix miracles with ideals.

Great deprivations and great illusions alter a person's nature to such an extent that what seems impossible now becomes possible and what is unattainable now becomes attainable.

If you were to allow this – just as do historians – that great people lead humanity to the attainment of well-known goals, then it is impossible to explain the aspects of history without understanding of accidents and genius. "An incident causes a situation ; a genius takes advantage of it," so history records. The words – incident and genius – do not designate anything actually existing and so cannot be specifically defined. These words only designate a known level of the understanding of situations.

Indifference is psychological meanness. Indifference evolves from the nasty side of our soul. It does not earlier sense that attaining it is accompanied with the loss of everything that resides in us that is beautiful.

It seems to me that the human mind in each unique individual passes through its development along the path by which it is developed as part of entire generations. Thoughts serving as the basis of various philosophic theories compose the indivisible parts of the mind. But each person more or less clearly comprehended them even earlier than he knew about the existence of philosophic theories.

More willingly than all else, destiny laughs at the ideals and prophecies of the mortal, and we must remember that this statement contains a great wisdom.

New thoughts, even personal ones, will not quickly win over our sympathies. It is better to first adjust to them.

People are terribly economic and frugal entities. They want to know even more and purchase their information even cheaper if possible.

People often begin to strive toward great goals when they feel that they do not have the strength to accomplish small objectives. But on occasion there are results.

Sages do not know more than the stupid. They only have more bravery and self-confidence.

The best and most convincing means of proof is to begin your deliberations with harmless ones that everyone is capable of accepting.

The creators of great ideas have a very neglectful attitude toward their compositions and worry little about their fate in the world.

The dilemma of philosophy is to teach a person to live in oblivion, and specifically that person who fears popularity more than all else and hides from it because of different doctrines.

The most important and significant convictions and revelations appear in the world totally naked, without a verbal shell. It is a special and very difficult matter to find words for them, it is an art in itself.

The most reliable means of freeing yourself from truths that annoy you to no end is to stop paying them the usual tribute of respect and reverence and begin dealing with them plainly, even with some inclusion of familiarity and contempt.

There is no more a repulsive and objectionable scene than the scene of an educated person who seems to feel he understands everything there is to understand and has a response to whatever question he is presented.

There is sufficient basis to have a distrustfulness attitude toward life. It has deceived us so much in even the most of dependable expectations.

We live in a realm of illusions and fear the possibility of somehow violating the triumphant harmony of the fairy-tale kingdom more than all else on earth.

What is important and needful to us, that which we value and definitely love, we seldom brag about.

When a person notices some type of shortcoming in himself, and from which he cannot escape by any means, there is nothing left for him except to pass his shortcoming off as a quality.

You cannot be in discord with the present. You know that if the past was this way and that way, then the present needs to be this way and that way and a result this will lead to this future. You need to reconcile yourselves only with your individual and particular understanding and your explanation.

BORIS PETROVICH VISHISLAVTZEV

1877 – 1954

Educator, Theologian

Boris Vishislavtzev was born in Moscow on October 3, 1877. He competed law school at the Moscow University in 1899, and then beginning in 1917, he taught law at the same school, his subjects being the philosophy of law, history of philosophy, ethics and religion. His work served an important role in the Russian cultural renaissance of the turn of the 20th century.

In 1922 he was exiled from Russia. He then lectured on the philosophy of religion at different academies in Berlin, Paris and Geneva. While in Paris, he taught at the Theological Institute. His final years were spent in Geneva, where he died October 10, 1954 of tuberculosis.

Vishislavtzev named his personal concept – the Philosophy of the Heart. His most famous book was *The Heart in Christian and Hindu Mysticism*, published in 1929.

A person without a heart is a person without love and without religion. The state of being irreligious will leave a person in the final end heartless.

The hidden region of the heart, which appears as clandestine, and subsequently, subconscious, should not necessarily be exalted and brought close to God. The reason is that from it, and often unexpectedly and unconsciously for every person, evolve both good and bad actions. The good person from the good treasury of his heart provides good, while the bad person from the bad treasury of his heart provides bad. Luke 6:45, Matt 12:35. The subconscious presents itself in this manner as the sphere of endless possibilities, from which both vice and virtue will sprout. It is a material that can accept either a beautiful or an ugly form.

Vice is created from the identical material as virtue. There are no inherent drives of the soul and body that would be bad in themselves. They arise as bad only when they accept a special form, in particular, the form of moral corruption. The fundamental idea of the entire Greek Eastern asceticism and mysticism was the idea of apotheosis, which is the genuine sublimation of the entire substance of a person, all the drives of his body and soul, because the body of a human is the temple of the holy Spirit of God, I Cor 6:19, and just like its soul, it is subject to transformation and apotheosis. Origen provided a great merit when he taught apotheosis as a clandestine expression of Christ in the heart of the believer. It is as though Christ is born again in a person's soul. He transforms it according to His image as He moves into the soul and resides there. Such a transformation of the soul preserves all its drives and leads it to a higher sublimation. All Christian mystics and ascetics one way or another accept this classical form of sublimation.

Wherever you locate your higher treasure, there is your eros. The cosmos of love sprouts from the chaos of ambiguous erotic impulses. The eros of marital love permits sublimation in Christ and in the church and is the great mystery and a sacrament.

Beyond this, here is center of Christian mysteries, because all Christian symbols evolve from the eros: Father, Son, Mother, Brethren, Bride, Groom. If infatuation, wedding, motherhood, fatherhood, were something base or contemptible (as the Gnostic heretics think), then these symbols would not have surfaced in the Divine writings. The direction toward the possibility of potent sublimation of the eros is confined in them: the family is a smaller church, and the church is a larger family. If this eros was contemptible in some or another aspect, then why does the Songs of Songs reside in the canon of sacred books?

RUSSIAN TRADITIONAL PROVERBS

A bachelor that fights gets marries; the married man that fights – repents; the elder that fights - gets ready to die.

A hidden joy often resides in an altercation with people.

A person must never be ashamed or embarrassed of any type of work, no matter how unsanitary it may be, except for a idle life.

A person without a homeland is like a nightingale without a song.

A person without friends is like a tree without roots.

An ignorant person is a dull axe.

An intelligent lie is better than a stupid truth.

An intelligent person does not tell all he knows; while the stupid person knows little but tells all.

An intelligent person has the ability to learn from his enemies.

An intelligent person likes to learn, the stupid likes to teach.

An old stomach does not remember friends.

Animosity hates truth.

Begin every matter using your head.

Bitterness of the heart can be sweetened with a smile.

Conceit is not smart, but a misunderstanding.

Do not be obstinate, but be direct.

Do not depend on happiness, it is often superficial.

Do not fear the bitter, but fear the sweet.

Do not just fantasize about happiness, do it!

Do not live how you want, but live how you can.

Don't look at personalities. Look at the cash.

Earn while you are young, then spend when you are old.

Even behind a smile, poison can be hid.

For some, money is the whole point of life. Other people already have it.

God wants goodness for everybody, and so if you want goodness for everybody, meaning you have love for them, then God resides in you.

Greed is the lair of the evil enemy.

Happiness and unhappiness ride the same horse.

Happiness deceives many.

Happiness travels on crutches, while unhappiness flies with wings.

If you are sweet, people will lick you. If you are bitter, people will spit you out.

If you don't know, keep quiet. If you do know, hold your tongue.

If you hurry, people will laugh.

If you live for people, they will live for you. If you live collectively, you are better off waiting for the sky to fall.

If you love, remember that hate exists. If you hate, remember that love exists.

It is better to suffer corporeally than mentally.

Laugher without a reason is a sign of stupidity.

Life is provided for benevolence.

Love is like a ring, and a ring has no end.

Love provides people goodness, because it unites a person with God.

No one doesn't know how to live, like we don't know how to live.

One good deed is worth more than a hundred sermons on goodness.

One of Russia's great misfortunes is that it has fools showing which road to take.

Our people have been promised so much, but it is still not enough for them.

People died, but their good conduct outlives them forever.

People speak differently about God, but all feel and understand Him the same.

Repetition is the mother of education.

Smart people love to learn; fools love to teach.

Success is due to God; failure is due to people.

Summon happiness, but tolerate sorrow.

The eyes are the mirror of the soul.

The forbidden fruit is sweet.

The good student see the mistakes of his mentor, but respectably keeps silent about them, because these mistakes will be to his benefit in the future and guide him on a direct path of less mistakes.

The poor person is not who has little, but who contributes little.

The poor soldier is the one who has not aspirations to become a general.

The stupid person is the one who cannot get angry; the wise person is the one who does not want to get angry.

There is a toy for every individual's age.

There is no God for the person who does not seek Him. Seek Him and He will disclose Himself to you.

There is no honor in having a beard, even a goat has one.

To be a coward is shameful, but it is more shameful to brag of your bravery out of fear that someone will call you a coward.

To live is to serve your homeland.

To live for yourself is decay, to live for your family is to flare, to live for your nation is to shine.

To sin is human, to justify sin is diabolic.

To speak the truth you risk losing friends.

Unjustifiable relaxation exhausts a person worse than work.

RUSSIA'S WISDOM

Up to the age of 30 your wife will warm you; after 30 it takes a bottle of wine; and later in life not even a stove will help.

What you brag about when you are young, you will repent of when you are old.

What you do not have in your thoughts, you will not have in your eyes.

Whatever you acquire through diligence will brighten all.

When you are young have strong shoulders, when you are old have a strong head.

Who believes anything easy will succumb to anything easy.

Who is not healthy by 20, not smart by 30, and not wealthy by 40, has squandered his entire life.

Who loves to work, the people will admire.

Who sows to the wind will reap a storm.

Whoever starts a fight will be beaten the worst.

Woe to the person who does nothing good for anybody.

You will not wash a black soul with soap.

Russian Bibliography

Агеева, Елена, *Афоризмы, мысли и высказывания выдающихся Россиян*

Беляева, И.Б. *Энциклопедия Мысли*, в 2 томов

Василенко, Лионид Иванович, *Введение в Русскую Религиозную Философию*

Даль, Владимир Иванович, *Пословицы и поговорки русского народа*

Замалеев, А.Ф. *Антология Русской Философии*, в 3 томов

Замалеев, А.Ф. *История Русской Философии*

Замалеев, А.Ф. *Русская Религиозная Философия XI-XX вв.*

Зеньковский, Васили В. *История Русской Философии*

Зоберн, Владимир, *Православний Цитатник*

Ильф, Илья и Петров, Евгений, *Самые остроумные афоризмы и цитаты*

Корнилов, С.В. *Русские Философы*

Лосева, И.Н. *Русские Мыслители*,

Маслина, М.А. *Русская Философия – Энциклопедия*

Носков, В.Г. *Афоризмы, Серебряный Век*

Носков, В.Г. *Афоризмы, Золотой Век*

Носков, В.Г. *Афоризмы, Русские Мыслители*

Петруня, О.Э. *Виноград духовный*

Раневская, Фаина, *Случаи, шутки, афоризмы*

Толстой, Л.Н. *Путь Жизнь*

Филиппов, Анатолий Николаевич, *Православные притчи*

Шапошников, Л.И. и Федоров, А.А. *История Русской Религиозной Философии*

Яковенко, Борис В. *История Русской Философии*

RUSSIA'S WISDOM

www.ingramcontent.com/pod-product-compliance
Lightning Source LLC
Chambersburg PA
CBHW021822220426
43663CB00005B/104